GOVERNMENTS AND MULTINATIONALS

Governments
and
Multinationals
The Policy of
Control Versus
Autonomy

Edited by
Walter H. Goldberg
International Institute of Management
Science Center Berlin
in cooperation with
Anant R. Negandhi
University of Illinois at Urbana-Champaign

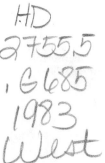
Oelgeschlager, Gunn & Hain, Publishers, Inc.
Cambridge, Massachusetts

International Standard Book Number: 0-89946-145-x

Library of Congress Catalog Card Number: 82-3591

Printed in the U.S.A.

Library of Congress Cataloging in Publication Data
Main entry under title:

Governments and multinationals.

  1. International business enterprises—Addresses, essays, lectures. 2. Industry
and state—Addresses, essays, lectures. I. Goldberg, Walter, 1924–   .
HD2755.5.G685   338.8'8   82-3591
ISBN 0-89946-145-x   AACR2

Contents

Foreword

The International Institute of Management of the Science Center Berlin (Wissenschaftszentrum Berlin) uses about 50 percent of its resources for studies of industrial structure, aiming at investigations of the reasons and the characteristics of structural change in industry as well as the policies and methods for inducing such structural change. This comparative study of the behavior and performance of multinational corporations was undertaken between 1976 and 1980. The first three books in the series were the following: A. R. Negandhi, in collaboration with B. R. Baliga, *Quest for Survival and Growth: A Comparative Study of American, European, and Japanese Multinationals* (Königstein/Ts.: Athenäum, and New York: Praeger, 1979); A. R. Negandhi (ed.), *Functioning of the Multinational Corporation: A Global Comparative Study* (New York: Pergamon Press, 1980); and A. R. Negandhi and B. R. Baliga, *Tables Are Turning: German and Japanese Multinational Companies in the United States* (Cambridge, Mass: Oelgeschlager, Gunn & Hain, 1981). This book is the fourth volume in the project, with additional volumes scheduled for publication. The present volume concentrates on the problem of the organization and efficiency of relations between national governments and multinational corporations in preventing, minimizing, or settling conflicts arising from the transfer of resources in the course of foreign direct investment.

The book concentrates on the degree of centralization versus decentralization and the consequent dependence or autonomy of MNC subsidiaries in the host countries; the question of making available new products and methods through centralized versus decentralized research laboratories; the question of financial transactions and their control; and investigations into the policy options available both to nation-states and to multinational corporations in order to structure and adapt their mutual relations in these respects.

The members of the International Institute of Management would like to thank the contributors to this volume, in particular Walter Goldberg, former director of the Institute, Anant R. Negandhi, who originated this timely, interesting, and fruitful research at IIM; and Mrs. Brigitte Schmidt, who has taken care of the manuscript through many stages and deserves particular recognition.

It is our hope that the publication will shed light on the functioning of multinational corporations.

The Science Center Editors
1982

Introduction: Global Rationalization Versus Adaptation to National Interest

THE URGENCY OF THE SUBJECT MATTER

This book is primarily concerned with the question of how relations between foreign direct investors and host governments are organized as well as how efficient these relations are so that conflicts of interest between MNCs and national governments can be prevented, minimized, or settled. The urgency of researching this subject has recently been attested to by one of the most knowledgeable researchers in the field of foreign direct investment (FDI), transnational corporations (TNCs), and multinational corporations, Professor John H. Dunning (Dunning, 1979a):

> ... in the case of a TNC which pursues a globally or regionally integrated strategy, decisions about what is best for the whole enterprise need not necessarily coincide with what is best for an individual foreign affiliate. Consequently, clashes of interest between the host country and the decision-taker, viz., the TNC occur—clashes which will be all the more pro-

nounced where FDI is undertaken in a monopolistic and oligopolistic market environment. It has been the divergence between the perceived social and economic welfare of *countries* and those of the *owners of FDI* where the debate over the TNC has been more vociferous in recent years.

It is not unreasonable to assume that countries wish to increase their economic welfare while retaining as much control over the use of the re- sources necessary to generate this welfare—whether these resources be indigenous or imported.

Researchers, . . . would do well to widen their horizons of inquiry and to pay special attention to newly developed forms of involvement, which, either because they are important agents of resource dissemination or be- cause they control the use of resources outside their national boundaries, may have a marked effect on the well-being of home or host countries.

This book takes up policy questions of this type, both at the national and enterprise levels. It focuses on the transfer of resources (as opposed to the transfer of goods), such as capital, technology, and management skills as well as the conditions of the transfer.

First, the interaction between alternative methods of resource transference and the goals of host countries requires careful analysis. Second, there is need to better identify the meaning of "control," and the conditions under which it is likely to be effective where exercised across national boundaries. What determines the locus of control? Can one identify the circumstances under which it is likely to be centralized or delegated by TNCs? A third area, yet to be seriously explored, is the interaction between TNCs and the production and dissemination of technology (Dunning, 1979a).

In listing and assigning priorities to these questions, Dunning also points out the problem of international *capital markets* and *capital movements*. He realizes that the transfer of *resources* is highly impor- tant but at the same time concedes that the subject is little researched.

A GENERAL THEORETICAL BASE UNDERLYING THE STUDIES

The implicit theoretical base of the contributions to this work is in essence what Dunning (1979b) calls the *eclectic theory of international production*. Its principal hypothesis is:

. . . that the propensity of a firm to engage in foreign direct investment rests on three conditions being satisfied. These conditions are as follows:

1. that it must possess net ownership advantages vis-à-vis a firm of other nationalities in serving particular (and, in practice, mainly foreign) markets. These ownership advantages largely take the form of the possession of intangible assets, which are at least for a period of time, exclusive or specific to the firm possessing them.
2. assuming (1) condition is satisfied that it must be more beneficial to the enterprise possessing these advantages to use them itself rather than to sell or lease them or the right to use them to foreign firms i.e. for it to internalize its property rights to an extension of its own activities rather than externalize them through contracts at arm's length prices with independent firms e.g. through licensing, management contracts, franchises, technical services agreements, turnkey projects, subcontracts.
3. assuming (1) and (2) conditions are satisfied, that it must be profitable to the enterprise to utilize these advantages in conjunction with at least some factor inputs (including natural resources) outside its home country; otherwise foreign markets would be served entirely by exports, and domestic markets by domestic production.

The greater the ownership advantages of enterprises . . . , the more the incentive they have to exploit these themselves and the more the economies of production and marketing favor a foreign location, the more a firm is likely to engage in foreign direct investment. (Dunning, 1979b, pp. 12–13.

Dunning specifies the three cornerstones of the eclectic theory in more detail on pages 13a and 13b of 1979b.)

Under such conditions the multinational (or transnational) corporation tends to maximize its yields through global rationalization and by taking full advantage of *internal conditions* (the large-scale exploitation of patents, production processes, managerial capacity, access to financial resources, applying a strategy of integration and specialization, etc. cf. Chapter 13) as well as *external* conditions (by ensuring access to physical resources and markets, by exploiting the shelters of governmental regulation, etc.).

The question whether firms are only short-term maximizers, as postulated in traditional economics, or instead take a longer perspective by attempting to maximize yields over longer (so-called strategic) periods, which means that in the short run they may deliberately and occasionally act in nonoptimal modes, is an old and traditional debate in economic research. This issue is very relevant to the present investigation. Company objectives in conflict with country objectives may lead to conflicts that force management to decide whether to choose short-term profit maximization or to adopt a longer perspective.

The question, to which several contributions are devoted, implies that the firm (i.e. its management) is the focus and level of observation chosen. However, of necessity there must be occasional shifts in emphasis, both to higher levels of management (corporate headquarters) and to the levels of industries or industry (as in the contributions on trade policies by Blair and financial center development by Reed).

THE ISSUES OF
MNC–GOVERNMENT RELATIONS

Governmental relations with industry go back to the era of mercantilism. When states or sovereigns wanted their countries to develop greater economic strength, steps were taken to encourage the development of manufacturing up to industrial levels. In many cases, this implied restrictions on international trade as well as restricting imports of foreign-owned resources (capital, technology, skills).

The economic history of the twentieth century is full of examples of governmental intervention in business, often aiming to *constrain* foreign activities or to *encourage* the investment of foreign resources in the host country. Thus governmental regulation frequently both repelled and attracted foreign business and manufacturing at the same time. Governmental dealings with industry, in particular large industry and foreign direct investment, had become more explicit during the last 10 to 15 years (a lucid record of this development is offered by Vernon, 1974). Governments have (re-) discovered the potential of industry in being instrumental in achieving national goals and implementing national policies. After this development particular attention was devoted to multinational corporations for several reasons: indigenous firms have their headquarters, that is, their bases of existence, "at home." They are likely to understand and comply with their home country's policy. Multinational enterprises, meanwhile, reach major decisions at a great distance and thus are likely to be much less responsive to the goals and policies of their host countries.

Many transnational corporations (TNCs) have grown so large that their size exceeds that of some nation-states (the annual turnover of General Electric is larger than the GNP of the Republic of Austria, etc.) Thus, a TNC could override, neutralize, or even counteract the political will of a nation-state. The mere potential to do so is enough to trigger countermeasures.

In summary, two properties of multinational corporations (MNCs)

—namely, their size and foreign nationality, or even transnationality —make them different from domestic large industry. They therefore become the focus of critical interest. Two factors may have contributed to this phenomenon: the dominance of U.S.-based MNCs after World War II and the vivid criticism of their behavior in developing countries. In conclusion, MNCs operating abroad have become the specific subject of interest, scrutiny, and regulation beyond and above the interest devoted to indigenous firms as means of implementing national policies.

In which spheres of policy or to what political instruments might multinational corporations be subjected to regulation in order to prevent or to attain specific behavioral modes?

The principal areas in which corporations frequently are expected to comply with government regulations are *foreign* policy (participation in nationally or internationally desirable development plans; participation in economic sanctions); *trade* policy (supporting or curtailing trade in certain categories of goods, certain industries, or vis-à-vis certain countries); *balance of payment* policies (e.g., export promotion; import substitution in order to impact upon the balance of payments, often to prevent or diminish a deficit; and in some spectacular cases, also to reduce a trade surplus); and other policies relating to the *monetary* system (e.g., participation in compensation deals).

Other relevant areas are as follows:

Policies aimed at *developing* or *restructuring* domestic industry; policies for the maintenance or exploration of *natural resources* (or to establish industrial processes beyond mere extraction of natural resources, e.g., through further refinement); and policies regarding *ownership*, that is, of equity and fixed property, land, and in particular of natural resources.

Financial policies such as taxation or profit-sharing policy (i.e., policies preventing transfer prices, license fees, etc., to be abused to transfer untaxed profits from country to country).

Antitrust and *competition* policies at national and international levels.

Policies aimed at *technology transfer* (or the prevention of technology transfer).

Social and *employment* policies (e.g., job creation, job maintenance, regulation of working hours, protection of the working environment, protection of underprivileged categories of workers, etc.) and *environmental* policies.

Policies based in the national *political system* (distributive measures, capital formation, participation or codetermination schemes, etc.).

Policies aimed at improving national *prestige* in economic, industrial, or social activities.

This enumeration of policies and regulations in which MNCs are expected to participate or by which they are affected is by no means exhaustive (cf. Root and Ahmed, 1978).

Obviously, distortions such as political instability or even revolution do not necessarily frighten away foreign direct investment, especially after a major physical investment has been made (cf. Kobrin, 1976; Kobrin, 1979; and Frank, 1981). What seems to be much more important are the forms of instability that are not necessarily revolutionary in character, such as changes in basic strategic conditions upon which the operations of MNCs are based: ownership, remittance regulation, complex and time-consuming procedures, or prospects of arbitrary and unpredictable alterations in the rules of the game after an investment decision has been made or implemented.

Unpredictability of the political environment stems mainly from changes in the host country's perceived or real bargaining power due to economic or market growth, which makes foreign direct investments very attractive, on the one hand, but tends to be taken by host country governments as a basis of strengthening power over industry in general, on the other hand. Quite often it is directed toward MNCs in particular, for example in attempts to make high technology enterprises indigenous.

National goals may change (as demonstrated in this volume by the case of Australia). Rapid industrialization may be a top priority in a state in order to lay the ground for general economic and social improvement. Industrialization is often supported by measures to ease entry into certain industries by foreign investors, for example by import tariffs and regulations on clusters of goods, the domestic production of which is favored (e.g.) for the sake of import substitution). Over time, other national objectives may be given higher priority at short notice (e.g., employment). The consequent shifts in policy may be in the direction of export drives (devaluation or inducements to export). These policies, in turn, may make it necessary to reduce certain import barriers; thus, at short notice, changing the basic conditions under which foreign direct investment (FDI) was undertaken in the country in question.

The Australian example in this volume concerns the raw material extraction sector in which many drastic changes have occurred during recent decades in many countries and in which the foreign investor, once a substantial physical investment has been made, is heavily constrained in strategic decisionmaking. Drastic changes in the economic climate (as in the structural changes of the second half of the 1970s) or failures in the course of realizing national goals and plans, may, as experience shows, often lead either to aggressiveness vis-à-vis foreign investors or to profound changes in the economic climate and policy of many (host) countries. Traditionally liberal countries, for example, may introduce regulations of various kinds. Frank (1981) also illustrates cases of scapegoating, for example, blaming foreign investors for the consequences of miscarriages, with which their operations had have little or nothing to do. Frank, in concentrating on less developed countries (LDCs), also points to the potential "succession of dilemmas" in referring to LDCs:

> Third world governments face a series of frustrating dilemmas as they seek to shape a national policy toward foreign direct investment. If multinationals repatriate the bulk of their profits, they are depriving the nation of the newly created wealth; if, on the other hand, the firms reinvest the bulk of their profits locally, they are further increasing their ownership and control of the economy of the host country. If multinationals pay local workers the standard wage, they are exploiting cheap labor and garnering excess profits; if, on the other hand, earlier and simpler technologies are introduced, they are shortchanging the local economy. Resolving the dilemmas naturally has entailed policy shifts and adaptations on the part of the developing countries in response to their changing perceptions of how to maximize their gains from the foreign investment process.

The present volume attempts to shed light on the relations between MNCs and host country governments in either preventing conflicts of this type or in settling conflicts that have emerged. The bulk of the literature on MNC–host country tensions is about relations between less developed countries and multinational corporations controlled from headquarters in highly developed countries. Much of the literature is theorizing in character. This book, focuses on MNCs operating in highly developed environments (and to some extent also in recently developed industrial nations such as Mexico) as the leveling off of postwar economic growth in general and the structural impact of the energy-pricing changes in particular have induced many highly industrialized countries to turn to new policies affecting industry and trade. Often, specific policies and measures were contemplated or applied to constrain or regulate the activities of foreign investors. The reasons, at least in certain respects, are similar to reasons ascertained from the discussion of LDC government–MNC relations, which had stirred up many minds during the 1960s.

Concerns about TNC behavior have brought about the establishment of the UN Commission, the Information and Research Center on Transnational Corporations; calling into action of the International Working Group of the Code of Conduct; and further development of codes of conduct by the Organization for Economic Cooperation and Development, as well as by the International Chamber of Commerce. The International Labor Organization (ILO) issued "Principles Concerning Multinational Enterprises and Social Policy." In addition, "regional" codes have been issued or adopted, for example, by the foreign ministers of the European Economic Community (ECC) or by the "Andean Group."

It should not be forgotten that nation-states (in particular the U.S. government), but also assemblies of nation-states (such as the EEC), on certain occasions have, more or less, virgorously requested their national or multinational corporations to act in foreign countries as if they were part of the government or subordinated to home government regulations in their overseas activities.

Finally, some smaller highly industrialized nations (Canada as a prime example) have found that their indigenous industries were at a disadvantage in their home countries because the (predominantly U.S.-owned) multinational corporations, with their ability and obvious attempts to "rationalize globally," outperformed the generally (much) smaller indigenous firms.

Thus there is ample reason to investigate MNCs operating in highly and semiindustrialized countries:

1. What requirements are voiced on both sides?
2. What are the major areas of concern, friction, or conflict?
3. What measures should be used to avoid, reduce, or settle conflicts?

In order to investigate these general assumptions, the following inferences must be made:

1. MNC–host government relations are to be adapted to indigenous conditions and requirements in various host countries.
2. Various "nationalities" of MNCs (or MNC top management operating abroad) must show different propensities to be involved in settling actual frictions.

Comparative studies of these problems were undertaken and will be reported throughout this book.

The contributions to this volume are organized into four parts:

Part I discusses the *behavioral aspects* of MNC–host government relations. in the economic theory of foreign direct investment, the individual firm is regarded as a "black box" that operates on rational grounds and has access to information on the environment and about available strategic options and their outcomes. Decisions that have been made are immediately implemented and effective. Uncertainty is sometimes but not always taken into consideration. Firms act in a uniform manner, and indigenous influences are non-existent. Reality and theory, however, diverge. Three reports from a major internationally comparative study shed light on the importance of a range of criteria, such as centralization versus de-centralization, autonomy versus dependence, nationality, and idio-syncratic organization and individual behavior, and how these factors, as well as others, influence MNC–government relations.

Part II focuses on one of the main criticisms of MNCs, that is, their *financial behavior*. In its extreme exaggeration, it has been claimed that large MNCs have the power to blackmail or, in financial terms, literally ruin small- and medium-sized nation-states. The findings reported here do not even support the "global rationalization" assumption for finance, even though it would be the easiest one to apply, as financial transactions can be implemented in a few seconds. They do not even require physical transfers.

Part III is concerned with the *location , intensity, and character of R&D*. A major reason for the existence and operation of MNCs is the availability of superior products or modes of production. MNCs can develop and survive only if they keep abreast of competition by this kind of superiority (cf. Dunning, 1979b, Rugman, 1980). In its attempts at global rationalization, the MNC is in a position to distribute its R&D costs over quantities of items produced world-wide, facing neither the cost nor the uncertainties of knowledge transfer national corporations would have to expect and meet (cf. Ronstadt, 1977). By constantly pushing their R&D efforts forward and also using profits that are richly flowing from production and distribution centers around the world to cover their overhead, MNCs could, in the end, outcompete indigenous corporations. This could be concluded on logical as well as theoretical grounds. (Reality is also different in this case, as innovations with the potential for high profits cannot be forced into appearance. Profitable innovation can be developed by any type of firm under-taking various kinds of R&D.)

For this reason there is a strong interest in how MNCs decide upon the location of their R&D activities, how indigenous cor-porations compare with MNCs in the efficiency of their R&D activities, and how the host government can influence the location decisions as well as the general conditions for R&D.

In this volume the concerns of two smaller, highly industrialized countries, Canada and Sweden, are investigated, although the conclusions are relevant to a much wider range of nations and corporations.

Part IV is devoted to *national policies* that attempt to influence MNC behavior, with recognition of how MNCs can and may adapt or react to certain policy options and instruments. This section is rich in new information because it discloses deliberations in government-induced investigations and the preparation of policy proposals, based on case studies as well as statistical analyses. It also attempts to systematize the available options. When this systematization is held against the generally believed conclusions that conditions differ from country to country, firm to firm, and time to time, it means that distinct steps in theory and practice of this crucial matter have been made.

Another conclusion that can be derived from Part IV (as well as from contributions in Parts I and III) is that MNCs produce welfare gains that the indigenous corporations obviously cannot nearly approach, no matter how they strive to. (This point was demonstrated in Chapter 10 on Belgian MNC policy and in Chapter 8 in comparing Canadian and U.S. firms operating in Canada). A principal question concerning foreign direct investment or multinational corporation *theory* and *policy* is how welfare gains stemming from MNCs (obviously operating at higher levels of efficiency, despite existing regulations) can be maximized and reasonably distributed. If they are regulated away, they may cease to exist altogether, and all parties participating in the game will therefore lose.

Items Not Covered

Space limitations make it impossible to cover all issues of (potential) tension between MNCs and nation-states. However, the exclusion of certain issues should not be interpreted as either neglect or an act of negative assessment. Highly urgent and important issues omitted here will either be discussed in forthcoming volumes of this study or are the concern of other specialized groups of researchers.

BIBLIOGRAPHY

Dunning, J. H. "Recent Developments in Research on Multinational Enterprises: An Economist's Viewpoint." In *Recent Research on the Internationalization of Business*, edited by L.-G. Mattson and F. Wiedersheim-Paul. Uppsala: Uppsala University, 1979a.

———. "Explaining Changing Patterns of International Production: In Defence of the Eclectic Theory," University of Reading *Discussion Papers in International Investment and Business Studies*, No. 46, November 1979b.

Frank, I. "Foreign Enterprise World-Wide." *Economic Impact* 33, No. 1 (1981): 8-10.

Kobrin, S. J. "The Environmental Determinants of Foreign Direct Manufacturing Investment: An Ex Post Empirical Analysis." *Journal of International Business Studies* 7, No. 2 (1976): 29-42.

———. "Political Risk: A Review and Reconsideration." *Journal of International Business Studies* (1979).

Ronstad, R. C. *Research and Development Abroad by US Multinationals*. New York: Praeger, 1977.

Root, F. R., and Ahmed, A. A. "The Influence of Policy Instruments on Manufacturing Direct Foreign Investment in Developing Countries." *Journal of International Business Studies* 9, No. 3 (1978): 81-93.

Rugman, A. M. "A New Theory of the Multinational Enterprise: Internationalization Versus Internalization." *Columbia Journal of World Business* 15, No. 1 (Spring 1980): 15-27.

Vernon, R., ed. *Big Business and the State: Changing Relations in Western Europe*. Cambridge, Mass.: Harvard University Press, 1974.

Behavioral and Organizational Aspects of MNC-Host Government Relations

Part I discusses further analyses of an international study of 39 MNC headquarters and 158 subsidiaries of U.S., German, British, and Swedish multinational corporations in highly developed and semideveloped (Mexico, Brazil, Iran, and India) countries. All of the corporations studied are active in the manufacturing sector.

This analysis, which comprises a subset from the above-mentioned study, is predominantly qualitative in character. Quantitative analyses of a wide range of aspects of this study were reported in A. R. Negandhi and B. R. Baliga's *Tables Are Turning* (1981) and *Quest for Survival and Growth* (1979). Further analyses will be published in forth coming studies by members of the International Team.

The approach here is complementary to the prevailing theory of international direct investment (e.g., Vernon, 1966; Kindleberger, 1961; Caves, 1971; see Chapter 1 by Negandhi and Chapter 2 by Baliga for full references.) insofar as these studies regard enterprises as "black boxes," with access to full information for risky decisionmaking and the carrying out of the decisionmaking in a strictly rational manner. Such studies, therefore, cannot explain differences in performance on grounds other than either resource availability or measurable contingencies in the national environment. The studies of the International Team investigate differences in behavior caused by conditions or contingencies in the various host countries that cannot be measured or assessed in strict economic terms. In addition, the team investigates the impacts of national idiosyncracies upon MNC performance and MNC–government interactions in the host countries.

The aim of the first three studies in Part I is to investigate the nature of decisionmaking, organizational structures, the levels of dependence or independence between headquarters and the subsidiaries and the resulting effectiveness of internal relations, and, finally, the types and impact of MNC–nation-state relationships.

Gladwin and Walter (who are not members of the International Team) offer an analytical scheme as an aid to characterizing (potential and actual) conflicts. They develop this scheme into an aid for management in making strategic choices when approaching conflicts of various types.

Negandhi concentrates on examining the components of the global rationalization process adopted by U.S., West German, and Japanese MNCs, emphasizing the levels of formalization of policies and practices, degrees of centralization versus decentralization, and the relative influence of headquarters and the subsidiaries in decisionmaking. Furthermore, he studies critical issues and problem areas in the headquarters-subsidiaries relationship, the nature of external problems encountered by U.S., German, and Japanese MNCs in certain host countries, and finally the implications of the global rationalization process on the internal efficiency of the MNCs as well as on the maintenance of effective external relations with the host countries in question.

The first aspect of the internal functioning of the MNCs studied is the level of formalization of policies and practices, the degrees of centralization versus decentralization, and the relative influence of headquarters and the subsidiaries in decisionmaking, headquarter-subsidiary relationships, with an emphasis on critical issues and problem areas. Differences in behavior based on the nationality of the MNCs are fairly consistent. Almost 90% of the U.S. MNCs, but only approximately one-third of the German and just over 10% of the Japanese subsidiaries, were dependent on manuals, policies, and procedures issued by headquarters. Thus, the influence of these subsidiaries on strategic and policy matters is very different among the three nationalities, granting much freedom to the Japanese and very little to the American chief executive officer (CEO) abroad.

Consequently, almost all the American subsidiaries, and approximately two-thirds of the German and Japanese subsidiaries, were expected to provide up-to-date information on balance sheet, profit and loss figures, production output, market share development, cash and credit positions, inventory levels, and sales per product. Also in line with this characterization is the frequency of reporting, which is highest for the U.S. subsidiaries. Interestingly, the highest emphasis for the U.S. subsidiaries is on reporting short-term performance, while only moderate requirements are made for reporting on personnel as well as external socioeconomic and political conditions.

When comparing the structures and procedures of Japanese MNCs to those of the Western MNCs, one should keep in mind that the social network habits of Japan place less emphasis on formal reporting than is expected in Western corporations, even though the American pattern has been widely copied.

A proxy of the relative influence by subsidiaries on decisionmaking is their dependency on headquarter decisionmaking. As to be expected, American subsidiaries are least autonomous, Japanese subsidiaries enjoy the greatest autonomy whereas the Germans are ruled on the liberal side of the mean, but still at some distance from the Japanese degree of autonomy.

To make strategic and tactical decisions comparable, a weighting procedure was adopted. In general, the dependence on headquarters by subsidiaries for strategic decisionmaking is much higher than for tactical decisionmaking (as it should be). Nevertheless the following "distribution pattern" remains: high dependence for the U.S. subsidiaries and only moderate dependence for the German and Japanese subsidiaries.

When discussing critical issues and problem areas between headquarters and subsidiaries, approximately half of the subsidiary CEOs seemed to live in a problem-free world, regardless of nationality. In resolving issues between headquarters and subsidiaries, about half of the time the subsidiaries were asked to make the final decision. Here again, the "distribution pattern" between the nationalities resembled the pattern already reported.

The influence of firm and country contingency factors on decisionmaking and their consequences upon the degree of autonomy are preliminarily reported upon.

In support of the global rationalization hypothesis there is a relatively high degree of interdependence between headquarters and subsidiaries because of the intercorporate transfer of technology and semifinished and finished goods.

Subsidiaries in developing countries tend to have lower autonomy, whereas those in competitive markets tend to have higher autonomy, regardless of the size of the subsidiary or the nature of the product line.

There is a weak relationship between a firm's profits, growth, and general performance and its subsidiary autonomy. Tightly controlled subsidiaries perform better financially than autonomous subsidiaries, although subsidiaries with a high degree of autonomy are better accepted by the host country as to their operations thus improving their eventual growth and survival potential.

Given the prevailing trend over the last 20 years, during which the activities of many multinational corporations have been under close scrutiny, obviously the dichotomy between short-term performance versus long-term viability is an important issue. There is no uniform pattern discernible, although the principal character of the issues can be divided by placing the highly industrialized countries on one side, the semi-industrialized on the other, and the less developed countries in a third group. Although political issues today travel rapidly between the countries, matters of external concern to the MNC subsidiaries still differ widely. In West Germany the issue of codetermination was and still is a hot issue, whereas in many other highly developed countries, job creation, export potential, balance of payment support, and productivity as well as innovation in industry are some of the preferred performance criteria against which host country politicians and pressure groups assess the behavior and performance of their MNC guests.

Negandhi provides a fairly detailed record of large-scale comparative research. When evaluating the recent examples of foreign direct investment control and regulation in Canada and the United States, Negandhi foresees the development of a tougher climate for multinational activities throughout the world. Negandhi also reports that the German and Japanese multinationals have greater flexibility in adapting to host country governments, which has given them a faster growth and better bargaining position than would have been expected considering the tougher times and the periodic negative attitude of the host countries vis-à-vis American MNCs.

Negandhi concludes by conjuring that there will be a growth in protectionist trade and investment policies, which will constitute a challenge to MNCs in general. He leaves open the question if the more open and long-term oriented strategic behavior of Japanese and German MNCs will make it possible for them both to accommodate the global rationalization goal, which is the economic backbone of the multinationals' activities and simultaneously ease their survival under hardening conditions.

Baliga investigates the behavior of U.S.-controlled MNCs and the relations between those MNCs and certain host countries. He begins by discussing the conditions for the MNCs' initial success and the possible reasons for their later decline. He finds support for the "failure of success syndrome" (proposed by Marrow, 1974), which claims that the same factors that generated the spectacular success for U.S. MNCs carried the seeds for their later decline.

Baliga conjectures that differences in the "mind sets" of MNC executives (i.e., differences in formal rules under which they act as well as differences in their attitudes toward various factors in the host country environment) can lead to three syndromes that can jeopardize their success in the host countries. These differences are:

1. Recognition of the global nature of the environment (e.g., MNC attempts at global rationalization may conflict with local or national interests as well as differences in infrastructure, political, legal, and other conditions). A major reason why U.S. MNC subsidiaries failed to recognize these phenomena lay in the high level of centralization applied to U.S. MNCs and the consequent bureaucratization of their local behavior.

2. Understanding the nature of business–government relations. In the same way that U.S. corporations tend to criticize their home government whenever it intervenes into their economic affairs, they tend to take a similar stand abroad. At home, they can rely upon trade associations, lawyers, and press releases in dealing with public affairs. Abroad, however, these instruments are either unavailable or are not nearly as effective as in the United States. At the same time, U.S. MNCs are obviously not flexible enough to develop personal relationships with governmental bodies abroad. MNCs and their executives from other countries generally are better equipped to understand the various kinds of government–business relations and have smoother means to deal with them. They tend to be less inclined to voice dissent in public or to try to "play a power game."

3. Applying appropriate control systems. U.S. subsidiaries were more often organized as profit centers than other MNC subsidiaries, as a means of centrally controlling decentralization. Performance criteria usually are designed for the short term, and as a result internal executive behavior is also short-term oriented. Consequently, external behavior, and in particular MNC–government relations, will most likely also become short-term oriented, with "here and now" results more important. Because MNCs of other nationalities usually apply long-term as well as short-term performance criteria, they often have acquired better images than their U.S. colleagues and competitors.

In concluding, Baliga poses the question whether the U.S. MNCs could regain the lead they once had (and which, according to some researchers, they may have lost). His answer is affirmative, provided the managers are willing to change their behavior. Baliga provides a short guideline that might lead management to renewed success.

Welge investigates German-based MNC relations in Mexico. Confining his report to only one host country is motivated by his experience from the multicountry study, in which it was shown that host government interactions specifically depend upon the host country in question. The author uses a dynamic bargaining model to explain the gradual shift of the power balance from the multinational corporations to the host countries, based on the cornerstones of joint maximization, uncertainty (which is reduced over time), and learning.

The environment for MNC activities is characterized as being highly regulated, but at the same time permissive. A significant amount of influence from Mexican authorities and co-owners is compulsory. The climate for foreign direct investment in Mexico is considered quite good, with the Mexican domestic market being expected to grow very rapidly. This seems to be the major reason why many firms stay in the country and continue to invest by ploughing back their profits there. However, the profitability of the Mexican operations is not overly high, mainly because of price regulation.

In terms of the dynamic bargaining model, MNCs generally seem to perceive the future market potential as Mexico's foremost bargaining strength. Because of expected growth rather than present profits or resource availability, firms comply with the regulations and decide to remain in Mexico.

Welge investigates expectations and adaptation to government rules and policy by six German and four U.S. MNCs. German subsidiaries tend to choose an adaptive strategy, because this is also what they do in their home country and because they anticipate future gains from market growth. The most difficult problem seems to be union relations and the lack of collective-bargaining arrangements in Mexico. The German subsidiaries usually handle the situation by negotiating, whereas the American firms tend to take a slightly tougher stand, both vis-à-vis the government and the unions. This may be a consequence of the longer experience of U.S. subsidiaries with the Mexican environment.

In measuring centralization versus decentralization and headquarters' control over its subsidiaries, U.S. MNCs are the most centralized, the Japanese the least, and the Germans inbetween. The German subsidiaries are quite decentralized and tend to centralize only key strategic decisions, with local operative decisions being made by the management of the subsidiary. This strategy permits flexible adaptation to host country expectations and requirements at the subsidiary level. These findings are astonishing similar to those reported by Baliga. German subsidiaries also were able to soften the de facto application of host country regulations by behaving "better" than prescribed in certain instances (e.g., higher integration, and higher export shares than requested). Although such behavior may lower operational profits in the short run (which has not been proved), it also may lay the groundwork for cooperation between the host government and the MNC subsidiary. (It may, however, induce the host government to put new pressures on the "less well behaving" subsidiaries. This latter conclusion, however, is beyond those of the author.)

Gladwin and Walter analyze how TNCs can manage social conflict in host countries (e.g., human rights issues, bribery and corruption, consumer protection, the natural environment, tax avoidance) against the background of a rich case collection. Their first conclusion is that managers of TNCs generally are ill-equipped to manage social conflicts even though TNCs often are more exposed to tensions in the social sphere than are national firms. The authors develop algorithms to diagnose such conflicts as well as contingency plans for handling them. The pragmatic character of the proposals is demonstrated by the maxim that management has to be concerned with obtaining satisfactory outcomes of conflicts but must not necessarily resolve the conflicts itself (as this may be outside of its reach).

As the analytical scheme is anchored in the *stakes*, a TNC may place the outcome of a conflict on one side (the stakes in a conflict will be high if much may be won or lost) and its relative *power* or *leverage* in the conflict on the other side. These concepts are explained and exemplified; they are related to the integration and nationally responsive strategies of TNCs described in Chapter 13.

In summarizing the conclusions drawn from authentic cases, the key determinants of management behavior in TNC–host country conflicts are arranged in the model. Attention is paid to the fact that issues in the "motivational structure" (stakes and interest interdependence) usually have greater weight and importance than factors in the "capability structure" (i.e., the power, leverage, and quality of relationships). Five basic behavioral alternatives are related to the conditions in the cases under study:

Competitive (assertive, uncooperative) responses, aiming at dominance.

Avoidance (unassertive, uncooperative) responses, to escape a major problem or situation.

Collaborative approaches, in cases where both sides agree on achieving the same objectives, but where they differ on the means to be employed.

Accommodation (unassertive, cooperative) responses aiming at appeasement.

Compromise (moderately assertive, moderately cooperative) in cases where the goals are important, but are not worth the effort of more assertive behavior.

The authors point out that TNC–host country conflicts tend to become "integrated"; several, often loosely related issues are brought together and treated as a single entity. Disentanglement of the issues is, if at all possible, highly recommended so that smaller "chunks" can be dealt with, thus making it possible to apply a different strategy to each issue.

Attention is also drawn to the fact that conflicts frequently develop dynamically over time. Conflict management strategies should be geared to this fact in order to prevent "snowball effects." Consequently, the original taxonomic model is being developed into a dynamic conflict outcome-seeking model in an attempt to lay the ground for dynamic conflict management. The authors, with the support of their model, would like management to analyze conflict situations in order to disclose possible patterns (all of which can not possibly be reflected in the model). In this way management can avoid merely reacting to emerging situations and instead act strategically. The authors also stress that conflict management must involve TNC headquarters in most cases so that the consequences of the steps taken at one site can be assessed for the entire corporation.

The authors predict that in the foreseeable future TNCs will increasingly create, collide with, and be victimized by nonmarket tensions and contradictions.

Chapter 1

External and Internal Functioning of American, German, and Japanese Multinational Corporations: Decisionmaking and Policy Issues*

Anant R. Negandhi†

The quest of multinational corporations for global reach has led them to rationalize and unify their production, financial, research and developmental, and marketing activities. To facilitate such unification in strategies and policies, the American multinational corporation (MNC) has changed its organizational structure for managing international business from a mere export department to an international division, to a multinational structure with area and/or product concentration, to a matrix organizational form, and eventually to a transnational enterprise structure.[1]

A similar trend for European and Japanese multinational corporations has been predicted by Franko[2] and Yoshino.[3]

Although the global rationalization concept has been advocated

*This chapter is part of the large-scale study undertaken in 16 countries with 158 subsidiaries and 39 headquarters of American, British, German, Japanese, and Swedish multinational companies. The research is being supported by the International institute of Management, Science Center Berlin, and the Institute of International Business of the Stockholm School of Economics, Sweden. The research team consisted of A. R. Negandhi (University of Illinois); Ram Baliga (Texas Tech University); Anders Edstrom, Gunnar Hedlund, and Lars Otterbeck (Stockholm School of Economics); and Martin Welge (Fernuniversität Hagen, West Germany).

†University of Illinois at Urbana–Champaign.

and is being implemented, the real attributes, such as the nature of decisionmaking, levels of centralization-decentralization in specific areas, the relative influence of headquarters and overseas subsidiaries and the resulting effectiveness or tensions in their relationships, and the impact on the MNC-nation-states relationships have not been explored systematically by many researchers.

The purpose of this chapter is to examine some of the components of the global rationalization processes that are being adopted by the American, German, and Japanese multinational companies. More specifically, the following elements are examined in more detail:

1. Levels of formalization of policies and practices.
2. Degree of centralization-decentralization and the relative influence of the headquarters and subsidiaries in decision-making.
3. Headquarters-subsidiary relationships and the nature of the critical issues and problem areas between them.
4. Nature of the external problems encountered by the three types of multinationals in the countries studied.
5. Implications of global rationalization processes on internal efficiency and the maintenance of effective external relationships with the host countries.

Prior to the analysis and discussion of the results of this study, a word about research methodology and sample may be in order.

THE RESEARCH METHODOLOGY AND SAMPLE

The project was conceived in a comparative vein; we endeavored to study American, German, British, Japanese, and Swedish multinationals and their subsidiares. Our aim was to collect detailed information on many aspects of multinational operations, both at headquarter and subsidiary levels. Subsidiaries of 158 American, British, German, Japanese, and Swedish multinationals operating both in Europe (West Germany, United Kingdom, Spain, Portugal, Belgium, and the Netherlands), and in the United States, Mexico, Brazil, India, Iran, and their respective 39 headquarters were studied. Our sample was restricted to firms that were engaged in some form of manufacturing activity. Hence, firms in travel, banking, and other service sectors were omitted from consideration. Firms that were studied were selected from various investment directories and listings provided by the Chambers of Commerce, governmental agencies, and trade associations.

It is appropriate to make some remarks on the type of sample that was utilized in the analysis. Ideally, in order to have some confidence (statistically) in the results, the sample needed to be large enough and drawn randomly. Matching was impossible as the historical patterns of American, British, German, Japanese, and Swedish investments are all quite different; with Japanese multinationals being a much more recent phenomenon. Accordingly, a conscious, random sampling procedure was not feasible. In order to increase the generalization and external validity of the study, considerable supplemental information was obtained concerning the activities of the multinational corporations in these countries. Despite these efforts, the reader is cautioned to bear the limitations of the sample in mind when reading through the analyses and discussions.

In-depth interviews were conducted with the chief executive officers and other managerial personnel from all firms that had agreed to participate in the study. A semistructured interview guide was utilized to conduct the interviews. Each interview lasted an average of between four and eight hours; and in most cases included luncheon and dinner sessions. These sessions proved to be extremely valuable as the executives tended to relax, and, in narrating episodes related to the organizational functioning, they revealed significant, although subtle, aspects of their operations.

This chapter analyzes the results of the study conducted with 120 subsidiaries of American, German, and Japanese multinational corporations. The characteristics of these companies are given in Table 1.1.

INTERNAL FUNCTIONING OF THE
MULTINATIONAL CORPORATIONS

We first examine the level of formalization of policies and practices, degree of centralization-decentralization, and the relative influence of the headquarters and the subsidiaries in decisionmaking, the headquarter-subsidiary relationships, and the nature of the critical problems between them. As noted earlier, our aim of examining these elements was to assess the extent of the global rationalization strategies utilized by the three types of multinational corporations, namely, American, German, and Japanese.

In the next section, we examine the implications of these practices on the effectiveness of the firm at both the internal and the external levels.

Table 1.1 Profile of the Companies Studied

	Country of Origin		
	United States (N = 34)	Germany (N = 45)	Japan (N = 41)
Type of Industry			
Heavy engineering	12	14	2
Light engineering	5	6	14
Chemical and pharmaceutical	7	21	4
Electrical and electronics	0	2	6
Automobile	6	2	2
Tires and rubber products	3	0	0
Foods	1	0	1
Mixed—diversified trading companies with manufacturing investments	0	0	12
Ratio of Equity			
Wholly owned	32	44	31
Majority ownership	2	0	1
50–50 ownership	0	1	5
Minority ownership	0	0	4
Size: Number of Employees			
5000 and more	5	6	2
1001 to 4999	11	11	2
501 to 1000	4	9	4
201 to 500	4	4	9
101 to 200	3	8	3
100 or fewer	1	3	5
Information inadequate		26	

LEVEL OF FORMALIZATION

To assess the level of formalization in the American, German, and Japanese multinational companies, three aspects are examined:

1. The dependence of the subsidiaries on the manuals, policies, and procedures supplied by the headquarters;
2. utilization of these policies and procedures for decisionmaking; and;
3. the nature and the frequency of reporting required by headquarters.

Table 1.2 shows the extent to which the subsidiaries of the American, the German, and the Japanese multinational companies depended upon the written policies of the headquarters. An overwhelmingly large number of the American subsidiaries (88 percent) relied on

Table 1.2 Extent to which Subsidiaries Depend on the Written Policies
from Headquarters

MNC Ownership	Great Deal (%)	To Some Extent (%)	Very Little to Not at All (%)
American (N = 33)	88	6	6
German (N = 44)	32	20	48
Japanese (N = 40)	12	22	66

Level of significance = 0.0001.
Number of missing observations = 3.
Total number of observations = 120.

policies of headquarters. Approximately one-third of the German subsidiaries did so, while merely 12 percent of the Japanese subsidiaries utilized the policies supplied by their headquarters. Conversely, only 6 percent of the American, 48 percent of the German, and 66 percent of the Japanese subsidiaries indicated very negligible influence on strategic and policy decisions affecting their operations.

A similar picture emerges when we examine the influence of the written policies and procedures (whether supplied by the headquarters and/or modified by the subsidiaries) on actual strategic and policy-level decisions (see Table 1.3).

One can also evaluate the relative influences of headquarters on the subsidiaries' operations by examining the nature and frequency of reporting required of the managers of the subsidiaries.

As can be seen in Table 1.4, almost all of the American subsidiaries and approximately two-thirds of the German and Japanese subsidiaries were required by their respective headquarters to provide up-to-date information on balance sheet, profit and loss figures, production output, market share, cash and credit positions, inventory levels, and sales per product. The frequency of reporting was greater for the

Table 1.3. Extent to which Subsidiaries Depend on Manuals, Policies, and
Procedures for Strategic and Policy-Level Decisions

MNC Ownership	Great Deal (%)	To Some Extent (%)	Very Little to Not at All (%)
American (N = 33)	88	3	9
German (N = 44)	32	16	52
Japanese (N = 40)	10	32	58

Level of significance = 0.0001.
Number of missing observations = 3.
Total number of observations = 120.

Table 1.4. Nature and Frequency of Reporting by the Subsidiaries to the Headquarters in Various Areas

Type of Report	American (N = 33)				German (N = 44)				Japanese (N = 40)			
	Weekly	Monthly	Quarterly	Ad Hoc Yearly	Weekly	Monthly	Quarterly	Ad Hoc Yearly	Weekly	Monthly	Quarterly	Ad Hoc Yearly
Balance sheet		97	24	–	5	49	32	14	2	42	24	32
Profit and loss statements	6	91	3	–	–	49	35	16	–	42	32	26
Production output	6	94	–	–	13	50	29	8	6	47	25	22
Market share	3	70	24	3	2	48	29	21	3	31	33	33
Cash and credit statement	–	100	–	–	2	41	36	21	2	39	27	32
Inventory levels	3	88	9	–	5	46	26	23	5	38	23	34
Sales per product	3	88	9	–	2	37	26	35	5	44	19	32
Performance review of personnel	3	9	3	85	–	15	5	80	–	2	–	98
Report on local economic and political conditions	6	33	6	55	5	32	17	46	5	12	7	76

American (usually monthly) than for the German and the Japanese subsidiaries.

It is revealing to note from this table that the only items with which the subsidiaries were less bothered were the performance reviews of their personnel and local socioeconomic and political conditions. In other words, stress is placed more on aspects that affect the short-run financial picture of the company rather than on factors that affect the firm's long-term survival and growth.

The analyses of the above three aspects of formalized reporting clearly indicate the increasing levels of formalization being introduced by American MNCs. Although the German MNCs seem to be catching up with the Americans, the Japanese companies, however, are still relying on their informal network of reporting.

THE RELATIVE INFLUENCE ON DECISIONMAKING

Centralization versus subsidiary autonomy is a perennial and conflicting issue for most multinational companies. On the one hand, increasing competition in the world market requires some measure of rationalization of production and marketing processes at a global level, thus requiring a higher degree of centralization of decisionmaking at the headquarter and/or regional headquarter levels. On the other hand, however, satisfying the increasing demands from the host as well as the home countries of the multinationals necessitates some measure of subsidiary autonomy in strategic decisionmaking.

To assess the relative influence of the headquarters and subsidiaries in decisionmaking, we examined the following factors:

1. Training programs for local employees
2. Laying off operating personnel
3. Use of expatriate personnel
4. Appointment of a chief executive
5. Maintenance of production facilities
6. Determining aggregate production schedules
7. Pricing decisions
8. Expansion of production capacity
9. Use of a local advertising agency
10. Servicing of products sold
11. Introduction of a new product for the local market
12. Choosing a public accountant
13. Extension of credit to major customers
14. Use of cash flow by the subsidiary
15. Borrowing from local banks

Tables 1.5 and 1.6 provide the raw score and difference in means between the influences of the subsidiary and headquarters on decision-making. Here again, as can be seen from the tables, American subsidiaries have the least autonomy, the Japanese the most with the German subsidiaries in the middle.

However, the picture of greater autonomy for the subsidiaries changed when we compared the role of strategic versus routine decisions. As shown in Table 1.7, the relative score becomes negative for all three types of subsidiaries when measuring the influence of strategic decisions.

To probe further, we computed an overall delegation index by assigning different weights to strategic versus routine decisions. Strategic decisions were weighted three times as much as routine

Table 1.5. The Relative Influence of Subsidiaries in Decisionmaking[a]

	Mean Scores		
	United States	*Japan*	*Germany*
Personnel training program for your subsidiary	3.8	4.6	4.5
Layoffs of operating personnel	4.4	4.9	4.4
Use of expatriate personnel from headquarters	2.7	3.6	2.4
Appointment of chief executive of your subsidiary	1.5	2.8	1.7
Maintenance of production facilities at subsidiary	3.3	4.3	4.8
Determining aggregate production schedule	3.2	4.2	4.3
Expansion of your production capacity	2.5	3.5	2.7
Use of local advertising agency	3.9	4.7	4.5
Servicing of products sold	4.4	4.7	4.7
Pricing on products sold on your local market	3.0	4.5	4.0
Introduction of a new product on your local market	2.6	4.1	3.1
Choice of public accountant	2.7	4.6	4.4
Extension of your credit to one of your major customers	3.7	4.5	4.3
Use of cash flow in your subsidiary	3.2	4.2	3.4
Your borrowing from local banks or financial institutions	3.2	3.6	3.4
Average (means)	3.21	4.19	3.77

Source: Authors' interviews.

[a]The responses were precoded from "1" for "Very Little to No Influence" to "5" for "Very High Influence."

Table 1.6. Relative Influence over 15 Decision Areas:
Mean Score Differences[a]

	Differences in Means		
	United States	*Japan*	*Germany*
Personnel training . . .	1.1	3.1	2.4
Layoffs . . .	2.6	3.3	2.7
Expatriates . . .	−0.7	0.2	−1.7
Appointment of CEO . . .	−3.0	−1.6	−3.0
Maintenance . . .	0.1	1.8	2.4
Production Schedule . . .	−0.1	1.2	1.9
Expansion . . .	−1.4	−0.2	−1.2
Advertising . . .	1.4	2.7	2.7
Servicing . . .	2.5	2.9	3.1
Pricing . . .	−0.5	1.9	1.3
New Products . . .	−1.2	0.8	−0.6
Choice of CPA . . .	−0.5	1.8	2.4
Credit to Customers . . .	1.2	2.4	2.5
Use of Cash Flow . . .	0.1	1.7	0.3
Borrowing from Banks . . .	0.1	0.5	0.1
Average (means)	0.11	1.50	1.02

Source: Authors' interviews.

[a]The figures in the table represent the differences in means between the rated *subsidiary* and *HQ* influence for each of the decision items, the means taken over the companies in the identified country category. A positive number implies a relatively greater influence on the part of the subsidiary, while a negative number indicates greater HQ influence.

decisions. The weighting factor reflected the approximate ratio of feedback time for strategic decisions as compared to routine decisions. Table 1.8 presents the findings for the overall delegation index and the extent of delegation provided to the subsidiary management along with a set of decisions.

As can be seen from Table 1.8, the overall delegation index is fairly low in absolute terms. Despite the acknowledgement of head-

Table 1.7. Relative Influence over 15 Decision Areas:
Selected Strategic Decisions

Item	*Overall*	*United States*	*Japan*	*Germany*	*Sweden*	*United Kingdom*
Appointment of CEO	−2.1	−3.0	−1.6	−3.0	−0.4	−1.7
Expansion	−0.8	−1.4	−0.2	−1.2	−0.5	−0.2
New Products	−0.2	−1.2	−0.8	−0.6	−0.4	0.4
Mean	−1.3	−1.87	−0.33	−1.6	−0.17	−0.50

Source: Authors' interviews.

Table 1.8. Comparison of Delegation in the Various Areas for U.S., German, and Japanese MNCs

	United States (N = 34)		Germany (N = 45)		Japan (N = 41)	
	Mean	S.D.	Mean	S.D.	Mean	S.D.
Overall delegation index	-1.68	4.33	0.14	3.72	2.89[a]	3.38
Local personnel decisions	2.40	1.46	2.85	1.24	3.51[b]	0.93
Expatriate personnel decisions	-2.10	1.67	-2.49	1.60	-0.65[b]	2.00
Routine production decisions	-0.04	2.63	2.59[a]	1.43	2.24[a]	1.84
Strategic production decisions	-1.78	2.21	-1.54	2.21	0.07[b]	2.26
Routine marketing decisions	1.27	1.62	2.42[a]	1.19	2.85[a]	1.11
Strategic marketing decisions	-1.58	2.14	-0.83	2.42	1.14[a]	2.35
Financial decisions	0.30	2.00	1.61[a]	1.50	1.90[a]	1.00

Key:

-4	0	+4
maximum HQ influence	equal influence	maximum subsidiary influence

[a] $p \leqslant 0.001$
[b] $p < 0.05$

quarters of a less than perfect understanding of the subsidiary's operation and its environment, the subsidiary's influence on strategic decisionmaking is minimal.

CRITICAL PROBLEMS BETWEEN
HEADQUARTER AND SUBSIDIARY
OPERATIONS

During interviews with the senior executives of both headquarters and the subsidiaries, we probed into some of the critical problems encountered in headquarters–subsidiary relationships. Besides examining the nature and intensity of focal issues between headquarters and the subsidiaries, we also attempted to assess the relative influence of headquarters and the subsidiaries in resolving these issues.

Approximately half of the subsidiaries of the American, German, and Japanese multinational companies studied indicated that there were no serious problems in their relationships with headquarters. Of the 48 critical issues narrated by the executives of the subsidiaries, roughly a third were concerned with the lack of the subsidiary's autonomy in dealing with their problems in the host countries and approximately a quarter were concerned with capital investment decisions. Table 1.9 shows the range of problems between headquarters and the subsidiaries.

In measuring the relative influence of headquarters and the subsidiaries in resolving issues, our results indicated that in approximately half of the cases, headquarters made the final decisions whereas in less than a third of the cases the subsidiaries' viewpoint prevailed. Among the three types of subsidiaries studied, the German and Japanese seem to have greater influence in resolving issues.

IMPACT OF SPECIFIC FACTORS OF
THE FIRM AND COUNTRY ON
DECISIONMAKING AND THE
CONSEQUENCES OF AUTONOMY

Both in organizational theory and international business, it has been shown that specific factors of the firm, such as size, technology, and type of industry, as well as specific factors of the country, such as levels of industrial and economic development, market and other economic conditions prevailing in a given country, and the level of government control on industry, may affect not only the

Table 1.9. Nature of Critical Issues Existing Between Headquarters and Subsidiaries

Ownership of MNC	Capital Investment	Sales and Financial	Home Country Policies	Host Country Policies	Organizational Autonomy	No Issues	Total
	$N/q_0^1/q_0^2$	$N/q_0^1/q_0^2$	$N/q_0^1/q_0^2$	$N/q_0^1/q_0^2$	$N/q_0^1/q_0^2$	$N/q_0^1/q_0^2$	
United States	3/10.3/27.3	2/6.9/22.2	1/3.4/14.3	1/3.4/16.7	5/17.2/33.2	17/58.6/27.9	29
Germany	5/12.2/45.5	3/7.3/33.3	2/4.9/28.6	2/4.9/33.3	8/19.5/53.3	21/51.2/34.4	41
Japan	3/7.7/27.3	4/10.3/44.4	4/10.3/57.1	3/7.7/50.0	2/5.1/13.3	23/59.0/37.7	39
Column Total	11	9	7	6	15	61	109

Source: Authors' interviews.

Key: q_0^1 refers to row percentages.

q_0^2 refers to column percentages

Chi square = 6.35   10 D.f.   Significance = 0.78

centralization decisions, but also the impact of these decisions on the firm's efficiency.[4]

At the present time my colleagues collaborating in this project and I are analyzing our composite data further to examine the effects of these factors on the subsidiary's autonomy and the consequences of autonomy on the firm's efficiency.

Our preliminary analysis suggests the following trends:*

1. When there is a large amount of intercompany transfer of technology, raw materials, and semifinished and finished goods with a high degree of interdependence between headquarters and the subsidiary, there is a lower level of subsidiary autonomy.
2. Subsidiaries located in the developing countries tend to have somewhat lower autonomy.
3. Subsidiaries operating in competitive markets tend to have higher autonomy.
4. The size of the subsidiary does not affect the level of autonomy.
5. The nature of the product lines has a very marginal effect on the subsidiary's autonomy.
6. Subsidiary autonomy has some effect, although it is not very significant, on the firm's profits, growth, and other performance criteria. Tightly controlled subsidiaries are relatively better performers, financially, than the autonomous subsidiaries. However, a subsidiary with higher autonomy has a more positive impact on the host country's acceptance of its operation, thereby improving its eventual growth and survival potential.

This last finding thus provides support to the advocates of the processes of rationalization and unification for MNCs. However, at the same time it raises an intriguing question about the utility of such centralization processes under rapidly changing socioeconomic and political conditions in industrialized as well as in developing countries. To explore this question further, we first examine the changing conditions in the industrialized countries and then discuss the implications of such changes on MNC strategies, policies, and structure.

FAST-CHANGING CONDITIONS IN INDUSTRIALIZED COUNTRIES

Although many of the industrialized countries are operating as "free and open markets" and are generally very congenial to foreign

---

*The summary results are drawn from the twin papers of Johnny K. Johansson et al., "Autonomy of Subsidiaries in Multinational Corporations," in *The Management of Headquarter–Subsidiary Relationships in Multinational Corporations*, edited by Lars Otterbeck (London: Gower, 1982).

investors, recently they, too, have begun to question the utility of unchecked foreign investment. In other words, the governmental decisionmakers as well as other public groups (e.g., labor unions, consumer advocates, and environmentalists) are discovering that national needs, ambitions, and objectives can be at variance with the objectives, goals, and strategies of MNCs.

The range, nature, and intensity of these issues, of course, differ considerably from country to country, depending upon the prevailing political climate and economic conditions (e.g., unemployment, inflation, or balance of payments position) and the level of industrial and economic development. For example, in a study of MNCs in developed countries, Fry[5] reported that the issue of worker participation ("Mitbestimmung") was most prominent in West Germany, and the traditional issues, such as providing new techonology, employment, upgrading wages, and developing local resources, were considered secondary by the governmental officials.

In contrast, in Belgium the major issues pertaining to MNC activities were related to employment capabilities, potential effect on the balance of payments position, research and development activities (or lack of), development and utilization of local resources, and worker participation in management. Simultaneously, however, MNCs emphasized their importance in terms of increasing the entrepreneurial spirit, providing new technology, and producing consumer goods at lower prices. These differences in expectations between the host government and MNC priorities are clearly highlighted in Table 1.10.

Especially since the oil crisis of 1973 most of the industrialized nations have experienced a downturn in their economic growth and prosperity, which in turn has created considerable hostility, not only toward foreign multinationals but also among the opposing groups in a given society (e.g., management against labor, domestic multinationals against foreign multinationals, and multinationals against their own subcontractors). For example, when faced with declining sales of U.S. automobiles, the three largest U.S. auto companies (General Motors, Ford, and Chrysler) began to denounce auto imports from Japan and the European countries asked the U.S. Congress and the President to help them. At the same time, their own subcontractors have publicly accused the auto companies of being "double talkers" by asserting that "it is not just imported cars, it's imported parts that are causing problems."[6] The growing complaints over Detroit's policies of importing parts for domestically assembled cars have now reached Washington. Consequently, congressional proposals that were originally designed to limit imports of autos are being amended to also place restrictions on imported parts.[7]

Table 1.10. Expectation Differences Between Multinational
Corporations and Nation-States

Impact	Government Wants More	Firms Give More
Germany		
Worker participation	X	
Increased competition		X
Capital inflows		X
Increased skilled employment		X
Create entrepreneurial spirit		X
Belgium		
Increased general employment	X	
Increased skilled employment	X	
Balance of payment effects	X	
Increased R&D efforts	X	
Develop local resources	X	
Worker participation	X	
Increased quality of consumer services	X	
Social and cultural values		X
Increased entrepreneurial spirit		X
Provide new technology		X
Create lower prices		X

Source: David E. Fry, "Multinational Corporations–Host Government Relationships: An Empirical Study of Behavioral Expectations," D.B.A. dissertation, Kent State University, 1977.

The results of our own large-scale study, reported in Table 1.11, illustrate the nature of demands made by MNCs in West Germany, the United Kingdom, Spain, Portugal, and France.

As can be seen from this table, economic stagnation, triggered by the oil crisis, has generated traditional economic demands even in the more industrialized nations of the world. However, except in the case of Spain and Portugal, the European countries, in which this field research was undertaken, have not yet legislated these demands.

However, one thing appears clear: the less economically developed a country, and/or the more intensive its economic problems, the greater are the demands placed on MNCs and the more willing is the country to legislate these expectations.

Table 1.12 shows the nature of the problems faced by the American, German, and Japanese MNCs in various industrialized countries. The labor force seems to be the source of almost half the problems faced by the multinationals. However, U.S. and German subsidiaries have, proportionately, more labor problems than Japanese companies. The underlying theme of labor–management problems is, however, quite different in the various countries. In Germany, for instance, industry representatives were involved in challenging the constitutional

Table 1.11. Nature of Demands Made on Multinational Corporations in Selected Industrialized Countries[a]

	Germany (N/%)	United Kingdom (N/%)	Spain (N/%)	Portugal (N/%)	France (N/%)	Total
Technology transfer	0/0.0	2/21.4	0/0.0	0/0.0	0/0.0	3/5.3
Exports	0/0.0	1/7.1	0/0.0	0/0.0	1/12.5	2/3.5
Employment	0/0.0	2/14.3	0/0.0	0/0.0	0/0.0	2/3.5
Economic development	3/23.1	5/35.7	10/90.9	9/81.8	7/87.5	34/59.6
Ambivalent	1/7.7	0/0.0	0/0.0	0/0.0	0/0.0	1/1.8
No specific demands	9/69.2	3/21.4	1/9.1	2/2.18	0/0.0	15/26.3
	13/22.8	14/24.6	11/19.3	11/19.3	8/14.0	57/100

Source: Interview data collected by the authors.
[a] Raw chi square = 43.19530 with 20 degrees of freedom. Significance = 0.0019.

validity of the "codetermination" laws as well as influencing the election of representatives who were against the codetermination laws. The U.S. multinational subsidiaries, owing to stipulations about the size of the workforce in the law, were most susceptible to the laws. Given the confrontational nature of management–labor relations in the United States, American multinationals initially had a difficult time accepting the collaborative philosophy.

Except in Germany and a few other countries, all multinationals, especially the larger U.S. and German MNCs, have been the target of leftist-oriented labor unions. This has been particularly true of Spain and Portugal, where rising nationalistic expectations have made these issues even more difficult to handle. Japanese multinationals appear to have avoided serious problems with labor, to some extent, by their smaller size and their willingness to enter into joint ventures with either government organizations or private entrepreneurs. This finding is interesting in the light of the fact that, despite being involved in joint ventures or minority holdings in the developing countries, Japanese organizations have had considerable problems with labor.[8] These problems have stemmed mainly from efforts made by the Japanese to impose their management style, and—in South and Southeast Asia—from animosities rooted in recent history. Apparently the Japanese MNCs have learned from their experience in the developing countries of Asia and South America and therefore have restricted the use of a Japanese management style (such as lifetime employment and demanding loyalty to the company) in the industrialized countries.

Japanese subsidiaries were involved, however, in conflicts with the EEC Commission. Problems were centered around charges of

Table 1.12. Problems Faced by the Multinationals in Industrialized Countries

	Host Government (N/%)	Labor (N/%)	Political Groupings (N/%)	Local Competitors (N/%)	Multiple Sources (N/%)	No Problems (N/%)	Regional Economic Grouping (N/%)	Total
U.S. MNCs	1/25.0 1/4.3	11/40.7 11/47.8	1/100.0 1/4.3	1/100.0 1/4.3	1/100.0 1/4.3	8/38.1 8/34.8	0/00.0 0/0.0	23/100
German MNCs	0/0.0 0/0.0	12/44.4 12/80.0	0/0.0 0/0.0	0/0.0 0/0.0	0/0.0 0/0.0	3/14.3 3/20.0	0/0.0	15/100
Japanese MNCs	3/75.0 3/15.7	4/14.8 4/21.0	0/0.0 0/0.0	0/0.0 0/0.0	0/0.0 0/0.0	10/47.6 10/52.6	2/100.0 2/10.5	19/100
Total	4/100 4/7.0	27/100 27/47.4	1/100 1/1.8	1/100 1/1.8	1/100 1/1.8	21/100 21/36.8	2/100 2/3.5	57/100

"dumping" by Japanese organizations, despite the fact that the accused Japanese companies had manufacturing subsidiaries in the EEC countries. The Japanese organizations responded by adopting a legalistic stance while simultaneously emphasizing their local manufacturing activities in efforts to make the dumping charge untenable.

As noted earlier, although the industrially developed countries have, thus far, constrained themselves in enacting limiting legislation against foreign private investments and multinational corporations, the public debates and discussions are moving closer to this end at a faster speed than would have been anticipated. For example, the recent establishment of the Foreign Investment Review Agency in Canada[9] and their pronouncements about expected corporate behavior, as seen in Table 1.13, come very close to what the developing countries have been demanding from foreign investors during the last two decades.

In turning to the United States, it is apparent that unemployment and inflation continue to undermine the people's confidence in national economic conditions, the legislators both at the state and national levels have begun to introduce legislation to curb the activities of foreign investors and multinational companies. For example, in the last few years approximately half of the 50 states have introduced legislation to restrict foreign investment in agricultural land. At a lesser end, as mentioned earlier, the subcontractors of U.S. automobile companies as well as the labor unions have begun to question the virtue of multinational investments and their general strategies of global rationalization.

Our results, on the other hand, clearly show the increasing trend toward global rationalization and centralization in decisionmaking. Thus, the question must be asked whether the German and Japanese multinationals are flexible enough to turn the tide and maintain their flexible structures and responses, as they have been able to do in the developing countries, once circumstances demand that they do so in the industrialized countries.

Even the American multinationals, champions in evolving progressive organizational structures for managing expanding international business (from export departments to international divisions, regional structure, worldwide product setup, and the matrix system) have been warned about the swiftly changing environmental conditions in both the developed and the developing countries.

Business International,[10] a reputed consulting firm in international business, recently identified some of the major economic and political changes that will affect the need for changes in present organizational forms utilized by American and other multinational companies.

Table 1.13. Canada's 12 Good Corporate Behavior Principles
(as They Relate to Alleged Objectionable U.S.
Subsidiary Policies)

Guiding Principle Summary	*Alleged Objectionable Practices*
1. Full realization of the company's growth and operating potential in Canada.	1. U.S.-based corporate planners institute expansion and cutback plans without regard for Canada's plan and aspirations.
2. Make Canadian subsidiary a self-contained, vertically integrated entity with total responsibility for at least one productive function.	2. The Canadian subsidiary is primarily an assembler of imported parts or distributor of goods produced elsewhere so operations can be easily shut down or transferred.
3. Maximum development of export markets from Canada.	3. Filling export orders to third-country markets from the U.S. country stock earns credits for U.S. balance of payments rather than Canada's.
4. Extend processing of Canada's raw materials through maximum number of stages.	4. Have as few as possible materials-processing stages in Canada to minimize political leverage.
5. Equitable pricing policies for international and intracompany sales.	5. Negotiated or spurious prices by Canadian U.S. subsidiaries are designed to get around Canadian income taxes.
6. Develop sources of supply in Canada.	6. Preference for U.S. or third-country sources for purposes of corporate convenience or political leverage.
7. Inclusion of R&D and product development.	7. The concentration of R&D and product design in the United States means Canada can never develop these capabilities.
8. Retain substantial earnings for growth.	8. Profits earned in Canada do not remain to finance Canadian expansion.
9. Appointment of Canadian officers and directors.	9. Use of U.S. officers and directors to prevent development of local outlook in planning and execution.
10. Equity participation by Canadian investing public.	10. Creation of wholly owned subsidiaries denies policy determination and earnings to Canadians.
11. Publication of financial reports.	11. Consolidation of Canadian operating results into parent company statement or failure to publish any relevant information.
12. Support of Canadian cultural and charitable institutions.	12. Failure locally to support such causes as the United Appeal where parent corporations give generously to comparable U.S. campaigns.

Source: David J. Ashton, "U.S. Investments in Canada: Will the Other Shoe Drop?" *Worldwide P & I Planning* (September–October 1968): 57.

DECLINING OR STAGNANT ECONOMIC GROWTH IN INDUSTRIALIZED COUNTRIES

On the average, Canada, France, West Germany, Japan, the United States, and the United Kingdom will experience their real growth in GNP drop from about 3 percent in 1979 to 1 percent in 1980. The U.S. GNP growth may drop from 2 percent in 1979 to 1.25 percent in 1980; Japan from 6 percent to 4.75 percent; West Germany from 3 percent to 2 percent; Canada from 2.75 percent to 1.5 percent; and the United Kingdom from 0.5 percent to 2 percent.[11] While growth rates in major industrialized countries are declining, inflation continues to soar. Thus, the poorer future outlook and the higher inflation rates are likely to reinforce protectionist forces in the United States and other developed countries.[12]

Given such changing economic and political conditions, Business International warns that multinational corporations will have to create a responsive organizational structure that could combine the centralization of strategies and policies with the increasing decentralization of subsidiary operations.[13]

Whether the German and Japanese companies, in their quest for adopting the American model of global rationalization, will be able to achieve a marriage between the centralization of strategies and policies (as required by the global rationalization concept) and the needed decentralization or higher autonomy of the subsidiary operations is an open question awaiting the attention of the academic scholars as we move into the 1980s.

NOTES

1. Stopford, John, and Wells, Louis. *Managing the Multinational Enterprise.* London: Longmans, 1972.
2. Franko, Lawrence. "The Move Toward a Multi-Divisional Structure in European Organizations." *Administrative Science Quarterly*, 19 (1974): 493–506.
3. Yoshino, Michel. *Japan's Multinational Enterprise.* Cambridge, Mass.: Harvard University Press, 1976.
4. Pugh, Derek, et al. "The Context of Organization Structures." *Administrative Science Quarterly* 14 (1969): 91–114. For international aspect see Vernon Raymond, *Storm Over the Multinationals: The Real Issues.* Cambridge, Mass.: Harvard University Press, 1979, especially chapters 1 and 2, pp. 1–33.
5. Fry, David E. *Multinational Corporations–Host Government Relationships:*

An Empirical Study of Behavioral Expectations. DBA dissertation, Kent State University, 1977.

6. *Wall Street Journal* LX, 149 (May, 14, 1980), p. 1.
7. Ibid.
8. Negandhi, Anant R., and Baliga, B. R. *Quest for Survival and Growth: A Comparative Study of American, European and Japanese Multinationals.* Königstein, West Germany: Athenäum, and New York: Praeger, 1979.
9. Safarian, A. E., and Bell, Joel. "Issues Raised by the National Control of the Multinational Enterprise." In *Multinational Corporations and Governments: Business–Government Relations in an International Context,* edited by Patrick M. Boardman and Hans Schollhammer, p. 74. New York: Praeger, 1975.
10. Business International. "Pressures on Management Call For Coordination and Innovative Twists." *Business International* (January 4, 1980), pp. 1, 7, 8.
11. Ibid.
12. Ibid.
13. Ibid.

Chapter 2

U.S. Multinational Corporations: A Lesson in the Failure of Success

The decades of the 1960s and 1970s witnessed considerable debate and dialogue on the role of multinational corporations, especially U.S. MNCs, in the world economy. The rapid growth of American multinational corporations generated fears of dominance and control not only in the developing countries but also in the developed countries of Europe (Vernon, 1971; Moran, 1974; Sampson, 1973; Barnet and Mueller, 1975; Mikesell, 1971; Turner, 1973; Servan—Schreiber, 1968; Sauvant and Lavipour, 1976). The situation, today, is significantly different from that of the 1960s and 1970s. The rate of growth of American multinationals has slowed down and is being surpassed by the German and Japanese multinational corporations (Franko, 1976; Yoshino, 1976; Tsurumi, 1977). What has caused this turnabout? What are the factors behind the rapid growth of German and Japanese multinational corporations? These are some of the fundamental questions being asked by researchers on multinational corporations (Yoshino, 1976; Franko,

*This research is predominantly funded by the International Institute of Management, Science Center Berlin, and involves collaborative efforts by researchers from Germany, Sweden, and the United States.

†Texas Tech University.

1976; Tsurumi, 1977; Johnson and Ouchi, 1974). Many studies, including this one, adopt a comparative perspective for understanding the differences and similarities in the functioning of multinational corporations from different countries, with the objective of providing some prescriptions to executives. This particular study was concerned with examining the structuring of multinational corporations headquarters–subsidiary relationships, modes of maintaining external reationships, and some aspects of decisionmaking. Approximately 200 organizations—U.S., German, Japanese MNCs and their subsidiaries— were studied through in-depth interviews with top management. In this chapter, we report some of the findings pertaining to U.S. MNCs, and wherever appropriate, comparisons will be made with German and Japanese MNCs. It should be emphasized that many of the findings reported here are based on the content analysis of the interviews, while other findings are based on quantitative analysis. This was a deliberate part of the research strategy adopted as we felt that studies predominantly utilizing questionnaires miss the subtle aspects of organizational functioning. In the following section, we discuss, briefly, other details of the methodology employed in conducting the investigation.

RESEARCH METHODOLOGY

The data utilized in the current paper were obtained as part of the larger study, "Multinational Corporations in Developed Countries," alluded to earlier. Reflecting the diverse interests of the collaborating group, the study sought to gather detailed information on practically every aspect of corporate functioning. In-depth interviews were conducted with personnel from headquarters and subsidiaries of German, Japanese, and U.S. MNCs operating in Europe, the United States, Mexico, Brazil, Iran, and India. The multinational corporations studied were identified from investment directories and listings provided by the various Chambers of Commerce and manufacturing associations. We also limited our investigation to firms in the manufacturing sector. While every effort was made to ensure that a random sample was obtained, lack of cooperation on the part of some identified multinationals and other realities of field research in international business made it impossible to obtain a rigorous random sample. These factors lead us to emphasize that the findings reported in the study are more indicative than definitive. We feel, however, that the findings merit serious consideration as sufficient corroborating evidence has appeared in recent literature (Charan and Freeman, 1980; Hayes and Abernathy, 1980; Northrup and Rowan, 1979; Suzuki, 1979; Vernon, 1977).

THE CREATION OF "FAILURE OF SUCCESS" MIND SETS

It is our fundamental contention that the current malaise of U.S. multinational corporations can be found in the "failure of success" (Marrow, 1974) syndrome. The very processes that generated the tremendous success for U.S. MNCs in the 1960s carried the seeds of its decline. We now analyze some of the factors that were responsible for the dramatic growth of U.S. multinational corporations.

Numerous theories (Vernon, 1966; Kindleberger, 1961; Caves, 1971; Aliber, 1970; Johnson, 1970; Magee, 1977; Kojima, 1978) have been advanced to explain an organization's decision to grow internationally. Of these, theories such as need to engage in defensive foreign direct investment (Knickerbocker, 1973) and the product life cycle theory (Vernon, 1966) have been considered particularly appropriate to U.S. multinational corporation expansion overseas. Rugman (1979) has, however, demonstrated that these are all subsets of a general theory of internalization.

Regardless of the particular theory favored, it would be difficult to deny that U.S. government policies directed at the reconstruction of the economies of Europe and Japan played a considerable part in foreign direct investment by U.S. corporations. American corporations that were growing comfortably in a vast domestic market, fueled by high income levels, were literally prodded abroad. Despite this incentive and shelter, a number of companies failed to appreciate the value of their overseas activity (*Business Week*, 1980). As a consequence, many of the U.S. businesses failed to acquire the international perspective that has become so essential to survival and growth today. Even today the number of U.S. corporations that realize the value of international operations is woefully small (*Business Week*, 1980).

The reconstruction efforts also contributed to the image of the superiority of the "American System or the American Way of Life." Thus, products, systems, processes, and strategies that had proven to be considerably successful at home were transferred abroad with little or no modifications. We feel that many of these were accepted abroad initially, not because of their inherent worth or as a result of satisfying a particular need, but because there were very few options available. By this time, however, U.S. companies had become very smug and were blinded by their own success. Strategic marketing (Abell and Hammond, 1979) efforts almost came to a standstill.

The rapid growth of the U.S. MNCs was generally equated with the superiority of American management know-how. When Servan-Schreiber's (1968) book apparently supported this belief, U.S. multinational corporations undertook a process of spreading the "Gospel according to the Harvard Business School" with a missionary zeal. Unfortunately, while many of these systems may have contributed greatly to increasing efficiency they were also simultaneously responsible for decreases in effectiveness in a number of instances. In our opinion, the biggest single problem that U.S. MNCs face today is that of maintaining effectiveness.

U.S. corporate executives had also become accustomed to managing their systems for growth in the context of a relatively laissez-faire economy. They encountered similar conditions in their early investments in Europe and were able to exploit these investments successfully. However, as the economies were reconstructed, nationalism increased and many of the European countries began to develop their own systems of government. In a number of instances, these systems had objectives (industrial democracy, for example) that were quite different from those pursued in the United States. Rather than reacting to these newer objectives set by the host governments in a positive manner, U.S. MNC executives viewed these changes as "capricious, unwarranted and irrational." Caught up in the supremacy of their own functioning, they failed to develop the appropriate responses to these changing circumstances.

One may very well question at this juncture "What of the U.S. direct investment in Latin American and Canada?" Initially, the technical and financial know-how possessed by the U.S. MNCs provided them with sufficient bargaining power to limit the role of the host governments. Recently, however, with the increase in nationalism and options available to host governments, U.S. MNCs have run into a number of conflicts (U.S. State Department, 1974; Negandhi and Baliga, 1979; Gladwin and Walter, 1980).

Executives of U.S. corporations have also grown accustomed to managing organizations with a considerable degree of "slack" (Galbraith, 1977). Many organizational systems were geared to the availability of this slack to absorb organizational errors. The decline in slack witnessed in the late 1970s has created numerous problems for MNC managers. By contrast, German and Japanese system executives who had developed mechanisms to cope with little or no slack are better suited to cope with these reductions in slack. As much of the foreign direct investment in the coming decades is going to be concentrated in the relatively slack poor countries of Asia and Africa, we feel that the German and Japanese MNCs have a decided advantage in maintaining their edge over U.S. MNCs.

MIND SETS AND THEIR IMPACT ON ORGANIZATIONAL FUNCTIONING

It should be evident by now that historic successes have created a mind set in U.S. MNC executives that is parochial, myopic, and better suited to analytical problem solving than problem recognition (Livingstone, 1971). The question that then arises is "To what extent does the mind set affect corporate functioning?" It is our contention that this mind set has considerable impact on both strategic and operational decisions. It should be pointed out that many of the theories utilized to explain MNC activity (Vernon, 1966; Kindleberger, 1961; Caves, 1971; Aliber, 1970, for example) do not consider mind sets. As a matter of fact, the corporate executive is treated as a perfect information channel between the environment and the firm (Spender, 1978). We feel, however, that the differences in the various mind sets of MNC executives from different countries account for the differences in organizational performance observed. For instance, we feel that the element of "harmony with the environment" that is apparently an integral part of the Japanese mind set (Nakane, 1970) enables the Japanese MNCs to function with less intense conflict. Likewise, a number of environmental members (e.g., government executives and representatives of trade and manufacturing associations) interviewed during the study felt that U.S. MNC executives were "less willing to act" in a particular situation as compared to their European or Japanese counterparts. To paraphrase Drucker (1954), U.S. executives always appear to be searching for ways to do things right rather than to do the right thing.

The net result of this mind set has been the generation of three distinct "failures" that have contributed in a substantial manner to the overall decline in the competitive position of U.S. MNCs. These failures are:

1. A failure to recognize and/or react to the global nature of the environment while respecting the unique characteristics of the subenvironments.
2. A failure to recognize the inherently adverse nature of foreign business–government (host) relationships.

3. A failure to develop appropriate management and control systems.

We consider these failures in greater detail below.

FAILURE TO RECOGNIZE THE GLOBAL NATURE OF THE ENVIRONMENT

It would not be an exaggeration to state that as a corporation ventures abroad the number and variety of environments that it faces become progressively more complex. Issues such as nationalism and the nation-state–corporation interaction come to the forefront. Simultaneously, the multinational corporation, if it desires to derive benefits from its multinational operations, is confronted with pressures for global rationalization of its operations. In many instances, the economic demands of rationalization conflict with the "unique" demands of the environment. For example, economic considerations may dictate that a particular manufacturing facility be sited in a particular country, and yet the host government may set "unreasonable" conditions for investment, such as limits on the raw materials imported or demanding the use of local labor and managers. If the multinational corporation tries to deal with such situations in a manner similar to that which it adopts at home, its efforts will invariably fail. Because of their mind set, U.S. multinational corporation executives try to handle such conflicts either from a "power" perspective (i.e., assuming that they have considerable bargaining power in the situation) or from a rational legal perspective (i.e., the manner that they would most likely resort to in dealing with government intervention in the United States). In many instances, however, the appropriate response would be "political," one that requires acceptance of a less than optimum economic strategy. Unfortunately, very few U.S. MNC executives have learnt to do so. Having become accustomed to dealing with the relatively nonpolitical U.S. environment on a technical and economic basis, U.S. MNCs have failed to develop the necessary skills to cope with "political, irrational demands." With increasing inflationary pressures coupled with low economic growth, a number of the more industrialized nations are being forced to reexamine their developmental programs. Such a reexamination has generally led to more direct government intervention. For example, the National Reconstruction Board in Britain has been responsible for propping up a number of internationally noncompetitive enterprises in the automobile industry. Similar support has been provided to industries in France and Italy; and with the virtual bailout of the Chrysler Corporation, the U.S. government also appears to be creating the necessary precedent for government intervention in the future. Many U.S. MNCs have not yet made significant responses to these developments in the environment. By contrast, Japanese companies have proposed setting up joint ventures with government-backed corporations. For example, Honda has proposed a joint venture with British Leyland (BL) in Britain and also with Alfa Romeo in Italy.

More often than not, when U.S. multinational corporations have ventured abroad, the orientation of MNC executives has been to try to suppress the uniqueness of the host environment and strive to create a "mini-American" environment in order to manage their operations conventionally. In the process of creating mini-American environments and cushioning themselves from the unique demands of the host environment, U.S. MNCs have failed to think in strategic global terms. By externalizing the blame in the event of poor performance they have "reinforced the domestic perspective of international operations." In this process, U.S. MNCs have also transferred, with little or no change, conventional organizational structures and processes that have been successfully employed in their domestic operations to their overseas subsidiaries. Thus, if rigid bureaucratic control systems were the norm at headquarters they were extended to the subsidiary without thinking about the appropriateness of such systems to the different environments confronting the multinational corporation subsidiaries. Approximately 80 percent of the U.S. MNC subsidiary executives interviewed reported heavy reliance on manuals and written policies in contrast to 13 percent of the Japanese MNCs studied. Management information systems and financial control systems were the predominant integrating mechanisms in U.S. MNCs whereas informal channels of communication and control systems were employed by Japanese MNCs. Interestingly enough, U.S. MNC headquarters personnel placed greater reliance on outputs of the management information and control systems than on personal inputs or feedback from subsidiary executives. This fact is emphasized when one notes that only 30 percent of U.S. MNC subsidiary executives reported any substantial involvement in strategic planning decisions at headquarters.

Table 2.1 presents the relative levels of influence on a number of decisions. These findings are perceptions made by U.S. MNC subsidiary and headquarters personnel. The table appears to confirm the fact that American subsidiary personnel felt the heavy impact of the

Table 2.1. Relative Levels of Influence in Decisionmaking

	Perception of Subsidiary Executives		
	Subsidiary	*Headquarters*	*Difference*[a]
Personnel training program in subsidiary	4.286	2.524	1.762
Layoff of operating personnel	4.762	1.095	3.667
Expatriate personnel usage	2.429	1.810	0.619
Chief executive appointment	1.810	4.476	-2.666
Maintenance of facilities	3.000	3.000	0.000
Aggregate production schedule	2.952	3.190	-0.238
Production capacity expansion	2.762	3.381	-0.619
Use of local advertising agency	4.000	2.190	1.810
Servicing of products sold	4.619	1.524	3.095
Pricing of products	3.381	3.238	0.143
Introduction of new products	3.238	3.381	-0.143
Choice of public accountant	2.619	3.190	-0.571
Extension of credit	3.762	2.286	1.476
Use of cash flow	3.619	2.714	0.905
Borrowing from local banks	3.571	2.762	0.809

Scale key:

1	3	5
little or no influence	moderate influence	considerable influence

[a]Positive differences indicate greater subsidiary influence.

corporate superordinate objective of global rationalization of operations. They had a fairly restricted influence on aggregate production schedules, capacity expansion, and introduction of new products. Practically all U.S. subsidiary executives interviewed exhibited a considerable amount of frustration at having the discretionary component of significant decisions reduced to a minimum. Some typical instances from our interviews highlight this sense of frustration:

> The CEO of an American subsidiary in Britain complained bitterly about the price of his exports being determined by the marketing manager at the European headquarters. Yet the subsidiary was responsible for meeting profit targets.
> The subsidiary of a U.S. firm in France wanted to set up a profit-sharing system with its employees as consistent with the practice in the region. Headquarters refused the subsidiary's request despite repeated pleas by subsidiary management. The subsidiary was subsequently plagued by a series of strikes as a result.

While the benefits of bureaucratization in dealing with fairly stable environments cannot be denied, we feel that such rigidity cannot be justified for the variety of environments in which U.S. MNCs function.

Ironically, the overreliance on formalized reporting and control systems has further undermined what little delegation was provided to the subsidiary executives. As can be seen from Tables 2.1 and 2.2, U.S. subsidiary executives appear to underestimate the influence they exercise (or have the potential of exercising) on key decisions. This overreliance has also desensitized corporate management from recognizing the importance of environmental differences and their impact on performance. The general response of most of the American MNC corporate personnel to poor performance by subsidiary executives was to change subsidiary personnel. They did not question whether the evaluation criteria employed were appropriate to the particular environment confronting the subsidiary.

THE FAILURE TO UNDERSTAND THE NATURE OF BUSINESS–GOVERNMENT RELATIONSHIPS

U.S. corporations in general, and multinational corporations in particular, tend to blame government intervention in economic affairs for the majority of their woes (*Business Week*, 1980; Hayes

Table 2.2. Relative Levels of Influence in Decisionmaking

	As Reported by Headquarters	As Perceived by Subsidiary Executives	Difference[a]
Subsidiary borrowing from local banks	1.222	2.762	−1.540
Extension of credit to major customers	3.222	2.286	0.936
Introduction of new product in subsidiary market	2.556	3.381	−0.825
Use of local advertising	3.111	2.190	0.921
Expansion of production capacity	2.444	3.381	−0.937
Maintenance of production facilities	4.000	3.000	1.000
Appointment of subsidiary chief executive	3.000	4.476	−1.476
Layoffs of operating personnel	4.444	2.762	1.682

Scale key:	1	3	5
	little or no influence	moderate influence	considerable influence

[a]Positive values indicate greater subsidiary influence.

and Abernathy, 1980). U.S. MNCs claim that they have been considerably hampered by U.S. government antitrust laws and the Foreign Payments Act in their ability to compete effectively on the international scene. They also blame host governments for intervening unnecessarily in their operations and making incessant and unreasonable demands. Such statements really signal an inability on the part of both headquarters and subsidiary executives to develop political strategies and maintain effective external relations. As can be seen from Table 2.3, U.S. MNC executives relied considerably on trade associations, press releases, and outside lawyers (emphasis on impersonal dealings) to conduct their external relations. These are very public and highly visible modes of maintaining relationships. While such an approach may be fairly relevant in the context of the U.S. environment, which has a very vocal and powerful press and judicial system, we feel that the approach is quite problematic in a number of countries that prefer a low-key and less visible approach. Franko (1976) has indicated that one of the primary causes for hostility to U.S. MNCs in a number of host countries is the lack of discretionary dealing by MNC executives. An earlier study of multinational corporations in the developing countries confirmed that U.S. executives reacted to government pronouncements more on a legalistic basis than on their underlying intent (Negandhi and Baliga, 1979). Franko (1976) has on many occasions referred to the "discretion" exercised by European MNCs and governments as being the key determinant of the success achieved by European MNCs. He asserts that U.S. MNCs are quite indiscreet and that this creates problems for governments, both home and host. As one host government official remarked:

> The Americans are very fond of washing their dirty laundry in public. When this is done we are forced to respond owing to pressures generated

Table 2.3. Modes of Maintaining External Relations

	Mean	Standard Deviation
Personal contact by top-level executives	2.667	1.197
Public relations department	3.619	1.244
Contact through legal department	3.333	1.065
Collective action through trade associations	4.524	0.814
Press releases	4.476	0.602
Outside laywers	4.524	0.602

Scale key:	1	5
	Very little or none at all	Very great deal

by our political constituents. There are many occasions when I wish that we could iron out our differences in a closed session.

A major factor that creates such problems for U.S. MNCs in managing relationships with government agencies and their personnel is "objectivity." U.S. executives apparently find it very difficult to comprehend the "nonrational" or emotional dimensions in decision-making. As an example, a senior executive of a U.S. MNC had the following to say about the company's decision to close a manufacturing facility in Europe:

I do not understand why . . . [the] government should be so upset at closing this plant. After all it was the government's decision to join the EEC, which made the plant noncompetitive.

Similar remarks were voiced by a number of MNC executives who were interviewed.

It is easy to see from the above that economic considerations dominate strategic decisionmaking in U.S. MNCs. This is because U.S. corporations in general have made little or no effort to legitimize the "political" component of a manager's role. Instead they have consistently sought to reinforce economic performance (generally short term as will be discussed in a following section) in their compensation structure (Hayes and Abernathy, 1980; Charan and Freeman, 1980).

FAILURE TO DEVELOP
APPROPRIATE
CONTROL SYSTEMS

As U.S. MNCs have grown, their organization structures have evolved from the simple functional form to highly decentralized structures. This process has been accompanied by the creation of profit centers. In a number of multinational corporations, the boundaries of an overseas subsidiary coincide with that of the profit center. As has been alluded to earlier in this chapter, the creation of profit centers has generated considerable pressure for "quantifiable" and "objective" methods of assessment, which have invariably culminated in the use of short-term financial measures like return on investment (ROI). The net effect has been a kind of urgency displayed by practically all the managers interviewed. Unfortunately, in a number of instances this has translated itself into hasty short-term decisionmaking. There is considerable reluctance on the part of the managers of profit centers to make capital investment decisions with long payback periods as such decisions will "make me look bad and make my successor look good." Such an attitude generally results in subsidiary managers turning in excellent performances oriented toward "efficiency" but with a sacrifice of long-term effectiveness. An unpleasant consequence of such behavior, emphasizing recovery of investment in the shortest possible time, was the creation of a feeling or perception of "profiteering" and "exploitation" in the eyes of the public. These feelings become all the more intense and bitter when U.S. subsidiary actions are compared to those of German and Japanese MNCs whose executives are not confronted with pressures for short-term performance. The rapid growth of European and Japanese MNCs is due in no small measure to a willingness by management to accept innovative technologies, marketing programs, and capital investment decisions.

THE LEVERAGE ISSUE

It is our contention that underlying the three major failures discussed is the limited understanding of U.S. MNC executives of their leverage or bargaining power vis-à-vis the environment. There can be little or no argument about the relative decline in leverage of the U.S. MNCs over the years. In the post-World War II era through the 1960s, U.S. MNCs had considerable leverage derived from their financial resources, technology base, and management know-how. Host governments were generally willing to make concessions in order to obtain access to this resource base. In most cases, however, the concessions were reluctantly made and representatives of these nations were biding their time to modify, in their favor, the perceived imbalances in the relationship. For the industrial countries this opportunity arose following reconstruction of their war-ravaged economies. For the third world countries, the resurgence of the economies of Europe and Japan provided alternative sources of resources. They (LDCs) were only too willing to favor European and Japanese MNCs in exchange for the opportunity to rid themselves of or reduce the power of the "exploitative" Yankees. Unfortunately, many of the U.S. MNC executives have failed to recognize and react to this decline in leverage. They have also failed to develop the necessary political skills to deal with the more recent power equations.

CONCLUDING REMARKS

It is interesting to note that Franko (1971) identified the following factors, among others, as being substantially responsible for the success of American business:

1. The innovative fertility of U.S. companies
2. The happily ruthless spirit of competition in the United States
3. The U.S. tradition of "corporate openness"
4. The U.S. managerial tradition of organizational experimentation and flexibility

Ironically, a decade later the mind set of U.S. MNC executives discussed earlier had served to nullify the fertility. The spirit of competition is now confined to tinsel changes. The control systems employed have progressively reduced flexibility and the desire to experiment. Finally, an imprecise understanding of leverage has created numerous problems with corporate openness. For U.S. MNCs, the question now, of course, is "Can we regain our position of dominance in the International Arena?" We believe that the answer is a qualified "yes." The first course of action that multinational corporation executives would have to undertake would be to step back and evaluate their position objectively and realistically. This would entail a rejection of attributing all success to oneself and all failures to others. We believe that if this is done, MNC executives will understand the three basic failures discussed and the underlying mind set that has generated these failures. Simultaneously, they should try to understand their relative leverage and work within its constraints. For its part, corporate management should realize and reward "political strategies" and encourage risk-taking strategic behavior on the part of subsidiary executives. Recently, we have begun to see isolated instances of development of political strategies by major U.S. MNCs. Both Ford and General Motors tried to wrest a great many concessions from the governments of France, Spain, Germany, and Austria in exchange for locating plants in these countries. A major factor to be borne in mind in implementing political strategies is that the loser may become antagonized and supplementary strategies should be developed to deal with such situations.

These recommendations will necessitate fundamental changes in organizational policies: longer tenure for subsidiary executives; increased involvement of subisdiary executives in strategy management; and increased job rotation programs to provide the executives with a comprehensive understanding of their complex roles and, most of all, increased global strategic thinking. The interdependency of economic systems, and the realization of a global environment, may necessitate MNC executives to take a lead in educating the government regarding the need to provide a measure of flexibility in its rules and regulations, that is, rules and regulations that are indicative rather than binding and prescriptive. We also contend that the current educational processes that potential U.S. MNC executives are exposed to are very "parochial" and "isolationist" and this needs to be drastically changed if the myopic mind set is to be overcome. If such efforts are not forthcoming in the future we will continue to see the decline of U.S. multinational corporations.

REFERENCES

Abell, D. F., and Hammond, J. S. *Strategic Market Planning: Problems and Analytical Approaches.* Englewood Cliffs, N.J.: Prentice-Hall, 1979.

Aliber, R. Z. "A Theory of Foreign Direct Investment." In *The International Corporation*, edited by C. P. Kindleberger. Cambridge, Mass.: M.I.T. Press, 1970.

Barnet, R. J., and Mueller, R. E. *Global Reach: The Power of the Multinational Corporations.* New York: Simon and Schuster, 1974.

Business Week. Special Issue: "The Reindustrialization of America," June 30, 1980, esp. pp. 68-70.

Caves, R. E. "International Corporations: The Industrial Economics of Foreign Investment." *Economica* 38 (1971):1-27.

Charan, R., and Freeman, R. E. "Planning for the Business Environment of the 1980s." *The Journal of Business Strategy* 1, No. 2 (Fall 1980):9-19.

Drucker, P. *The Practice of Management.* New York: Harper & Row, 1954.

Franko, L. G. *The European Multinationals: Discretion Breeds Success.* Stamford, Conn.: Greylock Publishers, 1971.

——. *The European Multinationals: A Renewed Challenge to American and British Big Business.* New York: Harper & Row, 1976.

Galbraith, J. *Organization Design.* Reading, Mass.: Addison-Wesley, 1977.

Gladwin, T. N., and Walter, I. *Multinationals Under Fire: Lessons in the Management of Conflict.* New York: John Wiley, 1980.

Hayes, R. H., and Abernathy, W. J. "Managing Our Way to Economic Decline." *Harvard Business Review* 58 (July-August 1980):67-77.

Johnson, H. G. "The Efficiency and Welfare Implications of the International Corporation." In *The International Corporation*, edited by C. P. Kindleberger. Cambridge, Mass.: M.I.T. Press, 1970.

Johnson, P., and Ouchi, W. "Made in America: Under Japanese Management." *Harvard Business Review* 52, No. 5 (September-October 1974): 61-69.

Kindleberger, C. P. *American Business Abroad: Six Lectures on Direct Investment.* New Haven, Conn.: Yale University Press, 1968.

Knickerbocker, F. T. *Oligopolistic Reaction and Multinational Enterprise.* Cambridge, Mass.: Harvard University Press, 1973.

Kojima, K. *Direct Foreign Investment: A Japanese Model of Multinational Business Operations.* London: Croom Helm, 1978.

Livingstone, J. S. "Myth of the Well Educated Manager." *Harvard Business Review* 49 (January–February 1971):79–87.

Magee, S. P. "Multinational Corporations: The Industry Technology Cycle and Development." *Journal of World Trade Law* 11 (July–August 1972):297–321.

Marrow, A. *The Failure of Success.* New York: American Management Association, 1974.

Mikesell, R. F., et al. *Foreign Investment in the Petroleum and Mineral Industries: Case Studies in Investor Host Country Relations.* Baltimore: Johns Hopkins University Press, 1971.

Nakane, C. *Japanese Society.* London: Wiedenfeld and Nicolson, 1970.

Negandhi, A. R., and Baliga, B. R. *Quest for Survival: A Comparative Study of U.S. European and Japanese Multinationals in the Developing Countries.* Königstein/Ts.: Athenäum, 1979.

Northrup, H. R., and Rowan, R. L. *Multinational Collective Bargaining Attempts: The Record, Cases and the Prospects.* Philadelphia: Industrial Research Unit, The Wharton School, University of Pennsylvania, 1979.

Rugman, A. *Internalization as a General Theory of Foreign Direct Investment: A Reappraisal of the Literature.* Graduate School of Business, Columbia University, Working Paper No. 218 A, April 1979.

Sampson, A. *The Sovereign State of ITT.* New York: Stein and Day, 1973.

Sauvant, K., and Laviour, R. W., eds. *Controlling International Enterprises: Problems, Strategies and Counterstrategies.* Boulder, Colo.: Westview, 1976.

Servan-Schreiber, J. J. *The American Challenge.* New York: Atheneum, 1968.

Suzuki, R. "Worldwide Expansion of U.S. Exports: A Japanese View." *Sloan Management Review* 20, No. 3 (Spring 1979): 67–70.

Tsurumi, Y. *Multinational Management: Business Strategy and Government Policy.* Cambridge, Mass.: Ballinger Publishing Co., 1977.

Turner, L. M. "There's No Love Lost between Multinational Companies and the Third World." *Business and Society Review* 11 (Autumn 1974):75–78.

U.S. State Department. "Disputes Involving U.S. Foreign Investment: July 1, 1971 through July 1, 1973." Washington, D.C.: Bureau of Intelligence and Research, 1974.

Vernon, R. "International Investment and International Trade in the Product Life Cycle." *Quarterly Journal of Economics* 80 (May, 1976):190–207.

——. *Sovereignty at Bay.* New York: Basic Books, 1971.

——. *Storm Over the Multinationals: The Real Issues.* Cambridge, Mass.: Harvard University Press, 1977.

Yoshino, M. *Japan's Multinational Enterprises.* Cambridge, Mass.: Harvard University Press, 1976.

Chapter 3

Decisionmaking in German Multinationals and Its Impact on External Relationships

*Martin K. Welge**

PURPOSE

This chapter examines specific external and internal practices of German firms, both at headquarters and at their subsidiaries operating in Mexico. The reason for limiting our analysis to a single host country is that during our interviews in various host countries we realized that problems and aspects of MNCs (i.e., host government interactions) are very specific to individual host countries. Although Mexico is not yet a highly industrialized country, it is certainly in the process of becoming so, and it therefore seems interesting to use such a country as an example.

In order to bring more conceptual clarity to the discussion of MNC—host government relations, we first develop a conceptual framework based on the notion of a *dynamic bargaining model.* We then try to describe the bargaining position of Mexico vis-à-vis foreign investment generally and German foreign investment specifically. This description is based on published material from various Mexican official institutions as well as from our interviews with government officials and business people in Mexico. We next analyze various aspects of the decisionmaking process of German MNCs in detail as they attempt to cope with host government's demands and expectations.

*Fernuniversität Hagen.

THE CONCEPTUAL FRAMEWORK:
A DYNAMIC
BARGAINING MODEL

Several paradigms and hypotheses were developed to describe the pattern of interactions between host countries and multinational corporations. Some of them attempted to explain the interaction pattern by concepts such as neocolonialism, center–periphery domination, or by the consolidation of underdevelopment. None of these theories is able, however, to explain the slow but steadily increasing change in the balance of power during the last 30 years, which has changed in favor of the host countries, becoming detrimental to MNCs. Both theoretical and practical attempts have been made to describe the interaction pattern between MNCs and host governments under such perspectives as the joint maximization of mutual advantage or the fundamental harmony of interests. Although theories built on these paradigms tend to be static, they ignore the problem of the exercise of power and tend to confound postponement of conflict with conflict resolution.

For these reasons, more recent theories are based on game theory and bargaining models, particularly the bilateral monopoly model (cf. Stigler, 1961; Shelling, 1963; Kindleberger, 1965, 1969; Mikesell, 1971). The *foreign investor* controls the knowledge, the experience, market access, and financial resources a country needs for its economic development. The *host country* has control over raw materials, labor, market potentials, and taxes. All of these factors can be combined into an attractive investment climate for the foreign investor. When a host government is not receptive to foreign investors regardless of how they behave, on the one hand, and when it does not want to keep out foreign investors at any cost, on the other hand, a problem of *joint maximization* arises. Since both parties tend to increase their share of benefits from an industry or project, each can threaten and/or offer advantages. This struggle also goes on when distributing profits from an industry (project) proportionately to the MNC and the host government. This is not a zero-sum game, for the absolute amount of profit is a function of the relative shares held by each of them. Certain collaborative strategies can increase the size of the cake to be distributed, as well as the absolute profit for all participants.

The bargaining model just described is extended by the role of *uncertainty* as an independent variable. The foreign investor begins from a position of monopolistic control with the capability to implement a particular project. There is uncertainty among the participants about the success of a project as well as its production costs. Consequently, during this phase of agreement in circumstances can be characterized by monopolistic control and high markups for risk and uncertainty. The foreign investor is in a stronger bargaining position, and the investment terms will be favorable for the investor. If the project turns out to be successful, the MNC–host government relations will change considerably. The terms no longer meet the reality; there will be increasing pressure for new negotiations with the foreign investors. The more uncertainty is reduced, the stronger becomes the bargaining position of the host country.

Another factor influencing MNC–host government relations is the host country's *learning curve*. At the beginning of the internationalization process, the host country does not have the capability to evaluate the feasibility studies and reports of foreign investors. There is usually no existing bureaucracy with this kind of professional knowledge and expertise; when projects turn out to be successful, however, there is a motivation in the host country to build up this knowledge and expertise. This process will be reinforced by the fact that increasing demands force government agencies to participate more in the results of economic progress. The bargaining power of the foreign investor becomes weaker and, simultaneously, the host country's position is strengthened.

In summary, joint maximization can be seen as a process of continuous mutual adaptation. Foreign investors will act in their own interests if they are in the stronger bargaining position, and they will show more adaptive behavior if they are in the weaker position. The same behavioral pattern is true for the host countries (also see Moran, 1974, p. 153; a similar view is taken by Gladwin and Walter, 1980, p. 45).

MEXICO'S BARGAINING POSITION AS A HOST COUNTRY FOR FOREIGN DIRECT INVESTMENT

Mexico, with 64.6 million inhabitants (1977 estimate), has a federal and democratic constitution designed after the U.S. Constitution. Within this framework, the president is the most dominant decisionmaker. His term of office is for six years, and he cannot be reelected. The members of the Senate and the House of Representatives usually approve the president's decisions. For almost half a century this system has created a comparatively stable political situation, not counting the political unrest between 1968 and 1971. The

Partido Revolucionario Institucional (PRI), the strongest political party in Mexico, has dominated all elections since 1929. The PRI is more or less a reservoir of different interest groups, whose major cohesion comes from total loyalty to the president.

NATURAL RESOURCES

Mexico is well endowed with natural resources, the utilization of which appears to be of decisive importance for its further economic growth and development. First, the *oil reserves* should be mentioned. According to the Constitution and federal law, the state-owned PEMEX company is in charge of the Mexican oil and gas industry (including exploration, refining, and distribution) as well as production and distribution of basic petrochemical products and certain derivatives. The primary petrochemical industry is controlled by PEMEX, too. The policy of the current administration is to use the oil money for the development of a diversified local industry in order to create jobs in the country and to achieve balanced growth with moderate rates of inflation.[1] Without a doubt, the oil wealth strengthens Mexico's bargaining position vis-à-vis the United States, whose investment in Mexico amounts to more than 70 percent of all total foreign investment.

Besides oil, Mexico has great resources of silver, copper, lead, zinc, gold, manganese, mercury, and sulphur. In 1975, Mexico exported mineral products worth $297 million, not including silver and oil. Until 1960, the extractive sector was dominated by foreign investors. Since the late 1960s, however, a Mexicanization strategy has been enforced, which means that there has to be local participation of 51 to 66 percent in new projects, depending on the type of extractive industry. This Mexicanization policy has been implemented step by step. Today, 96 percent of the extractive sector is controlled by Mexicans.

LABOR FORCE

One of the most serious problems is unemployment. The annual birth rate of 3.2 percent is one of the highest in the world, and every year about 800,000 people enter the job market. It is only because of the massive emigration of workers to the United States that the current rate of unemployment of about 19 percent has not been transcended.[2]

In order to fight the uneven distribution of income and unemployment, industrial decentralization programs were decided upon. These programs promote industries, especially in the northern part of Mexico. Striving for a more balanced regional economic development was also the reason given for the intensive promotion of the "Industria Maquiladora," offering massive incentives to foreign investors for investments in the northern part of Mexico. Major benefits for these job-processing companies are comparative wage advantages and the export of finished goods.

Mexico's great reservoir of labor is especially attractive to foreign investors using labor-intensive technologies. More than 40 percent of the total workforce is paid the minimum wage, which is guaranteed by the government. Between 1974–1976, however, wage increases for organized workers were an average of 20 percent per year; an attempt by the government to restrict wage increases to 10 percent in 1977 failed, with wages actually increasing by 30.4 percent.

MARKET SIZE AND MARKET GROWTH

By following a policy of balanced growth, Mexico achieved impressive growth rates in its gross national product, averaging 6.8 percent a year since World War II. In 1979 the growth rate was 8 percent. This trend is contrary to that seen in most of the developed countries, all of which showed a decline in growth except for Japan. In the past decade, the annual GNP growth has been greater than the annual growth rate of the population, which means that there has been an improvement in per capita income. Economic growth is based on a high rate of capital accumulation, averaging as high as 20.6 percent of the GNP and financed with local resources of about 87 percent. The rest came from additional credit and foreign investment. Gross national product by industry is shown in Table 3.1.

Industrial production has been the major basis for the impressive growth of the GNP. The government has supported this process by following a policy of industrialization and by credit and import substitution programs. The percentages of different sectors in the GNP are listed in Table 3.2.

Growth rates that are considerably above the average of most industrialized countries, the growth of its population, and increasing per capita income are undoubtedly factors that make Mexico attractive to foreign investors. According to Connor (1977), foreign investors have earned far above average returns on their investment—

Table 3.1. Gross National Product by Industry

	1972		1976	
	Pesos	*%*	*Pesos*	*%*
Agriculture, forestry, hunting, and fishing	52.9	10.3	110.3	9.0
Mining and quarrying	18.9	3.7	51.5	4.2
Manufacturing	120.2	23.6	298.6	24.5
Construction	27.3	5.3	74.9	6.1
Electricity, gas, and water	7.3	1.4	14.9	1.2
Transport, storage, and communications	14.6	2.8	36.5	3.0
Wholesale and retail trade	162.4	31.7	375.3	30.7
Other services	108.7	21.2	258.8	21.3
Gross domestic product	512.3	100.0	1,220.8	100.0

Source: U.N. Monthly Bulletin of Statistics.

more than 16 percent in the case of American MNCs—which, of course, increases the attractiveness of Mexico as a host country for foreign investment.

THE FRAMEWORK OF ECONOMIC POLICY

The second half of 1976 was characterized by a devaluation of the peso, a massive escape of Mexican money into foreign currencies, and dramatic wage and price increases, all of which created great uncertainty. The nomination of President Portillo, however, was responsible for an improvement in economic conditions. The economic planning of the new administration can be characterized by the following factors:

Creation of more investment opportunities.
Strengthening of public financial institutions.
Introduction of steeper progression of tax rates for corporate and private incomes.
A higher share of taxes collected given to the states and communities.
Improved coordination between the federal government, states, and communities.
Improve conditions for workers brought about by social and social-legal means.
Prevention of tax evasion.

In the framework of this new economic policy, the government passed

Table 3.2. Percentage Change for the Manufacturing Industry as a Share of the Gross National Product

	1960-70	1971-75	1976	1977
Foodstuffs	6.1	3.8	7.2	-2.4
Textiles and clothing	7.9	5.9	2.3	-0.1
Paper and paper products	9.1	3.5	14.0	4.5
Chemicals and raw materials	15.7	10.0	6.9	8.2
Iron and steel	10.0	6.3	4.7	2.0
Machinery	14.1	4.5	—	—
Automobiles and parts	14.8	12.0	-9.2	-11.6

Source: Banco National de Mexico.

a number of laws and decrees, of which the following are directly or indirectly relevant to foreign investors:

Allowing temporary imports of raw materials in order to increase exports of finished goods in the job-processing industries.

Reform of income taxation in order to encourage the reinvestment of capital and the export of technology.

Inducements to encourage industrial development in the underdeveloped regions of the country.

Law for Promoting Mexican Investment and the Regulation of Foreign Investment (1973).

Law for the Registration of the Transfer of Technology and the Use and Exploitation of Patents and Trade Marks (1973).

Under President Echeverria, the state share of investment in industry increased from 33 percent in 1970 to more than 50 percent in 1976 and private investors were frightened by the devaluation of the peso and the high amount of deficit spending. Through its "alliance for production" policy, the Portillo Administration encourages private investors by providing state loans and interest inducements, as well as a reduction in bureaucratic red tape. This also holds true for foreign investors, who are encouraged to invest because the government handles the investment laws flexibly. Thus, we can conclude that there is a favorable investment climate in the context of the current economic framework.

FRAMEWORK FOR THE REGULATION OF FOREIGN DIRECT INVESTMENT

The import of capital and technology by foreign companies is controlled by two laws: the Law for Promoting Mexican Investment and the Regulation of Foreign Investment, and the Law for the Registration of the Transfer of Technology and the Use and Exploitation of Patents and Trade Marks. The explicit objective of both laws is that foreign investment and technology are desirable only when they conform to the new development strategy by accelerating economic progress, complementing internal savings, or being useful in promoting the national economic effort. A prerequisite is that foreign investment and technology must always fully respond to the interests, policies, and economic objectives of the country. If one considers that only 5.5 percent of the total investment in industry is by foreign firms, it becomes clear that the objective of the law is the supportive integration of foreign direct investment into the country's developmental strategy, rather than restraining or controlling foreign capital.

LAW FOR PROMOTING MEXICAN INVESTMENT AND THE REGULATION OF FOREIGN INVESTMENT

The basic idea of this law is the required approval and registration of foreign investment. Essentially, the following issues are regulated:

Ownership
Responsibilities of the National Commission for Foreign Investment
Criteria for investment projects
Expansion of existing enterprises
Registration of foreign investment

The criteria, applied by the National Commission for Foreign Investment when approving an investment project and in determining the ownership share to be held by the Mexican equity (private or public), are of particular interest here. The following criteria and characteristics are taken into consideration:

1. To limit foreign control over the use of resources.
2. To promote national security (e.g., border zone prohibitions).
3. To stimulate local ownership and control.
4. To avoid concentration of foreign ownership (by sector or region).
5. To encourage foreign investment complementary to national investment.
6. To avoid displacement of national business.
7. To produce a positive impact on the balance of payments.
8. To produce a positive impact on exports.

9. To produce a positive impact on employment and wage levels.
10. To stimulate skill transfer.
11. To stimulate use of local products in manufacturing.
12. To encourage use of foreign finance.
13. To encourage diversification.
14. To encourage regional integration.
15. To encourage development of less developed zones.
16. To encourage competition.
17. To encourage technology transfer.
18. To discourage inflation of prices.
19. To improve the quality of products.
20. To limit external political pressure.
21. To encourage compliance with national development policy objectives.
22. To encourage respect for the country's social and cultural values.
23. To encourage that investment be important in the context of the Mexican economy.

The enumeration of these criteria does not, of course, mean that all characteristics have to be met satisfactorily for an investment project to be approved. Instead, it serves as a checklist for evaluation, with the final decision being based on the total value of the positive versus the negative aspects of the project. On the one hand, these criteria contain positive requirements for the project (i.e., export promotion), and on the other hand, they imply constraints or "prohibitions" on the project (i.e., monopolization or the displacement of national business), or negative properties, which depreciate the value of a project.

Although, as a general rule, the law restricts foreign ownership to 49 percent, the majority of the firms we interviewed were 100 percent owned. The explanation is that in the case of outstanding compliance with certain criteria, foreign participation beyond 49 percent can be approved. A subsidiary that exports more than 50 percent of its production has a good chance to receive approval for 100 percent ownership. Approval is most likely when the product has a high technological standard, when there is a high local content percentage (i.e., when the value added in Mexico is high), and/or if the plant is located in an underdeveloped zone of Mexico. A good indication that the law is flexibly applied by the commission is that 74 out of 103 exceptional requests for ownership have been approved (cf. Robinson, 1976, p. 186). The commission can also allow the firm up to five years to look for a Mexican partner, for example; during this time, the Mexican shares are held by a trustee.

LAW FOR THE REGISTRATION OF THE TRANSFER OF TECHNOLOGY AND THE USE AND EXPLOITATION OF PATENTS AND TRADEMARKS

In article 1 of this law a National Registry of Technology Transfer is provided for. According to article 7, legal transactions of the following kinds cannot be registered, and are, therefore, not legally valid:

1. If the technology is freely available in Mexico.
2. If the price is excessive.
3. If payment constitutes an excessive burden on the economy.
4. If supplier is given management rights.
5. If there is a free grant-back.
6. If limits are imposed on local R&D.
7. If there is a tied-buying provision.
8. If exports are restricted.
9. If complementary technology is prohibited.
10. If there is a production or sales limit.
11. If there is an obligation to sign an exclusive sales or representation agreement.
12. If duration is over 10 years.
13. If claims are to be submitted to foreign courts.

According to article 8, this list is substantially modified in the sense that the Ministry of Industry and Trade can approve registration despite the fact that the transaction implies one or some of the above-mentioned characteristics. Approval can be received if the transfer of the particular technology is of special interest to Mexico. Exceptions are not possible, however, for items 1, 3, 5, 6, 8, 11, 12, or 13. According to the current interpretation of the law, transactions based on oral agreements or factual existing legal transactions (a situation that seems to be typical of transactions between parent companies and their subsidiaries) are treated in the same way as written legal transactions because nonregistration would be contrary to the purpose of the law. Figure 3.1 summarizes the entry conditions for foreign technology.

THE REACTION OF FOREIGN INVESTORS

The General Reaction

It is difficult to judge the general impact of the laws just described on the flow of direct investment. Estimates of official sources appear

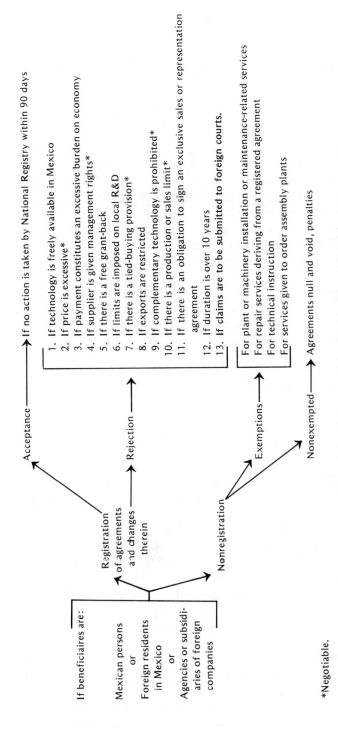

Acceptance ⟶ If no action is taken by National Registry within 90 days

1. If technology is freely available in Mexico
2. If price is excessive*
3. If payment constitutes an excessive burden on economy
4. If supplier is given management rights*
5. If there is a free grant-back
6. If limits are imposed on local R&D
7. If there is a tied-buying provision*
8. If exports are restricted
9. If complementary technology is prohibited*
10. If there is a production or sales limit*
11. If there is an obligation to sign an exclusive sales or representation agreement
12. If duration is over 10 years
13. If claims are to be submitted to foreign courts.

Registration of agreements and changes therein ⟶ Rejection

For plant or machinery installation or maintenance-related services
For repair services deriving from a registered agreement
For technical instruction
For services given to order assembly plants

Exemptions

Nonexempted ⟶ Agreements null and void, penalties

Nonregistration

If beneficiaires are:

Mexican persons
or
Foreign residents in Mexico
or
Agencies or subsidiaries of foreign companies

*Negotiable.

Figure 3.1. Entry conditions for foreign technology.

67

to be contradictory. Mexican government officials maintain that the flow of direct investment has remained unimpaired; the U.S. Department of Commerce, however, believes that U.S. direct investment suffered a backstroke in 1973 after three years of steady decline. Predictions of the Department of Commerce also show, however, that the impact of the investment laws on U.S. direct investment will be moderate in the following years. It appears to us that there has been a decline in foreign investment in 1971 and 1972 because of the uncertainty created by the new laws; when the new "rules of the game" became known, a normalization occurred. This view seems to be substantiated by the figures of the Mexican–German Chamber of Commerce, indicating that foreign investment increased by 26 percent in 1974 as against 1973. The estimate for 1975 is that foreign investment was worth approximately 5 billion pesos.

It seems fairly safe to conclude that Mexico's bargaining position was strong enough to control foreign direct investment by relatively restrictive investment laws. Despite these restrictive rules, foreign investors obviously perceived enough chances and opportunities to achieve their corporate goals.

Data from Interviews with Mexican Subsidiary Managers

Robinson studied 20 Mexican subsidiaries of U.S. MNCs in 1974, and found that 85 percent of the companies indicated that they planned to extend their investment in Mexico despite the new rules. Only 10 percent planned to reduce their investment. The majority of the subsidiaries indicated, however, that they would finance their new investment projects only with retained profits. Robinson explains this behavior by what he calls the "racetrack syndrome," which means that a dollar earned in Mexico is different from a dollar earned in the United States (cf. Robinson, 1976, p. 192).

Our own interviews, conducted in 1976 with German subsidiaries in Mexico, revealed a similar response pattern. The majority of the companies responded to the question of whether they were planning to extend their investment in the future with "a definite yes." The interpretation given by one of the respondents seems to be typical of this attitude. Because Mexico's population doubles every 20 years, economic progress has to be maintained. Thus, there will be a highly attractive market potential in the future. The answer of the CEO of one subsidiary, active in the pharmaceutical industry was somewhat atypical, but nevertheless very understandable. Under no circumstances was this company willing to invest in the future. Because of strict price controls in the pharmaceutical industry, this company had been suffering from high losses for a couple of years already.

The overall response pattern seems very interesting if *subsidiary success* is taken into account. Eighty percent of the German subsidiaries perceived their goal achievement as either unsuccessful or as neither successful nor unsuccessful. The most likely explanation to us seems to be that corporate headquarters judges the potential for future profits as more important than current profits and that being present in the market is currently more important than showing a short-term profit. Our data show a similar response pattern for the *American subsidiaries* in Mexico. Although all of them reported unsatisfactory goal performance, the majority (75 percent) reported that they would extend their Mexican investment in the future.

In terms of our dynamic bargaining model elaborated above, the multinationals seem to perceive the *future market potential* as a major bargaining strength of the host country, and in order to be able to take advantage of this future market growth the companies follow a strategy of *compliance*.

In order to give a more detailed picture of the interaction pattern between the multinationals and Mexico as a host country, we next draw attention to individual variables that describe the *external relationships*.

First is the respondents' perception of the *host country expectations* (see Table 3.3). The majority of the companies felt that the host government expects them to provide capital, advanced tech-

Table 3.3. Perceptions of Host Country Expectations (*N* = 10)

	Subsidiary Responses (%)	
Host Country Expectations	*Germany*	*United States*
1. Capital inflow	—	—
2. Providing advanced technology and R&D	16.7	—
3. Exports and import substitution	—	—
4. Use of local inputs	—	25.0
5. Employment	16.7	—
6. All of the above or any combination of the above	66.7	75.0
7. Host country's expectations are not known	—	—
8. Showing our good credentials by declaring realistic profits and inter/intra pricing	—	—
	100.0%	100.0%

Source: Author's interviews.

nology and R&D, export and import substitution, use of local inputs, and employment.

The quality of relations certainly depends upon the *extent to which these expectations have been met* by actual performance (see Table 3.4). Looking at the overall response pattern, it becomes evident that the companies feel that they have met these expectations.

When examining the individual answers in more detail, the picture becomes more differentiated. One respondent, pointing out the reduction of unemployment as the most important host country expectation, very frankly admitted that his company has hardly contributed to the solution of this problem. Regarding the 10 million people without work, of whom 50 percent are under 20 years of age, providing 1100 jobs seems to be more than a modest contribution. Another respondent from the same industry (electrical engineering) pointed out that his company has doubled its production capacity and also has plans for further investments. The company faced great difficulties, however, in meeting its export requirements because of the low degree of integration typical of new products as well as the noncompetitiveness of the products on the world market.

All respondents from the chemical and pharmaceutical industries mentioned providing world standard technology as their most important contribution. In one case, the company was even ready to provide technology because of the perception that Mexico would like to recieve the technology without cost, and despite the fact

Table 3.4. Extent to Which Host Country's Expectation Are Met (*N* = 10)

Actions Taken to Meet Expectations	Subsidiary Responses (%)	
	Germany	United States
1. Nothing specific to show	16.7	50.0
2. Providing high technology	16.7	—
3. Providing high employment	—	—
4. Exporting a great deal	—	—
5. Establishment of training centers for use of local community	—	—
6. Using very high proportions of local inputs	—	—
7. Combination of items 2 through 6	66.7	50.0
8. They do not expect anything specific from us	—	—
9. Have kept our book clean with respect to pricing and profits	—	—
	100.0%	100.0%

Source: Authors' interviews.

that the company suffered severe losses in the last couple years. Explaining this seemingly paradoxical behavior, the subsidiary manager explained that giving up the Mexican market would cause competitors to step into the market, and would also create negative spillover effects on other countries. The respondents from the chemical industry agreed that they are little able to provide a direct positive contribution to unemployment because of their capital-intensive technology. In one example, it was exemplified, however, that indirect impacts can be substantial. For example, shoe soles were produced from polyurethane, and thus an industry with 6000 jobs was developed.

A good example of an almost ideal reaction to the host government's expectations was given by an automobile company. In the automobile industry, a minimal degree of integration of 50 percent is requested, and for 1982 a quota of 80 percent is recommended.

The company has achieved a degree of integration greater than that requested, and it also has a higher export share than it was expected to have. In addition, the company raises capital from the parent company instead of the local financial market. This perfect behavior has significantly improved the company's bargaining position. In negotiations with government officials the company managed to win approval for price increases, although prices had been fixed because of the high rate of inflation.

This pattern clearly shows that most of the companies felt that they have met host country expectations, and some of them had even been able to change their bargaining position in a favorable way, rather than simply following a passive strategy of compliance or accommodation.

As another aspect of external relations we analyzed *company expectations* (see Table 3.5). Fifty percent of the affiliates expected the host country to stabilize the economy, thus freeing it from controls, such as remittance of profits and exchange controls, as well as inflation. A third of the companies had no particular expectations. The data seem to indicate that the companies take the rules set by the Mexican government for granted, and they expect the host government to create stable economic conditions.

The description of MNC–host country relations thus far may have created the impression that these relations were free of problems, conflicts, or tensions. This is, of course, not true. For example, the German subsidiaries experienced their greatest problems with labor unions. Actually almost 70 percent of the companies reported problems with labor unions. The difficulty resulted from not having an organized labor union system and the lack of organized collective

Table 3.5. Company Expectations (*N* = 10)

Company Expectations	Subsidiary Responses (%)	
	Germany	*United States*
1. Providing infrastructure facilities	—	—
2. Providing conducive labor legislation	—	—
3. Providing conducive business–government relationships	16.7	25.0
4. Permitting flexible expansion and diversification and other incentives including taxation	—	—
5. Stabilizing and freeing the economy from controls such as remittance of profits, exchange controls, and inflation	50.0	—
6. Strengthening price control and/or lifting price control	—	—
7. Political stability	—	25.0
8. Combination of any of the above	—	50.0
9. Nothing in particular	33.0	—
	100.0%	100.0%

Source: Authors' interviews.

bargaining. One respondent complained that the opinions and strategies of the union representatives vary from one hierarchical level to another, thus creating problems in labor negotiations. This executive felt that there was no way to achieve fair play with the union leaders. The issue of the unions is basically money: both wages and fringe benefits.

The typical *mode of conflict resolution* for the German subsidiaries was negotiation (see Table 3.6). In these negotiations the subsidiaries generally followed the rules and regulations set by the Mexican government. The companies, for example, were not prepared to grant wage increases that were significantly beyond the guidelines issued by the government. Interestingly, most of the American firms reported problems with host government itself, and for them the dominant mode of conflict resolution was legal action rather than negotiation.[3]

Table 3.6. Mode of Conflict Resolution (*N* = 10)

Mode of Conflict Resolution	Subsidiary Responses (%)	
	Germany	*United States*
Negotiation	100.0	0.0
Legal action	0.0	50.0
Unresolved	0.0	50.0

Source: Authors' interviews.

Beyond problems with the unions and labor relations, the German affiliates also reported problems with the host government and its agencies. The dominant issue for the German firms was the control of the expansion of their activities. Controls on foreign exchange remittance and on profits were not so often considered an issue. Again, the American pattern was somewhat different; they complained more about limitations on foreign exchange that was required for the importing of spare parts, machinery, and raw materials.

We also asked whether the companies made any *changes in policy* to deal with the environmental protection agencies. Of the German companies, 83 percent reacted in such a way that they decided to keep the lines of communication open. They felt that open channels of communication and open dialogues would be the best way of resolving problems with the host country's agencies and public. The majority of the American companies, however, reported no strategy changes. All the Mexican affiliates—American and German—were in total agreement by pointing out that they had not perceived any strategy changes in their counterparts.

In summarizing our findings about external relationships, we would like to emphasize that the German MNCs in Mexico basically follow *a strategy of adaption* because they feel that they are in the weaker bargaining position. For them, this strategy seems to be the only way to take advantage of the prospects for future growth and profit that all of them anticipate will come very soon. The most difficult problem in the entire interaction seems to be dealing with the unions. The lack of collective bargaining, a mechanism that functions well at home, is perceived as very disadvantageous. The general reaction to this type problem is to *negotiate* within the framework of rules issued by the government.

Generally speaking, we did not get the impression from our interviews that external relationships were as problematic as we had anticipated they would be in view of the tight investment laws. Obviously, the companies managed to feel somewhat satisfied within the given situation. This condition, however, requires particular structures and processes within the MNC system, which we describe below.

In our earlier research (cf. Welge, 1980, pp. 192), we studied the internal structures and processes of German MNCs and their foreign subsidiaries in the chemical industry. When interpreting subsidiary dependence according to the theoretical notion of *coordination intensity*, we found that all companies had a globally integrated structure with respect to *structural coordination*. The two dominant patterns were either worldwide responsibility for product divisions or two- or three-dimensional grid structures (for similar results see

Franko, 1976, p. 203). For *personal coordination*, the following pattern emerged: extensive use of expatriates in executive positions; highly centralized international personnel decision; and significant importance of visits in terms of frequency, the hierarchical position of visitors, and purpose. With regard to *technocratic coordination*, we observed a preference for 100 percent ownership and highly centralized investment decisions. Credit decisions as well as profit transfer decisions, however, were much more decentralized.

In our ongoing research (cf. Negandhi and Welge, 1981) subsidiary autonomy was studied in more detail than in our earlier study. The results are in Table 3.7. The table clearly shows that the American subsidiaries are the most centralized, the Japanese the least centralized, and that the German subsidiaries occupy a middle position. Only in four decisionmaking areas, use of expatriates, appointment of the CEO, expansion of production capacity, and new product introduction, was the influence of headquarters perceived to be higher than that of the subsidiary. The data seem to support the view that German MNCs tend to centralize key strategic decisions, and that in operative decisions the subsidiaries enjoy a large amount of freedom and autonomy. This strategy, of course, allows subsidiary management the necessary flexibility and discretion to respond to environmental demands and expectations. Consequently, the German MNC system tends to follow a strategy of compliance in the host country.

This hypothesis can be supported by looking at the level of formalization within the MNCs (cf. Negandhi and Welge, 1981, Chapter 2). Table 3.8 shows the extent to which the subsidiaries of American, German, and Japanese MNCs depend on written policies from headquarters.

An overwhelmingly large number of the American subsidiaries (88 percent) relied on the policies of headquarters. Approximately a third of the German subsidiaries did so, whereas only 12 percent of the Japanese subsidiaries indicated a very negligible influence of the policies of headquarters on their individual operations.

A similar pattern emerges when the influence of written policies and procedures on actual strategic and policy decision is examined (cf. Negandhi and Welge, 1981, Chapter 2). In other words, whereas American MNCs seem to drive toward unification and the integration of policies and procedures, the German companies seem to prefer to operate with more flexibility. This again seems to be a favorable structural aspect, keeping the subsidiary flexible and adaptive enough to respond to local environmental demands and being able to reach workable compromises with local stakeholders. Both autonomous

Table 3.7. Means and Standard Deviations for the Different Decisions According to Countries

Decisions	United States x̄	SD	x̄	SD	Germany x̄	SD	x̄	SD	Japan x̄	SD	x̄	SD
1. Personnel training	3.8	1.0	2.7	1.0	4.5	0.8	2.0	1.1	4.7	0.8	1.4	0.8
2. Layoffs of operating personnel	4.4	1.0	1.7	1.1	4.4	1.1	1.6	1.0	4.9	0.7	1.3	0.7
3. Use of expatriates[a]	2.7	1.5	3.4	1.5	2.4	1.1	4.0	1.3	3.5	1.4	3.3	1.4
4. Appointment of chief executive[a]	1.5	0.7	4.7	0.5	1.7	1.0	4.7	0.8	2.8	1.1	4.2	1.1
5. Maintenance of production facilities	3.3	1.2	3.2	1.3	4.8	0.7	1.9	1.1	4.4	1.0	1.9	1.1
6. Aggregate production schedule	3.2	1.1	3.3	1.3	4.3	0.9	2.1	1.2	4.0	1.2	2.5	1.2
7. Expansion of production capacity[a]	2.5	1.2	4.1	1.1	2.7	1.1	4.0	1.3	3.6	1.0	3.5	1.3
8. Use of local advertising agency	3.9	0.9	2.4	1.0	4.5	0.8	1.7	0.9	4.6	0.7	1.7	1.0
9. Servicing of products sold	4.4	0.7	1.8	0.8	4.7	0.8	1.5	0.9	4.8	0.5	1.5	0.9
10. Product prices[a]	3.0	1.3	3.5	1.2	4.0	1.1	2.6	1.3	4.3	0.8	2.3	1.1
11. New product introduction[a]	2.6	1.2	3.8	0.9	3.1	1.2	3.7	1.3	3.9	1.0	3.2	1.3
12. Choice of public accountant	2.7	1.6	3.2	1.5	4.4	0.9	2.0	1.1	4.7	0.5	1.8	1.2
13. Providing credit to major customers	3.7	0.7	2.4	0.9	4.3	0.8	1.8	0.9	4.4	0.7	1.8	0.8
14. Use of cash flow[a]	3.2	1.1	3.1	1.2	3.4	1.2	3.0	1.2	4.1	0.9	2.3	0.9
15. Capital borrowing	3.2	1.1	3.1	1.1	3.4	1.2	3.2	1.4	3.7	1.0	2.8	1.0
	N = 34				N = 45				N = 41			

Source: Authors' interviews.

Key: 1 = very little or no influence; 2 = little influence; 3 = medium influence; 4 = high influence; 5 = very high influence.
[a] strategic decisions

Table 3.8. Extent to Which Subsidiaries Depend on Written Policies
from Headquarters (in Percents)

MNC Ownership	Great Deal			To Some Extent			Very Little to Not at All		
	1	2	3	1	2	3	1	2	3
American (N = 33)	88%	84%	100%	6%	8%	—	6%	8%	—
German (N = 44)	32	34	22	20	20	22%	48	46	56%
Japanese (N = 40)	12	11	14	22	26	14	66	63	72

Source: Authors' interviews.

decisionmaking and comparatively low levels of formalization are necessary prerequisites for an intelligent and successful strategy of adaptation and adjustment.

CONCLUSION

In this chapter, we used a dynamic bargaining model for analyzing MNC–host government relations. Mexico and basically German MNCs were examined as partners in the interaction process. In terms of its natural resources, labor force, market size, and market growth potential, as well as the legal framework controlling the interaction process, Mexico's bargaining position vis-à-vis German MNCs was considered strong. The German companies we investigated managed to live with the strict investment laws by following a strategy of accommodation and adjustment. By using intelligent tactics, for example, higher integration than was required or higher export shares, some companies were even able to achieve a bargaining position that was favorable to them. Owing to their comparatively high degree of autonomy with respect to operative and sometimes even strategic decisions (i.e., product prices), as well as the comparatively low degree of formalization of policies and procedures, they had enough flexibility to respond to environmental threats and opportunities quickly. For them, this behavior of accommodation and adjustment is the only realistic strategy to use in paving the way for future participation in the growth potential of the Mexican economy.

NOTES

1. According to the Banco de Mexico, the rate of inflation was 20 percent in 1979. Economic research institutes, however, calculated a 25–30 percent rate of inflation.

2. According to the Bundesstelle für Aussenhandelsinformation" (1980) the number of unemployed and underemployed was estimated at 47 percent in 1978. Reliable official statistics are not available.
3. This observation is also supported by the research of Negandhi and Baliga (1979).

REFERENCES

Baliga, B. R. "An Investigation into the Functioning of German Multinational Corporation Subsidiaries in the United States." DBA Dissertation, Kent State University, 1979.

Bundesstelle für Aussenhandelsinformation. *Investitionen in Mexico*, 2nd ed. Cologne, 1980.

Connor, J. M. *The Market Power of Multinationals: A Quantitative Analysis of U.S. Corporations in Brazil and Mexico.* New York: Praeger, 1977.

Deutsch-Mexikanische Industrie- und Handelskammer. *Mexico 1970–1976.* Wirtschaftsentwicklung. Edition 132, December 1976.

Franko, L. G. *The European Multinationals.* New York: Harper and Row, 1976.

Gladwin, T. N., and Walter, I. *Multinationals Under Fire: Lessons in the Management of Conflict.* New York: John Wiley, 1980.

Kindleberger, C. P. *American Business Abroad: Six Lectures on Direct Investment.* New Haven: Yale University Press, 1969.

Leroy, G. *Multinational Product Strategy: A Typology for Analysis of Worldwide Product Innovation and Diffusion.* New York: Praeger, 1976.

Mikesell, R. F., et al. *Foreign Investment in the Petroleum and Mineral Industries.* Baltimore: Johns Hopkins Press, 1971.

Moran, T. H. "Multinational Corporations and the Politics of Dependence: Copper in Chile." Princeton, N.J.: Princeton University Press, 1974.

Negandhi, A. R., and Baliga, B. R. *Quest for Survival and Growth: A Comparative Study of American, European, and Japanese Multinationals.* New York: Praeger, 1979.

Negandhi, A. R., and Welge, M. K. "Power Against Power: Global Rationalization Strategies of American, German, and Japanese MNCs versus National Needs" (manuscript in preparation).

Robinson, R. D. *National Control of Foreign Business Entry: A Survey of Fifteen Countries.* New York: Praeger, 1976.

Welge, M. K. *Management in Deutschen multinationalen Uternehmungen.* Stuttgart: Poeschel Verlag, 1980.

———. The Effective Design of Headquarter–Subsidiary Relationships in German MNCs." In *Headquarter–Subsidiary Relationships in Multinational Corporations*, edited by L. Otterbeck, p. 79. London: Gower, 1982.

Chapter 4

How Multinationals Can
Manage Social Conflict

Thomas N. Gladwin* and Ingo Walter*

Recent years have seen a marked rise in the incidence of social conflict that affects the management of multinational companies. Conflict falling outside the conventional scope of the marketplace covers an amazing array of issues—human rights, bribery and corruption, consumer protection, the natural environment, terrorism, nationalism, economic boycotts, technology transfer, tax avoidance, and political subversion are just a few of them. Management's opponents are equally diverse, ranging from heads of state, regulatory bodies, and religious groups to labor unions, terrorists, and international organizations. Compared with domestic companies, multinationals have to operate in a setting in which the rules of the game are far more ambiguous, contradictory, subject to rapid change, and sometimes entirely absent. In examining hundreds of cases of social conflict involving multinationals, we are convinced that the consequences for the firm can be serious indeed.[1] Besides nationalization and expropriation they include increased operating costs, losses of market share and managerial control, and enormous chunks of executive time. And it turns out to be mismanagement of conflict, and not conflict itself, that is so dangerous for the firm.

More often than not, managers are poorly equipped to handle

*Graduate School of Business Administration, New York University

78

social conflicts in a multinational setting. The issues involved are often new, or emerge suddenly in an unfamiliar foreign setting with a chemistry all their own. Social conflict in one country sometimes has repercussions at home, or in other countries in which the company operates. Actions taken now may come back to haunt management a few years down the road, often in greatly amplified form. The 1980s and 1990s will, in our view, see an intensification of social conflicts facing multinationals. Growing resource scarcity, powerful national and group interests, increased awareness of risks and returns, and mounting regulatory pressures will be responsible. Companies that do well in this emerging environment will have to develop a sort of "technology of social policy" for managing the myriad sources of conflict that fall outside the confines of the marketplace. What we suggest here is a way to diagnose such conflicts, develop contingency plans for handling them and think about an organizational design appropriate to the task.

WHAT ARE THE OPTIONS?

In deciding how to handle a particular social conflict, management has to be concerned with obtaining a satisfactory outcome— not necessarily with resolving the conflict itself. It also has to be concerned with its relationship with the opposition. Management's behavior should be determined in large measures by the emphasis it places on each of these dual concerns. We can begin with Figure 4.1. "Cooperativeness" defines the extent to which management is willing to help satisfy the concerns or interests of the other party(ies) in conflict. This can be viewed as a continuum, with very hostile or uncooperative behavior and very cooperative or helpful behavior at the opposite ends of the scale. "Assertiveness" defines the extent to which management is willing to take a high profile to attain its own ends in a conflict—again one can think of the continuum extending from very passive or unassertive behavior to very aggressive behavior at the two ends of the scale. Assertiveness is important in determining the investment of time, manpower, and other resources that management ends up investing in a particular conflict.

Consider the varied reactions of Sperry Rand and Dresser Industries to the export–control actions of the Carter Administration undertaken during the summer of 1978 to express displeasure with the Soviet trials of political dissidents and American journalists. Sperry Rand was denied an export license to ship a $6.8 million computer system to TASS, the official Soviet press agency. At about the same

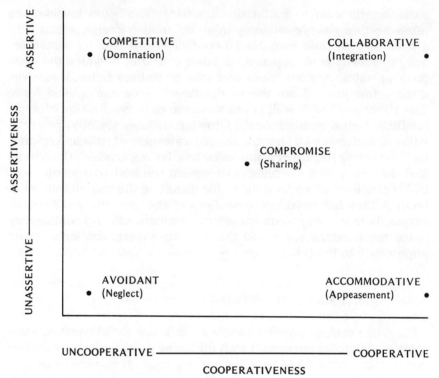

(*Source:* Kenneth W. Thomas, "Conflict and Conflict Management," in *Handbook of Industrial and Organizational Psychology*, edited by Marvin D. Dunnette (Chicago: Rand McNally, 1976), p. 900.

Figure 4.1

time, all American exports of oil technology to the Soviets were placed under government control. J. Paul Lyet, Sperry Rand's chairman, reportedly greeted the denial with "Bah, humbug," but added that the company had always complied with the wishes of the U.S. government on "where and with whom" the company traded, and would "continue to follow that policy." Dresser's reaction was almost the opposite of Sperry Rand's relatively unassertive and cooperative stance. Carter's oil decision was labeled "sheer idiocy," and John V. James, Dresser's chairman, speedily and bluntly attacked efforts by the President's senior advisers and a special review panel convened at the request of Defense Secretary Brown to stop the firm's $150 million contract to build a drill-bit plant in the Soviet Union. The highly combative approach helped produce a go-ahead for the Dresser sale. Carter's decision on the Sperry sale was quietly reversed nine months later; but in the meantime the Russians had found a new supplier—CII-Honeywell-Bull of France.

There are, of course, many possible combinations of cooperativeness and assertiveness, but five behavioral "zones" stand out in Figure 4.1. Management can chose to *compete* tooth-and-nail (assertive-uncooperative), with the hope of overcoming the opposition. It can opt to *avoid* (unassertive–uncooperative) conflict and withdraw from the fray. Or it can choose to *accommodate* the opposition (unassertive-cooperative). And it can *collaborate* (assertive–cooperative) actively with hope of satisfying both sides of the issue. Finally, there is always the option to *compromise*, in order to "split the difference" in a bargaining context, which represents an intermediate position in terms of both assertiveness and cooperativeness. We should emphasize that these options are ways of coping with conflict, not necessarily ways of *resolving* conflict—only collaboration and compromise involve conflict resolution in the sense that both opposing parties obtain satisfaction. Crushing an attempt by unions in Europe to bargain on a multinational basis, terminating business in payoff-prone regions such as the Middle East, or temporarily halting bank loans to the South African government may enable the firm to suppress or bypass the open expression of conflict, but they do not really resolve the underlying issues involved.

HOW TO DECIDE WHEN TO FIGHT

Suppose there are demands to get out of South Africa, stop marketing powdered infant formula in Haiti, or cut the price of tranquilizers in Great Britain. How might management go about deciding how assertive to be? What factors ought to determine the resources it should invest in the hope of obtaining a favorable conflict outcome? The answers depend on the *stakes* management places on that outcome, together with the relative *power* or leverage of the enterprise in the conflict situation.

Stakes

The stakes of a multinational enterprise in any given conflict are obviously high when a great deal can be won or lost. Just how much does obtaining a specific outcome really matter to the firm? How much would be jeopardized or forfeited if the outcome goes completely against management's position? Stakes are a product of the expected difference in value between the outcome that satisfies management's goals and one that totally frustrates them. Conflict stakes can generally be assessed subjectively, but perhaps never rigorously pinned down, and therefore a great deal depends on management's own perceptions. It was relatively painless, for example, for Procter & Gamble (Folger Coffee) and General Foods (Maxwell House) to end their U.S. importation of Ugandan coffee in 1978 in response to pressure from human rights groups and U.S. congressmen aimed at ending American's business connection with Idi Amin's regime. Ugandan supplies amounted to only 6 percent of U.S. coffee imports. The story certainly would have been different had the supplier in question been Brazil. Tough competition, rather than accommodation, surely would have been the result.

Probably the most important factor in determining a multinational's stakes in a particular conflict is management's own global strategy. Conflict outcomes that weaken the heart of that strategy—damaging the firm's distinctive competence, competitive edge, degree of control, or unique capabilities—are likely to be those that management wants most to avoid. While multinationals often pursue multiple strategies in different product or geographic divisions, it seems possible to distinguish between different kinds of strategies and show how the stakes in any particular conflict depend on them. Firms that concentrate on exploiting technological leads, such as IBM, usually consider it essential to maintain an exceptionally strong R&D program, high quality standards, tight control of technological skills, and close supervision of marketing strategy. Other multinationals see themselves as comparatively efficient in the development of innovative leads in many product lines and markets—although technological preeminence in any one may not be assured. Thus the need for a tight rein on production and marketing is not as critical in conflicts over ownership of affiliates, technology transfer, or quality control. For example, companies like Honeywell, Westinghouse, ITT, an L.M. Ericsson have been relatively calm when faced with pressures for local ownership participation in countries like France or Brazil, while IBM has fought these same pressures every step of the way.

Multinationals in the oil, copper, aluminum, and chemicals industries tend to pursue strategies resting on the advantages of large scale, with barriers to entry, coordination of decisions at various stages of production, security of raw materials supply, and stability in product demand being their particular "jugular veins." Whenever governments or other opponents take actions that threaten them, the stakes are likely to be viewed as high. Multinationals in the food and pharmaceutical industries, meanwhile, rely on strategies based on advanced managerial and marketing skills, proprietary know-how, strong trade names, or massive promotional expenditures. Tight control of marketing programs is usually viewed as absolutely essential, and conflicts that affect them are assigned with high stakes. And there are other strategies that rest on the multinational's global scanning capability and well-integrated, efficient logistical system. In the automobile and electronics industries, for example, where returns are achieved from low-cost production locations and effective global marketing, tight internal control is needed to tie together this kind of multinational network and threats to that network involve high stakes.

Besides such strategic factors, stakes are affected by the firm's financial condition. If the enterprise is very well off, it may be prepared to offer greater concessions to its opponents than if it is close to collapse. During the winter of 1975–76, for example, Chrysler was able to translate its financial weakness into what some observers labeled a "triumph of negotiations" in the United Kingdom. Heavy-handed threats to liquidate its failing British subsidiary enabled management to squeeze an aid package of $360 million out of the labour government—five times the amount the government first proposed.

Other determinants of stakes include sunk costs, precedents that may be established, and accountability to third parties—joint venture partners, industry associations, suppliers and customers, or government regulators. At the same time, perceived stakes may be reduced in various ways. One is insurance, as is provided to U.S. companies by the Overseas Private Investment Corporation against seizure of overseas property by foreign governments, inability to repatriate profits, or acts of war. Another is the existence of options. A third is the joint ownership of capital-intensive facilities, such as aluminum smelters, copper mines, oil fields, natural gas pipelines, and petrochemical complexes, which tend to create a common cost structure and common exposure to risk for the firms involved. If a consortium facility is impaired or expropriated, competitive relationships may remain more or less intact and losing a conflict does not necessarily set one firm back relative to its rivals.

In trying to ascertain its stakes in a conflict outcome, management also has to factor in a time element. As time pressures increase, perceived stakes in obtaining the most desirable conflict outcome may fade—urgency tends to increase "decision costs," prompting management to soften its demands, reduce its aspirations, or increase its concessions. Such was the case in Standard Oil Company of Ohio's (52 percent owned by British Petroleum) ill-fated attempt to construct a tanker terminal in Long Beach, California, and pump Alaskan crude oil to Texas refineries. The urgency of servicing the company's huge debt associated with the Trans-Alaska Pipeline and finding a way to get petroleum products cheaply to its Midwest markets caused Sohio to become an "Environmental Santa Claus." The company even agreed to spend $78 million to reduce pollution at a Southern California Edison generating plant as part of a pollution offset arrangement in the hope of gaining a quick green light for the project. Five years of delay, however, eroded the $1 billion project's economics, and it was abandoned in 1979.

Whether attributable to strategic requirements, financial condition, precedent, available options, or urgency, when the stakes are perceived to be high it seems logical that management will want to be assertive in a particular conflict situation, and it should be willing to expend considerable time and energy either to steamroller the opposition or to pursue avenues of collaboration. With low stakes, major outlays of corporate financial and human resources simply may not make sense.

Power

While stakes succeed in defining management's motivation in social conflict, they do not go very far toward suggesting appropriate conflict strategies without reference to the firm's relative power position. This depends both on the multinational's own characteristics and the situation in which it finds itself, and can differ enormously from one conflict to another. Power can be defined in terms of the range of conflict outcomes through which it can push another party such as a labor union or a national government, and viewed as a continuum extending from a significant power advantage to significant power disadvantage at the endpoints of a scale. That relative power positions can change rapidly was nicely demonstrated by the rapid and dramatic decline in bargaining leverage of most multinationals operating in Iran following the overthrow of the Shah.

What are the sources of a multinational's power or leverage position? Management may possess information not known to the opposition, or can point out contingencies about which the other party has little or no awareness. Or it may be able to emphasize its common interests with the other side to engender feelings of solidarity. It may also be able to convince the opposition that it is justified in making a particular demand on grounds of precedent, reciprocity, or fair play. Management may be able to convince the other party that it has superior knowledge or abilities, and hold out the promise of benefits such as new investment or job creation, whereby it is clear that the reward depends on a conflict outcome that is favorable to the enterprise. Or it can threaten a pullout if the conflict is not favorably resolved. In short, the ingredients of power include firm size, financial base, human resources, expertise, leadership quality, prestige, communication and persuasion skills, access to the media, cohesiveness, prior experience in waging conflict, intensity of commitment, degree of trust and legitimacy, and risk-taking ability.

Another important ingredient of relative power in multinational corporate conflict is coalitions, which are especially likely to form in multiparty battles when one party or another considers it useful to join forces with protagonists with complementary objectives. Examples would include 63 major U.S. multinationals and banks joining together in the early 1970s to form the "Emergency Committee for American Trade" to lobby aggressively against the highly protectionist AFL–CIO backed "Hartke-Burke" bill; more than a hundred firms agreeing to endorse the principles of Rev. Leon Sullivan aimed at eroding apartheid and promoting fair employment practices in South America; 170 firms represented on the Business Roundtable joining together to bargain with American Jewish groups on the Arab boycott issue; or 3 major companies and 30 industry associations going to court in 1977 in West Germany in an attempt to get that country's new codetermination law overturned on constitutional grounds.

The site of a conflict may also affect relative power. Multinationals play most of their conflicts "away" rather than "at home," and usually have to contend with opponents on their own territory, where they are more familiar with the local environment and often enjoy the ability to control or influence it. The foreign enterprise, as a guest, may be constrained in its assertiveness by a need for caution in an unfamiliar setting—although the firm can occasionally obtain assistance from its home government. Not least important, multinational corporate power is strengthened by the existence of options. One example is dispersion of production. Enterprises that rely on well-diversified supply sources are less vulnerable to embargoes or nationalizations and are perhaps more resilient in conflicts in general than firms that rely on more concentrated sources. They gain in leverage from limitations in the ability of governments or other opponents to reach out for alternative sources of technology or capital. In manufacturing industries, power can derive from breaking down the production process so finely that threats to the firm become meaningless—a government's expropriation of a screwdriver-type electronics components assembly operation, putting together imported inputs for export, would yield little.

In the last analysis, multinationals attain power through a degree of indispensability, that is, by possessing something unique to offer or withhold when a conflict arises. And if the ingredients of power are complex, they are also the primary determinants of the feasibility of different types of conflict behavior. A clearly superior power position is likely to favor relatively assertive behavior in conflict situations. This can either take the form of a straightforward competitive stance or one of active collaboration, where the firm's problem-solving resources imply a position of strength and low risk. An inferior power position inhibits management's ability to compel the other side to negotiate or make concessions, and unassertive behavior (avoidance or accommodation) may be most appropriate.

A classic case occurred in the early 1970s when some of the richest oil fields in the North Sea were discovered in the Shetland basin by multinational oil firms including Shell, British Petroleum, Conoco, Burmah, Exxon, and Total. It became evident to the residents of the Shetland Islands, some 100 miles due west of the field, that the companies would be seeking permission to pipe the oil ashore at Shetland, the nearest possible landing point. But very few of the Islands' 19,000 inhabitants wanted oil development encroaching on their way of life. Seizing the initiative, the Shetland Island Council pushed an unprecedented piece of private legislation through the British Parliament in 1974 that gave the Council extensive rights to control and participate in oil-related development. With the Shetland landfall and tanker terminal vital to the economic exploitation of the fields, the oil companies were in no position to argue and yielded at almost every turn to the Council's demands on siting, facilty design, and inflation-hedged royalties.

WHEN TO WORK WITH THE OTHER SIDE

Careful definition of stakes and power elements can help management decide how assertive to be in conflict situations, but it also has to decide how cooperative to be. This depends fundamentally on the interdependence of interests between the multinational and its conflict opponent—are we playing a "zero-sum" or a "positive-sum" game? And whether the need to cooperate can be translated into action is principally a matter of "relationship quality" between management and the other parties in conflict.

Interest Interdependence

Convergence or divergence of interests in conflicts can arise from interdependence of both "goals" and "means." A purely cooperative goals situation can be defined as one in which the various parties sink or swim together, while in a purely competitive situation if one swims, the other must sink. Means interdependence exists when the methods that one party needs to reach its goal affect those available to the other. Management often finds that, even though both it and the opposition are in general agreement on a common goal, there is basic disagreement on how it should be accomplished. Mining companies like AMAX, Rio-Tinto Zinc, and International Nickel, for example, have often found themselves in general agreement with governmental agencies and citizen groups on the desirability of exploiting a particular mineral resource, but nonetheless engaged in severe squabbles on how to go about it—fast or slow, small or large scale, one extractive method or another, and so on.

Goal and means incompatibility in conflicts often focuses on joint dependence on common pools of resources. Multinationals inevitably touch on a wide range of politically sensitive areas in countries where they operate—economic growth, employment, prices, technical change, income distribution, taxation, dependence on external markets, pollution control, balance of payments, national security, and reliance on foreign resources are a few of these. Actions that are perceived to threaten these interests are likely to represent points of incompatibility with host governments or interest groups. Especially for developing-country governments, a multinational's activities may be perceived as harmful to national identity or autonomy. Or a local labor group may perceive threats to its negotiating position. Social action groups may view the multinational as inimical to human rights, the quality of life, or consumer protection. In 1976, Dow Chemical found itself the target of severe criticism from Italian Communist Party economist Eugenio Peggio for "dismantling" the research and sales operations of its 70 percent-owned Italian pharmaceutical subsidiary, Gruppo Lepetit S.A., and placing them under the Dow umbrella. The result, according to Peggio, was that "if Dow decides to leave, what is Italy left with?" In his view, those multinationals that "devour and dismember Italian companies for their own benefit" had to be opposed.

Perhaps the most fundamental source of diverging interests is incompatibility between the *global* views of management and the essentially *national* perspective of most of the institutions with which it comes into conflict. We normally view the world as macroeconomic policy at the national level setting the conditions within which the microeconomic functions of the firm are carried out. With multinationals, however, we have the global microeconomics of the firm often influencing the parameters of macroeconomic policy at the national level. And while the multinational has interests that extend beyond the border of any single country, its managers worry about the problems that arise from overlapping national jurisdictions, particularly their affiliates being used as political tools, conduits, and hostages by competing sovereign states. At the same time, public opinion, moral suasion, and interested third parties such as conciliators, mediators, arbitrators, and fact-finders can help push conflict behavior toward cooperation.

In general, management is likely to be best able and most highly motivated to behave in a cooperative manner in conflicts when both goals and means are positively interdependent and coordination of convergent interests through collaborative or accommodative effort seems appropriate. Some multinationals, for example, have chosen to meet the third world call for "appropriate technologies" by engaging in product innovation for the special conditions and needs of developing nations, such as Ford Motor's "developing nations tractor" or GM's "basic transportation vehicle."

Relationship Quality

Conflicts may occur even when there is no perceived or actual divergence in goals or means among the parties. Often this is a result of prior relations and attitudes. A positive relationship will generally serve to foster mutual trust, recognition of the legitimacy of the other party's interests, open communications, and an increased willingness to respond helpfully to the other party's needs—as opposed to suspicion, poor communications, threats, and intimidation. Hostility tends to feed upon itself, triggered by factors like isolation, stereotypes, failure or disillusionment in prior conflicts, mutual ignorance, racial differences, distorted perceptions, and institutional barriers. Local ideologies and values may reject the multinational enterprise as an institution—socialism as an ideological commitment, and concepts of capitalist exploitation, imperialism, and class struggle will naturally place a burden on constructive conflict resolution. So will anti-American, anti-German, or anti-Japanese paranoia, and questionable behavior on the part of a handful of multinationals like ITT in Chile can likewise severely erode the foundation of mutual trust needed for positive relations.

Perhaps the foremost sources of negative relations for multinationals in conflict situations are ethnocentrism and nationalism. Ethnocentrism reflects an inability to appreciate the viewpoint of others whose cultures have, for example, a different morality, religion, or language, and turn up in an unwillingness or inability to see the common problems that lie beneath variations in social and cultural traditions. Nationalism, as an extension of ethnocentrism, adds a strong chauvinistic and emotional component to many conflicts involving multinationals. For instance, surges of nationalist sentiment have spurred Canadian governments from time to time to impose protectionist measures aimed at the flow of U.S. influence into Canada. One industry particularly affected has been publishing, with classic battles emerging over government attempts to drive *Time* and *Readers Digest* out of the country.

Factors that can lead to positive rather than hostile relations between multinationals and their opponents in conflict situations include experiences of successful prior interactions, perceived similarity in beliefs, common values and attitudes, recognition of existence and legitimacy, good communications, and concerns of the parties about their ability to work together in the future. Management is most likely to exhibit a high degree of cooperativeness (collaboration or accommodation) when relations are open, friendly, and trusting. The annals of MNC conflict contain plenty of examples of hostility—Nestlé vs. the Third World Action Group over infant formula promotion in developing nations, Firestone vs. The Young Americans for Freedom over plans for a synthetic rubber plant in Rumania, Mobile vs. the Center for Social Action of the United Church of Christ over alleged petroleum supplies to Rhodesia, and ITT vs. the Senate Foreign Relations Subcommittee on Multinational Corporations over its Chilean activities.

PUTTING IT ALL TOGETHER

Figure 4.2 summarizes the key determinants of management behavior in multinational corporate conflicts. The framework suggests that, in any given conflict, behavior is likely to be a product of the interaction of our four situational factors—outcome stakes, relative power, interest interdependence, and relationship quality—resulting in some combination of assertiveness and cooperativeness in conflict strategy. As we have seen, outcome stakes and interest interdependence are driving forces of conflict management, but must be modified by the firm's relative power and relationship quality with its opponents in order to ascertain optimum behavior as measured by the degree of assertiveness and cooperativeness appropriate to the conflict situation at hand. The five points on the grid represent the extremes of what could be called behavioral "zones"—a competitive zone, an avoidant zone, a collaborative zone, an accommodative zone, and a compromise zone. It is our view that multinationals

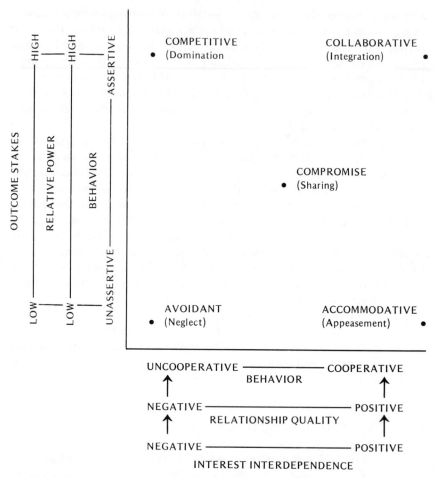

Figure 4.2. Determinants of appropriate conflict behavior.

regularly encounter conflict situations of a relatively pure form, where the four situational variables combine to suggest unambiguously a corporate conflict–management position.

We should emphasize that the four situational factors may not be equally important. For instance, the "motivational structure" of conflict (stakes and interest–interdependence) is probably a more important determinant of conflict behavior than the "capability structure" (power and relationship quality). This is because capabilities are more readily changeable than the underlying motives. And there may be certain linkages among the situational factors themselves—parties who dislike one another are apt to emphasize or develop incompatible goals. It is not hard to understand, for example, why most multinationals have been unwilling to engage in a dialogue with representatives of the World Council of Churches—the WCC declared its vehement opposition to multinationals in 1977 on the grounds that they are accomplices of "repressive states, predatory local elites, and racism," and thus pillars of a system that "oppresses, excludes, and exploits." And as the stakes in conflict outcome increase, so does the incentive to utilize every source of power that may be available to each side.

Our framework suggests that a *competitive* (assertive, uncooperative) response to conflict is appropriate when a multinational's stakes and power are relatively high, and when interest interdependence and relations are relatively negative. The objective is domination. Such is the case in the uranium cartel dispute involving two Pittsburgh neighbors—Westinghouse Electric and Gulf Oil. Westinghouse brought suit against Gulf and 28 other uranium producers charging them with creating an international cartel that forced the price of uranium from $8 a pound to more than $40 a pound over a two-year period. This thorny legal imbroglio—dubbed the "laywers full employment case" by a federal judge—went to trail in late 1980 and it is likely to take at least a decade before all the motions, counterclaims, and appeals are finally decided.

An *avoidant* (unassertive, uncooperative) approach to handling conflict is useful when the firm's stakes and power are relatively low, and when interest interdependence and relations are relatively negative. The objective is to throw in the towel or move on to greener pastures at lowest possible cost. A clear example would be Exxon, Ford Motor, Otis Elevator, Coca-Cola, General Motors, among other firms, quietly pulling out most of their U.S. executives from Argentina in 1973–1974 when the executive kidnap rate in that country reached 10 per month. Avoidance can be useful in many kinds of situations, such as when alternate projects or markets are readily available, when the issues in conflict are trivial and represent only minor annoyances, or when potential disruption and negative publicity seem to outweigh the benefits of conflict resolution.

A *collaborative* (assertive, cooperative) approach to handling conflict is likely to be best when the multinational's stakes and power are relatively high, and when interest interdependence and relations with the opposition are relatively positive. The widely publicized experiment in workplace innovation in the Volvo assembly plant at Kalmar, Sweden, represents a case in point. The goals, not yet fully achieved, are to upgrade worker tasks into tasks that are more creative and satisfying for the individual, thereby leading to a higher level of worker motivation, greater productivity, reduced absenteeism, and reduced strike activity. Collaboration is especially effective when both sides want to achieve the same objective but differ over the means.

An *accommodative* (unassertive, cooperative) response to conflict is suitable when stakes and power are relatively low, and when interest interdependence and relations are relatively positive. The objective is appeasement, and this makes sense when issues are more important to others than to the firm itself, when the firm finds itself outmatched and losing the battle, when management finds that it has been wrong on matters of substance, and when organizational energy is needed for other conflicts where the stakes are higher. How else can one explain the recent unprecedented "orgy of self-flagellation" during which some 400 American-based multinationals voluntarily disclosed to the Securities and Exchange Commission that they were making a total of almost $1 billion in questionable payments abroad?

Finally, a *compromise* (moderately assertive and cooperative) tends to be useful when the firm's stakes are moderate and power advantage or disadvantage is slight, and when interest interdependence and relations are mixes of positive and negative elements. The objective is to "split the difference," especially when conflicts involve differences in goals, attitudes, and values, and when many issues are involved that are given different priorities by the two parties. During 1976-1977, for instance, the American Jewish Congress (AJC) negotiated agreements with a number of major U.S.-based multinationals regarding the Arab boycott of Israel. Gulf Oil, Bethlehem Steel, Goodyear Tire & Rubber, Standard Oil of California, and Tenneco were among those who agreed to provide requested information about boycott practices and/or to revise corporate policies in return for the AJC's withdrawing its shareholder resolutions on the matter. Compromise makes sense when goals are important, but not worth the effort or potential delays associated with more assertive kinds of behavior. It can produce expedient solutions under time pressure as well as temporary settlements to complex issues. And it can be a primary backup when collaboration or competition is unsuccessful.

DIVIDE AND CONQUER

One of the reasons why multinational corporate conflicts can become so protracted is that the bones of contention become fused into a monolithic whole that is not easily broken apart. Each side comes to view the issues as so interconnected and the resulting complex as so overwhelming that the give-and-take process of compromise and concession appears impossible. The likehihood of reaching a satisfactory solution to a conflict can often be increased by separating or "fractionating" the large issues involved into smaller and more workable ones. The issues can often be manipulated—sized up or down, hooked together, broken apart, or stated in different language. They can be differentiated in terms of importance and relatedness, and different conflict management techniques applied at the same time. Some questions can be avoided, others compromised, and still others subjected to intensely assertive behavior on the part of management. Fractionation of issues in conflict can help alleviate the stultifying effects of excessive commitment often associated with attempts to deal with large and complicated conflicts.

Opponents can also be fractionated—often necessary when the opponents themselves have divergent interests. Enka Glanzstoff, for example, the fiber subsidiary of the Dutch chemical firm AKZO, announced plans in 1975 to close fiber operations in three countries and eliminate 6000 jobs by 1977 to hopefully regain profitability. AKZO's two major Dutch and German unions, inspired by the International Federation of Chemical, Energy and General Workers Unions, called for discussions with the company to be held only on an international basis, hoping to set a precedent in multinational labor cooperation against multinationals. Dutch Prime Minister Joop den Uyl pubicly supported the union demands. But AKZO steadfastly refused to talk on a multinational basis and successfully shattered the front orchestrated by Charles Levinson of the International Federation by appealing to the desires of small Dutch unions who did not want an all-out confrontation during a recession. AKZO was thus able to netotiate the plant closings with its labor unions in each country separately.

Certainly unique to conflicts facing multinational companies are issues involving parties in different nations, and it can easily become the "monkey in the middle." Because of its "double identity," and questions of overlapping and conflicting jurisdiction, management often finds itself wedged between the hauling and pulling of parties in several countries whose interests point in fundamentally different directions. Consider Fruehauf's majority-owned subsidiary in France, sandwiched between conflicting U.S. and French government positions in 1965 regarding shipment of truck trailers to China; Volkswagen angering the Brazilian government during the 1975 recession when the company reassigned an export production order from its Brazilian subsidiary back to Germany to appease workers at home; Gulf Oil confronting incompatible demands, with respect to disbursement of royalty payments from its Angolan operations in 1975, exerted by the Ford Administration and the three factions vying for control during the Angolan revolution; and British Petroleum losing its assets in Nigeria to nationalization in 1979 when it got caught in the middle of a dispute over the African policies of the government of Prime Minister Margaret Thatcher.

Even in single-country conflicts management may find it advantageous to use different conflict-handling strategies simultaneously to block the formation of powerful opposing alliances, encourage countercoalitions, or promote division or contention among weaker parties. Boeing, for example, found it useful to collaborate with the State Department while competing with the SEC on disclosure of the names of its agents and consultants abroad who had received more than $70 million in questionable payments. Boeing refused to comply with the SEC demands, claiming that the disclosure of "proprietary and confidential information" could cause "substantial, irreparable harm." The company gained the support of the State Department, which in a document filed with the U.S. Appeals Court stated that disclosure "could reasonably be expected to cause damage to the foreign relations of the U.S."

ROLLING WITH THE PUNCHES

Conflicts are dynamic. They usually do not appear suddenly, but pass through a series of progressive stages during which the degree of conflict may either escalate or abate. Conditions related to stakes, power, interest interdependence, and relations with opponents often shift significantly from one time period to the next. It stands to reason that conflict management strategy should be adapted accordingly. The saga of IBM in India, which followed a path of collaboration–competition–compromise–avoidance illustrates the point. The company collaboratively responded to an invitation of Jawaharlal Nehru to establish an accounting machine plant in Bombay in 1951. IBM went on to dominate the Indian computer industry, and eventually the Indian government pressed the firm both to reduce its 100 percent ownership to 40 percent and to extend its computer design and manufacturing operations in India for the domestic as well as export markets. IBM was initially highly reluctant to consider any deviation from its traditional global policy of keeping all of its foreign affiliates under 100 percent IBM ownership. An equally rigid position on the part of the Indian government forced IBM to propose a range of concessions in the hope of compromise. But they were not enough for the Indians, and IBM's proposals were rejected. The company concluded that the equity dilution demanded "would seriously impair its ability to manage an international high technology company requiring sharing of resources and know-how across national borders" and thus announced its withdrawal from the nation on November 15, 1977.

Even the elements we have used as our guides to conflict management can be consciously altered as time goes by. Values, beliefs, and perceptions of the opponents can be changed through communication and persuasion. The quality of a relationship can be improved through skillful public relations. The power balance may be shifted by working on the firm's leverage or the effectiveness with which it is used. Coalitions can be formed to offset an initial power disadvantage. Perceptions of the stakes involved in a conflict can change dramatically as management's or its opponents' options change. And perceptions of interest interdependence can be altered by substitute goals, third-party intervention, reformulating the issues involved, or introducing "superordinate" goals or threats that outweigh the existing hostility and divergent objectives.

There may also be changes in conflict circumstances beyond the control of the parties concerned. This is perhaps best illustrated by the inevitable cycles that appear in the bargining strength of multinationals and governments of developing countries in the natural resource industries, where contractual arrangements between the firm and the government tend to become obsolete over time. After the capital has been sunk and the initial risks have been taken, attitudes may change. Management may perceive the project as offering even more promise than before, but the government—with the project now "captured"—may come to view the original terms of the agreement as unreasonable. Knowing that the terms needed to retain the essential benefits of the project are much less now than those needed to attract it in the first place, it presses for renegotiation. The ingredients of conflict management for both sides have changed. There are many examples of this "obsolescing bargain" phenomenon. The government of Papua New Guinea, for example, demanded a renegotiation of terms of the Bougainville copper mining agreement with Bougainville Copper Ltd. (Rio-Tinto Zinc) just one year after the world's fourth largest copper mine had been in operation—partly a consequence of extraordinarily large profits earned during the first year.

Figure 4.3 illustrates 16 potential paths of change in conflict behavior. Several of these "vectors" may be appropriate in any conflict, although the "opening moves" in the form of offers, gestures, and

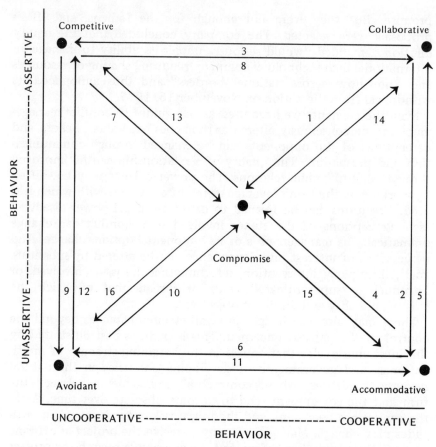

Figure 4.3. Sequential patterns of mode utilization.

actions are often critical in the creation of the psychological setting that may prevail throughout. It is at this early stage that rules and norms are first implanted, issues such as trust and toughness are considered for the first time, and each party's preferences, intentions, and perceptions are exposed.

From a managerial point of view, it might be reasonable to recommend initial use of the collaboration mode whenever possible. This is because outcomes of such behavior are likely to come close to outcomes that are viewed as substantively "fair" or in the "public interest," arrived at by procedurally "equitable means." Our assumption here is that over the long term the interests of the enterprise will best be safeguarded if they coincide with perceptions of public interest. But joint problem-solving efforts are fragile and may break down. And so path 1 (collaborate → compromise) may be needed to resolve remaining issues. If the breakdown is severe enough, and if management finds itself in a weak bargaining position, then path 2 (collaborate → accommodate) may be necessary to maintain a positive working relationship with the opposition. If the multinational's power base is sufficiently strong and the relationship is viewed as expendable, then path 3 (collaborate → compete) may be a viable last resort when irreconcilable differences emerge.

When a multinational confronts an issue associated with intense and aggressive feeling, *accommodation* may be very useful as a starting point. If management can fully understand and empathize with the other side, this approach may establish a relationship that can eventually employ either compromise (path 4) or possibly even collaboration (path 5). Accommodation may facilitate influence by gradations—the "foot-in-the-door" technique—or even induce guilt or obligation in the other party, making it less likely to resist the more uncooperative or assertive behavior that follows. A shift from accommodation to avoidance (path 6) may be necessary when the enterprise is pushed too far or when things just do not work out. To illustrate, readers may recall the case of Polaroid Corporation in South Africa. In 1971 demonstrations, sit-ins, and an attempted product boycott in the United States led management to acquiesce to some of the demands of the Polaroid Workers Revolutionary Movement. The company, as part of a widely publicized "Experiment," required its independent distributor in South Africa to improve wages and job opportunities for blacks and banned sales of its products to the South African government. but in 1977 Polaroid was forced to pull out of the country altogether when it confirmed reports from exiled black activists that its local distributor had been selling film to the government in violation of the earlier understanding.

Competitive opening behavior on the part of management may be necessary to bypass premature cooperation that can lead to a superficial, unsatisfactory, or unstable agreement before the underlying issues in a conflict have really been worked through. Competition, with its threat of losses to both sides, may occasionally be a necessary precondition to motivate the parties eventually to engage in a cooperative process. By starting out tough, management can systematically soften its position by making positive concessions, either in part (path 7) or in full (path 8). This was observed in the head-on clash between Hoffmann-LaRoche and the U.K. Monopolies Commission and Department of Health and Social Services over the pricing of Librium and Valium. Roche chose to get involved in a battle of "epic proportions" in order to prevent the spread of price-cutting demands in a dozen other nations. But the stakes declined as the tranquilizers went out of patent and Roche compromised not long afterward. And with competitive behavior the enterprise always has the option to throw in the towel when the going gets rough or too costly (path 9). Such was the case in Coca-Cola's recent withdrawal from India in the face of government demands that it disclose its secret formula, Firestone's termination of a Rumanian rubber plant deal as a result of the protest orchestrated by the Young Americans for Freedom, and Shell Oil Company's departure from the State of Delaware after a bitter "To Hell With Shell" campaign by environmentalists fighting the firm's refinery construction plans.

Avoidance-oriented behavior often makes sense for openers when the firm's stakes or power are low, where a zero-sum game is involved, or where there is a great deal of hostility. Management lets it be known that it would not touch the issue with the proverbial "ten-foot pole." Yet if it backs off and lets the situation cool down, it is possible that a basis may emerge at a later time for meaningful dialogue and negotiation (path 10). It became known in 1976, for example, that Coca-Cola's independent bottler in Guatemala had engaged in repressive actions against employees exercising their right to union representation. Faced with church group demands that it terminate the franchise agreement, Coca-Cola argued that it was not the owner of the plant and had no control over its labor practices, and thus tried to disassociate itself from the conflict. The pressure of a shareholder resolution eventually led the company to agree to investigate the charges in exchange for a withdrawal of the church action. Church sponsors even visited Guatemala in 1978 and witnessed the signing of an agreement between the bottler and the workers. But murders, the use of riot squads, and abductions reportedly continued, and this lead church groups to again press Coca-Cola into adopting a "code of minimum labor standards" that would be required of its franchisees around the globe. The company then once again adopted an uncooperative stance, restating that allegations involving independent bottlers were none of its business. Unlike the Coca-Cola case, when and if the relationship improves or interests converge, a transition to accommodation may be appropriate (path 11). If the stakes go up or the power balance reverses, then a switch to competition (path 12) may become the logical course of action.

It might even make sense occasionally to move away from an opening position of *compromise*, especially when negotiations are moving slowly or additional leverage is needed and the enterprise finds it expedient to introduce some threats into the picture (path 13). Goodrich in 1976, for instance, was attempting to reorganize the profitless non-tire section of Rubberfabriek Vredestein N.V. of

Holland, which it had acquired in a bitter takeover battle with Goodyear in 1971. The unions protested the proposed reorganization, which would have meant layoffs of 762 out of 4700 employees. This brought the Dutch government into the dispute. Negotiations ambled along until Goodrich, fed up with the slow pace, delivered an ultimatum—it offered to sell Vredestein to the government in June 1976 and announced it would sell off or close down if no agreement could be reached. The pace then quickened with negotiating teams flying back and forth between Akron and The Hague, and a fade-out agreement was reached in October 1976.

In other cases the very experience of "good faith" bargaining and development of mutual trust between a multinational and another party may allow compromise to evolve into collaboration (path 14). Faced with intensifying nationalistic pressures in Guyana in the 1960s, Booker Sugar Estates, a subsidiary of Britain's Booker McConnell Ltd., embarked upon a comprehensive program to win Guyanese acceptance by drastically increasing its contribution to the local economy. Working closely with government departments, the company promoted the formation of new business ventures, encouraged the expansion of independent cane farming, helped develop local government infrastructure, sought local equity participation, progressively "Guyanized" its management, and generally attempted to reduce the industry's traditional paternalism. Booker's efforts to embody Guyanese goals in its corporate strategy allowed the company to operate unscathed until 1976, when a government takeover was negotiated.

A decline in power or a desire to maintain a particular relationship may call for a movement toward accommodation (path 15). A classic case here would be that of the oil majors and OPEC. With the entry of lean and hungry independents into the Middle East, the leading firms lost their ability to set the terms of doing business. As a result, decisions that were the product of compromise in the 1950s and 1960s became products of accommodation in the 1970s. And if bargaining fails to produce an acceptable agreement, management always has the option of pulling out (path 16). In early 1979, for example, the Swiss banking subsidiaries of Citicorp and Dow Chemical withdrew at the last minute from a syndicate that was floating a $33 million loan to Algeria. The eleventh-hour exit was prompted by a complaint made public by a manager of Banque Rothschild of Paris that his bank had been excluded from the syndicate because of its Jewish connections. Withdrawal was the only way in which the two American firms could comply with U.S. antiboycott laws that outlaw discimination in the underwriting of loans.

The point is that conflicts are not static, and therefore conflict management cannot be static either. Many of them track all over the grid we have developed. Yet the "pathology" of many of the conflicts we have observed in our research often varies dramatically from what our model would suggest is optimal for the firm. Some representative cases might include Nestle's mishandling of demands that it change its infant formula promotion practices in the third world, ITT's heavy-handed direct political involvement aimed against Allende in Chile, General Dynamics' failure to reach a negotiated settlement with the Quebec government over ownership of the Asbestos Corporation, Hitachi's faulty public relations in connection with its attempt to establish a color TV plant in the United Kingdom, Citibank's handling of the so-called David Edwards' affair in which the dismissed employee alleged that the bank had "parked" funds to minimize taxes, and Mercedes-Benz's quick and full capitulation to ransom demands of terrorists holding one of its executives in Latin America. Such deviations from "appropriate" conflict management, we maintain, tend to be costly and disruptive for the multinational enterprise. Our model is intended to make it easier for management to focus on the essentials of conflicts, and by using such a "filter" stay closer to that elusive path.

FROM THEORY TO PRACTICE

Developing a guide to management to conflict over social issue is one thing. Putting it into practice is quite another. Of primary importance, we feel, is sensitivity—the ability of management to zero in on the essentials of a conflict and understanding what makes opponents tick. This demands accurate assessment of each side's stakes and power positions and the consequences for each side of the various possible outcomes. It is a skill not easily learned or transferred from the one environment to another, nor is it something that can be very far removed from the strategic planning core of the enterprise. Ways have to be found to inculcate such sensitivity in successive generations of top management at both headquarters and the affiliate level, and to combine it with substantive staff and consultancy expertise on a range of issues extending from pollution control and consumer affairs to terrorism and human rights. The act of constructive conflict management can be advanced both by adjusting the incentive systems under which managers operate, and creating the task systems essential to effective implementation.

Decisions also have to be made about where to place responsibility. Many conflicts can be managed only from headquarters, because outcomes in one country inevitably affect the firm's fortunes in another. Other conflicts can be handled far more effectively at the affiliate level. All require close monitoring and open channels of communication between headquarters and the affiliate. And staff or consultant expertise on substantive conflict issues should be available to jump in at a moment's notice.

A true "technology of social policy" in a multinational company thus requires the right kinds of human resources, experience, and network of accountability and responsibility. It represents "internalized" corporate know-how not really very different from the knowledge of how to build a petrochemical plant or an aircraft and make it work right the first time. Yet it is far more diffuse, complex, and intractable. Partly for this reason management often considers it unimportant, a bunch of unconnected bridges to be crossed when we come to them. If we are right about the setting of international business in the 1980s and 1990s—our prediction is that multinationals will increasingly create, collide with, and be victimized by nonmarket tensions and contradictions—this view is certainly wrong. It may also be dangerous.

NOTE

1. Gladwin, Thomas N., and Walter, Ingo. *Multinationals Under Fire: Lessons in the Management of Conflict*. New York: John Wiley, 1980.

PART II

Financial Behavior Issues

As with many other studies in this volume, *Gentry* begins by confronting the global rationalization model as the basic motive for MNC operations, as opposed to the interest of nation-states and their attempts to exercise influence on the activities of multinational corporations. National policy by necessity must impinge on the internal behavior of MNCs and their possibilities of achieving and maintaining global coordination and control of widely dispersed resources.

Between global rationalization and the opposing adjustment theory falls a compromise strategy. This theory assumes that MNCs have modestly altered their policies and strategies to meet host country demands but still continue to operate under the global rationalization model, based on centralized management of production and marketing processes.

Gentry investigates whether presently applied MNC financial management practices fall in line with the global rationalization model. One should assume that financial management lends itself most easily to global rationalization, as compared to other functional fields of corporate management.

The author asks if MNCs take lower operating risks than corporations serving only national markets, and if stock markets appraise MNCs as being less risky than national companies. He *hypothesizes* that MNC credit strategies and policies result in the selection of customers and suppliers from a significantly lower risk level than would apply in national companies, and that the risk measure determined by the stock market is significantly lower for MNCs than for national corporations.

Gentry first reviews the international finance literature, concentrating on valuation, by means of the capital asset pricing model, which he developes into the enlarged model. He attempts to compare the proxies of trade credit policies for MNCs to those of national companies, and stock market measures in a similar comparison. The model is then applied to a cluster of 260 companies, of which 76 are industrial MNCs and 153 industrial national corporations. In addition, there are (national) transportation companies and 4 multinational and 16 national trading corporations.

The data are analyzed stepwise. In an analysis of cash inflows, the test measuring the risk categories of the credit customers and the predictability of cash inflows indicates a similar performance for multinational as well as for national corporations. The presence of a global rationalization behavior cannot be traced. In analyzing cash outflows, a similar conclusion is reached.

Next, the behavior of financial officers was investigated, again showing no difference between the degree of centralization of functional business activities for MNCs and national corporations, as hypothesized in the global rationalization theory.

Similar negative findings were derived from an investigation of market-determined risks.

To repeat briefly, Gentry's assumption was that, because of centralized coordination and control of international resources by means of a more efficient managerial system, which attempts to rationalize globally, MNCs, as compared to national corporations, would be in a preferred bargaining position in trade credit management and in financial markets. Because of reduced uncertainties in receiving supplies of critical resources and customers with lower risk ratings, both of which lead to a higher predictability of cash inflow and outflow, and also because of the centralization of financial decisions, MNCs would be able to acquire capital at lower interest than the national corporations. At the same time the stock market would value MNC stock higher than that of national corporations.

After applying sequential tests to the above conjectures, item by item, no such differences could be established. The implications of these findings are manifold.

MNCs do not have a superior financial management that permits them to exploit possibilities of global rationalization. Thus, there is a potential for improvement of managerial efficiency in MNCs. By implication, the accusation that claims MNCs shift capital from country to country and thus jeopardize the sovereignty of the nation-states in control of their own currency actually does not take place (or takes place only in exceptional cases). For establishing policy, therefore, this would mean that generalized restrictions on inter-MNC capital flowing from country to country would either not be necessary or should be geared to individual cases.

Another possible interpretation may be that the lower risks assumed in the Gentry study are compensated for by higher risks in other spheres that were not investigated, for example, political risks or regulation risks.

Gentry, in concluding, raises a number of policy questions that still remain unanswered.

Reed investigates the role of financial centers in the international transfer of capital in which multinational corporations are assumed to participate to a considerable extent. Reed attempts to shed light upon whether MNC capital transfers have had an impact on the development of new international financial centers or upon obvious shifts in importance a number of these centers have experienced since World War II. He tests the hypotheses of whether international financial centers are preeminent in their daily operations, as well as long-term strategic objectives of multinational corporations and nation-states. Reed identifies and examines the organizational structure and rank of international financial centers over time and the determinants or factors required to build infrastructures and preeminence.

Reed first reviews the current theories concerning the eminence, formation, and the markets of international financial centers.

The author investigates the movements in the top ranks of international financial centers, attempting to explain their principal movements. An important conclusion is that a previous analysis of international financial center development and eminence has left unexplored their role as information centers and their role in the management of the world's global capital portfolio, which he then illuminates.

Reed characterizes the issue conflicts between multinational corporations and highly industrialized nation-states primarily as macro problems concerned with international order, centering around inflation and employment. In turn these categories comprise issues of balance of payments (as influenced by international trade and capital flows), economic growth, supplier and consumer satisfaction, and levels of assistance to developing countries. The issue conflicts between MNCs and developing countries, meanwhile, center around foreign ownership, local borrowing, exporting requirements, transfer pricing, profit repatriation, contribution to local know-how and technology advancement, and so on. The author develops the MNC–nation-state conflict model, caused by global rationalization on one side, and attempts to achieve national optimization on the other side. He introduces the product life-cycle theory in international trade and investment (Vernon) and claims that nation-states should use the international product life cycle as the basis for developing their political economy strategies by elaboration and monitoring of life cycles of major importance to the nation-state. This monitoring must not necessarily be at the expense of multinational corporations. Rather, through properly understanding the life cycles, it could ease the tensions between the potential antagonists. The author then ties the MNC–nation-state model and the international product life-cycle model together with the international monetary system. He proposes a model that would enable the International Monetary Fund to adjust the currency basket represented by special drawing rights (SDR) to reflect changes faster and more accurately in the participating countries' economic structure and performance. He develops a ranking score in which the collective importance of a given country's international financial centers is also reflected.

The proposed SDR basket structure would make the SDR more attractive in terms of capital value and marketability to the international financial center community than the present structure. The capital value of the SDR would be competitive with any other individual currency included in the basket. Reed concludes that international financial centers could serve as bridges between the nation-states and the multinationals and bring about increased operating efficiency and effectiveness, which would benefit the entire world. The proposed systems would drastically reduce the propensity for conflict between MNCs and nation-states because it would minimize the ability of MNCs to affect substantially the policies and goals of one nation-state at the expense of another.

Chapter 5

Global Rationalization and MNCs' Trade Credit Policies: Policy Issues

*James Gentry**

In recent years there has been a change in international economic and political environments resulting in part from the shrinkage of international space and an expansion of new business opportunities in foreign markets [38, p. 1]. Multinational corporations (MNCs) have entered new foreign markets, but the opportunity to expand into foreign markets has been matched by threats and actual intrusions by foreigners into previously safe home territory [38, p. 5]. Since 1955, international trade has accelerated rapidly and it has produced a growing interrelationship among the world economies. The interdependence has created the most pain for the less-developed countries, who view the shrinking of international space as increasing their dependence on products manufactured in the North [23]. The outcome has been increased tension and anxiety on the part of many nation-states and multinational firms.

There are various theories concerning the reaction of MNCs to the increasing demands of nation-states. The global rationalization theory is based on the idea that planning and decisionmaking activities are highly centralized in corporate headquarters. Centralized decisionmaking allows MNCs to achieve global coordination and control of widely disbursed resources. Having the flexibility to coordinate and control international resources efficiently allows management to reduce production uncertaintites related to the shortage of materials, supplies, labor, and power, and to lower market uncertainties related to market share and size.

*University of Illinois at Urbana–Champaign.

There is an opposing adjustment theory that holds MNCs have significantly adjusted their strategies and policies related to production and marketing in order to accomodate the demands of host countries [30]. Also there exists a compromise strategy that falls in between global rationalization and the adjustment strategy. The compromise strategy assumes MNCs have modestly altered their policies and strategies to meet host country demands, but continue to operate under global rationalization theory where centralized management of production and marketing processes is maintained [26, p. 6]. The compromise reflects a softening of the global rationalization concept and suggests MNCs are pursuing unique policies and strategies in their trade relations with host countries.

Do current financial management practices of MNCs support the existence of a global rationalization theory? Assuming that global rationalization exists in the financial management of MNCs does observable data show that MNCs take lower operating risks than companies serving only national markets? Does the stock market appraise MNCs as being less risky than national companies (NCs)? The following two hypotheses provide an approach for investigating the preceding questions. First, trade credit strategies and policies of MNCs result in the selection of customers and suppliers from a significantly lower risk level than is found in national companies (NCs). Second, the risk measure determined by the stock market is significantly lower for MNCs than NCs.

The objectives of this chapter are to review briefly the finance literature on trade credit policy and the capital asset pricing model; to explain the methodology of the study; to analyze and interpret the data used to test the two hypotheses; and, finally, to identify key trade policy issues related to MNCs.

LITERATURE REVIEW

Valuation is a unifying theme for theories focusing on long-term corporate finance policy issues dealing with investment, financing, and dividend decisions. The capital asset pricing model (CAPM) provides a theory for explaining the premium financial markets are willing to pay for risk. The value of the firm is directly related to the risk premium. The CAPM provides a framework for measuring risk and the tradeoff between risk and return. Mossin [25], Hamada [19], Bogue and Roll [7], Weston [40], Weston and Brigham [41], Van Horne [35, 36], and others have extended the CAPM to measure the risk–return tradeoff of capital investment projects.

The CAPM is an economic model based on a critical assumption that capital markets are efficient during a one-period time horizon. Theoretically this means the expected market rate of return on an asset accurately reflects the actual outcome of management's investment and financing decisions.

Imbedded in the CAPM framework is the assumption that the investment and financing decisions of management are optimal. Furthermore, it is assumed that the strategic objectives of management are clearly defined and remain stable. This implies the ability of management to identify changes in markets, sources of raw materials, and technology and to adjust plans and operations to incorporate these new developments. In essence the CAPM assumes stable market conditions and that the operations of a firm are managed efficiently.

The CAPM is developed in a hypothetical world in which the following assumptions are made about investors and the opportunity set [11, p. 160]:

1. Investors are risk-averse individuals who maximize the expected utility of their end-of-period wealth.
2. Investors are price takers and have homogeneous expectations about asset returns which have a joint normal distribution.
3. There exists a risk-free asset such that investors may borrow or lend unlimited amounts at the risk-free rate.
4. The quantities of assets are fixed. Also, all assets are marketable and perfectly divisible.
5. Asset markets are frictionless and information is costless and simultaneously available to all investors.
6. There are no market imperfections such as taxes, regulations, or restrictions on short selling.

The CAPM model assumes there is a linear tradeoff between risk and return. Thus high-risk investment alternatives are expected to generate higher returns than riskless projects, and this difference is the risk premium. The degree of risk perceived by the market for a specific asset or portfolio becomes the cost of risk to the firm. Structuring the above into equation form highlights the essentials of the CAPM.

$$\overline{k}_j = R_F + (\overline{k}_m - R_F)\, \text{Beta}_j \qquad (5.1)$$

where $\overline{k}_j$ = expected rate of return on asset j
P_F = risk-free interest rate
$\overline{k}_m$ = expected rate of return on the market portfolio
$\text{Beta}_j = \text{Cov}/(k_j, k_m)/\text{Var}_m{}^2$, the measure of volatility of the return of an individual security relative to market returns

The CAPM has implications for short-run financial management. There is a belief that cash, accounts receivable, inventory, and accounts payable involve less risk than plant and equipment. The rationale for this belief is that unlike capital investment decisions, working capital decisions are routine and reversible over time [16]. The CAPM provides a framework for including short-run assets and liabilities that have lower risk.

Initially, the CAPM did not allow for decisions related to the management of financial assets such as receivables and payables because of the limiting assumptions underlying the model. The CAPM assumed away transactions costs of all types, plus cost of information, indivisibilities, and divergent borrowing, lending rates, and sometimes taxes [9]. The assumption of perfect financial markets implied perfect competition in financial markets. Although these assumptions were believed crucial for handling investment and capital structure decisions, they closed the door on any questions related to short-term financial management. The problems of managing receivables disappears under the perfect financial market assumption [9], which also precludes any discussion of an optimal credit policy [24]. The perfect market theory inferred that receivables would not provide excess returns to management, but like all financial assets would produce only a certainty equivalent return equal to the risk-free rate of interest (R_f). Furthermore, the perfect market assumption implies a firm can borrow at any time at the certainty equivalent cost of R_f. Additionally, there is no incentive to use trade credit rather than borrowing from a bank or selling commercial paper.

Although the CAPM provides a useful theoretical framework, financial markets are not perfect, but are imperfect instead [9]. A few examples will illustrate the imperfections. There are transaction costs involved when doing business in the financial markets and, even more apparent, the future is not known with certainty. In the management of corporate cash flows, one can observe that a firm's actual sales may be either greater than or less than forecasted, and a firm's actual costs are not equal to the forecasted costs. The result is either an excess or a shortfall in net cash flow. Short-term lending or borrowing provides the mechanism for adjusting the firm's financial position [17]. These few observations highlight the need for integrating short-run financial planning variables into the long-run planning model, which would result in a unified theory of corporate finance.

Cohn and Pringle [9] provide the rationale for including working capital decisions in the CAPM. They show that the assumption of perfect financial markets must be dropped and market imperfections introduced explicitly. Cohn and Pringle cite the extension of the

CAPM by Vasiek [37], Black [6], Fame [14], and Brennan [8] in demonstrating that the basic conclusions of the CAPM hold under divergent borrowing and lending rates. In particular, the expected return on a risky asset remains a linear function of the covariance of the asset's return with that of the market portfolio [9, p. 39]. The primary contribution of Cohn and Pringle is that working capital management can be used to keep the firm's shares in a given risk class [9, p. 39]. The firm faces shifts in its risk class because of the lumpy nature of long-term investment and financing decisions and also because of forecasting errors. Cash, marketable securities, and short-term borrowing are used to offset or moderate cash flow shortfalls. Also it is apparent that receivables, payables, and inventories can be managed to reduce the market-determined risk of a firm.

The introduction of working capital components into the CAPM has been utilized by several authors. Bierman, Chopra, and Thomas [5] have assumed that the level of receivables and inventories can affect operating earnings. They suggest a method for integrating the current asset level into the CAPM. Copeland and Khoury [10] focus on the risk–return tradeoff involved in changing the level of investment in accounts receivable. The use of a firm's credit policies to increase its receivables and the value of the firm is an implicit assumption of the two preceding articles. Also Beranek [4, Chapter 10] and Cyert, Davidson, and Thompson [12] have developed the nuances that are related to the changing of credit policies when managing accounts receivable. Finally, several authors have explored the implication of changes in cash discount policy [1, 15, 20] credit period and credit policy standards [3, 13, 22, 28, 42] and the effect of each on the value of the firm.

Haley and Higgins [18] emphasize the importance of accounts payable as a primary source of funds for financing inventories and the contribution a trade credit surplus has on a firm's net cash flows. The authors implicitly recognize the importance of a firm's trade credit policies that are negotiated with its suppliers. Additionally, Robichek, Teichroew, and Jones [31] introduce the subtleties of stretching accounts payable to achieve an optimal short-run financing decision.

An objective of short-run financial planning is to acquire cash inflows as early as possible and to hold onto the cash as long as possible. The inflow and outflow of cash through a firm resembles the flow of liquid through a pipeline. The speed and the level of the flow of cash through the firm are two critical measures of financial performance. The timing of inflows and outflows are determined by the credit terms that are negotiated prior to any sales, purchase, or production contracts. Strategically, management would prefer to synchronize cash inflows and outflows as closely as possible. The synchronization of cash flows would reduce the need for short-term borrowing to offset a shortfall in cash. the best strategy is to receive the inflows early in the production process and disburse cash at the conclusion of the process. A firm in a strong bargaining position may be able to achieve this strategy. However, a firm in a weak bargaining position may find it necessary to pay out cash before materials arrive and may not receive cash inflows until a long period after the goods are delivered. Thus the credit terms negotiated with customers and suppliers reflect the bargaining power of each firm.

With this background concerning the effect trade credit terms have on cash inflows and outflows, we shall compare the proxies of trade credit policy for MNCs to those of national companies. Also the stock market measures of MNCs are compared to those of NCs.

METHODOLOGY

In designing the original questionnaire, cash flow literature was reviewed and several corporate executives from a cross section of industries were interviewed. The interviews aided in refining the questionaire used to examine management's perceptions of bottle-necks in the cash flow forecasting process. The questionnaire was pretested and executives involved in the pretest were interviewed to modify the questionnaire.

The initial sample was composed of the 1978 *Fortune* 1000 largest industrial companies, the 50 largest transportation companies, and the 50 largest retail companies [43]. The second screen selected all companies from the initial list of 1000 that had five years of continuous return data on the CRSP file from January 1975 to December 1979. This reduced the list to 690. Questionnaires were sent to the highest financial officer in each company.

There were three mailings sent to the 690 companies between June and September 1980. For this paper the returned responses from 260 companies provide the basis for the empirical study. These companies compose 37.5 percent of the 690 companies included in the final mailing. There were 76 industrial MNCs and 153 NCs that represented 26.9 and 10.6 percent, respectively, of the total sales of the Fortune 1000. The 11 transportation companies were all NCs. They represented 27 percent of the total sales of the Fortune 50. There were 4 MNC and 16 NC retail companies that composed 14 and 36 percent, respectively, of the total sales of the Fortune 50 retailers.

The market risk measure (Beta) for each company was calculated by regressing monthly rates of return of each company against monthly rates of return of a market index. Monthly returns plus dividends for each company and the index were acquired from the CRSP files for the period January 1975 to December 1979.

ANALYSIS

Credit extension is a key marketing and finance decision that reflects tradeoffs and compromises by management. Credit management takes into account the standards established by the industry, the current economic and business conditions, the economic outlook of the company, previous credit experience, and the bargaining position of a company relative to its customers and suppliers. In industries that are not perfectly competitive the bargaining position of a supplier is reflected in the decision of which customers will receive credit, the amount of credit to be extended, and the terms [29]. If the bargaining power of a supplier is superior to a customer, the former will not extend trade credit to the latter if it increases the risk or lowers the return of the receivables portfolio. Under these conditions the supplier is dominant in establishing who receives credit, how much, and the terms of the trade. However, if the prospective customer has the dominant bargaining position due to industry competitive forces, the terms of the trade will reflect the importance of the bargaining power of the customer. Because many industries are not perfectly competitive, the extension of credit is based on the bargaining power of a supplier or a customer.

In the context of a global rationalization theory, the MNCs would have stronger bargaining power in the extension of trade credit than the NCs. Theoretically, a MNC would have a larger market size and a larger share of the total world market than the NCs. If the market size is growing and the market share of the MNC remains constant, the MNC does not have to extend credit to higher risk accounts. However, in a growing market an NC would be willing to accept a higher level of risk in order to either make an entry or expand its market share.

Another important dimension underlying the credit extension process is the relationship between the predictability of cash inflows and riskiness of the receivables portfolio. The larger the portion of the receivables portfolio held in low-risk accounts, the higher the realibility of the predictions concerning cash inflows. Alternatively, the larger the portion of the receivables in high-risk accounts, the lower the reliability of the predictions concerning cash inflows.

One objective of the survey was to measure management's perception of its company's credit-granting operation. The questions related to receivables management provide an appraisal of the policies and strategies that underly the credit extension operation. The hypothesized relationship is that the risk level of MNC credit customers is significantly lower than the credit customers of NCs. Also it is hypothesized that the reliability of predictions related to cash inflows will be significantly higher for the MNCs when compared to the NCs.

Cash Inflows

To test if global rationalization exists in the management of cash inflows, financial managers were asked to respond to four separate questions. These questions are the basis of the analysis related to cash inflows.

How do financial managers perceive the distribution of their credit customers? They were asked to respond to the following questions:

> In your largest business unit what percentage of your credit customers are considered to be:
> a. Low risk?
> b. Average risk?
> c. High risk?

The responses of the MNC and NC financial managers are summarized in Table 5.1. There were 67 responses from MNCs and 138 responses from the NCs. A one-way analysis of variance (ANOVA) was used to determine if there is a significant different between the risk class distribution of MNC and NC credit customers. The data in Table 5.1 shows that the low-risk credit customers represent 59%, ±28%, of the total for MNCs and 57%, ±29%, for the NCs. The F value of the ANOVA test shows there is no significant difference between the MNCs and NCs at the .05 level of significance. Because the sample size of the two groups are vastly different, the Duncan test [21, pp. 133–144] was used to determine if a bias in the sample size affected the statistical results. The .05 and .01 critical values for the Duncan test are 5.01 and 5.65, respectively. The Duncan test statistic is not significant, which indicates the difference in sample size did not have an effect on the ANOVA statistics.

The responses of the financial managers to the percent of credit customers considered to be average risk was a mean of 31%, ±24%, for the MNCs and a mean of 35%, ±25%, for the NCs. The percent

Table 5.1. Risk Distribution of Credit Customers, Multinational Compared to National

	Multinational			National			ANOVA F value	Duncan Test
	Mean (%)	S.D. (%)	N	Mean (%)	S.D. (%)	N		
Credit Customers								
% Low risk	58.76	28.22	67	56.54	29.13	138	0.40	1.97
% Average risk	31.27	23.91	67	34.77	25.09	138	0.67	1.40
% High risk	9.97	14.32	67	8.69	12.08	138	0.19	0.26
% Customers Providing								
80% of credit sales	31.42	21.07	40	34.58	25.51	86	0.09	3.08
Largest Credit Customers								
% Low risk	82.05	21.43	41	72.78	31.69	119	0.87	3.06
% Average risk	15.22	18.91	41	22.44	27.55	119	1.80	0.89
% High risk	2.73	5.08	41	4.78	1.22	119	0.83	0.12

of the customers rated as high risk was 10%, ±14%, for the MNCs and 8.7%, ±12% for the NCs. The ANOVA and Duncan test were not significant. Thus the data indicate that there is no difference in the distribution of the risk classification of credit customers of MNCs and NCs.

A second measure of credit policy is to determine the concentration of credit sales. How do financial managers perceive the concentration of their credit sales? Frequently, financial executives observe that there is a skewed distribution in their accounts receivable. That is, 20 percent of their customers account for 80 percent of the credit sales, which is commonly referred to as Pareto's law [2, 33]. They were asked the following question:

In your largest business unit, approximately what percentage of your customers provide 80 percent of your total credit sales?

Although only a small number of the respondents answered this question, 40 MNCs and 86 NCs, Table 5.1 shows their responses were quite similar, 31%, ±21%, and 35%, ±26%, respectively. The ANOVA test indicates that there is no significant difference at the .05 level, and the Duncan test results were not significant. The mean statistics are supportive of the skewed distribution suggested by Pareto's law.

The managers were asked to indicate the risk class distribution of these largest credit customers. They were asked the following question.

What percentage of these largest credit customers are considered to be:
a. Low risk?
b. Average risk?
c. High risk?

The ANOVA tests show no statistical difference between the MNCs and the NCs. The Duncan test is not significant. Table 5.1 shows 82%, ±21%, of MNC's largest customers were considered as low risk, while 73%, ±32%, of NC's largest customers were rated as low risk. The MNC managers indicated 15%, ±19%, of their largest customers would be average risk and the NCs estimated 22%, ±28%. The MNCs reported 3%, ±5%, of their largest customers were in the high-risk category while the NCs registered 5%, ±1%. The results of these tests show a similarity among MNCs and NCs in the selection of credit customers.

The predictability of cash inflows is related to a firm's credit policies and strategies. Well-designed and efficient credit systems should have a higher reliability of cash inflow predictions than poorly designed and less efficient systems. The global rationalization theory allows us to hypothesize that the tight centralization of decision-making by MNCs should produce a more efficient management of corporate resources than is present in NCs. Therefore, one would expect the reliability of cash inflow predictions of MNCs to be substantially higher than in NCs. How do financial managers perceive the reliability of their predictions concerning cash inflows? They were asked to respond to the following question:

> Currently, how would you rate the reliability of your largest business unit's predictions related to cash inflows?

The respondents had six choices—very high, high, average, low, very low, and not estimated. The distribution of the responses for the MNCs and the NCs are presented in Table 5.2. Approximately 42 percent of the MNCs and 49 percent of the NCs considered the reliability of their cash flows to be high or very high. For the total distribution the F value of the ANOVA test shows that there is no significant difference between the MNCs and the NCs. The Duncan test is also not significant at the .05 level.

In summary, the tests measuring the risk categories of the credit customers and the predictability of cash inflows indicate a similarity

Table 5.2. Reliability of Predictions Related to Cash Inflows and Outflows
Multinational compared to National

	Multinationals		Nationals			
	Frequency Mean (%)	N	Frequency Mean (%)	N	ANOVA F value	Duncan Test
Cash Inflows						
Very high	12.7	79	12.8	172	0.05	0.97
High	29.1		36.0			
Average	48.1		39.0			
Low	6.3		8.1			
Very low	3.8		2.3			
Not estimated	0.0		1.7			
Cash Outflows						
Very high	10.3	78	8.8	171	0.01	0.86
High	29.5		36.3			
Average	48.7		42.1			
Low	9.0		9.9			
Very low	2.6		1.2			
Not estimated	0.0		1.8			

among the MNCs and NCs. These indirect tests do not support the presence of a global rationalization theory in the selection of credit customers or the management of cash inflows.

Cash Outflows

Do MNCs manage cash outflows significantly differently from NCs? The objective of this section is to determine if global rationalization provides a theoretical rationale for distinguishing between MNCs and NCs. To test for the presence of global rationalization in the management of cash outflows, financial managers were asked four questions. An analysis of the responses provides a basis for evaluating the presence of global rationalization in the management of cash outflows.

How do financial managers perceive the bargaining position they hold with their suppliers? They were asked the following questions:

> With what percentage of the accounts payable in your largest business unit is your bargaining position (the ability to alter payment schedules) considered to be:
> a. Superior?
> b. About equal?
> c. Inferior?

The responses are summarized in Table 5.3. The MNCs indicated they had a superior bargaining position with 33%, ±30%, of their suppliers. The NCs observed they maintained a superior bargaining position with 31%, ±29%, of their suppliers. The bargaining position appeared about equal for 55%, ±32%, of the MNCs and 56%, ±31%, of the NCs. An inferior position was perceived by 12%, ±19%, of the MNCs and 13%, ±19%, of the NCs. The responses from the two groups are quite similar, and the F value of the ANOVA test indicates there is no significant difference between the MNCs and the NCs. The Duncan test is also not significant at the .05 level.

To determine the concentration of accounts payable, the financial managers were asked:

> In your largest business unit approximately what percentage of your suppliers account for 80 percent of your total trade debt (accounts payable)?

Only 34 MNCs and 85 NCs answered this question. Pareto's law [2, 33] suggests this distribution may be skewed, for example, 20 percent of the suppliers account for 80 percent of the payables. The responses of the MNC managers shows 31%, ±22%, of their suppliers

Table 5.3. Bargaining Position with Suppliers, Multinational Compared to National

	Multinational			National			ANOVA F value	Duncan Test
	Mean (%)	S.D. (%)	N	Mean[a] (%)	S.D. (%)	N		
Bargaining Position with Suppliers								
Superior (%)	32.91	29.69	48	30.97	29.47	107	0.01	1.59
About equal (%)	55.19	32.02	48	56.33	31.50	108	0.01	2.08
Inferior (%)	11.90	19.25	48	12.70	18.91	107	0.00	0.57
% Suppliers accounted for 80% of accounts payable	31.35	21.74	34	29.76	21.99	85	0.38	2.98
Bargaining Position with Largest Suppliers								
Superior (%)	31.97	33.45	39	30.49	21.99	90	0.03	1.90
About even (%)	51.10	34.99	39	53.83	33.45	90	0.02	2.43
Inferior (%)	16.92	27.57	36	15.68	24.54	90	0.30	1.03

[a]Data rounded up slightly to equal 100% in the two categories.

accounted for 80 percent of the payables and the responses of the NCs was 30%, ±22%. The mean statistics are supportive of the skewed distribution suggested by Pareto's law. The *F* value of the ANOVA test shows that the responses of the MNC and NC managers are similar. Also the Duncan test is not significant.

How did the two sets of managers appraise the risk distribution of these largest suppliers. They were asked the following questions:

> With what percentage of your largest suppliers is your bargaining position (the flexibility to alter payment schedules) considered to be:
> a. Superior?
> b. About equal?
> c. Inferior?

There were 39 MNC managers and 90 NC managers responding to this question. Table 5.3 shows that there was no statistical difference in the responses of the two sets of managers in evaluating their bargaining position vis-à-vis their suppliers. In summary, the bargaining position of MNCs and NCs with their suppliers did not provide empirical support for a theory of global rationalization.

The final test of managing cash outflows focused on the reliability of predictions. How do the financial managers appraise the reliability of predicting cash outflows? They were asked the following question:

> Currently, how would you rate the reliability of your largest business unit's predictions related to cash outflows?

There were six possible responses—very high, high, average, low, very low, and not estimated. The distribution of the responses of the MNCs and the NCs are presented in Table 5.2. The *F* value of the ANOVA test indicates that the responses of the two groups are similar. Approximately 87 percent of the responses of both groups considered the reliability of the predictions, which ranged from very high to average. The average rating was selected by 49 percent of the MNCs and 42 percent of the NCs.

The preponderance of the evidence indicates the MNCs and NCs have similar bargaining positions with their suppliers and similar perceptions about the reliability of cash outflow predictions. Global rationalization is not supported in the bargaining position with suppliers or the management of cash outflows.

In conclusion, the empirical data in the management of cash inflows and outflows do not support global rationalization as a viable theory for explaining the decisionmaking behavior of MNCs.

Centralization

Centralization of decisionmaking allows MNC management to achieve improved economic efficiency through global coordination and control of their widely disbursed international resources. The centralization concept is a fundamental assumption underlying global rationalization, and therefore one would expect to find financial operating decisions to be more centralized at MNCs than NCs. Financial managers were asked the following questions:

In your company, do you use a centralized or decentralized approach in the management and control of:
Accounts receivable?
Accounts payable?
Purchasing?
Production?
Cash (investment and borrowing)?

A summary of the responses to the questions is found in Table 5.4. The responses show the management of cash is highly centralized. Almost 98 percent of the MNCs and 99 percent of the NCs indicated that there was a centralization of cash management. Smith and Sell [32] also found a similar centralization of cash management. The ANOVA tests show there is no difference between the MNCs and NCs in the centralization of cash management.

In the management of receivables, Table 5.4 shows that 52 percent of the MNCs and 42 percent of the NCs utilize a centralized approach. More than half of the MNCs and NCs have decentralized payables and purchasing systems. Production was the most decentralized activity for both groups, that is, 72 percent of the MNCs and 77 percent of the NCs. The *F* values of the ANOVA tests were not significant for any of the questions and neither were the Duncan tests.

Does management use a centralized or decentralized approach in preparing inputs for monthly, quarterly, or annual cash flow forecasts? Global rationalization would suggest that the MNCs are more centralized than the NCs. The responses to this question are found in Table 5.5. For the 80 MNCs responding, 48 percent used a centralized approach, 42 percent decentralized, and 10 percent used both approaches. The response of the 178 NCs were 51 percent, centralization, 45.5 percent decentralization, 2 percent both approaches, and 1 percent did not forecast. These responses between MNCs and NCs are not significantly different according to the *F* value of the ANOVA test. The Duncan test is not significant.

Table 5.4. Centralized Versus Decentralized Control for Various Areas, Multinational Compared to National

	Multinational Frequency			National Frequency			ANOVA F value	Duncan Test
	Mean Centralized (%)	Mean Decentralized (%)	N	Mean Centralized (%)	Mean Decentralized (%)	N		
Accounts receivable	52.5	47.5	80	41.7	58.3	178	2.59	0.25
Accounts payable	47.5	52.5	80	44.0	56.0	175	0.27	0.25
Purchasing	44.7	55.3	76	36.4	63.6	176	1.56	0.24
Production	27.8	72.2	79	23.3	76.7	163	0.58	0.19
Cash (invest and borrow)	97.5	2.5	81	98.9	1.1	177	0.65	0.02

Table 5.5. Approach Used in Preparing Inputs for Cash Flow Forecast, Multinational Compared to National

	Multinational Frequency Mean (%)	National Frequency Mean (%)
Centralized	48.1	51.1
Decentralized	42.0	45.5
Do not forecast		1.1
Both approaches	9.9	2.2
N	80.0	178.0
ANOVA F value	3.07	
Duncan Test	0.53	

In summary, the statistical tests show that there is no difference between MNCs and NCs in the centralization of the functional business activities as was hypothesized by the global rationalization theory. At this juncture the empirical data do not support the presence of a global rationalization theory in the financial management activites of MNCs.

Market-Determined Risk

The CAPM provides a market-determined framework for evaluating and comparing the market risk measures (Betas) of MNCs and NCs. The global rationalization theory suggests that MNCs should have lower risk measures (Betas) than NCs. A beta was calculated for each company and a one-way ANOVA was used to compare the risk measures of the MNCs to the NCs. The results of tests are reported in Table 5.6. To insure that the difference in sample size did not bias the ANOVA results the NCs were subdivided randomly into four groups of 45 and the betas of each group were tested against the MNCs. The results of each of the four groups were nearly identical to the test results reported in Table 5.6. The sample size bias was found to be nonexistent.

Table 5.6. Market Risk Measures of MNCs and NCs

	MNCs	NCs
Mean	1.241	1.348
S.D.	0.456	0.433
Range	0.433–2.729	0.267–2.664
N	80	180
ANOVA F value	3.271	
Significance of F	0.072	

The average risk measure of the 80 MNCs was 1.24, ±0.45, and it was 1.35, ±0.43, for the 180 MNCs. The F value of the ANOVA test was 3.271, which is not significant at the .05 level. A plotting of the beta distributions revealed right skewness for both groups. The betas were unusually high; therefore the algorithm for retrieving the data and performing the regression was carefully checked for accuracy. The conclusion is that rates of return in the years 1975 through 1979 were extremely volatile and the sample has a few extreme betas in excess of 2.0. The result was an average risk measure for the two groups that was substantially above average.

For the period 1975–1979 the stock market appraised the riskiness of the MNCs and the NCs as being relatively similar. Nevertheless, the test of the differences between risk measures did not support the global rationalization theory. Rather the test provided further evidence to support earlier findings that there was no differences between MNCs and NCs.

CONCLUSIONS AND POLICY IMPLICATIONS

A basic notion underlying this study was that global rationalization provided MNCs with a preferred bargaining position in trade credit management and in financial markets. It was assumed that centralized coordination and control of international resources provided a more efficient managerial system. This preferred position reduced the uncertainties facing MNC management in the acquisition of raw materials and in the expansion of global markets. To determine if the presence of global rationalization affected financial management practices of MNCs, it was hypothesized that when comparing MNCs to NCs, the MNCs would have a portfolio of customers with lower risk ratings, a superior bargaining position with their suppliers, a higher predictability of cash inflows and outflows, a greater centralization of financial operating decisions and forecasting activities, and a lower risk measure in the stock market. In testing each of the hypothesized relationships, the analysis found that there was no difference between MNCs and NCs. Thus, the advantages of global rationalization are not perceived to exist by MNC financial managers or in the financial markets. What are the policy implications of this finding? The following questions evolved from the analysis.

Is it reasonable to expect MNCs to be more efficient than NCs because of global rationalization? If the answer is yes, MNCs need to focus on improving the productivity of their marketing, production, and purchasing activites. Should the government introduce legislation related to investment, financing, and tax incentives that will motivate MNC management to improve their financial productivity?

If there is no difference in the risk level of customers of MNCs and NCs are NCs providing the necessary credit to higher-risk companies in the national marketplace? Should NCs be taking greater risks in credit extension? If so, why will NCs change the risk–return tradeoff of their current receivables portfolio? Should the government be designing policies to improve the risk-taking capacity of NCs in credit managment?

Alternatively, is it possible MNCs are taking greater risks in their trade credit decisionmaking than is necessary? If the MNCs were to reduce the risk level of their customers will the financing needs of the higher-risk customer be met by NCs or will their financing need shift directly to the banking community?

If global rationalization does not or should not exist in the financial management operations of MNCs are there compelling reasons why MNCs cannot meet expanded trade credit or production needs of third world countries? If MNCs are in a unique position to expand trade credit to less developed countries should this rate of expansion to higher-risk customers be increasing?

The answers to these policy questions are complex and will not be resolved easily or quickly. The discussion of the key issues should lead to improved decisions by MNCs, NCs, and government policy leaders.

REFERENCES

1. Gordon J. Alexander and James M. Gahlon. "An Approach to Determining The Firm's Optimal Cash Discount Policy." *Journal of the Midwest Finance Association* 9 (1980):40–46.
2. Maurice Allias and Vilfredo Pareto. "I. Contributions to Economics." In *International Encyclopedia of the Social Sciences*, edited by David L. Sills, Vol. 11, pp. 399–411. New York: Macmillan and Free Press, 1968.
3. Joseph C. Atkins and Yong H. Kim. "Comment and Correction Opportunity Cost in the Evaluation of Investment in Accounts Receivable." *Financial Management* 6 (Winter 1977):71–76.
4. William Beranek. *Analysis for Financial Decisions.* Homewood, Ill.: Richard D. Irwin, 1963.
5. Harold Bierman; K. Chopra; and L. Joseph Thomas. "Ruin Considerations: Optimal Working Capital and Capital Structure." *Journal of Financial and Quantitative Analysis* 10 (March 1975):119–128.
6. Fisher Black. "A Capital Market Equilibrium with Restricted Borrowing." *Journal of Business* 45 (July 1972):444–455.

7. Marcus Bogue, and Richard Roll. "Capital Budgeting for Risky Projects with 'Imperfect' Markets for Physical Capital." *Journal of Finance* 29 (May 1974):601-613.

8. Michael J. Brennan. "Capital Market Equilibrium with Restricted Borrowing and Lending Rates." *Journal of Financial and Quantitative Analysis* 6 (December 1971):1197-1206.

9. Richard A. Cohn, and John J. Pringle. "Steps Toward an Integration of Corporate Financial Theory." In *Readings On The Management of Working Capital*, 2nd ed., edited by Keith V. Smith, pp. 35-41. St. Paul: West Publishing Co., 1980.

10. Thomas E. Copeland, and Nabil T. Khoury. "Analysis of Credit Extension in a World With Uncertainty." In *Readings on the Management of Working Capital*, 2nd ed., edited by Keith V. Smith, pp. 323-330. St. Paul: West Publishing Co., 1980.

11. Thomas E. Copeland and J. Fred Weston, *Financial Theory and Corporate Policy*. Reading, Mass.: Addison-Wesley, 1979.

12. Richard M. Cyert; H. J. Davidson; and G. L. Thompson. "Estimation of the Allowance for Doubtful Accounts by Markov Chains." *Management Science* 8 (April 1962): 287-308.

13. Edward A. Dyl. "Another Look at the Evaluation of Investment in Accounts Receivable." *Financial Management* 6 (Winter 1977):67-70.

14. Eugene E. Fama. "Risk, Return and Equilibrium." *Journal of Political Economy* 79 (January-February 1971):30-55.

15. Seymour Friedland. *The Economics of Corporate Finance*. Englewood Cliffs, N.J.: Prentice-Hall, 1966.

16. James A. Gentry; Dileep R. Mehta; S. K. Bhattachanyya; Robert Cobbaut; and Jean Louis Scaringella. "An International Study of Management Perception of the Working Capital Process." *Journal of International Business Studies* 10 (Spring-Summer, 1979):28-38.

17. James A. Gentry. "Integrating Working Capital and Capital Investment Processes." In *Readings on the Management of Working Capital*, 2nd ed., edited by Keith V. Smith, pp. 585-608. St. Paul: West Publishing Co., 1980.

18. Charles W. Haley and Robert C. Higgins. "Inventory Control Theory and Trade Credit Financing." *Management Science* 20 (December 1973):464-471.

19. Robert S. Hamada. "Portfolio Analysis, Market Equilibrium and Corporate Finance." *Journal of Finance* 24 (March 1969):13-31.

20. Ned C. Hill and Kenneth D. Riener. "Determining the Cash Discount in the Firm's Credit Policy." *Financial Management* 8 (Spring 1979):69-73.

21. Geoffrey Keppel. *Design and Analysis: A Researcher's Handbook*. Englewood Cliffs, N.J.: Prentice-Hall, 1973.

22. Yong H. Kim and Joseph C. Atkins. "Evaluating Investments in Accounts Receivable: A Maximizing Framework." *Journal of Finance* 33 (May 1978): 403-412.

23. Philip Land. "Impact of Trade and Debt on the Developing Countries." In *Growth With Equity*, pp. 175-208. New York: Paulist Press, 1979.

24. Wilbur E. Lewellen; John J. McConnell; and Jonathan A. Scott. "Some Theorems on Trade Credit Policies." Working Paper No. 699, Krannert Graduate School of Management, Purdue University, May 1979.

25. Jan Mossin. "Security Pricing and Investment Criteria in Competitive Markets." *American Economic Review* 59 (September 1979): 749-756.
26. Anant R. Negandhi, ed. *Functioning of the Multinational Corporation*. Elmsford, N.Y.: Pergamon Press, 1980.
27. Anant Negandhi and B. R. Baliga. *Quest for Survival and Growth*. New York: Praeger, 1979.
28. John S. Oh. "Opportunity Lost in the Evaluation of Investments in Accounts Receivable." *Financial Management* 5 (Summer 1976):32-36.
29. Michael E. Porter. "How Competitive Forces Shape Strategy." *Harvard Business Review* 57 (March-April 1979):137-145.
30. C. K. Prahalad and Yves Doz. "Strategies, Policy-Making and Organization Adaptability of Multinational Corporations." In *Functioning of the Multinational Corporation*, edited by Anant R. Negandhi, pp. 77-116. Elmsford, N.Y.: Pergamon Press, 1980.
31. Alexander Robichek; Daniel Teichroew; and James M. Jones. "Optimal Short Term Financing Decision." *Management Science* 12 (September 1965): 1-36.
32. Keith V. Smith and Shirley Blake Sell. "Working Capital Management in Practice." In *Readings On The Management of Working Capital*, 2nd ed., edited by Keith V. Smith, pp. 51-86. St. Paul: West Publishing Co., 1980.
33. Joseph Steindl. *Random Processes and the Growth of Firms: A Study of the Pareto Law*. London: Griffin; New York: Hafner, 1965.
34. Bernell K. Stone. "The Payments Pattern Approach to the Forecasting and Control of Accounts Receivable." *Financial Management* 5 (Autumn 1976): 65-82.
35. James C. Van Horne. "An Application of the Capital Asset Pricing Model to Divisional Required Returns." *Financial Management* 9 (Spring 1980): 14-19.
36. ———. *Financial Management and Policy*, 5th ed. Englewood Cliffs, N.J.: Prentice-Hall, 1980.
37. Oldrich A. Vasiek. "Capital Asset Pricing Model with No Riskless Borrowing." Unpublished memorandum, Wells Fargo Bank, San Francisco, March 1971.
38. Raymond Vernon. *Storm Over the Multinationals*. Cambridge, Mass.: Harvard University Press, 1977.
39. Tirlochan S. Walia. "Explicit and Implicit Cost of Changes in the Level of Accounts Receivable." *Financial Management* 6 (Winter 1977):75-78.
40. J. Fred Weston. "Investment Decisions Using the Capital Asset Pricing Model." *Financial Management* 2 (Spring 1973):25-33.
41. J. Fred Weston and Eugene F. Brigham. *Managerial Finance*, 6th ed. Hinsdale, Ill.: Dryden Press, 1978.
42. J. Fred Weston and Pham D. Tuan. "Comment on Analysis of Credit Policy Changes." *Financial Management* 9 (Winter 1980):59-63.
43. "Directory of the 1000 Largest Industrial Corporations." *Fortune*, May 8 and June 19, 1978.

Chapter 6

International Financial Center Preeminence In MNC and Nation-State Interaction

*Howard Curtis Reed**

The study of international financial centers in the years following World War II has declined markedly. Commenting on the decline, Kindleberger has noted that it is a curious fact that the formation of financial centers is no longer studied in economics.[1] He suggests that the reason may be because the study falls between two reasonably distinct areas: urban and regional economics, which concerns itself, primarily, with cities and the location of commerce, industry, and housing; and money and capital market development, which emphasizes building financial infrastructure and its relationship to economic growth and development. This view is echoed by Cheng who observed that there appears to be no obvious way to apply the factor endowment approach (developed by Heckscher-Olin) or the distance-from-center approach (developed by von Thünen) used in regional and urban economics to explain the location of regional financial centers.[2] Studies that have analyzed the roles of money and capital markets in economic development leave largely unexplored the question of the location of financial centers and the functional links between them. There is also no mention of the intermediating

A large part of this research was supported by a grant from the Institute for Constructive Capitalism at The University of Texas at Austin.

*University of Texas at Austin.

function (and role) of international financial centers between industrial (multinational corporations) and political (nation-states) entities.

The purpose of this research is to test the hypothesis that international financial centers are preeminent in the daily operations and long-term strategic objectives of multinational corporations (MNCs) and nation-states. Testing the hypothesis requires identification and examination of international financial center organizational structure and rank (over time); and (2) determinants, that is, the factors that are required to build infrastructure and preeminence. This research will use multivariate statistical techniques (hierarchical cluster analysis and stepwise multiple discriminant analysis) to test the hypothesis. The multivariate techniques are employed with the intent of improving the quality and usefulness of the analysis and its results. The literature on international financial centers is void of quantitative measures of the infrastructure relationships—within centers and between centers.

The study of international financial centers, and their preeminence, is important for several reasons. It provides insight into what is required to build financial infrastructure, such as institutions and markets. It provides insight into, if not complete answers about, the organization, distribution, and influence of these centers. It encourages a better understanding of the relationship between centers by evaluating their impact on such factors as communications, inflation, savings, capital flow, and investment. Such study is helpful to governments in formulating and implementing policies designed to affect the activities and/or status of a particular center (or centers). In addition, if the process is allowed to proceed without substantial government interference, the direction and magnitude of a center's development will be predictable.

To accomplish the objectives of this research, nine banking and finance variables (Table 6.1) are used to measure—determine the organizational structure and rank—of 76 centers.[3] Hierarchical cluster analysis is used to determine structure by classifying centers into groups. Stepwise multiple discriminant analysis verifies the cluster analysis grouping (organizational structure), determines what factors (variables) caused the particular groupings, and ranks the centers. After the centers have been measured, the impact of capital flows, capital formation, communications, industrial position (as measured by the assets of large industrial corporations), inflation, investments, and trade on international financial structure and rank are examined. The results of the analysis provide a framework in which the relationship of international financial centers to multinational corporation and nation-state activity is discussed in some detail.

Table 6.1. Variable Measures

Local Bank Headquarter: Large internationally active commercial banks headquartered in the center.

Local Bank Direct Links: Foreign international financial centers with direct links to the international financial center through the large internationally active local banks headquartered in the center.

Private Bank: Private (merchant or investment) banks with an office in the center.

Foreign Bank Office: Large internationally active foreign commercial banks with an office in the center.

Foreign Bank Direct Links: Foreign international financial centers with direct links to the international financial center through the large internationally active foreign banks with an office in the center.

Foreign Financial Assets: The total amount of foreign financial assets of the international financial center (allocated on the basis of the total assets of the center's local bank headquarters).

Foreign Financial Liabilities: The total amount of foreign financial liabilities held in the international financial center (allocated on the basis of the total liabilities of the center's local bank headquarters).

Local Bank Branch/Representative Direct Links: Foreign international financial centers with direct links (i.e., branches and representative offices) to the center through local banks (headquartered there).

Foreign Bank Representative Office: Large internationally active foreign commerical banks with branches or representative offices in the center.

Sources: Rand-McNally International Bankers Directory, Chicago; *The Bankers Almanac and Year Book*, London; *Moody's Bank and Financial Manual*, New York; and *International Financial Statistics*, IMF, Washington, D.C.

INTERNATIONAL FINANCIAL CENTERS

Financial centers are thought of as hierarchically structured central places whose purpose it is to coordinate and clear financial transactions. The efficiencies of a centralized location are thought to exist in connection with the economies of scales of such functions as:

1. Quick and easy access to the knowledge and services of complementing and competing institutions.
2. Clearing and exchange process for checks, drafts, and stock certificates.
3. Availability of larger and cheaper amounts of capital for borrowers.
4. Greater liquidity for lenders.

The attributes of financial centers are lucidly summarized by Kindleberger.[4]

> Financial centers are needed not only to balance through time the savings and investment of individual entrepreneurs and to transfer financial capital from savers to investors but also to effect payments and to transfer savings between places. Banking and financial centers perform a medium of exchange function and an interspatial store-of-value function. Single payments between separate points in a country are made most efficiently through a center, and both seasonal and long-run surpluses and deficits of financial savings are best matched in a center. Furthermore, the specialized functions of international payments and foreign landing or borrowing are typically best performed at one central place that is also [in most instances] the specialized center for domestic interregional payments. . . .

Present theory suggests that the factors that give impetus to the development of "national" financial centers also give rise to their eventually becoming international centers. The speed of international development and the level of international activity are apparently dependent on how readily national financial centers broaden and fine tune their financial infrastructure. Within this context, it follows that international financial centers evolve from and are mere extensions of national financial centers. However, traditional financial center theory leaves largely unexplored perhaps their most important attributes—the gathering, analyzing, and disseminating of information, and the management of the world's global capital portfolio. It is in these two areas that international financial centers have their greatest impact.

Eminence Theories

Kindleberger argues that the same forces that produce a single dominant financial center within a country ultimately produce a single worldwide center. This thesis has led him to conclude that London was preeminent during most of the nineteenth century. In the twentieth century, preeminence shifted to New York but is now shifting away from New York back to the Eurodollar market. In his view the market is spread all over the world, but its heart beats in the American and British banks in London.[5]

Other scholars generally agree with the thesis that a hierarchy among international financial centers does exist. Kindleberger's single preeminent center theory is challenged, indirectly at least, by those who place both London and New York at the peak of the international financial hierarchy.[6] The single center thesis looks primarily to economies of scale for its justification. The desire to minimize time differences and costs (e.g., capital, communications, transport) to increase liquidity through broader markets and to do away with certain subjective evaluations such as unfamiliarity and other cultural factors are also used to substantiate this argument.

Fernand Braudel has also, from time to time, discussed centering and decentering in a way that suggests that one and only one financial center dominates.[7]

A world economy has a pole or a center, represented by one dominant city, in the past a city-state, today a capital city—that is an economic capital, New York rather than Washington, D.C. In addition, two centers can exist simultaneously and for a prolonged period within a single world economy, as did Rome and Alexandria under Caesar Augustus, Anthony, Cleopatra; Venice and Genoa before the war of Chiogga (1378-81); or London and Amsterdam during the 18th century, before the definitive exclusion of Holland. For one of these two centers is always eliminated in the end. Thus, in 1929 after some hesitation, the center of the world unquestionably shifted from London to New York.

Mundell has at times linked financial preeminence with political domination. In his view the monetary order created at Bretton Woods (1944-1946) was an open acceptance of the stunning twentieth-century emergence of the United States as a supereconomy. As a result of the Bretton Woods Agreement the U.S. dollar became the world's principal currency, replacing the pound sterling and even gold. This scholar attributes the economic rise of the United States and the strategic role of the dollar to the rise of the United States as a hegemonic power.[8]

Formation Theories

Just as scholars differ as to the hierarchical structure of international financial centers, they also emphasize various formative factors to differing degrees. Kindleberger, and to a lesser extent Haegele and others, spell out the prerequisites for becoming an international financial center with care and detail.

Kindleberger places considerable importance on the number, size, and international experience and expertise of the center's banks.[9] In his view, banks start out to serve the needs of sovereigns and nobles; develop connections with the commercial sector; then become less personally involved in governmental finance; then develop ties to transport, including shipping, canals, turnpikes, and railroads; then build connections with industry; and finally develop intermediation services for insurance, mortgages, consumer financce, factoring, pension funds, and the like. The borrowing and lending pattern starts locally, extends to the national level (perhaps including intermediate regional stops), and finally becomes international. As markets become more hierarchical, their instruments and functions become more specialized. Sociopolitical forces of significant magnitude, such as chronic inflation, depression, or war, distort or intensify the pattern. Various more localized factors are essential to this evolutionary process. First, savings are necessary so that dealers can make a market, lend when the rest of the market is borrowing, and sell out of inventory when the rest of the market is buying. Financial centers are needed not only to balance the savings and investments of individual entrepreneurs through time and to transfer financial capital from savers to investors, but also to effect payments and to transfer savings between places. Second, face-to-face contact between bankers, lawyers, security dealers, borrowers, and lenders is needed to minimize the uncertainty that generally accompanies transactions that take place by telephone, telex, and the mail. Finally, a well-developed transport system that provides relatively easy access to the center's services is important.

Haegele emphasizes the historical character of the location. First, the center must have played a major historical role in international commerce in order to have established international contacts and linkages. Second, the center's nation must have a history of nonconfiscatory policy, favorable regulation, and political stability. All are important factors in establishing the level of confidence needed to become a depository of funds.[10]

Vernon believes that high levels of financial activity are reached only after a location has become an active commercial center. The port of New York attracted the wholesalers, who in turn attracted the financial institution, who then attracted the principal offices of national corporations.[11]

Importance of Financial Markets

The importance of broad and efficient financial markets to an international financial center is underscored by Ragazzi.[12] In studying the movements of portfolio and direct investment capital between the United States and Western Europe during the 1960s, Ragazzi discovered that the large flow of U.S. direct investment in Western Europe was matched by sizable purchases of U.S. long-term portfolio assets by private European residents. He attributed the large outflow of portfolio capital to two characteristics of the European securities markets (the United Kingdom excepted). First, the European portfolio investor does not receive continually updated information. Public auditing of corporations is not so well developed in Europe as it is in the United States. This lack of information theoretically increases the risk of possible deviation from the expected rate of return for the portfolio investor. On the other hand, because the direct investor is in control of the company and therefore has immediate and direct access to all information, the risk is limited to the "industrial" risk inherent in the operations of the company. A second factor is the narrowness of the European securities market, again with the exception of the United Kingdom. This contracted state causes the fluctuations in prices of securities to be much larger than justified. Ragazzi concluded:[13]

> ... even if the determinant of portfolio and direct investments are different, flows of the two forms of capital are likely to be partly substitutes. Thus, an outflow of portfolio capital, for instance, will discourage direct investments. This could happen to the extent that; (a) it reduces the supply of risk capital to local firms and increases that supply to foreign firms; (b) it pushes up the market value of securities of foreign firms, increasing the cost of take-overs of foreign firms by domestic firms; and (c) it pushes up the exchange rate of the foreign country, increasing the cost of direct investment in that country.

Kindleberger believes that not enough attention is given to the importance of financial markets. He notes that perhaps too little is made of the fact that the broader the financial market, the greater the liquidity of security issues, with the result that lenders and borrowers from other regions will transfer to that market their gross demands and supplies, not only their excess demand or supply. The borrower pays a lower rate of interest and/or is able to issue a larger loan. The lender acquires a qualitatively different investment because it is traded on a broader secondary market, which is why the lender is willing and often eager to accept a lower interest rate.

The primary purpose of this brief literature review was to point out the academically established areas of agreement and disagreement with regard to the theories explaining the factors that influence the growth and development of international financial centers, as well as to point out the many factors that are essential to the eminence, formation, and markets of international financial centers. All three of these areas of discussion can be significantly clarified, in my opinion, by using hierarchical cluster analysis and stepwise multiple discriminant analysis to measure the relative impact of these many factors. In order to meet the objectives of their study, the analysis must measure the numerous variables over a significant time span. Therefore, the analysis covers the 25-year period, 1955–1980, and the centers are measured in 5-year intervals.

ORGANIZATIONAL STRUCTURE, RANK, AND DETERMINANTS

There are two time periods after 1955 in which the hierarchical structure and rank of international financial centers changed significantly, 1965 and 1975. The hierarchical organizational structure and rank score for the two time periods, and for 1955 and 1980, are shown in Tables 6.2 and 6.3, respectively.

Table 6.2. Organizational Structure of International Financial Centers[a]

1955 (4 Groups)
Group 1 New York
    2 London, Paris
    3 Hong Kong, San Francisco, Osaka, Tokyo, Montreal, Amsterdam, Bombay, Calcutta, Singapore, Frankfurt
    4 62 centers

1965 (3 Groups)
Group 1 London, New York
    2 Paris, Tokyo, San Francisco, Hong Kong, Frankfurt, Hamburg, Rome
    3 67 centers

1975 (5 Groups)
Group 1 London
    2 New York, Tokyo, Paris, Frankfurt
    3 13 centers
    4 14 centers
    5 32 centers[b]

1980 (5 Groups)
Group 1 London
    2 New York, Tokyo
    3 Paris, Frankfurt, Zurich, Amsterdam, San Francisco, Chicago, Hamburg, Hong Kong
    4 30 centers
    5 39 centers[b]

---

[a]Centers are listed according to their rank order. The group structure (i.e., 3 groups or 4 groups) chosen for each time period is the group structure that precedes the largest statistical error increase as the number of groups are reduced to the next hierarchical cluster level (e.g., from 4 groups to 3 groups, or from 3 groups to 2 groups).

[b]Group 5 contains "host international finance centers." They are distinguished from financial centers by the cluster analysis mainly on the basis of local bank headquarter activity, and are generally not headquarters for large internationally active banks.

Table 6.3. Rankings of International Financial Centers[a]

Centers	Rank Score	Centers	Rank Score
1955 (1946)[b]		*1965 (1962)[c]*	
New York	100	London	100
London	99	New York	96
Paris	86	Paris	79
Hong Kong	78	Tokyo	77
San Francisco	78	San Francisco	77
Osaka	76	Hong Kong	74
Tokyo	75	Frankfurt	73
Montreal	74	Hamburg	71
Amsterdam	73	Rome	69
Bombay	73		
Singapore	71		
Frankfurt	70		
1975 (1974)[d]		*1980*	
London	100	London	100
New York	95	New York	85
Tokyo	90	Paris	83
Paris	90	Tokyo	78
Frankfurt	87	Frankfurt	78
		Zurich	76
		Amsterdam	75
		San Francisco	74
		Chicago	72
		Hamburg	71
		Hong Kong	71

[a]The rank score is calculated from the discriminant function. The data (independent variables) are standardized, and the minus signs of the standardized discriminant coefficients are ignored. The minus signs are ignored because it is presumed that a high score on all independent variables is a positive factor in being highly ranked.

[b]1946 is the year that New York becomes "the" preeminent international financial center. A center is considered preeminent if it is a member of the apex of the hierarchy.

[c]1962 is the year that London becomes the world's top-ranked international financial center.

[d]1974 is the year that London becomes "the" preeminent international financial center.

In 1955, the organizational structure was determined by foreign financial assets[14] and local bank direct links. The importance of foreign financial assets reflect the fact that most of the world was recovering from the devastation of World War II. The United States, the world's economic and political hegemon, was the only country capable of supplying recovery and development capital to the rest of the world. The rankings were not significantly influenced by any one particular variable. There were five variables that had percentage contributions to the discriminant function of at least 14 percent. The largest contributor was local bank direct links with 24 percent.

By 1965, London not only had become a member of the apex of the hierarchy but it was also the world's top-ranked center. The organizational structure was determined by local bank branch/ representative direct links and foreign financial liabilities. The importance of local bank direct links is a natural evolution of the foreign lending of institutions to enlarge their overseas office network to supervise and better manage their foreign loan portfolios. While direct links are an important determinant to the overall structure, it had no impact on London's rejoining New York at the pinnacle. Even though London had remained a distant second to New York in foreign lending after World War II, it had maintained a slight edge in direct links mainly as a result of existing and former colonial ties (i.e., Bombay, Calcutta, Hong Kong, Kuala Lumpur, Melbourne, Rangoon, Singapore, and Sydney). London's ascendancy was due to its narrowing the gap to New York, in foreign lending, but mostly it was due to its surpassing New York in the amount of foreign financial liabilities kept there. In 1955, London's foreign financial liabilities amounted to $2 billion; in 1960, it was $6 billion; and in 1962, it was $19 billion. New York's total for the three periods was $6, $9, and $11 billion, respectively. Four variables had a significant impact on ranking the centers in 1965: local bank direct links, 29 percent; foreign financial liabilities, 24 percent; foreign financial assets, 15 percent; and local bank branch representative direct links, 14 percent.

By 1975, London was the only international financial center at the apex of the hierarchy. The organizational structure is determined by (1) foreign financial liabilities; (2) local bank direct links; and (3) foreign bank direct links. Foreign financial liabilities clearly separates all groups except group 3 from group 5 (see Table 6.2). When local bank direct links enter the analysis at step two, statistically significant separation is only enhanced among the groups clearly separated. Groups 3 and 5 are statistically separated when foreign bank direct links enter the analysis at step three (see Table 6.2). Five variables had a significant impact on ranking the centers—local bank direct links (21 percent), foreign bank direct links (20 percent) foreign bank offices (15 percent), foreign financial liabilities (14 percent), and foreign bank representative offices (13 percent).

In 1980, London's position at the paces of the international financial center hierarchy had improved significantly. The rank score of its nearest challenger, New York, dropped from 95 in 1975 to 85 in 1980. And the number of centers in group 2 had been reduced by 50 percent—only New York and Tokyo remained (Table 6.3). The organizational structure was determined by (1) local bank headquarters except for groups 1 and 2. When foreign financial liabilities enter the analysis in step two, statistically significant separation is obtained between group 1 (London) and group 2 (New York and Tokyo). Therefore London's preeminence in international finance is clearly the result of its ability to attract large amounts of foreign financial liabilities.[15] The rank is determined by foreign financial liabilities (29 percent contribution), foreign financial assets (26 percent contribution), and local bank headquarters (16 percent contribution). The large number of hierarchical tiers reflects, perhaps, the substantial disruptions in financial, economic, and political order during the 1970s.[16]

The widely held notion that New York emerged from World War II as the unchallenged preeminent center for international finance—and that it held that position unquestionably until 1964-1965, after the United States initiated a series of capital controls—is not fully supported by the analysis. New York did emerge from World War II as the preeminent international financial center 18 months before the first capital control measure was initiated.[17]

The data (Table 6.4) clearly show that large increases did occur in London's foreign financial assets (FFA) after U.S. capital control measures went into effect, but the data also show that equally large increases in London's FFA had taken place before 1962. Furthermore, by 1969 (year-end), London's foreign financial liabilities (FFL) were 73 percent larger than New York's total FFL; in 1955, London's FFL had been 67 percent smaller than New York's. In 1962, the year London became the top international financial center, its FFA was substantially smaller (91 percent) than New York's. And, London's FFL, which had become larger than New York's in 1962, was losing percentage points: the differential between London's FFL and New York's had actually decreased from 73 percent to 67 percent. In other words, the data clearly indicate that London would have regained the top position among international financial centers irrespective of the U.S. capital control measures.

HOME NATION INFLUENCE ON STRUCTURE AND RANK

In addition to the specific measures, it is useful to determine if there are home nation variables that also influence the organizational structure in international financial centers. A stepwise multiple discriminant analysis was used to determine if 13 home nation measures

Table 6.4. Foreign Financial Assets (FFA) and Foreign Financial
Liabilities (FFL) (billions of U.S. dollars)

	FFA	FFL
1955		
London	3	2
New York	22	6
1960		
London	5	6
New York	21	9
1961		
London	5	11
New York	23	11
1962		
London	8	19
New York	22	11
1963		
London	8	20
New York	22	13
1964		
London	9	23
New York	23	15
1965		
London	11	25
New York	21	15
1966		
London	13	27
New York	23	20
1969		
London	34	48
New York	25	35

(Table 6.5) had a significant impact on international financial center organizational structure.

The home nations were assigned to groups on the basis of the group location of their highest-ranked international financial center and measured for the test years of 1955, 1965, 1975, and 1980. The organization structure of the home nations duplicated the international financial center structure in 1955 and 1965. In 1970 and 1980 the United Kingdom's status did not complement London's preeminence. When an analysis of centers is performed using only banking variables (excluding foreign financial assets and foreign financial liabilities), the organizational structure of centers and home nations is exactly the same in all four test periods.[18] Home nation organizational structure was determined (in all four test periods) by interna-

Table 6.5. Home Nation Variable Measures

Variable
1. Industrial corporations among the world's 200 largest that are headquartered in the international financial center's home nation.
2 The total assets of the industrial corporations among the world's 200 largest that are headquartered in the international financial center's home nation.
3. Five-year total of short-term capital flows (net) of the international financial center's home nation.
4. Five-year total of long-term capital flows (net) of the international financial center's home nation.
5. Five-year total of total capital flows (net) of the international financial center's home nation.
6. Cumulative total of foreign direct investments (net) of the international financial center's home nation.
7. International reserves of the international financial center's home nation.
8. Five-year average of money supply as a percent of the gross national product of the international financial center's home nation.
9. Change in five-year average of money supply as a percent of the gross national product of the international financial center's home nation.
10. Merchandise exports of the international financial center's home nation.
11. Merchandise imports of the international financial center's home nation.
12. The number of phones per 100 in the international financial center's home nation.
13. The number of international telegrams (sent and received) in international financial center's home nation.

tional telegram activity, cumulative foreign direct investments, and assets of industrial corporations.

There are at least two important findings in the results of the home nation analysis. First, the fact that London emerged, after 1974, as the world's only preeminent international financial center without the United Kingdom also becoming preeminent clearly indicates that there are other (less quantitative) variables that are important to organizational structure and rank. Second, the international banking machinery of centers is less volatile and more representative of the *country's* long-term international power and influence. The next section discusses the significance of these two findings.

ADDITIONAL INFLUENCE ON
STRUCTURE AND RANK

London's experience since 1955 strongly suggests that such leadership variables as tradition, familarity, and confidence are important determinants of international financial center organizational structure and rank. New York's failure to maintain international financial preeminence after 1960 was not the result of U.S. capital control measures. As we have seen, London's upward move to become top-ranked (and share preeminence) in 1962 would have occurred irrespective of U.S. controls. The controls may have restrained New York's competitive vigor between 1962 and 1974 by enhancing the growth and significance of the Eurodollar market. But the argument can be made that the growth and importance of the Eurodollar market would have occurred (along its present lines) because of London's superior international banking machinery and its demonstrated ability to overtake New York by 1962.

Perhaps the answer can be found in the amorphous realm of leadership. When a country is as thoroughly dominant in as many areas as the United States was at the end of World War II (i.g., military might, industrial capacity, the world's preeminent currency), it would seem reasonable to expect its dominance to last more than a decade or two. However, the following events occurred shortly before New York's loss of financial preeminence and further eroded U.S. dominance: the Bretton Woods system of fixed exchange rates broke down, leading to a continually weakening U.S. dollar; and U.S. political hegemony deteriorated markedly as a result of activities in Southeast Asia, the Middle East, and Cyprus. These events led to a general decline in international order—political, economic, and financial. Although U.S. aspirations at the end of World War II—to lead the world to economic prosperity, political freedom, and peace—were surely noble and just, they were not successful. Despite having emerged from World War II as the indisputable leader of the noncommunist world with enormous advantages, the United States failed to secure these endowments and therefore drifted ever further away from its once "natural" leadership role.

The residual leadership emanating from the memory of Great Britain's colonial era appears to be the source of London's international banking and international financial legacies. Since 1900 (when measured in five-year intervals), Bombay, Calcutta, Hong Kong, Shanghai, Singapore, and Tientsin frequently appear on the list of the top ten. They were all, at one time, ports of the British Empire (Hong Kong still is). Other centers that were almost always ranked in the top twenty and that once were a part of the British Empire and therefore have their principal links to London are Johannesburg, Kuala Lumpur, Melbourne, Sydney, and Rangoon. No other center comes close to rivaling London in this respect. It seems reasonable, however, to assume that New York could have replaced London at the end of World War II as the principal link for these centers if it had understood the significance. The linkage between these former colonies and London largely explains the rapid recovery and growth of London's foreign financial liabilties, as London was still being used as a reserve center.

London's status as the sole occupant of the apex of the international financial center hierarchy in 1974 was the result of certain OAPEC (Organization of Arab Petroleum Exporting Countries) cash management decisions. When OAPEC quadrupled oil prices during 1973–74, thereby dramatically increasing their cash inflow, the members of OAPEC had to decide how and where to employ their cash reserves. They initially chose to employ these reserves primarily in Eurodollar day money accounts in London. OAPEC used the day money vehicle because they feared that Eurobanks would somehow confiscate their reserves. For a number of months after the oil price increases, the OAPEC countries moved their funds daily from one bank to another as a means of minimizing their perceived risks. Because the oil price increase was, at first, a political action taken to punish the United States for supporting Israel, OAPEC members never seriously considered placing their cash reserves in New York. Incidentally, day rates in New York during the months immediately following the 1973 oil price increase were considerably higher than similar rates in the Eurodollar market (see Table 6.6).

The addition of these nonquantifiable variables substantially enhances the understanding of the evolution and development of international financial center eminence.

INTERNATIONAL FINANCIAL CENTER SIGNIFICANCE

The analysis clearly identified the financial center variables most responsible for organizational structure and rank, and the home nation variables most responsible for structure. The three most important financial center variables are local bank direct links, foreign financial liabilities, and local bank headquarters. In addition, the three most important home nation variables are international telex activity, cumulative foreign direct investments, and assets of industrial corporations. What clearly emerges from the analysis is that the previous studies and theoretical explanations of international financial center development and eminence have left the role of these centers in two important areas largely unexplored: first, the gathering, analyzing, and disseminating of information; and second, the management of the world's global capital portfolio.

Table 6.6. Comparable Day-to-Day Deposit Rates

| | 1973 | | 1974 | | | | | |
	Nov.	Dec.	Jan./Feb.	Mar./Apr.	May/Jun.	Jul./Aug.	Sept./Oct.	Nov.	Dec.
New York	10.03	9.95	9.47	9.93	11.62	12.46	10.70	9.45	8.35
Eurodollar	9.45	9.50	8.69	9.52	11.36	11.80	10.33	9.26	8.35
Δ	0.58	0.45	0.78	0.41	0.26	0.66	0.37	0.19	0.00

Information Centers

The importance of direct links (provided by local and foreign banks) and international telex activity clearly indicates that international financial centers are also *information centers*. The basis for this contention is twofold. First, the greater the number of direct links, the greater the quality of unfiltered information available to the center.[19] It is further presumed that unfiltered information is transmitted at a greater speed and at higher levels of accuracy and quality than filtered information. Therefore, direct links can be viewed as indicators (if not measures) of the speed with which information is transmitted between centers and of the accuracy and quality of that information. Second, the volume of international telex activity is an indicator of a center's international influence as a financial and information center. International telex facilities are used to the exclusion of nearly all other communication systems by bankers and businessmen, and to a lesser extent by news organizations and governments.

The level and quality of information available in international financial centers is important to governments, central bankers, multinational corporations, and international organizations. These entities must be able to assess the status of international financial centers. Given a particular purpose or strategy that necessitates intervening in financial markets, the question comes down to "Where?" Should the interventions be in more than one center? If so, what should the level of intervention be in each center? Governmental and quasi-governmental authorities also need to know where to go on an informal basis to get the most trustworthy information on current financial, economic, industrial, and political affairs.

The importance of informal (unfiltered) information networks and the personal interaction fundamental to such communication is demonstrated by the following anecdote. A few years ago, a high-ranking U.S. Treasury official wanted to start the rumor that the United States had officially decided to raise the price of gold. The official chose to share this inside information with a person who had strong connections in the London financial community in order to have the greatest possible impact on the international financial market. A week after the rumor had been started, the Treasury official indicated in a speech that he knew nothing about the rumor that the United States had no intention of raising the official price of gold. By using the powerful informal information network within the international financial community, the United States gained enough maneuvering time to implement its strategy for supporting the dollar.

Private financial institutions also consider it important to know the relative status of international banking and financial centers. When a financial institution office is located in a center that clearly has more status than the center in which the institution's headquarters are located, evidence suggests that the ranking center has more impact on the institution than the center in which it is headquartered. The reason behind this apparent paradox is that financial institutions assign their "best" people on the basis of perceived center status.[20]

Portfolio Management Centers

The importance of foreign financial liabilities (and foreign financial assets), local bank headquarters, cumulative foreign direct investments, and assets of industrial corporations to international financial center structure and rank appear to confirm the importance of information. These four variables clearly indicate that an international financial center is important for the following factors:

1. Financial sourcing and allocation.
2. Evaluating the policies, strategies, and activities of nations (i.e., the evaluation is reflected immediately in the foreign exchange, spot and forward, market value of currencies, and later on, in the nation's cost of capital).
3. Industrial project evaluation and pricing.
4. Monitoring the activities (and updating their assessments) of financial center clients.
5. Providing money and capital management services.

Without question, the level of efficiency with which a center can perform these functions is dependent on its astuteness in gathering, evaluating, and utilizing information from around the world. A center's astuteness is largely dependent upon the number (and size) of its locally headquartered banks, the acumen of these institutions, the collective connections (to other centers) of these institutions, and the industrial power (and reach) of the nation's corporations. The successful performance by a center of the five international financial center functions is defined here as portfolio management.

The financial sourcing and allocation function of the international financial center requires that the center have a sufficient and well-managed infrastructure to provide liquidity and competitive return on investments. Since there are never enough liquid reserves to cover liabilities, at any given time, the quality (risk vs. return, and maturity schedule) of a center's asset portfolio is paramount to the investor, governments of the investors, and the home nation government. Evaluating the policies, strategies, and activities of nations is necessary for several reasons: first, nations (their firms and citizens) are large, and active, users of the products and services of centers; second, as a result of the highly interdependent nature of the industrial country's markets, a shift in policy, strategy, or predicted activity could substantially alter the portfolio quality of the center, and in turn, of its investors; and third, to properly evaluate and price industrial projects that are targeted for investment in foreign countries, or projects that are dependent upon cash flow emanating from that country, industrial project evaluation is important for the initial pricing of the borrowed capital. Monitoring its progress is necessary so that the current value of the outstanding principal can be assessed. The quality of the money and capital management services offered by the center is a function, largely, of how well the other functions are managed.

IMPLICATIONS OF FINDINGS

The issue conflicts between the multinational corporations (MNCs) and the highly industrialized nation-states has little to do with the traditional areas of conflict that characterize MNC and developing country relationships, that is, foreign ownership, local borrowing, exporting requirements, transfer pricing, profit repatriation, and so forth. The conflicts between the MNCs and the highly industrialized nation-states (hereafter referred to as nation-states) are primarily *macro* problems concerned with *international order*.[21] The macro issues center around two broad categories: inflation and employment. These broad categories embody the more specific issues of balance of payments (international trade and capital flows), economic growth, level of assistance to developing countries, and supplier and consumer satisfaction (i.e., price, quality, delivery, and service).

The source of MNC and nation-state conflict is largely the result of their modus operandi and strategic objectives. The MNC operates in a *global* market, and it is significantly independent of national governments. But the MNC is responsible to each government in that it must develop an organizational structure and operating procedure that permits maximization of its global objectives. The general strategic objective of the MNC is for maintenance of a strong competitive (and eventually a dominant) position in global markets. This objective implies a strong competitive (to dominant) market share position as a purchaser (of raw materials, labor, capital, etc.) and supplier; and a relatively high level of profits. The nation-state, on the other hand, is responsible only to itself. As a result, the nation-state objective is the singleminded pursuit of the *national interest* at the expense of all others. The general strategic objective of the nation-state is for maintenance of a strong competitive (and eventually a dominant) position within the system of nation-states. This implies a strong competitive (to dominant) balance of payments and military position, which usually requires high levels of employment and economic growth (i.e., real output, incomes, and government revenue)—all of which lead to a stable political environment for the nation.

The two objectives differ primarily on the human and social dimensions of the level of employment. Essential to the nation-state's power is an internally stable environment. Perhaps the most important prerequisite is a relatively low level of unemployment and a perception (at least) of improving prosperity. The MNC is also sympathetic to the human and social benefits of high levels of employment. But efficiency, that is, the introduction of labor-saving or -replacing technology usually takes precedence. New industries are eventually developed to absorb the surplus labor. The the time lag is such that the threat of social unrest causes the political system to attempt to redistribute income in a way that compensates the nation's unemployed and underemployed. This attempt at the redistribution of income, more often than not, brings about an imbalance in the economic relationships between labor, industry, and society as a whole, which leads to unusually high rates of inflation and social unrest. The next step is for the nation-state to initiate policy actions that, in effect, are designed to export the nation's unemployment, inflation, and social unrest. Retaliation (from other nation-states) soon follows and the result is a tension-filled, disorderly, world.

Allowing the Product Life Cycle to Run Its Course

Consumption (or the ability to consume) permeates the contemporary nation-state system. Figure 6.1 shows the cyclical relationship between consumption, production, employment, the introduction of labor-saving or -replacing technology, savings, capital formation, and the formation of a new industry. The desire of the nation-state to achieve high levels of employment begins with consumption. Increasing consumption leads to increased output, which increases the level of employment. The production increases and the increasing labor force leads the MNC to look for more efficient ways to increase output to decrease per unit cost and reduce prices to increase market share; and to increase per unit profit (the price reduction to increase market share is less than the cost savings).[22] The required capital investment may come from retained earnings, borrowed capital

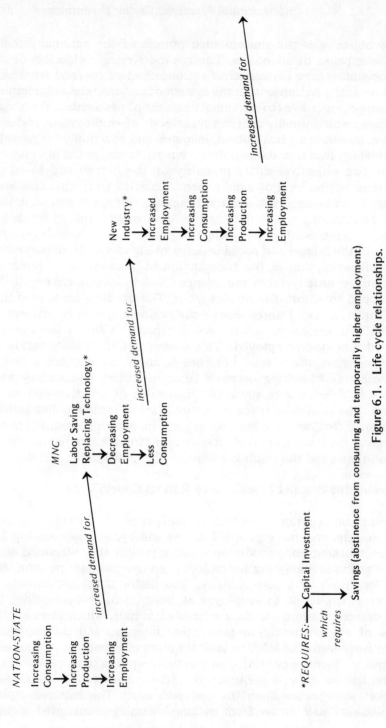

Figure 6.1. Life cycle relationships.

NATION-STATE

Increasing Consumption → Increasing Production → Increasing Employment

increased demand for

MNC

Labor Saving Replacing Technology*

Decreasing Employment → Less Consumption

increased demand for

New Industry* → Increased Employment → Increasing Consumption → Increasing Production → Increasing Employment

increased demand for

REQUIRES: → Capital Investment → Savings (abstinence from consuming and temporarily higher employment)

which requires

(domestic or foreign), or equity capital (domestic or foreign). The introduction of the new labor-saving or -replacing technology leads to increased unemployment, which leads to less consumption. The combination of decreasing employment and less consumption encourages the MNC community to develop new industries, which will increase employment substantially in the formative stages, which leads to increased consumption to increasing production to additional increases in employment.

The conflicting actions and objectives of the MNCs and the nation-states are not purposely antagonistic. The MNCs (i.e., manufacturing and high technology firms) have been shown to follow, what is sometimes referred to as, the "international product life cycle."[23]

> The product life cycle states that new products tend to evolve out of high income countries, mainly the United States, which allocate large expenditures on education of the work force and to research and development activities. These expenditures generate new products, processes, and technologies, which are initially marketed and sold domestically. As the produduct, etc., matures its production techniques are perfected, production costs are lowered and its utilities become appreciated by consumers abroad lending to profitable export operations. As the exports penetrate deeper and deeper into the foreign markets, the more feasible it becomes to establish a local production facility. The advantages associated with local production are that it substantially reduces any cost advantages that local competitors may have had if the product were being exported to the market where tariffs, transportation costs, etc., serve as a barrier to foreign imports. This process will continue until it has moved from the more-advanced to the less-advanced countries. Eventually the point is reached where it is feasible and profitable to export the product back to the country where it was developed.

If the premise is accepted that under the present system, managed by nation-states, there will be cyclical periods of unusually high rates of inflation and unemployment, then the international product life cycle offers a solution. The solution would require that the community of nations agree to allow the industrial and technological life cycle to run its course without substantial interference.

The proposed solution recognizes the inefficiencies and efficiencies of both the MNC and the nation-state. A MNC is a enterprise that operates at the *global market level* within the world economy.[24] The MNC organizational structure permits it to coordinate sourcing and marketing to achieve desired degrees of customization for an individual country, integrated community, or region without sacrificing economies of scale and specialization of its sourcing and marketing activities. The nation-states, on the other hand, do not have a multinational political organization to rival the MNC. Each nation-state is inhibited from pursuing global strategies and policies. The myopic view of the nation-state system is primarily the result of its organizational structure, which permits domestic political issues to dominate foreign policy initiatives: the antithesis of the MNC.

The specific proposal has two dimensions. First, the nation-states should use the international product life cycle as the basis for developing their political economy strategies. By monitoring the cycle and identifying the stage in which a particular industry is in (domestically and globally), the industry's remaining useful life within a particular country can be estimated. A carefully designed plan for phasing out the industry (within the country) can be implemented.[25] The severity of market disruptions, human suffering, social cost, and strained relationships among nations should be substantially less pronounced.[26] Second, the proposal is information dependent. The nation-states must have access to a common pool of information so that decisions can be made about: What to do? When to do it? And how to do it? Answers to these three questions embody an evaluation procedure that judges the status of an industry at all five market levels of the world economy—local, regional–national, national, regional–international, and global.

This type of evaluation and monitoring is continually being done within the community of international financial centers. Nation-states are (and have been) large and active users of financial center services. The nation-state can also find it convenient to use these centers to adjust their financial positions to counter the sociopolitical pressures resulting from high inflation and unemployment. It therefore seems reasonable to conclude that the success of the proposal requires monitoring and continuing financial, industrial, political, and trade evaluations being rendered by the community of international financial centers.

The International Financial System

The product life cycle proposal is, as are most other policy proposals, dependent on negotiated agreements being reached by the community of nation-states on the sovereign issues of economics and politics. For years George Ball has considered the present world system managed by nation-states as being old fashioned and inappropriate for the present complex world.[27] He argues that the only way for the world to take full advantage of the benefits of the multinationals is to modernize the world's political structure. Barnet and Miller call for comprehensive and coordinated government regulations of the multinationals (including complete corporate disclosure, local community control, and worker sovereignty) by the nation-states.[28]

The proposals require that nation-states multilaterally negotiate specific issues pertaining to international trade and investments, and also domestic monetary and fiscal policy actions. History has clearly shown that negotiated agreements of this magnitude are difficult to accomplish and even more difficult to adhere to for any sustained period of time, primarily because there is little flexibility (i.e., an automatic adjustment mechanism) built into the agreed-upon structure. Therefore each major adjustment requires additional negotiations. The result is that the process is continually held hostage to each nation's desire to show its citizens, after each round of negotiations, that it was a winner. Negotiations at this level always produce a result that reflects the hierarchical relationship among the participants. Thus the feeling of equality is rarely, if ever, felt by all (or even most) of the participants—whether it is justified or not. If the policy(ies) agreed to is not warmly embraced by all, it surely will not succeed.

The international economic policy of nation-states has always focused on the nationalistic objective of obtaining advantages in trade and investment relationships. These policies invariably lead to conflict. The multinationals and the nation-states recognize that their long-run interests are best served when trade and investment conflicts are avoided. Nevertheless, nation-states throughout history have pursued policies that, at times, have severely strained their relationships with other countries; and the multinationals have eagerly sought to take advantage of these conflicts to enhance their own status by increasing their total earnings, return on investments, common stock multiple, market power, and so forth.

The common denominator in the nation-state versus nation-state and the nation-state versus the multinational corporation is the foreign exchange value of each country's currency. The foreign exchange value determines, to a large extent, the magnitude and direction of trade and investment, which in turn directly affect the nation-state's level of employment, inflation, and overall economic growth. The multinational corporations, as a result of their global sourcing and production and marketing activities, must manage their portfolio of currencies in much the same way that they manage their product portfolio, without regard for the national policies (and objectives) of any single nation-state. Therefore the initial policy action should be directed at the international financial system [International Monetary Fund (IMF)].

The importance of the U.S. dollar in international finance is not an accurate indicator of the present status of American economic, industrial, and political power.[29] A number of recommendations for reducing the dollar's role as a reserve currency have been made. The most talked about is the IMF/SDR Substitution Account. Under the provisions of the account, the world's central banks would voluntarily deposit a portion of their dollar reserves with the IMF in exchange for special drawing rights (SDRs). Concern about the proposal within the international financial community centers around the attractiveness (use in trade, capital, and foreign exchange transactions), liquidity (no active secondary markets), and credibility (the account's ability to generate earnings large enough to service the SDR liabilities to central banks) of the SDR asset. The most important aspect of addressing these three concerns is the structure (composition) and value (weightings) of the SDR.

The IMF's present criteria for selecting countries for inclusion in the SDR basket is that they must be among the 16 largest exporters (in value) of goods and services. The weights are determined by each country's ranking in the value of exports of goods and services. Another reason for the monetary disorder is that the international financial system is dollar-heavy (i.e., the U.S. dollar's global reserve and liquidity role is far out of proportion to U.S. economic, industrial, and political power; U.S. GDP is 35 percent of the total of OECD countries and its foreign trade is 16 percent of the total). The international financial community, almost without exception, agrees that the U.S. dollar component in the global reserve and liquidity portfolios must be reduced. The only exception in the weighting procedure is accorded the U.S. dollar, which is given a weight more than twice its trade share to reflect its so-called financial role. J. J. Polak, Economic Counselor and Director of Research at IMF, noted that "the additional weight for the U.S. dollar is not compatible with the logic of the approach, but it was considered attractive by many countries in the light of the Special importance of the U,S. dollar in financial transactions.[30] Clearly the current method used to select and weigh the basket of currencies has serious flaws. It does not consider such important factors as capital flows, direct investments, industrial power (as measured by the assets of industrial corporations), and financial power.

The international financial center structure and ranking (determined by this study) reflect: first, the international financial power and influence of centers, and second, the country's (and its currency's) power and influence as measured by the home nation variables. As a result of this study, consideration should be given to structuring and valuing the SDR based on international financial center status, since it is generally agreed that monetary order (in particular) and political-economic order (in general) reflect the overall distribution of power.[31]

It appears that a selection and weighting procedure for the SDR basket based on international financial center organizational structure and rank is superior to the current IMF selection and weighting procedure. Using such a procedure, currencies would be selected on whether a country has a prominent international financial center (e.g., a center(s) with a rank score of 70 or higher).[32] The weight given to each selected country's currency should reflect the collective importance of that country's international financial centers.

There are 11 international financial centers with rank scores of 70 or higher. The 11 financial centers represent 7 different countries.[33] As a result the SDR basket will consist of 7 currencies. The weightings for each of the currencies are determined by taking the collective international financial center scores in each country as a percentage of the total. For example: United Kingdom 171/863 = 20 percent; United States (New York + Chicago + San Francisco) 231/863 = 27 percent; Japan (Tokyo) 78/863 = 9 percent, etc. Table 6.7 gives

Table 6.7. Comparison of SDR Baskets[a,b]

Present IMF System		Proposed IFC System	
Currency	*Weight*	*Currency*	*Weight*
U.S. dollar	33.0%	U.S. dollar	27.0%
German mark	12.5	British pound	20.0
Japanese yen	7.5	German mark	17.0
French franc	7.5	French franc	10.0
British pound	7.5	Japanese yen	9.0
Italian lira	5.0	Swiss franc	9.0
Dutch guilder	5.0	Dutch guilder	8.0
Canadian dollar	5.0		100.0%
Belgium franc	4.0		
Saudi Arabian riyal	3.0		
Swedish krona	2.0		
Iranian rial	2.0		
Australian dollar	1.5		
Spanish peseta	1.5		
Norwegian krone	1.5		
Austrian schilling	1.5		
	100.0%		

[a]Switzerland is not a member of the IMF but its importance in international financial activity is such that it (and its currency—the Swiss Franc) must be an integral part of the decisionmaking structure.

[b]On January 1, 1981, the IMF was to have reduced the size of the "basket" from 16 currencies to 5. This action appears to be just as arbitrary as the selection of the 16 currency basket. Therefore the principal thrust of my argument (proposal) remains valid. For a discussion of the IMF's selection criteria beginning January 1, 1981, see, *IMF Survey* (Washington D.C.: International Monetary Fund, October 13, 1980), pp. 297, 325–327.

the comparison between the present International Monetary Fund (IMF) system and the proposed International Financial Center (IFC) system.

The proposed SDR basket structure will make the SDR considerably more attractive (in terms of capital value and marketability to the international financial center community) than the present structure. Each currency has a home center(s) in which it is actively traded in the foreign exchange markets and in which it is the currency of denomination for money and capital market assets that are actively traded. As a result, the SDR yield (interest plus exchange rate gain or loss) is easily calculated on a current basis, and in turn a forward value can also be easily determined. In addition, the capital value of the SDR will be competitive with any other individual currency included in the basket.

Any country not willing to participate in the IFC/SDR system should be subjected to an enforcement mechanism that has the effect of contracting its international financial machinery. The enforcement mechanism would require that the country unwilling to participate be restricted (i.e., its financial institutions) from operating offices in the other basket currency countries; and the other basket currency countries (financial institutions) would cease to operate in the unwilling country. The premise here is that if a country is not willing to permit its currency to share global responsibility, then it is not entitled to operate the elaborate international financial machinery that has the potential of severely disrupting the existing order.

CONCLUSION

The problem-solving capacity of the nation-state is primarily unidimensional. The nation-state system is designed specifically to optimize the management of military and noneconomic political conflicts. In its desire to retain sovereignty over the domestic economy, the nation-state feels that it is forced to take action to control —what it sees—as the destabilizing activities of the multinational corporations. The multinationals, on the other hand, would prefer to operate as independent entities free of obligatory ties. Operating as they do, these global corporations find that it is not in their corporate interest to carry the banner (or even appear to) of nationalism for any nation-state. As a result the multinationals are not structurally capable of optimally managing noneconomic activities. The international financial centers can serve as the bridge between the nation-states and the multinationals and thus bring about increased operating efficiency (and effectiveness) that will benefit the entire world.

Determining, quantitatively, the organizational structure and rank of international financial centers provides a means for restoring monetary order to the international system. The IFC/SDE basket can be adjusted automatically, without negotiations, at regular intervals (perhaps every two or three years). Such a system permits international monetary responsibility to be shared equitably with the rules clearly defined. The basis for these rules is that each nation's internatinal financial and industrial infrastructure cannot be easily manipulated for short-term nationalistic objectives by nation-states, and that this system would minimize the multinational's ability to affect substantially the policies and goals of any one nation at the expense of another. In addition, a more orderly international financial system will make economic industrial policy formulation by nation-states easier; and the use of the product life cycle as an important element in formulating these policies will enhance the government's ability to manage the domestic political economy.

International financial centers, in effect, should serve as the nation-states' windows to the world (i.e., an economic and political barometer). If these centers are used for this purpose, the world economy will gain the two prerequisites necessary for order: first, a framework that creates harmony; and second, predictability. The international financial center organizational structure can be viewed as a hierarchical structure not only for finance but also for information and industrial and political evaluation. In this light, perhaps the most important function of an international financial center is to provide an environment that permits maintenance of global financial, economic, industrial, and political order.

NOTES

1. Charles P. Kindleberger, *The Formation of Financial Centers: A Study in Comparative Economic History*, Princeton Studies in International Finance, No. 36 (Princeton, N.J.: Princeton University, 1974), p. 1.
2. Hang-Sheng Cheng, "The U.S. West Coast as an International Financial Center," *Economic Review of the Federal Reserve Bank of San Francisco* (Spring 1976): 9–19.
3. The 76 centers (cities and city-states) were chosen on the basis of their reputations among knowledgeable groups such as economists, historians, political scientists, bankers, and businessmen as international financial centers. There are 40 countries, on six continents, represented. There are 38 European centers, 17 in Asia, 9 in Latin American, 5 in the United States, 3 in Africa, and 2 each in Australia and Canada. There were 80 centers analyzed in 1980.

   There are 68 commercial banks used in this study. It is believed that these 68 institutions were (and are) the world's most important internationally active banks. The names of many of these banks have been changed over the years, resulting from mergers, acquisitions, reorganizations, and so forth; these factors were recognized and accounted for in the analysis.

4. Kindleberger, *The Formation of Financial Centers*, p. 6.
5. Ibid., p. 4.
6. Gunter Dufey and Ian Giddy, *The International Money Market* (Englewood Cliffs, N.J.: Prentice-Hall, 1978), p. 35; Monroe Haegele, "Iran's Potential as a Finance Center," *International Finance* (New York: Chase Manhattan Bank, February 23, 1975); and Harry G. Johnson, "Panama as a Regional Financial Center," *Economic Development and Cultural Change* (January, 1976): 261.
7. Fernand Braudel, *Afterthoughts on Material Civilization and Capitalism* (Baltimore: The Johns Hopkins University Press, 1977), p. 82.
8. Robert Mundell, *The New International Monetary System* (New York: Columbia University Press, 1977), p. 238.
9. Kindleberger, *The Formation of Financial Centers*, pp. 9-10.
10. Haegele, "Iran's Potential," p. 7.
11. Raymond Vernon, *Metropolis, 1985* (Cambridge, Mass.: Harvard University Press, 1960), pp. 70-80.
12. Giorgio Ragazzi, "Theories of Determinants of Foreign Direct Investment," *Staff Papers* (Washington, D.C.: International Monetary Fund, July 1973), pp. 476-481.
13. Ibid, p. 480.
14. Data on foreign financial assets for London in 1946 are not available. Some information is available for 1949; it is estimated that less than $1 billion in foreign financial assets were on the books in London, compared with $24 billion in New York. Therefore, it is concluded that New York, in 1947, was also "the" preeminent international financial center. A center is considered preeminent if it is a member of the *apex* of the hierarchy.
15. The underlying causes of London's preeminence in 1975 and 1980 are primarily due to OAPEC (Organization of Arab Petroleum Exporting Countries) cash management decisions, beginning after the dramatic oil price increase in 1973. This will be discussed later.
16. The disruptions were: (1) ending the postwar fixed exchange rate system on August 15, 1971; (2) quadrupling of the world oil prices in 1973-1974—the price increases have continued and are presently more than 16 times what they were in early 1973; and (3) some loss of political standing of the United States in the world as a result of continuing conflict in the Middle East (which precipitated the oil price increases), losing Vietnam, and, more recently, the overthrow of the Shah of Iran.
17. The imposition of the Interest Equalization Tax (IET) in July 1963 and followed by the Voluntary Foreign Credit Restraint (VFCR) program in 1965 are cited, overwhelmingly, as the events that led to New York's demise as the world's top financial center.
18. In 1955, the group structures for the upper levels of the hierarchy are— Group 1: London, New York, Paris; Group 2: 34 centers; and Group 3: 39 centers. In 1965—Group 1: London, New York; Group 2: Paris, Tokyo,

Hong Kong, Hamburg, San Francisco; Group 3: 36 centers; and Group 4: 40 centers. In 1975—Group 1: London; Group 2: New York, Toyko, Paris; Group 3: 14 centers; Group 4: 15 centers; and Group 5: 43 centers. And in 1980—Group 1: London, New York; Group 2: 9 centers; Group 3: 33 centers, and Group 4: 36 centers.

19. Unfiltered information refers, in this instance, to the information transmitted between centers through direct banking links; filtered information transmitted between centers through relatively public networks. Unfiltered information is not necessarily transmitted *directly* from one center to another; it may be processed through an intermediary office (i.e., a regional office, corporate headquarters, or both), but the processing takes place within a single institution.

20. In recent interviews (summer 1979) with high-ranking officials of more than 50 large internationally active financial institutions (U.S. and foreign), it became clear that they select managers (and their staffs) to operate offices away from headquarters by attempting to match the manager's skill and competence with the perceived demands and requirements of the center in which the office is located.

21. Order is defined as an international system that has a workable framework (a prescribed set of rules) for solving the difficult problems of the political economy. The framework, when functioning properly, will: (1) create harmony in the inevitable diversity among the global financial, economic, industrial, and political systems; and (2) permit the direction and magnitude of future events (within the system) to be creditably predicted given a particular set of circumstances.

22. Two assumptions are made about MNCs. They are the (1) industrial engines of economic growth and prosperity for the world; and (2) manufacturing and/or high technology enterprises.

23. Vernon (1966) is given credit for pioneering the "product life cycle" theory. See "International Investment and International Trade in the Product Cycle," *Quarterly Journal of Economics,* 80 (1966):190-127.

24. The world economy consists of five distinct market levels: (1) global; (2) regional–international; (3) national; (4) regional–national; and (5) local.

25. Industries that are important to national security (i.e., steel) should not be completely phased out. Instead, a national level of inventories should be set and the industry should be maintained at levels necessary for an emergency. In this way the costs (social and economic) levels of maintaining inefficient industries will be shared by the nation (as a whole) but to a degree substantially less than what it is today.

26. Perhaps this phase of the proposal should be accompanied by various, complementary fiscal policies.

27. G. Ball, "The Promise of the Multinational Corporation," *Fortune,* June 1967, p. 80.

28. Richard J. Barnet and Ronald E. Miller, *Global Reach: The Power of Multinational Corporations* (New York: Simon and Schuster, 1974), pp. 283-290.

29. At year-end 1978, official international reserves (worldwide) amounted to $550 billion. Gold accounted for $230 billion of the total (at its prevailing free market price of $226 per ounce); special drawing rights (SDRs) and the International Monetary Fund's reserve position accounted for $30 billion; and the remaining $290 billion was foreign exchange holdings, of which the dollar accounted for 77 percent of the total. The remaining 23 percent of worldwide foreign exchange holdings were comprised of German marks, 9 percent; Swiss francs, 5 percent; Japanese yen, 5 percent; French francs, 2 percent; British pounds, 2 percent; and Dutch guilders, less than 1 percent. Global liquidity, as measured by the Eurocurrency market, at year-end 1978 amounted to approximately $480 billion (net), and the U.S. dollar accounted for 74 percent of the total. German marks accounted for 15 percent; Swiss francs, 5 percent; Japanese yen, 2 percent; French francs, 2 percent; and the British pound and Dutch guilder, 1 percent each.

30. J. J. Polak, "The SDR as a Basket of Currencies," *Staff Papers*, Washington, D.C.: International Monetary Fund, December 1979, p. 636.

31. See, for example, the essays in David P. Calleo, ed., *Money and the Coming World Order* (New York: New York University Press, 1976).

32. The rank score of 70 is somewhat arbitrary in that the cutoff score could be 71, 72, 73, etc. The esential ingredient is that it be agreed to by the International Monetary Fund. However, the cutoff score of 70, proposed here, appears to be a fair representation of global power and influence, and is therefore preferred.

32. Hong Kong, the British Colony, is part of the Overseas Sterling Area and therefore is considered to be a United Kingdom Center.

PART III

The R&D Centralization-Decentralization Issue

Doz lists the following advantages or raisons d'être of MNCs (over single national corporations):[1]

Economies of scale
Economies of experience (location- or firm-specific)
Economies of location
Product differentiation (by customer sets and product types)
Maintenance of channels for exports, sales, service, and maintenance, which also includes a corporate image
Financial flexibility, including access to capital
Technological intensity by product and process, including economies of R&D aggregation, possibilities of distributing R&D cost over large quantities of produced goods, and ease in transferring patterns, processes, licenses from unit to unit

Thus, a "natural" way of organizing R&D in MNCs is for centralization (at headquarters or elsewhere). This, however, is one of the main points of criticism against MNCs: MNCs as a rule do not contribute to the development of a host country's know-how as national corporations supposedly do. The decisions about R&D location and intensity therefore can create potential conflicts between MNCs and national governments, especially as MNCs most frequently operate in technology- and R&D-intensive industries. At the same time, the

MNCs often behave as "technological enclaves," that is, even if R&D laboratories are located in the host country, their spillover effects to the host country most often are negligible.

If a national corporation is being acquired in the course of direct investment in a host country by a foreign MNC, experience shows that chances of the locally operating unit's R&D division being closed after a short time are fairly high.

Another general finding is that the emphasis is on development rather than on research and that development often is constrained to adapting technology transferred within the MNC to local conditions and contingencies.

Håkanson begins with a discussion of findings about this point, concluding that more advanced and extensive R&D efforts are primarily undertaken in large subsidiaries operating in major markets (which do not necessarily have to be constrained to the boundaries of the host country).

The bulk of corporate R&D is aimed at the development of new and improved products. It is usually linked to major manufacturing plants. Basic and applied research unrelated to existing production often is concentrated in specific research centers, the location of which can be quite unrelated to that of the production units. For historical reasons such centers are often found in the vicinity of MNC headquarters. There are, however, exceptions, such as access to specialists either hired or available at major specialized research centers. Other secondary criteria also play a role.

Håkanson's contribution is a summary of research undertaken on behalf of the same Swedish governmental commission for which Vahlne is working. The main concern of Håkanson is how a little but industrially highly advanced country can perform in this context. Actually, the foreign-owned sector of the manufacturing industry in Sweden has grown rapidly between 1960 and 1975, mainly because of acquisition.

At the same time the R&D activities in foreign-owned subsidiaries have declined markedly (in 1977 the share of R&D performed in subsidiaries in Sweden was 6 percent, whereas the share of value-added was 7 percent. Compare the much more dramatic figures for Australia in Chapter 11 by Welsh and Wiedersheim-Paul. These figures cannot be compared to Sweden, however, as Australia is less developed industrially and at the same time much more regulated). As to be expected, development dominates over research, and is mainly devoted to adapting products and processes to the host countries' idiosyncracies.

Håkanson analyzes a cluster of 99 MNC subsidiaries (accounting for approximately 90 percent of value-added produced by foreign-controlled manufacturing subsidiaries) thoroughly. He found that only a few subsidiaries perform substantive R&D activities of their own, and are in low-integration export-intensive enterprises. In the other categories R&D intensity is the lowest in the highly integrated enterprises.

The application of regression analyses to the cluster of 99 firms demonstrates how difficult it is to capture a wide variety of strategic considerations and issues in a regression model. It explains less than half of the variation in R&D intensity between the firms. Well-supported conclusions are that the propensity to perform R&D in a foreign subsidiary increases with the subsidiary's age and size, and that R&D intensity is associated with the subsidiary's role in the international organization of production imposed by the MNC. Although R&D intensities vary among industries, organizationally autonomous subsidiaries producing for an international market tend to perform significantly more R&D than more tightly integrated subsidiaries oriented toward the local market. This is consistent with Ronstadt (1978), who distinguishes between Transfer Technology Units (TTU) as the lowest level, Indigenous TU (ITU), Global (GTU), and Corporate TU (CTU) in increasing order of level of generality of R&D Units.

Ondrack compares the responsiveness of MNC subsidiaries with that of indigenous Canadian firms in depth. The point of departure is the poor performance of Canadian industry in terms of industrial innovation and export sales, which in part is attributed to the comparatively high foreign ownership in Canadian industry. Independent laboratories (having little to do with local development) and local support laboratories were found to be predominant in Canadian-based MNC subsidiaries, neither of which contributes markedly to the international competitive power of Canadian industry. At the same time, R&D performance of the indigenous firms has not been impressive, which is attributed to the generally smaller size of these firms and to the fragmented domestic market.

Against this background, some policy options have attracted public interest: better focusing of fiscal support to R&D programs to promising areas of industrial development as well as directing such support to indigenous firms (and even to MNC subsidiaries that show unusual autonomy regarding R&D). Thus far, the results of governmental R&D policy seem to be that the general level of R&D spending (which is very low by international comparison) has remained stable over the last five to six years. During the same period, R&D in foreign-controlled MNC subsidiaries declined by as much as R&D increased in the indigenous firms.

Ondrack, after reporting on the state of knowledge in the literature (which is essentially that government innovation policy has little, if any, impact compared to other criteria, among which primarily the general business climate expectations seem to play a dominant role), investigates subsets of the machinery industry in 1974 and 1979. (It is widely spread over the country, has a high export potential, and is very dependent on R&D and innovation to remain competitive. Furthermore, it is one of the target industries of public industrial growth policies.) The cluster comprises Canadian as well as foreign-owned firms in comparable proportions.

Contrary to the general development reported above, Canadian firms reduced their R&D investment over the period under study, whereas MNC subsidiaries increased their R&D efforts. The most striking observation, however, is that at the same time few foreign firms but many Canadian firms took advantage of governmental R&D support. This also supports other findings reporting low responses from MNCs to national governmental support programs. *Subsidiaries*, regardless of whether they are indigenous or foreign, also show a generally low response to governmental programs.

Another interesting finding is that the project-type of R&D support programs in the firms studied lost drastically in participation over time, whereas tax incentives, obviously because of their general availability as well as their uncomplicated structure, were generally and increasingly taken advantage of (the study does not report on measures of effectiveness of any R&D support program).

In concluding, Ondrack conjectures that integrated MNC subsidiaries do not operate (aggressive) R&D programs and that they most likely will not respond to governmental policy measures unless they are sufficiently large to induce their headquarters to change their status, that is, from a technology transfer unit into an indigenous technology unit.

The main obstacle to industry responding to government R&D policy has been deficiencies in the programs themselves, deterring domestic and foreign-owned firms equally.

NOTE

1. Cf. Dunning (1979).

BIBLIOGRAPHY

Dunning, J. H. "Explaining Changing Patterns of International Production: In Defense of the Eclectic Theory." University of Reading *Discussion Papers in International Investment and Business Studies*, No. 46, November 1979.
Ronstadt, R. C. *Research and Development Abroad by US Multinationals.* New York: Praeger, 1977.

Chapter 7

R&D in Foreign-Owned Subsidiaries in Sweden

Lars Håkanson*

The research and development (R&D) activity in foreign subsidiaries is associated with technically advanced production, high skill intensity, and exports to third world countries. On this assumption, many host governments actively encourage foreign multinationals to establish R&D locally. However, as critics point out, the nature of multinational operations may set limits to the potential benefits of such policies.

Setting priorities for R&D and deciding how and where to exploit the results of R&D are rarely left to the discretion of local management, but rather are subordinated by the overall aims and policies of the corporation. The "strategic" importance attached to R&D is reflected by the fact that local R&D managers often report directly to technical departments at divisional or corporate headquarters, sometimes completely bypassing local management (Cordell, 1971, 1973).

Moreover, the ability of multinationals to transfer technology and allocate production on an international basis may prevent subsidiaries from fully exploiting the results of their own R&D. For this reason, detrimental effects are often feared when technically advanced firms are acquired by foreign-based multinationals.

*Institute of International Business, Stockholm School of Economics and Business Administration.

It has even been suggested that foreign-controlled R&D laboratories sometimes constitute a form of "brain drain":

> If the laboratories work on problems of the local environment, participate in university programs, enter joint research relationships with national laboratories, or rotate their personnel to other company locations for training, the country gains greatly from the laboratories' presence.
>
> But if the laboratories merely work in isolation and transmit their results to the parent company for worldwide exploitation, the country gains little more than some jobs for its science graduates. It may actually sustain a net loss if these graduates' services could have been better used on other problems of higher priority in the country. (Quinn, 1969, 156).

Clearly, the economic significance of foreign R&D units depends on the types of tasks to which they are assigned, the linkages they maintain with the local environment, and the manner in which their results are utilized. These functional characteristics, in turn, reflect the motives and considerations that lead multinationals to establish R&D at foreign locations, to retain such units in acquired companies, and in the manner in which such units evolve over time.

Drawing on a recent Swedish study,[1] this chapter analyzes the determinants of R&D in foreign subsidiaries in a small industrialized country. It makes no attempt to resolve the controversy regarding the balance of costs and benefits associated with multinational R&D. However, the chapter does attempt to provide one piece of the empirical and theoretical foundation on which such assessments should be made.

Following a brief discussion of the nature and evolution of foreign R&D units, a number of theoretical propositions emerging from the literature are examined in the light of the Swedish experience.

EVOLUTION OF FOREIGN R&D

The predominant motive for establishing R&D laboratories abroad is to help transfer technology from the parent company to its foreign subsidiaries (Cordell, 1973; Ronstadt, 1978). Such "technical support laboratories," or "technology transfer units," probably make up the vast majority of all foreign R&D establishments. Although these units may significantly contribute to the rate of innovation diffusion and productivity growth, only some of their work would qualify as R&D in the strict sense—most of it being technical service tasks associated with the introduction of new products or processes. However, adaptation of foreign technology to the local environment sometimes requires indigenous development, based upon local expertise and R&D capacity.

More advanced and extensive R&D is primarily found in large affiliates in major markets and also in acquired companies that had their own R&D at the time of acquisition. In these cases R&D operations were established or retained in order to facilitate the recruitment of qualified personnel and to exploit the competence and initiatives of local technicians. Typically, capacity for new product development is a response to initiatives and requests from local subsidiary management and evolve from smaller R&D units of the technology transfer type (Ronstadt, 1978; Håkanson, 1981).

Frequently, advanced R&D is associated with a "unique" competence within the corporate group, sometimes reflected in the formal allocation of global development responsibility for a certain line of production. Based on the accumulated experience of production and marketing, such special competence may reflect the particular characteristics of the local market, but it may originate in any indigenous innovation. R&D intensive subsidiaries often produce for an international market, but in certain industries characterized by low international mobility of goods (e.g., food and certain chemicals), the subsidiaries may also perform R&D for application in sister companies based abroad (SIND, 1977, the 209ff).

The bulk of corporate R&D refers to the development of new and improved products and is linked by location to major manufacturing plants. In contrast, basic applied research unrelated to existing production is sometimes concentrated in special "research centers," the location of which can be selected without reference to location of other corporate units (Malecki, 1980). Nevertheless, having typically evolved from technical departments of the parent company, research centers are usually located in the home country, often in the vicinity of the head office (Pavitt, 1971; Mansfield, 1974; Creamer, 1976). However, certain large multinationals have also established such units at foreign locations (Trier, 1967; Ducol, 1969, Ronstadt, 1978; SCB, 1977, p. 10ff; Granstrand and Fernlund, 1978). The principal motive for selecting a foreign location is to facilitate recruitment of foreign specialists and to establish a network of contacts with foreign universities and research institutions.

R&D IN FOREIGN SUBSIDIARIES IN SWEDEN

Aggregate Trends

From the beginning of the 1960s until the middle of the 1970s, the foreign-owned sector of Sweden's manufacturing industry had grown at a rapid rate, primarily through foreign acquisitions of domestic companies. Foreign manufacturing subsidiaries, accounting for 5.7 percent of the total manufacturing employment in 1977, are concentrated in parts of the chemical industry, the glass and glass products industry, and in the electrical and scientific instruments industry.

In spite of the growth of the foreign-owned sector during the first half of the 1970s, its share of R&D declined. In 1977 foreign subsidiaries performed 6 percent of the industrial R&D. This was less than their share of value-added, which came close to 7 percent. In the beginning of the 1970s the average R&D intensity was higher in the foreign-owned sector than in the domestic sector, but by 1977 this situation was reversed (Samuelsson, 1977, p. 174; Håkanson, 1980, p. 144ff). Average R&D intensity (R&D costs as a percentage of value-added) in domestic manufacturing companies is estimated at 4.3 percent, as compared to 3.2 percent in foreign subsidiaries.[2]

The data partly reflect changes in the industrial structure of the foreign-owned sector; a decline in the chemical industry has been balanced by foreign acquisitions in certain less R&D-intensive industries, notably food. It is also probable that some R&D functions have also been transferred from Sweden to foreign laboratories. Unfortunately, in the absence of time series for individual firms, the relative importance of such transfers cannot be determined.

The scope and purpose of R&D in foreign subsidiaries are very similar to those of domestic industry. New product development and improvements of existing products account for about three-fourths of R&D costs, although this share is higher in the foreign-owned sector. As a rule, production in foreign subsidiaries is based on parent technology. Hence a relatively large share of R&D resources can be allocated to product improvements to meet specific market needs.

However, a considerable share of foreign subsidiary R&D also refers to *new* product development and to research, especially in the engineering industry. Here, foreign subsidiaries devote an average of almost 13 percent of their R&D costs to "research," which is double the corresponding average for domestic firms.

Determinants of R&D in Foreign Subsidiaries

In view of the fact that foreign subsidiaries, in addition to their own R&D, have at least partial access to the R&D results and resources of the corporate parent and of sister companies abroad, the average

R&D intensity appear fairly high in the foreign-owned sector, especially in the food, electrical, and chemical industries. Moreover, although customer- and market-oriented product improvements account for a major share of R&D, R&D in the foreign subsidiaries does not appear to be significantly less "advanced" than in the domestic firms.

However, manufacturing and R&D in the foreign-owned sector are even more concentrated than in the entire Swedish industrial sector. Nine large foreign subsidiaries account for more than 40 percent of the production and three foreign firms for nearly half of the R&D. Aggregate data may therefore conceal significant differences between different types of subsidiaries. Specifically, prior expectations suggest that the relative size and scope of R&D vary with the size and age of the subsidiary and with its "role" in the international manufacturing organization.

Operations in small market-oriented subsidiaries are often limited to the final conversion of raw materials and imported components. Since manufacturing technology is largely obtained from the corporate parent, no, or only very limited, R&D capacity is needed. However, some technical development may be undertaken—especially in the producer goods industries—as part of technical customer service and adaptation of products to local market needs; when manufacturing processes are adapted to local conditions (Cordell, 1971; Bradbury, 1978).

Similar conditions are also often found in large- and medium-sized companies that produce for a wider European market. When such units have been established or acquired as part of a market development strategy, production frequently duplicates that of the parent company or of manufacturing plants in other countries. In order to facilitate coordination and control and to avoid duplication of R&D efforts, R&D tends to be concentrated in central laboratories, often in the home country. However, by using appropriate information and control systems, it may be possible to achieve organizational coordination without geographic centralization (Papo, 1971; Potter, 1971; Hanson and van Rumker, 1971; Granstrand and Fernlund, 1978; Terpstra, 1977; Fischer and Behrman, 1980).

More extensive and advanced R&D is primarily found in large and relatively autonomous subsidiaries, which often have a long history of operations in the market and also in the acquisition of technically advanced firms. Such subsidiaries have often been allocated responsibility for the development, production, and marketing of a specific product line for an international market, which is an expression of international rationalization of production and division of labor characterized by several large multinationals. In Europe, such organizational arrangements have been facilitated by the liberalization of trade, especially the creation of broad free trade areas. Subsidiaries, originally established to serve local national markets, have been able to extend their markets by developing specialization and concentration. Moreover, these tendencies accede to host country political demands for local production and exports.

In order to examine these hypotheses, the following analysis draws on cross-sectional data relating to 121 foreign subsidiaries in Sweden in 1977. The sample represents three-quarters of all the foreign manufacturing subsidiaries that employed more than 200 persons in any year from 1972–1977 and are still foreign owned in 1977. (In 20 cases, subsidiaries belonging to the same multinational group and operating in the same industry were aggregated to "subsidiary groups," each of which is subsequently treated as one observation.) The data were originally collected by the National Central Bureau of Statistics as part of the annual collection of financial statistics for firms and as part of the biannual R&D survey.[3]

The 99 units included in the analysis together employ around 55,800 persons and account for a value-added figure of 6,150 million kronor, corresponding to almost 90 percent of the total value-added in the foreign manufacturing sector. However, the sample includes some sales subsidiaries and the above comparison is not strictly valid; the employment figure is higher than the total reported in the manufacturing statistics for foreign subsidiaries.

R&D in "Types" of Foreign Subsidiaries

As a first step, the firms in the sample were classified along three dimensions: size, export propensity, and degree of integration or autonomy. Three measures of size were used: number of employees, value of sales, and value-added. Export propensity was measured by the export share of sales. Subsidiary autonomy was assumed to be reflected in the relative importance of intragroup transactions, that is, the share of resold goods in total sales and the share of intragroup exports in total exports.

By using a principal component analysis and computing the factor scores, a composite measure of each of the underlying dimensions was devised (Table 7.1).[4]

As indicated in the table, factor 1, absorbing more than half of the total variation, is primarily associated with size. Factor 2 is used to measure export propensity; thus market-oriented firms would tend to have low scores. Factor 3 is assumed to reflect the degree of inte-

Table 7.1. Foreign Subsidiaries in Sweden: Correlation of Factor Scores and
Manifest Classification Variables

Classification Variables	Factor 1	Factor 2	Factor 3
Number of employees	0.897	-0.177	-0.319
Values of sales	0.880	-0.032	-0.001
Value-added	0.890	-0.145	-0.237
Resale share	0.560	0.370	0.611
Export share	0.248	0.888	-0.257
Intragroup exports share	0.570	-0.195	0.523
Eigenvalue	3.076	1.018	0.923
share (percent)	51.3	17.0	15.4
Cumulative share (percent)	51.3	68.2	83.6

gration of the subsidiaries with corporate units abroad. It is positively correlated with both the relative share of resales and the share of intragroup transactions in exports. Low factor scores are taken as an indication of relative autonomy on the part of the foreign subsidiary.

Following visual inspection of a graphic plot of observations, seven classes of subsidiaries were identified. Nine were classified as large (factor L1), with the rest classified as small to medium sized (Figure 7.1).

The nine large subsidiaries differ primarily in factor 3, degree of integration. Three of them have low scores, indicating a relatively high degree of autonomy (group L1). All are active in technologically advanced industries and have been active in Sweden since before World War II. Three subsidiaries (L2) are characterized by low values for factor 2, export propensity, reflecting the low international mobility of goods in their respective industries. The remaining three large subsidiaries (L3) are distinguished by high scores for factor 3; resold goods account for a major share of their sales.

The 90 small- and medium-sized subsidiaries display a wide variation is the dimensions studied. In the absence of clear clusters, factor scores close to zero were selected somewhat arbitrarily as bases for dichotomization.

Two-thirds of the smaller subsidiaries show low export figures and appear to be oriented toward the Swedish market. Some of them supplement their local manufacturing with imports of finished goods (S3), but the majority of them (S2) do not. Both groups contain a high number of firms active in the food, chemical, and graphic industries, but group S2 also includes a number of smaller engineering companies.

About one-fifth of the smaller firms (S1) are relatively autonomous subsidiaries, characterized by high exports. The group is dominated

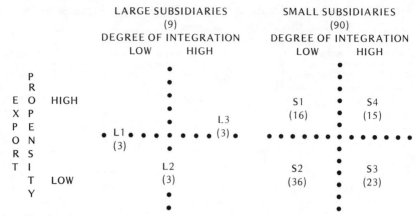

Note: Numbers in parentheses are the number of observations

Figure 7.1.   Classification of foreign subsidiaries in Sweden.

by medium-sized technology-intensive firms acquired from abroad, but is also includes a smaller number of firms oriented to raw materials.

The 15 companies in group S4 are similar to those in S3; differences in export tendencies are largely accounted for by reexports. In both groups, the bulk of local production is sold on the Swedish market. Only a few subsidiaries report significant amounts of intragroup exports. However, to the extent that such trade flows reflect international specialization and division of labor, some local R&D capacity can be expected. Nevertheless, the majority of firms in these groups probably rely more or less completely on technology developed abroad.

As indicated in Table 7.2, the difference between the propensity to perform R&D and the intensity of R&D performed varies considerably. More than half of the total R&D performed in the foreign-owned sector is accounted for by the three large R&D-intensive subsidiaries in group S1.

The overall pattern of R&D performance conforms to expectations. More than two-thirds of the export-oriented, autonomous firms in the small size category (S1) perform in-house R&D, a significantly higher share than in the other small- and medium-sized companies. The latter are characterized by small R&D departments and their average R&D intensities are low. This is especially true in the more integrated subsidiaries (S3 and S4), whose average R&D employment is significantly lower than in the more autonomous firms (S1 and S2). However, high standard deviations indicate considerable intragroup variation. Thus the difference between market-oriented firms in S2 and S3, respectively, it not statistically significant.[5]

Table 7.2. R&D in Seven Groups of Foreign Subsidiaries in Sweden

	Number of Subsidiaries		Man-years in R&D			R&D Intensity[a]	
Group	Total	R&D	Share	$\bar{x}$	s	$\bar{x}$	s
L1	3	3	52.6	205.5	57.5	6.4	1.6
L2	3	2	3.4	b	b	b	b
L3	3	0	0.0	0.0	10.7	0.9	1.7
S1	16	11	23.4	17.1	34.7	2.6	3.0
S2	36	11	15.4	5.0	10.7	0.9	1.7
S3	22^c	9	3.2	2.9	6.8	0.7	1.4
S4	15	6	2.0	1.6	2.9	0.6	1.1
Total	98^c	42	100.0	13.3	41.6	1.8	5.7

$\bar{x}$ = average, by observation.
s = standard deviation.
[a]Number of man-years in R&D as percentage of total employment.
[b]May not be disclosed.
[c]Excluding AB Leo. The Danish pharmaceutical company AB Leo has been excluded. This subsidiary differs from the others not only in its high R&D intensity but also in its organizational structure. The Danish parent, Kefalas A/S, is for all practical purposes a holding company and the group is managed from the Swedish subsidiary. The Swedish company, in turn, has several sales subsidiaries abroad and relatively high shares of intragroup exports, accounting for its classification among the more integrated subsidiaries.

REGRESSION ANALYSIS

The foregoing analysis broadly supports the hypothesized relationships. However, because of the small number of observations and large variance within each group, only weak statistical associations could be detected. In order to further explore the determinants of R&D in foreign subsidiaries, the hypotheses were combined in the following formalized model:

$$Y = f(S, E, I, T_i, A, E, H \ (. \ . \ . \ .) \qquad (7.1)$$
$$+ \ + \ - \ + \ + \ + \ -$$

The dependent variables (Y) denotes R&D intensity in a foreign subsidiary. As above, it is assumed to be positively related to size (S) and export propensity (E), but negatively dependent on degree of integration (I).

In addition, R&D intensity is assumed to also depend on the technological level of the industry (T_i). Since R&D is partly a reflection of the accumulated experience and the subsidiary's standing in the corporation (e.g., its negotiating strength in intragroup decision), a positive relationship to age (A) is assumed.

Moreover, acquired firms are expected to perform more R&D than established firms. Manufacturing units developed "from scratch" generally remain dependent on parent technology for a considerable time, whereas many acquired firms had their own R&D departments at the time of takeover.

Of course, the propensity to locate R&D abroad is also dependent on the characteristics of the multinational corporation of which the Swedish subsidiary is a part, for example, its size, geographic extension and degree of diversification (Håkanson, 1981). However, in the model only one such determinant is included, the country of origin (H). Specifically, it is assumed that U.S. and Canadian multinationals are more likely to locate R&D in Sweden than are their European counterparts.

The rationale for this hypothesis is twofold. First, it seems likely that the possibilities to perform technical service and other R&D-related functions in central laboratories on behalf of a foreign subsidiary are partly dependent on distance. It should be noted, however, that certain U.S. multinationals have—for this very reason—established special R&D units at central locations in Europe in order to serve their subsidiaries throughout the entire continent. Second, Samuelsson (1977) found that the Swedish subsidiaries of American multinationals more often produce for a wider European market than those of European groups, whose direct investments in Sweden are more often motivated by custom barriers, transport, and other transfer costs.

Operationally, R&D intensity (Y) was measured by the number of man-years in R&D as a percentage of total employment. For the independent variables, two alternative specifications were utilized. In the first case, the three first independent variables $(S, E, \text{and } I)$ were measured by the corresponding (mutually uncorrelated) latent variables defined in the principal component analysis (factors 1 and 3 in Table 7.1). In the second case, manifest variables were inserted, namely, value added, export share of sales, and share of resales in total sales.

In both regressions, the technological level of the industry (T_i) was measured by average R&D intensity (defined above) for all Swedish manufacturing firms in the subsidiary's industry in 1977. The age of the subsidiary (A) was measured by the number of years since manufacturing operations commenced in Sweden. Mode of establishment (E) was indicated by a "dummy" variable; $E = 1$ in acquired subsidiaries and $E = 0$ in established subsidiaries. Similarly, subsidiaries of European multinationals obtained $H = 1$, and for all others it was $H = 0$.

In the absence of clear hypotheses as to the relevant form of the assumed relationships, a simple additive association was tested by means of stepwise linear regression (OLS), yielding the following estimates:

Regression 1
Number of observations: 99 $R^2 = 0.47$ $F = 28.60$

$$Y = 0.99 - 0.474^{++}I + 0.692^{+++}T_I + 0.028^{+++}A$$
$$\quad\quad\quad (2.10)\quad\quad (8.47)\quad\quad\quad (2.82)$$

where I = factor 3 (degree of integration)
$\quad\quad T_I$ = average R&D intensity in the industry
$\quad\quad A$ = number of years since manufacturing was established in Sweden

Regression 2
Number of observations: 99 $R^2 = 0.49$ $F = 22.47$

$$Y = -1.41 + 0.004^{+}S + 1.260^{+}E + 0.675^{+++}T_I + 0.022^{++}A$$
$$\quad\quad\quad (1.69)\quad\quad (1.78)\quad\quad (8.26)\quad\quad\quad (2.19)$$

where S = value-added
$\quad\quad E$ = export share of sales
$\quad\quad T_I$ = average R&D intensity in the industry
$\quad\quad A$ = number of years since manufacturing was established in Sweden

The results confirm the previously observed similarity between foreign-owned and domestic firms; R&D intensity in foreign subsidiaries appears to be largely determined by industry. However, the estimates are also compatible with the assumption that the propensity to perform R&D is also related to the subsidiary's age and to its "role" in the multinational organization of production.

Regression 1 suggests that organization integration versus autonomy is an important determinant of R&D intensity.

Neither of the two estimates supports the assumption that R&D intensities are higher among acquired companies than among companies established from scratch. This result possibly reflects the fact that several of the most R&D-intensive subsidiaries are rather old, having been established before World War II, whereas the vast majority of all younger subsidiaries were acquired to serve as merely domestic firms.

Similarly, no support is found for the hypothesis that American multinationals more often allocate R&D to their Swedish subsidiaries than do European firms. It is suspected that if any such difference exists, it will have been absorbed by the role variables, that is, export propensity and degree of intengration.

CONCLUSIONS

Decisions about R&D investments are likely to be influenced by a wide range of strategic considerations that cannot possibly be captured in simple quantitative models. It is not surprising, therefore, that the regressions tested in this chapter manage to explain less than half of the variation in R&D intensity in foreign subsidiaries in Sweden. On the whole, however, the analyses support the argument that the propensity to perform R&D in a foreign subsidiary increases with the subsidiary's age and size, and that R&D intensity is associated with its role in the international organization of production imposed by the parent corporation. Although R&D intensities vary primarily according to industry, organizationally autonomous subsidiaries producing for export tend to perform significantly more R&D than do more tightly integrated subsidiaries oriented toward the local market.

However, the validity of the analysis presented here is impaired by the fact that no consideration is given to the nature and characteristics of the multinational organizations of which the studied subsidiaries are part. As indicated in a parallel study, corporate characteristics (size, degree of internationalization, diversification, etc.) significantly affect the share of R&D resources allocated abroad and the manner in which multinationals coordinate and control their R&D activities (Håkanson, 1981). The latter area awaits further exploration before any attempt can be made to assess the effects of multinational control and exploitation of technological change.

NOTES

1. See Håkanson (1980). The study was done at the Institute of International Business at the Stockholm School of Economics on behalf of the National Swedish Board of Industry.
2. In all industries for which comparable data could be obtained, average R&D intensities were higher in the domestic than in the foreign-owned firms. In 1977, the only exception was in the food industry (cf. SIND 1977).

3. The data are protected by law, and the right to use the material had to be granted by each individual firm. Permission was granted in all but one case, a company that in 1977 had passed into Swedish ownership. However, for 37 smaller firms (23 percent of the population by numbers), no data were available in the archives of the Central Bureau of Statistics.
4. For details, see Håkanson (1980:225ff).
5. Signifiance was computed using the Welch approximative *t*-test, with a required level of significance of 5 percent.

REFERENCES

Bradbury, F. R. "Technology Transfer," In F. Bradbury *Transfer Processes in Technical Change*, edited by F. Bradbury et al., pp. 107-118. Alphen aan den Rijn: Sijthoff & Noordhoff, 1978.

Caves, R. E. "International Corporations: The Industrial Economics of Foreign Investment." *Economica* (new series) 38 (1971):1-27.

Cordell, A. J., "The Multinational Firm, Foreign Direct Investment, and Canadian Science Policy," *Science Council of Canada, Special Study*, No. 22, December 1971.

Cordell, A. J. "Innovation, the Multinational Corporation: Some Policy Implications for National Science Policy," *Long Range Planning* 6, 3 (1973):22-29.

Creamer, D. *Overseas Research and Development by United States Multinationals 1966-1975: Estimates of Expenditures and a Statistical Profile*. New York: The National Conference Board, 1976.

Ducot, C. "The Laboratoires d'Electronique et de Physique Appliquée at Limeil-Brévannes near Paris: Origin—function—Activities." *Philips Technique Review* 30, 8/9/10 (1969):213-224.

Fischer, W. A., and Behrman, J. N. "The Coordination of Foreign R&D Activities by Transnational Corporations." *Journal of International Business Studies* 10, 3 (1979):29-35.

Granstrand, O., and Fernlund, I. "Coordination of Multinational R&D: A Swedish Case Study," *R&D Management* 9, 1 (1978):1-7.

Hanson, W. T., and Van Rumker, R. "Multinational R&D in Practice: Two Case Studies," *Research Management* 14, 1 (1971):17 51.

Hartmann, W. E., and Stock, W. *Management von Forschung und Entwicklung*. Berlin: Akademie-Verlag, 1976.

Hymer, S. H. *The International Operations of National Firms: A Study of Direct Foreign Investment*, 2nd ed. Cambridge, Mass.: MIT Press, 1976.

Håkanson, L. *Multinationella företag: FoU-verksamhet, teknik-överföring och företagstillväxt. En studie av svenska storföretag och utlandsägda företag i Sverige*. Stockholm: Statens Industriverk 1980:4, Liber förlag.

———. "Organization and Evolution of Foreign R&D in Swedish Multinationals." *Geografiska Annaler* 63 *B*:47-56.

Malecki, E. J. "Corporate Organization of R and D and the Location of Technological Activities." *Regional Studies* 14, 3 (1980):219-234.

Mansfield, E. "Technology and Technological Change," In *Economic Analysis and the Multinational Enterprise*, edited by J. H. Dunning, pp. 147-183. London: George Allen & Unwin, 1974.

OECD. *Trends in Industrial R&D in Selected OECD Member Countries 1967-1975*. Paris: Organization for Economic Cooperation and Development, 1979.

Papo, M. "How to Establish and Operate Multinational Labs." *Research Management* 14, 1 (1971):12-19.

Pavitt, K. "The Multinational Enterprise and the Transfer of Technology." In *The Multinational Enterprise*, edited by J. H. Dunning, pp. 61-85. London: George Allen & Unwin, 1971.

Potter, B. V. "Effective Information and Technology Transfer in Multinational R&D." *Research Management* 14, 1 (1971):20-27.

Quinn, J. B. "Technology Transfer by Multinational Companies." *Harvard Business Review* 47 (November-December):147-161.

Ronstadt, R. C. *Research and Development Abroad by US Multinationals*. New York: Praeger, 1977.

——. "International R&D: The Establishment and Evolution of Research and Development Abroad by Seven US Multinationals." *Journal of International Business Studies* 9, 1 (1978):7-24.

Samuelsson, H. F. *Utländska direkta investeringar i Sverige. En ekonometrisk analys av bestämningsfaktorerna*. Stockholm: Industriens Utredningsinstitut, Almqvist & Wiksell International, 1977.

SCB "Industrier med stor verksamhet i utlandet 1975." *Statistiska meddelanden*, Ser. F (1977):10.

——. "Forskningsstatistik 1977-1979. Teknisk och naturvetenskaplig forskning och utveckling inom industri, myndigheter, institut, organisationer och fonder," *Statistiska meddelanden*, Ser. U (1979):25.

——. "Svenska internationella företag." *Statistiska meddelanden*, Ser. F (1980):2.

Schwetlick, W. Forschung und Entwicklung in der *Organisation industrieller Unternehmen*. Berlin: Erich Schmidt-Verlag, 1973.

SIND. *Multinationella företag i svensk livsmedelsindustri*. Stockholm: Statens industriverk (SIND 1977:10), Liber Förlag.

Terpstra, V. "International Product Policy: The Role of Foreign R&D." *Columbia Journal of World Business* 12, 4 (1977):24-32.

Trier, P. F. "The Mullard Research Laboratories: An Outline of their Growth and Function." *Philips Technical Review* 28, 5/6/7 (1967): 129-135.

Vernon, R. "The Location of Economic Activity." In *Economic Analysis and the Multinational Enterprise*, edited by J. H. Dunning, pp. 89-114. London: George Allen & Unwin, 1974.

Chapter 8

Responses to Government Industrial Research Policy: A Comparison of Foreign-Owned and Canadian-Owned Firms

Daniel A. Ondrack *

Considerable research in Canada in recent years has been concerned with the relatively poor performance of Canadian industry in terms of industrial innovation, export sales, and secondary manufacturing in general. It would be impossible to cite all of the individual studies but recently major reviews of the situation have been conducted by several government task forces (The Watkins Report, 1968; The Gray Report, 1972; The Select Committee on Economic and Cultural Nationalism, 1974; and the Science Council of Canada, 1971). Two basic conclusions are that the comparative performance of Canadian industry is poor and that Canadian industry is unusually high in foreign ownership compared to other Western industrialized nations. Naturally, there is considerable interest in the possibility of linkages between the degree of foreign ownership and the industrial performance record in Canada.

One area of particular concern in Canadian industrial performance has been the record in industrial innovation and more specifically in industrial R&D (Bourgault, 1972; Cordell, 1971; Dickersen, 1978). The evidence of a relationship between the degree of foreign ownership and the degree of R&D spending in Canada has been mixed. A study by Safarian (1969) showed no statistically significant dif-

*Associate Professor, Faculty of Management Studies, University of Toronto.

ferences between the R&D expenditures of foreign-owned and Canadian-owned firms, but Safarian's study did not distinguish between firms in different industries. A later study by Globerman (1973) looked at differences between industries and found an industry effect between the R&D of foreign-owned and Canadian-owned firms. Globerman's conclusion was that public policies to stimulate increased industrial research must be industry-specific.

A detailed examination of the role of R&D activities in foreign-owned subsidiaries was made by Cordell (1971) to see whether the dollars spent on R&D by foreign-owned firms in Canada were used in the same ways as dollars spent by domestic firms. The following is a summary of Cordell's findings.

First, a multinational firm will seek to centralize control of the R&D program to develop an international research capability with laboratories operating around the world that respond to, and feed information to, centralized laboratories. Host country research operations may be undertaken for a wide variety of reasons; to take advantage of local skills, to obtain access to lower costs, to establish listening posts, and to transfer technology to local operations. Two general types of R&D operations seemed to be predominant in Canada, the *interdependent laboratory* and the *local support* laboratory. Similar typologies of R&D units were also developed by Ronstadt (1978).

An interdependent laboratory may be one of many laboratories scattered around the world that mainly conducts research and has little to do with local development. It is closely connected to the firm's international research program, may be directly supervised by the international head office, and may have little interaction with local manufacturing operations. On the other hand, a local support laboratory mainly acts as a technical service center to examine why a product may fail to operate in the Canadian market, to help adapt a product to the Canadian market, to translate foreign technology to local specifications, and to scale down production technology and engineering to shorter runs for the Canadian market. (This is the same as Ronstadt's technology transfer unit—TTU).

The critical aspect of the international interdependent laboratory is that while it is physically in Canada and may even be located adjacent to a subsidiary plant site, there may be little interaction between R&D personnel and local plant management and production (Globerman, 1973). The research performed may have little to do with new product innovation in Canada and often is very specialized, or confined to a specific stage of the R&D process. Innovation capability may be increased for the firm as a whole, but not directly for the Canadian economy, as any innovations that may occur are the property of the international head office (Britton, 1978; Quinn, 1969; Ronstadt 1978).

Local support or TTU research programs have little or no work allocated from world headquarters. The chief activities are adaptation and modifications of a product or process to Canadian conditions and transfer of production technology from the head office to the branch plant. Innovations here are generally confined to the successful introduction of a product into Canada that has been designed and successfully marketed elsewhere. While the difficulties and complexities involved in this type of innovation should not be underrated, it is not the same type of innovation as that required for new product development. If any of this latter type of innovation does occur in a local support laboratory, these innovations become the property of the international firm, subject to the decision of the international head office as to whether, and where, the innovation would be produced (Cordell, 1971).

Thus neither type of laboratory offers many opportunities for innovation in Canada (unless innovation is designated by the head office as part of the local role), and even if some innovations do occur, they do not necessarily result in any improvement in Canadian industrial production or exports. The situation can be summed up in another quote from Cordell's (1971) Science Council report: "In no case did we find a Canadian subsidiary that felt it had the freedom to enter foreign markets at will with a product which it thought it could be produced in Canada and competitively exported."

Studies by the National Industrial Conference Board (Duerr, 1970) and by Buckley and Pearce (1979) on the R&D activites of major multinational firms confirm most of the findings of Cordell. The tendency is for MNCs to centralize control of R&D, frequently in the United States, and to delegate lesser R&D roles to their foreign subsidiaries such as in the transfer of technology and the modification of products to suit local needs. The general conclusion that can be drawn is that the high degree of foreign ownership and control of the key industrial sectors of the economy and Canada's poor R&D performance must be seen as related.

The greatest potential for R&D jobs and for innovation in Canada, then, probably lies with indigenous, domestically controlled industry or with foreign-owned subsidiaries with considerable autonomy in R&D operations or indigenous technology units (ITU) (Ronstadt, 1978). However, the R&D performance of indigenous firms in Canada has not been particularly impressive so far, and this poor performance has been attributed by the Science Council to the generally smaller size of such firms and the fragmented Canadian market. Subsidiaries with highly autonomous or ITU research and development capabilities could offer considerable opportunities for R&D employment and for innovation, but future growth of such opportunities is tied to the willingness of foreign head offices to allow greater autonomy in host country subsidiaries.

THE POLICY SITUATION
IN PERSPECTIVE

Since the main issue is now fairly clear, what are the policy options to deal with it? The two main options most frequently discussed (Fayerweather, 1974; Britton, 1978) are:

1. Changing the basic pattern of distribution of government financial support for R&D programs; instead of the broad program of contributions to all sorts of R&D development in many industries, some current proposals run in the direction of deliberately aimed support for stronger efforts in specific industry sectors. The idea would be to identify particularly promising areas of industrial development and invest a greater part of government aid for R&D in major efforts to push these product areas.

2. Not only must support be more selective in terms of industry sector but it should also be aimed at Canadian-owned and -controlled firms in order to stimulate the development of domestic R&D operations. Support could also be given to foreign subsidiaries, but only to those with unusual R&D autonmy (McFetridge 1977)

In the face of these options it would be tempting for government policy in Canada to try both to reduce the degree of foreign ownership of industry and to try to encourage the development of R&D among the few remaining domestically controlled firms. An attempt at the first policy was made, arising from recommendations of the Gray Report (1972) on foreign ownership in Canada. This resulted in the creation of the Foreign Investment Review Agency (FIRA), which must review all applications for the foreign takeover of domestic firms and judge such applications on the basis of significant benefit to Canada (i.e., impact on domestic employment, secondary processing, level of exports, R&D, etc). The effect of this policy has not been to repatriate ownership of Canadian industry, but instead to reduce the rate of new takeovers and modify some of the terms of agreement.

In encouraging the development of R&D among firms in Canada, recent government policy has been twofold:

1. There is no discrimination in aid between foreign-owned and domestically owned firms.
2. A series of incentive programs to try to raise the overall level of industrial R&D to 1.5 percent of the Canadian GNP have been initiated.

About the time the federal government R&D incentive programs were introduced (1973), 56 percent of industrial research was done by foreign-owned firms and 44 percent by domestically owned firms. Total R&D at that time amounted to about 0.9 percent of GNP. The types of government incentive programs launched at that time were as follows (Mayer and Flynn (1973):

1. Industrial Research and Development Incentives Act (IRDIA)— a company could apply for a tax-free grant amounting to 25 percent of the capital cost of research and development done in Canada on a product, *provided* that the resultant products could be marketed abroad.
2. Program for the Advancement of Industrial Technology (PAIT) —any firm that had specialized knowledge in one area of technology and that could visualize strong commercial possibilities in the development of *cost-saving production processes* could apply for a cash grant of up to 50 percent of the development costs.
3. Industrial Design Assistance Program (IDAP)—any improvement in design quality that would enhance a firm's *competitive position abroad* was eligible for a grant of up to 50 percent of the design and administrative costs of the design program. The company had to design and produce the product in Canada and market it abroad within an agreed-upon time.
4. General Adjustment Assistance Program (GAAP), Building Equipment Accessories and Materials Program (BEAM), and Program to Enhance Productivity (PEP)—these programs were all designed to aid firms in seeking export sales and had little to do with encouraging R&D. Counseling Assistance to Small Enterprises (CASE) was oriented to the export problems of small business and had no provision for R&D.

From 1973 to 1978, the number of government aid and incentive programs increased in two directions: aid to R&D activities and aid to export activities. Additional government–industry–union task forces continued to study the dual problem of inadequate R&D and exports (Action for Industrial Growth, 1978; Action for Industrial Growth, 1979; Ontario Government Response, 1980), which culminated in an elaborate series of programs and policies to aid and encourage industrial R&D in Canada (see Appendix 8.1 for a complete list). Yet despite this proliferation of incentive programs, the national statistics bureau (STATSCAN) reported in 1979 that most developed nations, with the exception of Italy, spend more on industrial research than Canada and that Canada's total R&D expenditure still remained at about 0.9 percent of GNP. According to 1977 OECD data, less than 0.6 percent of industrial expenditures in Canada were for the research and development of new products and services compared to 1.9 percent for the United States, 1.29 percent for Sweden, and 1.35 percent for France. However, one change that did occur was that, by 1977, 56 percent of industrial research was done by Canadian-owned firms and 44 percent by foreign-owned firms, thus reversing the 1973 figures. The target of increasing R&D expenditures to 1.5 percent of GNP was still felt to be five years away when the Statscan report was published (1979).

Thus despite the array of government incentives offered to encourage growth in industrial R&D, Canadian industry as a whole failed to respond as actively or aggressively as had been desired. Foreign-owned firms' R&D in Canada even appeared to decline over this period relative to Canadian-owned firms.

INCENTIVE PROGRAMS

The experience of other nations with the use of incentives for increased R&D, import substitution, and exports has been mixed, with incentive programs being perceived by MNCs as "legal barriers" to freedom in business activities (Root and Ahmed, 1978). Dealing with foreign government bureaucracy is ranked as a high priority problem for MNCs (Ricks and Czinkota, 1979) and it is understandable that firms would want to minimize involvement in government regulation wherever possible. More importantly, MNCs make R&D investment decisions as part of the larger strategic management of the firm's operations. For example, Ronstadt concluded that foreign-based R&D "made U.S. multinationals more competitive in foreign and U.S. markets than they would have been if they had performed R&D only in the United States" (178, p. 23). Despite this fact, "the data suggest that foreign policy makers will be unable to attract investments in R&D unless good economic reasons exist for the investment." Thus a positive investment climate for the MNC's operations in general is seen as having more of an impact on the R&D investment decision than a series of specific R&D incentives (Root and Ahmed, 1979).

Consequently, there is considerable precedent in prior research and theory about MNC investment behavior to account for the apparent lukewarm response by MNCs to government incentive programs to encouarge greater industrial R&D and export activity in Canada.

THE STUDY

For more detailed information as to why this phenomenon occurred, a study was done on the machinery industry in Canada over the period of 1975-1979. The machinery industry was chosen because it is widely spread across Canada, it is a secondary manufacturing industry, it has a high potential for exports, and it is closely dependent on R&D and innovations for competitiveness. Moreover, the industry was identified by the Canadian Department of Industry, Trade, and Commerce as one of the high priority industries in Canada for development of a strategy for industrial growth (Mallory, 1978). The machinery industry has a fairly good R&D record as compared to other industrial sectors in Canada, accounting for 8 percent of total industrial R&D in Canada in 1977 as compared to 4 percent in 1967. In addition, R&D outlays by machinery firms have risen from an average of 1 percent of sales in 1965 to 1.5 percent of sales in 1975. Nevertheless, these expenditures are low when compared to U.S. machinery firms, which spend on the average of almost twice as much on R&D (Mallory, 1978).

A sample of 19 small- and medium-sized firms in the industry were originally surveyed in 1974-75 (Ondrack 1975). Interviews were conducted with senior executives and R&D personnel in 11 Canadian-owned firms and 8 foreign-owned subsidiaries. One of the objectives of the study was to assess the response of the firms to the R&D incentive programs at that time and to see how such programs fit into the firm's overall activities in R&D and innovation. A second study of the same firms was done in 1979 to follow up the progress of the firms over this period and to see if any changes had occurred in their responsiveness to the government incentive programs.

Table 8.1 shows some of the size characteristics of the sample from 1975-1979. It is apparent that a moderate trend toward growth in total sales and in total number of employees occurred for all types of firms. The samples of foreign-owned and Canadian-owned firms are approximately equivalent in terms of distribution over the size categories.

In order to analyze the behavior of the firms over the period studied, classification systems were developed in terms of autonomy of firms (or subsidiaries) and types of R&D activities. The classification system for autonomy has four categories that cover a continuum

Table 8.1. Size of Firms in Sample by Total Sales and Employees 1975–1979

| | Canadian Owned | | Foreign Owned | |
	(n = 11)		(n = 8)	
Total Sales	*1975*	*1979*	*1975*	*1979*
(in millions of $)				
Less than $10	7	6	4	1
10 – 20	1	–	2	2
20 – 30	1	2	1	2
30 – 50	2	1	1	1
50 +	0	2	0	2
Total Employees	*1975*	*1979*	*1975*	*1979*
100 – 200	5	5	2	1
200 – 300	3	2	3	1
300 – 400	1	0	2	4
400 – 500	1	1	0	0
500 +	1	3	1	2

ranging from "autonomous" to "integrated subsidiary." The classification system for R&D activity has four categories that cover a continuum ranging from "independent" to "dependent." These classifications necessarily involve a reduction of a series of complex relationships into a few global terms, but this degree of reduction was necessary for systematic analysis of behavior from essentially 19 case studies. A more detailed explanation of the classification system used is given in Appendix 8.2.

Table 8.2 shows the distribution of the sample over the typology of autonomy in 1975 and 1979. From the data in Table 8.2 it can be seen that by 1979 changes had taken place in the headquarters-subsidiary relationships in three Canadian and two foreign subsidiaries. Two Canadian subsidiaries changed from holding companies to profit center subsidiaries and one profit center changed to an integrated subsidiary. In all three cases the move is away from subsidiary autonomy toward greater involvement and control by headquarters. The reason for the shift was the same in all three cases: a falloff in

Table 8.2. Types of Autonomy and HQ–Subsidiary Relationships 1975–1979

		Autonomous Firm	*Holding Company Subsidiary*	*Profit Center Subsidiary*	*Integrated Subsidiary*
Canadian-owned firms	1975	5	3	3	0
	1979	5	1	4	1
Foreign-owned firms	1975	0	2	2	4
	1979	0	1	4	3

subsidiary performance, which resulted in headquarters asserting more control over subsidiary operations.

The changes in the status of the two foreign-owned subsidiaries followed different patterns and for quite different reasons. One subsidiary moved from a holding company to a profit center as part of the general strategy of headquarters to systematically acquire more control over the subsidiary and achieve a further integration of the subsidiary operations with global operations.

The second foreign-owned subsidiary had been an integrated subsidiary in 1975 but by 1979 had been reorganized into a profit center subsidiary. The reason for this change was that headquarters decided to create an international division to coordinate worldwide sales and to give some subsidiaries sole responsibility for the development and manufacture of some of the product lines. Eventually this subsidiary will have a "product mandate" for a certain sector of the total firm's product line with sole responsibility for R&D, manufacturing, and marketing. In Ronstadt's (1978) terms, the subsidiary will move from a technology transfer R&D unit (TTU), toward an indigenous technology R&D unit (ITU) as a result of the change in strategy at headquarters.

Table 8.3 shows the distribution of the firms over the four types of R&D activity. While one of the Canadian firms made a significant change in strategy from 1975 to 1979 for more commitment to independent R&D, otherwise a general pattern of retrenchment can be observed among the Canadian-owned firms. Firms that used to be active in R&D have now cut back to more conservative positions as a result of general economic setbacks. In contrast, some of the foreign-owned subsidiaries have actually moved to more aggressive types of R&D activity, which is in keeping with their moves to a more aggressive marketing strategy. It appears that certain Canadian-owned firms earlier took risks in trying to be aggressive in marketing and developing more self-reliance in R&D and then unfortunately suffered economic setbacks. The foreign-owned subsidiaries were more conservative in their operations at the onset of the study and

Table 8.3. R&D Activity in Firms from 1975–1979

| | | *Evolutionary* | | *or* | *Evolutionary* | |
		Independent	*Internal*		*External*	*Dependent*
Canadian-owned firms	1975	3	3		5	0
	1979	2	2		6	1
Foreign-owned firms	1975	1	1		2	4
	1979	2	2		1	3

did not seem to suffer the same sort of economic setbacks. Consequently, they are now in a good position to expand and be more aggressive while the domestic competition is in retreat.

Having examined the changes in sales, autonomy, and R&D of the firms over the study period, we are now in a position to examine the response of the firms to government R&D incentive programs. Data from the 1975 sample are examined first in Table 8.4.

From Table 8.4, it can be seen that a total of 9 out of the 19 firms had used or tried to use some of the R&D incentive programs up to 1975 and that most of these firms were Canadian owned (6 out of the 9). Thus there seems to be a strong relationship between foreign ownership and the lack of use of the R&D incentive programs. Of the 8 foreign-owned firms, only 3 used or tried the R&D incentive programs as compared to 6 out of the 11 Canadian-owned firms. Within the Canadian-owned subsample, principally the autonomous firms accounted for most of the usage of the R&D incentive programs. Thus subsidiaries in general, whether foreign or domestically owned, use the government incentive programs proportionately less than do autonomous firms.

From an examination of the detailed information in Appendix 8.3, a close relationship can be seen between R&D activity and use of the incentive programs, as 9 firms had R&D activities classified in independent or internal evolution and 8 out of these 9 firms used or tried incentive programs. Only one of the 6 firms with external evolution R&D activity used or tried an R&D incentive program and none of the firms with a dependent activity used or tried a program. Of the 9 firms that used or tried an R&D incentive program, 5 of them also used or tried some form of government program to aid export activity (ranging from assistance at trade missions to government agency financing or export sales). Only one firm in the sample used export aid programs and did not use or try an R&D incentive program.

Table 8.4. Response to Incentive Programs for R&D and Exports from 1975–1979 from 1975–1979[a]

		Used or Tried an R&D Program	Satisfied with R&D Program	Used or Tried an Export Program	Satisfied with Export Program
Canadian-owned firms	1975	6 yes, 5 no	1 yes, 5 no	4 yes, 7 no	2 yes, 2 no
(11)	1979	3 yes, 8 no	2 yes, 1 no	4 yes, 7 no	0 yes, 4 no
Foreign-owned firms	1975	3 yes, 5 no	0 yes, 3 no	2 yes, 6 no	1 yes, 1 no
(8)	1979	2 yes, 6 no	1 yes, 1 no	2 yes, 6 no	1 yes, 1 no

[a]Detailed information on individual firms from 1975–1979 is presented in Appendices 8.3 and 8.4.

Table 8.5. Usage of R&D Incentive Programs as a Function of Type of R&D
Activity and Type of Ownership

Type of R&D Activity	Tried or Used a Program	Type of Ownership	
		Canadian-owned	Foreign-owned
1. Independent or	Yes	5	3
internal evolution	No	1^a	—
2. External evolution	Yes	1^a	—
or dependent	No	4	5

^{a}Indicates an anomaly.

In summary, the two variables, type of R&D activity and type of ownership, account for the behavior patterns of 17 out of the 19 firms in the sample. Table 8.5 shows the distribution of the behavior of the firms according to these two variables for 1975.

The second feature of the 1975 data is the striking degree of dissatisfaction reported by firms that tried to use the R&D incentive programs, for 8 out of 9 users reported dissatisfaction. The reasons for this dissatisfaction are given in Table 8.6.

The most common problem was that the application processes were perceived as being too complex and too detailed. This feeling was especially true for smaller firms, which felt that the application process was beyond the capability or the patience of thinly stretched local management. The second major problem was that the government assessors were perceived as using inappropriately high scientific standards when assessing applications. While the terms of incentive programs such as PAIT and IRDIA seemed to be broad enough to allow for the kinds of projects submitted by the respondent firms, the assessors seemed to apply much more narrow frames of reference for what was appropriate for funding. After the investment of time and expense in preparing a demanding application, the experience of being rejected because a project was judged to be insufficiently sci-

Table 8.6. Reasons^a for Dissatisfaction with R&D Incentive Programs

Type of Firm	Unsuccessful Application	Too Science Restrictive	Provisions Too Limited	Applications Too Complicated
Canadian (6/11 users)	4	4	2	6
Foreign (3/8 users)	1	2	3	2
	5	6	6	8

^{a}Firms could cite more than one reason.

entific was very frustrating to the respondents. A third feature, particularly important to foreign-owned firms, was that the terms of some programs were too restrictive and therefore reduced the attractiveness of the program to MNCs. One provision was that developments that arose out of a sponsored program had to be produced and manufactured in Canada, which was seen as too limiting of the freedom of MNCs to allocate resources and operations to various parts of their international enterprise. In summary, despite the intentions of the R&D incentive programs, the administration of the programs was very discouraging to the firms that tried to use or had used the programs.

By 1979 the volume of programs offered (see Appendix 8.1) has increased tremendously, and ostensible efforts had been made to streamline the administration and to broaden the scope of various programs. Table 8.4 also shows the experience of firms from 1975 to 1979.

In the 1975 data 9 out of the 19 firms had tried or used R&D incentive programs and in 1979 this number had declined to a total of 5 firms. The decline in the number of firms using the incentive programs was actually greater when the behavior of individual firms is looked at in detail (see Appendix 8.4). Seven of the 9 original users dropped out but 3 additional firms began using programs by 1979, bringing the total up to 5. Of the 7 who dropped out, 2 no longer have R&D activity because of economic setbacks, while 5 continue to have R&D but do not bother with government incentive programs. Of the 3 firms added to the list of users, all started new R&D activities over the period of 1975–1979 due to changes in strategy of the firm. Only one of them actually tried to apply for formal R&D incentive programs, the remaining firms simply use the special R&D tax writeoffs available as part of the programs described in Appendix 8.1. Obviously, the 5 firms that have ceased to apply for R&D incentive programs and who have continued R&D activity also take full advantage of the tax writeoff provisions. Any firm that has R&D activity can take advantage of these provisions, and in two cases of foreign-owned firms, the tax writeoffs were a sufficient incentive to establish R&D activity in Canada where none had existed previously.

The high dropout rate from the R&D incentive programs suggests that the level of dissatisfaction observed in 1975 was sufficient to cause existing and potential users to abandon the programs and switch to self-reliant R&D activity. The tax writeoff provisions give support to firms willing to undertake the expense of R&D but is less of an incentive for firms not yet in R&D. The great attraction of income tax provisions as compared ot the R&D incentive program is vastly reduced paperwork, fewer problems of eligibility assessment, and fewer restrictions on the freedom of firms to make resource and operations allocation decisions, whether they are foreign or domestically owned firms.

CONCLUSION

A foreign-ownership effect on whether firms pursue R&D activities in Canada was found to the extent that integrated subsidiaries performed virtually no R&D in Canada. Obviously, such firms could not respond to federal programs with R&D or innvoation incentives unelss the incentive was large enough to cause the MNC headquarters to change its strategy toward the subsidiary. This is not likely to be the case, as has deen demonstrated by Ronstadt (1978). However, the R&D operations of an MNC may evolve over time from a technology transfer unit (TTU) to an indigenous technology unit (ITU) given appropriate market conditions in the host country. Ronstadt suggests that R&D incentives may have an effect if local subsidiary management is already trying to convince headquarters to authorize a shift from a TTU to an ITU and the local R&D incentives program may tip the balance in favor of such a decision. In such a circumstance, the subsidiary would likely no longer be an integrated subsidiary and would be of some other type. However, other types of foreign-owned subsidiaries (holding company, profit center) in this study had considerable autonomy and some chose to have R&D and others did not. Relatively autonomous subsidiaries could be in a position to respond positively to government incentive programs without conflicting with headquarters, although some degree of a foreign-ownership effect was still observed when headquarters policy was to avoid participation in government programs that place restrictions on the freedom of a firm to transfer technology or resources freely.

Among the Canadian-owned firms, the most active users of the incentive programs were autonomous firms and some holding company subsidiaries. It is understandable that autonomous firms would be active, as they generally need to be innovative to survive whereas a subsidiary can often afford to rely on the R&D capability of the parent firm. However, only two of the autonomous firms remained program users in 1979; the others chose to rely on the tax measures instead of putting up with the frustrations associated with the incentive programs.

As discussed earlier in this chapter, the experience with tax incentives for MNC investment in host countries has not been encouraging (Jolly, 1979; Rabino, 1980). At most, "competitive tax incentives would appear to be necessary, but not sufficient to attract foreign investment" (Root and Ahmed, 1978, p. 87). Furthermore, McFetridge (1977) has cautioned that in attempting to assess the impact of subsidies and tax incentives for R&D, it is necessary to distinguish between MNC R&D expenditures that would have occurred anyway and R&D that would otherwise not have been undertaken. For projects that would have been undertaken anyway, the effect of a tax incentive (or any other subsidy) is to substitute host country public funds for private MNC funds. Only if a subsidy is awarded to a project that would otherwise not have been undertaken is there an actual increase in value of resources devoted to R&D.

In summary, while a foreign-ownership effect can be observed in Canada that acts to limit activity in R&D (and presumably in innovation), the chief culprit in the lack of response to the government programs to aid and increase R&D activity has been the programs themselves. The complexities of the application procedures, the apparently inappropriate scientific evaluation criteria, and the restrictions associated with the programs have served to deter Canadian-owned and foreign-owned firms equally. A much more positive response seems to have been obtained from the use of increased and special tax write offs for R&D activities, which constitute only 3 out of the 27 items for R&D listed in Appendix 8.1. Of course not all of the items would be applicable to firms in this industry, and some of the programs are still too new to have had a fair trial.

Thus while one might still recommend the continuance of some special assistance programs for Canadian-owned firms, tax measures, despite their limitations, seem in the long run to be a more effective means of public policy for increasing the level of industrial R&D in Canada.

Appendix 8.1. Summary: Research, Innovation and Product Development

Program or Service	Purpose and Description	Form of Assistance
Information and Services		
National Research Council (NRC)	Assists and advises business on technological and scientific problems; also provides testing and research facilities.	Assistance is on request basis for problems in which NRC has expertise.
Technical Information Service (TIS)	Provides in-plant technological assistance and information services.	In-plant studies and advice.
Canadian Institute for Scientific and Technical Information (CISTI)	Collects scientific information and makes it available at minimal cost for specific requirements.	Tailored research reports available to individual firms.
Patent Office	Provides 17 years patents for new inventions (products and processes), and public disclosure of inventions and patentees.	Patents granted; new patents published; copies of new patents available.
Canadian Patents and Development Limited (CPDL)	Makes available to industry research findings, from government and nonprofit organizations, through patent licensing and other product development services.	Arranges licenses between inventor and user; assesses invention marketability and recommends further development. Supports Inventors' Assistance Program. Maintains an inventory of available inventions and government technology.
Trade Marks	Administration of Trade Marks Act, which gives owner of a registered trade mark 15 years exclusive right (renewable).	Trade Marks Office grants trade mark, maintains public record.
Registered Industrial Design	Administration of Industrial Design Act, which gives owner of registered industrial design 5 year exclusive right (renewable).	Industrial Design Office grants registration, maintains public record.
Support for Industrial Research, Innovation, and Product Development		
Industrial Research Assistance Program (IRAP) and Mini-IRAP Program	Aids industrial research in Canada and finances projects with high technological and economic payoff. IRAP supports in-house projects, and Mini-IRAP supports projects for smaller companies undertaken in research organizations.	Pays salaries, involving about 50% of research project costs.

Appendix 8.1. Summary: Research, Innovation and Product Development *(cont.)*

Program or Service	Purpose and Description	Form of Assistance
Scientific and Technical Employment Program (STEP) (also STEPEX)	STEP subsidizes hiring of unemployed scientists, engineers and technicians for new and significant initiatives. STEPEX subsidizes unemployed research staff hired by universities and research institutes for projects requested by private sector firms.	Subsidy per scientist, engineer or technician hired on approved projects for one year.
Industrial Post-Doctoral Fellowships	Subsidize costs of employing graduates in industrial research.	Subsidy of $13,000 plus travel costs for one year.
Industrial Energy Research and Development Program (IERD)	Encourages research on products and processes which reduce energy consumption.	Grants of up to 50% of project costs.
Enterprise Development Program (EDP)	Assists with product development costs, including high risk innovative projects, proposal preparation, and industrial design.	Grants of up to 75% of costs.
Design Canada	Encourages better Canadian design and product development.	Financial incentives, management training, technical advisory assistance, information seminars, and encouragement of design professions.
Standards Council of Canada	Promotes standardization.	Advice; contributions to organizations.
Defense Industry Productivity Program (DIP)	Sustains and develops technological capability for defense or civil export sales arising from defense production capability.	Grants of up to 50%, and loans, for development projects, financing of approved capital equipment.
Program of Assistance to Solar Equipment Manufacturers	Stimulates design, development and manufacture of solar equipment and systems.	Proposal and development contracts.
Canada–Saskatchewan Heavy Oil Development Agreement	To develop enhanced methods of recovering heavy oil.	Grants of up to 50% of capital costs of projects.
Fashion Design Assistance Program (FDAP)	To strengthen Canadian fashion design capabilities and promote Canadian fashion design.	Internships, training-in-industry experience, grants for special courses, promotions.
Tax Measures: —Immediate Write-Offs	Immediate 100% writeoff of current and capital expenses for R&D.	Expenses can be fully written off in year incurred.

Appendix 8.1. Summary: Research, Innovation and Product Development *(cont.)*

Program or Service	Purpose and Description	Form of Assistance
—Special Deduction for Increased R&D	Additional income deduction for companies which are increasing Canadian R&D efforts.	Deduction of 50% of increase over previous 4 year average, allowed until 1988.
—Investment Tax Credit	Deduction from corporate taxes for qualifying current and capital R&D expenditures.	10% or 20% tax credit; 25% for R&D by small Canadian private business corporations.

Industrial Research Facilities

Industrial Research Institute Program (IRIP)	University research institutes provide research services for industry.	Firms contract with the university on cost-recovery basis.
Centres for Advanced Technology	Provide advanced technology research capability for industry use.	Firms contract with the center on cost-recovery basis.
Industrial Research Associations	Provide research capability in specific fields (presently in welding, gas and sulphur industries).	Firms contract with the association on cost-recovery basis.
Rapeseed Utilization Assistance Program (RUAP)	Research and development for improving manufacture of rapeseed products.	Grants to Rapeseed Association of Canada, which funds research in universities and institutes.
Protein, Oil and Starch (POS) Pilot Plant Corporation	Develops technology for processing grains and oilseeds.	Offers facilities for development work.

Government Research and Technology Transfer

Contracting-out	Encourages private sector research for government requirements.	Department of Supply and Services manages contracting system and maintains lists of potential contractors.
Unsolicited Proposals Program	Funds research proposals developed independently by private sector, which further government research objectives.	Proposals are reviewed and may be funded initially by DDS for a sponsoring department.
Program for Industry/ Laboratory Projects (PILP)	Promotes transfer to industry of NRC research results, and development of their commercial potential.	Financial and other assistance, up to full underwriting of company's project/product development costs.
Cooperative Projects with Industry (COPI)	Extends PILP to Departments of Agriculture; Energy, Mines and Resources; Environment; Fisheries and Oceans; and Communications.	Financial and other assistance, up to full underwriting of company's project/product development costs.

Appendix 8.1. Summary: Research, Innovation and Product Development *(cont.)*

Program or Service	Purpose and Description	Form of Assistance
Project Research Applicable in Industry	Support to universities to encourage commercial exploitation of university research.	Grants.
Strategic Grants in Aid of Research	Support to universities for research in areas of national concern (e.g., energy, environment).	Grants.

Source: ABC—Assistance to Business in Canada. Ottawa, Board of Economic Development Ministers, 1979.

Appendix 8.2

Classifications of Autonomy and R&D Activity

a. *Autonomous firm*—where the firm has its own board of directors, has responsibility for arranging its own financing, and may issue publicly traded voting shares in Canada. Such a firm may also be controlled by a parent which owns a majority or a controlling minority position in the common stock but treats the holding as a portfolio investment. Headquarters normally makes no attempt in such cases to try to manage the subsidiary or to integrate the operations of the subsidiary with other subsidiaries. Instead the typical action of headquarters is to buy and sell such holdings as part of the management of its portfolio of investments. There were five Canadian-owned firms in this category and no foreign-owned firms.

b. *Holding Company subsidiary*—in this case the degree of HQ involvement in the subsidiary is a bit closer and there is a longer term interest in the performance of the subsidiary and in holding control of the subsidiary. The subsidiary normally operates in a highly autonomous manner but reports to a headquarters board or executive. Usually, such subsidiaries report only financial plans and results on an annual basis and operational plans are generally left to the responsibility of subsidiary management. HQ usually owns complete control of the subsidiary and financing is generally arranged through HQ. The subsidiary is generally responsible for determining product lines and markets as there is little or no attempt to integrate operations between subsidiaries. There were four Canadian-owned and two foreign-owned firms in this category.

c. *Profit Center subsidiary*—in this case, the subsidiary must submit detailed annual budgets and operations forecasts for approval to HQ and is free to operate within the designated limits of approved plans and budgets. HQ often determines the product lines and types of markets of the subsidiary and the subsidiary can only change these by negotiation with HQ. However, once an agreement has been negotiated, the subsidiary is then generally free to manage its own affairs as long as it stays out of trouble and delivers on the promises of its plan. HQ may try to encourage some form of integration between subsidiaries but many are left with the freedom to seek out the lowest prices for supplies or components and are not bound to purchase from or sell to a sister firm if the price is not competitive. There are two Canadian-owned and two foreign-owned firms in this category.

d. *Integrated subsidiary*—in this case the subsidiary is closely under the direction of HQ and is responsible for local administration and fulfilling the directives issued by HQ. Such a subsidiary usually operates as part of an integrated network of operations between a series of subsidiary sister firms, with considerable transfer of products from one subsidiary to another. One form of an integrated subsidiary may be simply as assembly plant with very few managerial functions in the subsidiary except those necessary for administering the assembly process. Another form may be simply a sales outlet handling an established line of products but with no local R&D, manufacturing or product development. An integrated subsidiary may be used when an MNC first enters a foreign market and needs to limit risk and closely control the local operations (Bilkey, 1978). However, an integrated subsidiary can also be used when an MNC has adopted a globally integrated production and marketing strategy and various subsidiary operations must be highly streamlined and integrated to achieve global economies of scale (Richman 1972). There were no Canadian-owned and four foreign-owned firms in this category.

R&D Activity.   Four types of R&D behavior were developed to describe a continuum of R&D activity from very conservative to highly committed. Extensive discussion of the differences in the four types of R&D behavior has been presented in the earlier report of this industry (Ondrack 1975), so only very brief definitions will be used here.

a. *Dependent*—almost complete reliance by the subsidiary on the parent firm for R&D.

b. *External/evolutionary*—basically a reliance on external sources of R&D (parent, competitor, customers, etc.), but over time the subsidiary or firm adds local modifications and improvements to its product lines so that eventually local expertise is developed.

c. *Internal/evolutionary*—a progression from (b) above to the point where the local subsidiary or firm expertise is quite advanced and there may even be some local investments in R&D equipment and personnel.

d. *Independent*—a progression from (c) above to the point where subsidiary or firm R&D largely is self-reliant and the local organization has considerable investment in R&D. A firm at this stage of commitment to R&D could still utilize any of the earlier strategies along with the independent strategy.

Appendix 8.3. Use of Incentive Programs for R&D (1975)

Firm	Autonomy	R&D Activity	Used or Tried R&D Program	Satisfied with R&D Program	Used Export Programs	Satisfied with Export Program
Canadian owned						
1.	Autonomous	Independent	Yes	No (PAIT)	Yes	Yes
2.	Autonomous	Internal evolution	Yes	No (PAIT)	No	—
3.	Autonomous	External evolution	Yes	Yes (IRDIA)	Yes	Yes
4.	Autonomous	External evolution	No	—	No	—
5.	Autonomous	Internal evolution	Yes	No (IRDIA)	No	—
6.	Holding company	Independent	Yes	No (PAIT)	Yes	No
7.	Holding company	Independent	Yes	No (IRDIA)	Yes	Yes
8.	Profit center	External evolution	No	—	No	—
9.	Holding company	External evolution	No	—	No	—
10.	Holding company	External evolution	No	—	No	—
11.	Profit center	Internal evolution	No	—	No	—
Foreign owned						
1.	Profit center	Independent	Yes	No (PAIT) (IRDIA)	Yes	No
2.	Holding company	Internal evolution	Yes	No (PAIT)	No	—
3.	Holding company	Internal evolution	Yes	No (IRDIA)	No	—
4.	Profit center	External evolution	No	—	Yes	Yes
5.	Integrated	Dependent	No	—	No	—
6.	Integrated	Dependent	No	—	No	—
7.	Integrated	Dependent	No	—	No	—
8.	Integrated	Dependent	No	—	No	—

Appendix 8.4. Use of Incentive Programs for R&D (1979)

Type of firm	Used or Tried 1975	Major Change Since 1975	Used or Tried 1979	Satisfied with R&D Program	Used or Tried Export Program	Satisfied with Export Program
Canadian						
1.	Yes	No	No	—	Yes	No (too complicated)
2.	Yes	No	No	(No R&D)	No	—
3.	Yes	No	Yes	Yes	Yes	No (foreign banks easier or cheaper)
4.	No	Yes[a]	Yes	No (New R&D)	Yes	No (foreign finance cheaper)
5.	Yes	No	No	—	No	—
6.	Yes	No	No	—	Yes	No (foreign finance cheaper)
7.	Yes	Yes[b]	No	(No R&D)	No	—
8.	No	No	No	Yes	No	—
9.	No	No	Yes[d]	(New R&D)	No	—
10.	No	No[b]	No	—	No	—
11.	No	Yes[b]	No	—	No	—

Appendix 8.4. (cont.)

Type of firm	Used or Tried 1975	Major Change Since 1975	Used or Tried 1979	Satisfied with R&D Program	Used or Tried Export Program	Satisfied with Export Program
Foreign						
1.	Yes	No	Yes	No	Yes	No (too complicated)
2.	Yes	Yes[c]	No	—	—	(HQ policy avoid restrictions)
3.	Yes	No	No	—	No	(HQ policy is to avoid restrictions)
4.	No	Yes[c]	No[d]	—	Yes	Yes
5.	No	Yes[c]	Yes[d]	Yes (New R&D)	No	(HQ policy is to avoid restrictions)
6.	No	No	No	—	—	(HQ policy)
7.	No	No	No	—	—	(HQ policy)
8.	No	No	No	—	—	(HQ policy)

[a]Change of ownership imposed change of strategy.
[b]Economic losses forced change of strategy.
[c]Reorganization by MNC HQ imposed change of strategy.
[d]Use of tax writeoffs only.

REFERENCES

Action for Industrial Growth: A First Response. Ottawa: Department of Industry, Trade and Commerce, November 1978.

Action for Industrial Growth: Continuing the Dialogue. Ottawa: Board of Economic Development Ministers, February 1979.

Bilkey, W. J. "An Attempted Integration of the Literature on the Export Behavior of Firms." *Journal of International Business Studies* 9, 1 (1978):33-46.

Board of Economic Development Ministers. *ABC: Assistance to Business in Canada.* Ottawa: Ministry of Supply and Services, 1979.

Bourgault, P. L. *Innovation of the Structure of Canadian Industry.* Ottawa: Science Council of Canada, Special Study No. 23, 1972.

Britton, J. N.; Gilmour, J. M.; and Murphy, M. G. *The Weakest Link: A Technological Perspective on Canadian Industrial Underdevelopment.* Ottawa: Science Council of Canada, 1978.

Buckley, P. J., the Pearce, R. D. "Overseas Production and Exporting by the World's Largest Enterprises: A study in Sourcing Policy." *Journal of International Business Studies* 10, 1 (1979):9-20.

Cordell, A. J., *The Multinational Firm, Foreign Direct Investment, and Canadian Science Policy.* Ottawa: Science Council of Canada, December 1971.

Dickerson, R. W., and Nadeau, P. A. *Report of the Royal Commission on Corporate Concentration.* Ottawa: Ministry of Supply and Services, 1978.

Doz, Y. L., and Prahalad, C. K. "How MNCs Cope with Host Government Intervention," *Harvard Business Review* 58, 2 (March-April 1980):149-157.

Duerr, M. G. *R&D in the Multinational Company: A Survey.* Montreal: National Industrial Conference Board, 1970.

Duerr, M. G. and Roach, J. M. *Organization and Control of International Operations.* Ottawa: The Conference Board in Canada, 1973.

Globerman, S. "Market Structure and R&D in Canadian Manufacturing Industries." *Quarterly Review of Economics and Business* 13, 2 (Summer 1973): 59-67.

The Gray Report. *Foreign Direct Investment in Canada.* Ottawa: Queen's Printer, 1972.

Jolly, V. K. "Transformation Regimes and Global Sourcing by Multinational Companies: The Case of India." In *Recent Research on the Internationalization of Business,* edited by L. G. Mattsson and F. Widersheim-Paul, pp. 36-54. Uppsala: Uppsala University, 1979.

Kates, Peat Marwick & Co. *Overview Report: Foreign Ownership, Corporate Behavior and Public Attitudes.* Toronto: Province of Ontario Select Committee on Economic and Cultural Nationalism, 1974.

Litvak, I. A., and Banting, P. M. "A Conceptual Framework for International Business Arrangements." In *Multinational Business Operations: Long Range Planning, Organization and Management,* edited by S. P. Sethi and J. N. Sheth. Pacific Palisades, Calif.: Goodyear Publishing Co., 1973.

Mallory, W. L. *Report by the Task Force on the Canadian Machinery Industry.* Ottawa: Department of Industry, Trade and Commerce, June 1978.

Mayer, C. S., and Flynn, J. E. "Canadian Small Business Abroad: Opportunities, Aids and Experiences." *The Business Quarterly* (Winter 1973):33-47.

McFetridge, C. G. *Government Support of Scientific Research and Development: An Economic Analysis.* Toronto: University of Toronto Press, 1977.

Ondrack, D. A. *R&D and Innovation in the Industrial Machinery Industry.* Ottawa: Department of Industry, Trade and Commerce, 1975.

——. *Innovation in the Machinery Industry, 1975-1979.* Ottawa: Department of Industry, Trade and Commerce, 1980.

Ontario Government. *Response to the Recommendations of the Federal Government Consultative Task Force on Canadian Industry.* Ontario: Ministry of Industry and Tourism, 1980.

Quinn, J. B. "Technology Transfer by Multinational Companies." *Harvard Business Review* 47 (November-December 1969):147-161.

Rabino, S. "Tax Incentives to Exports: Some Implications for Policy Makers." *Journal of International Business Studies* 11, 1 (1980):74-85.

Richman, B., and Copen, M. *International Management and Economic Development.* New York: McGraw-Hill, 1972.

Ricks, D. A., and Czinkota, M. R. "International Business: An Examination of the Corporate Viewpoint." *Journal of International Business Studies* 10, 2 (1979):97-100.

Ronstadt, R. "International R&D: The Establishment and Evolution of Research and Development Abroad by Seven U.S. Multinationals." *Journal of International Business Studies* 9, 1 (Spring-Summer 1978):7-24.

Root, F. R., and Ahmed, A. A. "The Influence of Policy Instruments on Manufacturing Foreign Direct Investment in Developing Countries." *Journal of International Business Studies* 9, 3 (1978): 81-94.

Safarian, A. A. *The Performance of Foreign Owned Firms in Canada.* Montreal: Canadian-American Committee, 1969.

Schreiber, J. C. *US Corporate Investment in Taiwan.* New York: The Dunellen Co., 1970, cited in V. K. Jolly.

Science Council of Canada. *Innovation in A Cold Climate.* Ottawa: Information Canada, 1971.

Sheth, J. N., and Lutz, R. J. "A Multivariate Model of Multinational Business Expansion." In *Multinational Business Operations: Long Range Planning, Organization and Management* edited by S. P. Sethi and J. N. Sheth. Pacific Palisades, Calif.: Goodyear Publishing Co., 1973.

Statscan. *Report on Industrial Research in Canada.* Ottawa: Ministry of Supply and Services, 1979.

Tang, S. C. "International Investments in Singapore." *Malayan Law Journal,* 1973, cited in V. K. Jolly.

Telling, J. *"Evaluation of Offshore Investment."* Ph.D. Dissertation, Harvard Business School, 1975, cited in V. K. Jolly.

The Watkins Report. *Report of the Task Force on the Structure of Canadian Industry.* Ottawa: Privy Council Office, 1968.

PART IV

National Policies for Transnational Corporations: Goals and Effects

The general policy section contains two contributions that were prepared in the course of policy development (Vahlne) or policy assessment (van den Bulcke). The chapters by Blair and by Welch and Wiedersheim-Paul are scientific analyses of the effects of trade policies on the propensity of national and transnational corporations to invest in certain countries.

A few years ago, the Swedish government decided to investigate the consequences of Swedish direct investment abroad, as well as the effects of foreign direct investment in Sweden. Sweden, like Belgium, has traditionally been a free trade country, but recently—given burgeoning economic difficulties—the political parties developed an interest in scrutinizing both the Swedish and foreign transnational corporations (thus questioning the free trade tradition). It was felt that if the investigations could uncover strong negative trends and consequences, legislation or regulation to cope with these alleged or obvious problems might result. *Vahlne* concentrates on the activities abroad of Swedish corporations, which have, during recent years, increased their direct investment in other industrialized countries. Vahlne demonstrates that the number of sales subsidiaries grew much faster than the number of manufacturing subsidiaries (as a result, the sales staff abroad increased much more than the number of production workers). In addition, the sales performance of

Swedish-based MNCs or TNCs abroad (as is also true for foreign TNCs operating in Sweden) is much stronger than that of corporations operating only at home.

The essence of Vahlne's thorough investigation is that simplified argumentation, based on only one or a few criteria, most frequently leads to wrong conclusions. (Unfortunately, most argumentation about TNC activities during the last few decades has been of the oversimplified conjectural type). Vahlne also demonstrates that Swedish legislation (of 1916) constraining foreign ownership of Swedish real estate as well as the OECD Capital Movement Liberalization Code (or exemptions from the code), even if they are liberally administered, obviously are efficient enough to prevent severe distortions (thus making further legislation essentially superfluous). Vahlne concludes that government policy affecting foreign direct investment (in both directions) cannot be separated from general industrial policy.

Belgium, which is also a very open economy, has a still higher degree (the highest in Western Europe) of foreign-owned corporations operating within its boundaries. An obvious reason is its geographically central position within Europe. Within the European Community it most likely applies the most liberal policy vis-à-vis TNCs. At the same time, comparatively few Belgian corporations operate abroad. When the Belgian government issued its "New Industrial Policy" in 1977, it both underlines the importance of foreign direct investment for the development of Belgian industry and requested foreign-owned MNCs to "keep in line" with the targets and aims of the new policy.

The chapter by van den Bulcke is aimed at the latter objective: How do foreign MNCs perform in Belgium? The principal method of investigation he uses is a matched sampling of (93) pairs of Belgian and foreign firms. MNCs generally hold larger shares of the Belgian market than Belgian firms. They feel less (static as well as dynamic) competitive pressure from (low-cost country) imports than their Belgian firms about the high cost of Belgian labor. Raising equity for new physical investment appears to be easier for the "foreigners" (because of access to internal TNC financial resources) than for the domestic firms. As most of the nationally desirable industrial development is in capital-intensive industry, the outlook for MNCs seems to be brighter than for Belgian firms. The concerns of government about increasing foreign dominance are well justified, therefore. Foreign corporations not only operate in R&D-intensive product sectors, but even if R&D intensity in such sectors is about comparable between indigenous and foreign firms, the latter have better access to R&D results, patents, and licenses than the domestic firms, and thus enjoy an advantage. Average value-added is also higher for MNCs than their Belgian counterparts.

MNCs in Belgium are both more market-oriented and export-minded than their Belgian counterparts. They contribute much more to balancing Belgium's trade than domestic firms do. Foreign-controlled MNCs created about 18,000 new jobs in Belgium between 1968 and 1975, while the Belgian manufacturing industry lost 30,000 jobs.

Some general conclusions from van den Bulcke's work are:

1. Foreign-controlled MNCs perform better in many aspects than their Belgian counterparts.
2. Belgian-controlled MNCs perform better than purely Belgian firms.

The government's decision to subscribe to the OECD guidelines of 1976–1979, claiming nondiscrimination, therefore seems to be well founded, for the Belgian consumer and taxpayer are participating in the welfare gains stemming from the presence of (foreign as well as Belgian-controlled) MNCs in Belgium. Their presence keeps up competition in several respects and encourages Belgian industry to take strategic measures toward survival. Several other contributions to this volume point in the same principal direction.

Welch and Wiedersheim-Paul investigate the performance of Australian versus foreign-controlled TNCs in Australia in a somewhat related manner. They concentrate on the mining industry, because the federal government in Australia has been trying to fight unemployment by pushing large-scale mining and mineral processing projects. TNCs also have been encouraged to participate in this aim, given the capital intensity required for such ventures. Australia, like Canada and Belgium, hosts a fairly large number of foreign-controlled TNCs. One historical explanation is the long Commonwealth affiliation and former colonial status of Australia and Canada.

Although the government during the 1970s introduced steps to restrict (the growth of) foreign control of industry, for example, by a formal application and screening procedure, the participation is growing.

For uranium projects a 75 percent rule of Australian participation is stipulated, whereas for new mining projects a 50 percent rule is generally followed. In the light of reality (i.e., availability of domestic equity), these hurdles have been temporarily lowered.

The above screening procedure applies only to new ventures. Expansion investments within an existing industry are not subject to control. The effect of federal control is further weakened by the fact that state interests, when it comes to creating new jobs, are usually given higher priority than national interests with regard to constraints on foreign holdings in the mining industries. The authors plead for more deliberate and long-range national policies to reduce the country's dependence on TNCs.

Some conclusions from the Australian case are:

1. National policies vis-à-vis TNCs are embedded into and part of general economic and industrial policy.
2. As policy priorities shift over time, the effectiveness of TNC policies will vary. Both national governments and TNC management have reason to assess the uncertainties arising from policy shifts (in the Australian case employment creation overrules attempts to increase the share of Australian equity in holdings and exploitation of natural and energy resources).
3. Because of its structure, the Australian economy is still heavily dependent on imported technology. The preferred mode of technology acquisition is TNC involvement.
4. Similar to the conditions in Sweden and Belgium, TNCs in Australia show a higher technological intensity (introducing new processes earlier and more frequently) than domestic industries (in particular, manufacturing industries). Conflicts may emerge over governmental attempts to create and save jobs and the high propensity of TNCs to introduce high technology and labor-saving techniques.
5. A tariff shelter aimed at nurturing domestic industries obviously attracts TNCs, which can quickly and easily bring in their technology and management to build up enterprises and to take over substantial market shares. The tariff shelter, however, also seems to imply that competition in manufacturing within industries is restricted, which, as a consequence, leads to low exports of manufactured goods. As a result, raw material resources become favored targets of TNC acquisitions in spite of national policy to restrict foreign dominance.

Blair deals with the relatively recent phenomenon of TNC exports of manufactured goods from production units in less developed countries (rather than producing for domestic markets there) to industrialized countries and relates it to trade policy options applicable to the host countries, using the United States–Latin American region as an example. Changes in trade policy are significantly and inversely influencing U.S. MNC direct investment flows of manufacturing into Latin America. The MNCs have not responded by investing in direct response to their growing export ratios. Thus, host country markets still seem to be the dominant motive for producing there. Consequently, although U.S. affiliate export sales seem to make up a larger share of the total sales, their overall contribution to the rapidly growing exports of manufactured goods from Latin America seems not to be significant. A conclusion important to the industrialized countries can be advanced: Blair's analysis indicates that claims that TNCs cause job losses in highly industrialized countries by moving their manufacturing activities to low-wage countries, that is, the less developed countries, lacks empirical support. The dominant motive for establishing manufacturing capacity in the LDCs is to serve the domestic markets, which otherwise would not be covered because of existing trade barriers. Blair's study covers only the Americas and should be extended.

Doz investigates the changes in TNC strategies in response to the establishment and development of the European Community market. He finds changes in the competitiveness of TNCs, increased interdependence among countries, and further erosion of governmental control over national economies. The creation of the European Market made possible specialization that leads to economies of scale (instead of small-scale production of the same product in many countries).

Doz distinguishes between two main strategies pursued by TNCs in their international environment:

Integrative strategies at global or regional levels, exploiting the advantages of specialization and economies of scale.

National responsive strategies, implying operating "local for local," behaving as national or local firms unable to exploit economies of scale but still taking advantage of some central TNC properties, such as pooling financial risks, spreading R&D cost over large sales volumes, coordinating export marketing efforts, and transferring specific skills between subsidiaries.

Between these "extreme" strategies one can find various degrees of strategy mix.

Doz investigates the advantages and disadvantages of these strategy alternatives. He concludes that a clear integration strategy seems to be the most favorable choice for TNCs. Still, in reality, not all TNCs integrate their operations, the main reason being their readiness to adapt to national governmental goals and policies. Doz gives examples why adaptation to national policies may be necessary, despite market internationalization. He analyzes the means and instruments governments and TNCs have at their disposal to partially offset the moves of their counterparts.

Against this background, Doz shows which industries will tend to adopt integrative, mixed, or nationally responsive strategies:

1. The more extensive government control is over the markets of an industry, the least likely it is that integrated strategies will be adopted.
2. Mixed strategies are attractive to smaller MNCs, when government control over markets is partial, and where governments are willing to provide subsidies and export assistance to joint ventures.
3. The larger the international market share of a company within an industry, the more likely it is that the company will adopt integrative strategies.

The policies adopted by European governments in limiting the extent of integration strategies in many industries suffer from strong opportunity costs. Significant economic inefficiency results from these policies. Overcapacity, underutilization, high unit costs, and high prices plague such European industries as aircraft, electrical power systems, and telecommunication equipment. In many industries the maintenance of a national orientation is unfeasible. Thus clear choices have to be made between internationalization through integrated TNC strategies and withdrawal. Integrated MNCs may be able to maintain relatively small-scale activities in many countries and still preserve their competitiveness by making them part of an integrated multinational network. Integration makes the need for sectoral specialization at the national level less acute and may thus serve the aims of European governments.

Doz concludes by analyzing the consequences of governmental policies vis-à-vis TNCs along the integration–national responsiveness dimension. Governmental TNC policies are related to general economic and competition policy.

Chapter 9

Foreign Direct Investments:
A Swedish Policy Problem

*Jan-Erik Vahlne**

There are many policy problems connected with transnational corporations (TNCs), and their resolution is all the more difficult as there are continuing differences about the effects of foreign investment in the home and host countries. This chapter, which is based on the work of an ongoing official investigation in Sweden, is limited to presenting some preliminary results about outgoing investments by Swedish TNCs in terms of long-term industrial policy. The results are then discussed from the point of view of Swedish policy.

The results and thoughts brought forward here are of a very preliminary nature. Furthermore, they are based on limited material. It may very well be the case that what is said here will have to be changed as the investigation continues.

SWEDEN AS A HOME AND HOST
COUNTRY FOR TNCS

Because it is a small country, it is only natural that Sweden has always had extensive exchange with the surrounding world. Exports and imports amount roughly to half of the industrial output

*Government Committee on Foreign Direct Investment, Stockholm (on leave from International Institute of Business, Stockholm School of Economics).

and a quarter of GNP. In addition, the foreign activities of Swedish-based transnational corporations (companies with producing subsidiaries in at least one foreign country) are extensive while the volume of foreign-controlled operations in Sweden is of lesser importance in an international perspective (see Tables 9.1 and 9.2).

If a corresponding relationship were calculated for the engineering industry, Sweden would come "close to the top of a ranking list" as this industry dominates Swedish foreign investment activities. The flows of direct investment are given in Table 9.3. Generally, outgoing investments are larger than incoming investments. Outgoing investments have also grown faster than incoming investments. Consequently, the volume of foreign operations of Swedish corporations has increased considerably between 1965 and 1974, as is shown in Table 9.4. It is interesting to note that while employment in Swedish industry rose by only 0.3 percent between 1960 and 1974, the corresponding figure for the foreign manufacturing subsidiaries of Swedish TNCs was 5 percent. Critical voices started to request harder regulations for capital export. TNC defenders then showed that the TNCs had managed better to keep up employment in Sweden than had purely national companies. Some critics, acknowledging the figures, claimed that this development was more a result of merger activities than of the creation of new jobs. This author argues that the simple descriptive figures do not lend themselves to this kind of conclusion, and instead must be based on a more thorough analysis.

In 1974 the share of Swedish industrial exports supplied by the Swedish foreign investors totaled at as much as 73 percent. The foreign investors sold 63 percent of their output in this year on the

Table 9.1. Value of Direct Investment Abroad of Developed Market Economies

Country	Relation Between Stock of Direct Investment Abroad and GDP 1976
United States	0.081
Great Britain	0.147
West Germany	0.045
Japan	0.035
Switzerland	0.332
France	0.034
Canada	0.057
Netherlands	0.109
Sweden	0.067
Belgium	0.054
Italy	0.017

Source: Transnational Corporations in World Development Re-Examined (1978); Konjunkturlaget (1978:2).

Table 9.2. **Share of Employment Represented by Enterprises or Establishment of Enterprises with Foreign Participation in Manufacturing Industry for Certain OECD Countries**

Country	Year	Percentage Employment
Australia	1972/73	23.6
Austria	1973	20.7
Belgium	1968	18.3
Canada	1972	52.4
Finland	1972	2.8
France	1973	14.9
Germany	1972	22.4
Japan	1972	1.9
Norway	1974	7.8
United Kingdom	1971	10.3
Sweden	1974	4.8

Source: OECD (1977).
Note: For all countries the foreign degree of ownership is at least 50 percent with the exception of Belgium and Germany for which it is unknown.

Table 9.3. **Flows of Direct Investment to and from Sweden, 1960–1978, Current Prices (million Swedish Kronor)**

Year	Foreign Direct Investment in Sweden	Swedish Direct Investment Abroad
1960	134	288
1961	167	346
1962	322	430
1963	754	391
1964	360	747
1965	320	537
1966	654	735
1967	584	877
1968	1039	673
1969	550	1696
1970	779	1093
1971	611	1255
1972	478	1903
1973	615	1503
1974	674	2430
1975	562	2303
1976	503	3476
1977	643	4315
1978	788	3005

Source: Bank of Sweden.
Note: The figures depict permissions to invest.

Table 9.4. The Size of the Foreign Operations Controlled by Swedish Industrial Firms

	Number of Subsidiaries			*Number of Employees (1000s)*		
	1965	*1970*	*1974*	*1965*	*1970*	*1974*
Manufacturing subsidiaries	329	428	481	148	183	220
Sales subsidiaries	583	905	1227	25	43	56
Sum	912	1333	1708	173	226	276

Source: Swedenborg (1976).

foreign markets. About a quarter of the output was manufactured abroad.

Although more than 100 Swedish corporations have manufacturing activities abroad, the foreign sector is highly concentrated. Whether one uses total assets as a measure, or number of employees, the 10 largest investors account for 75 percent and the 20 largest for 85 percent of foreign manufacturing activities (Swedenborg, 1973). Among these companies are Electrolux, SKF, LM Ericsson, Volvo, Sandvik, Swedish Match Company, Atlas Copco, Alfa Laval, and ASEA. In 1978, Electrolux, as the largest employer, employed 76,000 people, of whom 48,000 were abroad. SKF, the ball-bearing company, had 44,000 of its 54,000 employees abroad. For Sweden the relative importance of the engineering industry is also great in terms of foreign manufacturing. The forest industry has traditionally relied more on exports (Table 9.5).

The more controversial apparel industry, benefiting from low wages in other countries, has only a very small share. The 20 largest industrial companies in 1975 (in terms of employment abroad) employed

Table 9.5. Distribution of Employment in Manufacturing Subsidiaries, 1974 (%)

Food	1
Textile and apparel	3
Paper products and printing	3
Pulps and paper	2
Chemicals	11
Iron, steel, metals and metal goods	12
Machinery	33
Electric equipment	24
Transportation equipment	5
Other industries	6
	100

Source: Swedenborg (1976).

271,530 people in Sweden, and the corresponding figure for all of Swedish industry in companies with more than 50 employees was 825,998. The relative share of the 20 largest companies is thus a third of the total.

Although North America has recently received a growing share of Swedish foreign investment, Europe is by far the most important recipient (Table 9.6).

The right of foreigners to establish or acquire subsidiaries in Sweden is limited by a law dating from 1916, which states that they must obtain permission to buy real estate. However, this rule also applies in principle to Swedish joint-stock companies that do not have an "alien-ownership stock clause" in their articles of association. Such a clause stipulates that no more than 20 percent of the votes or 40 percent of the shares of stock can be controlled by foreigners. About 80 percent of the companies listed on the stock exchange have such a clause. The clause can be removed only by the government. In 1973 there was an amendment to the law stating that a removal of the clause would not be permitted if it would cause conflict with an essential public interest or if the company's shares would be acquired by a foreigner (or Swedish companies that did not have an "alien-ownership stock clause"). In practice, however, application of the 1916 law has been very liberal.

Outgoing direct investment is traditionally regulated by the Exchange Control Board of the Bank of Sweden because of the balance of payment consequences. Sweden has for many years received a yearly temporary exemption from the OECD capital liberalization code due to balance of payments difficulties. Since 1974, the Exchange Control Board is also empowered to take aspects of employment and general industrial policy into consideration. This regulation is also very liberally applied. For example, in 1977 only 13 out of 1340 applications were refused (Bank of Sweden). Of course, the existence of these criteria may affect the plans of the companies (or perhaps only the way in which the application is formulated).

Table 9.6. Geographical Distribution of Employees in Foreign- and Swedish-Controlled Manufacturing Companies, 1976 (%)

The European Economic Community	53
The European Free Trade Area	11
North America	7
Latin America	15
Rest of the world	14
	100%

Source: National Central Bureau of Statistics (1977:1).

However, one should remember that permission is not needed when the investment is financed abroad and is not guaranteed by the Swedish parent, or when the investment is financed through profits gained in the foreign subsidiary and is to be regarded as "normal consolidation." Therefore, our guess is that Swedish foreign direct investments are substantially larger than those given in the statistics for the Bank of Sweden in Table 9.3.

THE ONGOING OFFICAL INVESTIGATION

The rapid internationalization of the Swedish economy during the 1950s and 1960s caused the government to order an investigation into the implications of the activities undertaken by the TNCs. The resulting report, which was published in 1975, took an indifferent position vis-à-vis the TNCs, arguing that most of the problems connected with them would have occurred even in their absence in an open economy with a number of very large national firms. The unions especially reacted strongly against these conclusions, and the Swedish Trade Union Confederation, in a letter to the government, demanded that a new investigation be undertaken. In 1977, a committee was appointed (Committee on Direct Investments, DIRK) and directives were given for an investigation of the long-term effects of foreign direct investment by industrial firms on industrial policy.

The committee was asked to base its conclusions on empirical studies covering both foreign investment undertaken abroad by Swedish firms and investments in Sweden by foreign firms. The aspects of industrial policy, for which DIRK will evaluate the long-term consequences resulting from international investments, are as follows: technical development; international competitiveness; employment, both in terms of numbers as well as qualifications; volume of exports, productivity; and finally the regional balance in Sweden.

DIRK has a sister-committee investigating the effects of Swedish currency regulations, of which regulation of foreign direct investment is a part. The conclusions of this committee will partly be based on DIRK's studies.

DIRK's empirical work is currently being undertaken and will be completed in late 1982. Two different approaches are being used to arrive at an optimal combination of depth and generality. DIRK has ordered the collection of data through a postal survey of all Swedish industrial firms with manufacturing operations abroad. These data concern certain background information such as R&D intensity, degree of product diversification, and information describing the nature and size of the firm's international operations. Such data must be collected several times before it is possible to undertake cross-sectional as well as longitudinal studies. These studies will concern explanations both of foreign investments and their implications, for example, the degree of substitution between local production and exports from Sweden.

The broad studies of foreign investments brought into Sweden are mainly designed as comparisons between foreign-controlled and Swedish-controlled firms in many respects, such as R&D intensity, employment, investment, exports and imports, or performance, keeping other explanatory variables such as size and line of business under control. In this project DIRK relies upon the extensive data bank of the National Central Bureau of Statistics.

Although DIRK believes that the econometric method will produce reliable results, it decided to undertake in-depth studies to gain a better understanding of the role of foreign direct investment as one of several means to strenghthen the competitiveness. DIRK also felt it was necessary to have in-depth knowledge in order to apply the "alternative linkages" method in evaluating the consequences of foreign direct investments. This method is described below. The in-depth approach covers studies both of international oligopolies and of individual firms. Both types of studies are undertaken at the firm level. Altogether DIRK has studied six oligopolies in which one or several Swedish TNCs participate and ten individual firms, of which six are Swedish TNC's and four are foreign-controlled firms in Sweden.

SOME PRELIMINARY RESULTS

As stated earlier, most of the large Swedish TNCs are in the engineering industry and have been foreign investors for a very long time. The 20 largest (in terms of employment in producing subsidiaries abroad) are still the largest investors, as their share of Swedish-controlled producing activities abroad has remained stable since 1965. By now most of them do not have any, or perhaps only one, Swedish competitor. As the concentration process has also continued internationally, they are now members of international oligopolies. In some cases these oligopolies may even be called global oligopolies in the sense that the number of competitors is highly limited and the battlefield is the world market. This was the rationale behind one of DIRK's studies, which measured the effects from direct investments undertaken by a Swedish TNC, taking into consideration the customers and their criteria for choice of supplier, the competitors and their behavior, and finally the authorities and rules of the game institutionalized by them. That is, the object under study was the activities undertaken to serve a particular foreign market. The effect was defined as the *difference* between the outcome following the direct investment and another alternative that the firm would have chosen or would have been forced to choose, for example, exports from Sweden or licensing. In choosing the industries, we tried to vary certain important structural characteristics such as the degree of concentration, technological complexity, and current rapidity of technological change. Five industries were producing goods within the engineering industries undertaking mainly, but not exclusively, market-oriented investments. Most of the product groups in these five industries were characterized by high barriers of entry, such as product differentiation or scale economics. The firms in the sixth industry, apparel, mainly undertake resource-oriented investments in low-wage countries and then export the products back to Sweden.

We can say generally that the effects of the international competitiveness of the TNCs from their foreign investments were positive. Anything else would have been highly surprising. The effects on the part of the corporations located in Sweden are less obvious. We found that employment in and exports from Sweden were greater than they would have been if the foreign investments had not been undertaken. The corporations mainly keep R&D and the most advanced production activities in Sweden so that there is no negative effect on the skill mix of employment. In the long run, we found that direct investments were necessary ingredients in the competitive strategies within the international oligopolies; that is, as foreign competitors invest in foreign markets, the competitive ability of the Swedish TNCs is hampered unless they are allowed to undertake these investments. The nature of the competition is such that companies able to use large resources are favored. Therefore, a particular investment may be less interesting from the point of view of *where* the facility is located than to what extent it increases the competitive strength of the TNC. What has been said so far applies to *market-oriented* investments, normally providing for the manufacture of simpler parts and assembling them.

However, some companies have located important parts of their R&D activities abroad. We know that there is an increasing tendency to take advantage of the liberalization in trade and specialize by placing the different subsidiaries into different product groups to exploit scale economies. In some cases, this specialization is accompanied by locating management responsibility, including product development and advanced manufacturing activities, in the subsidiary in question. Of course, such changes are favorable to the TNC in question, but there is a possibility that the effect for the home country is negative: the country does not share the strengthening of the competitive advantages. This may be serious as the value of Sweden's traditional comparative advantages, such as the supply of raw materials and skilled manpower, are diminishing. Some observers think that the character of the comparative advantages are changing over to the area of knowledge: of markets, technology, and management. These factors are more closely tied to specific technologies, product groups, or individual companies than were traditional (superior raw materials, manpower skills) Swedish advantages. They are also more "footless" in the sense that they are tied to people who can more easily be moved to other countries (c.f. Laestadius, 1980).

There are also problems with conflicts in goals between what is best for the corporation and what is best for the country. Furthermore, we can expect this "new" type of internationalization with specialization between subsidiaries to continue. Even if the effects are positive, does that mean that there are no policy problems? As with many Western industrial economies, Sweden is now facing problems with unemployment and a growing difference between imports and exports. Industry is shrinking while most prescriptions for industrial health say that it should grow, the most important reason being the need to increase exports. Can we, then, in the name of efficiency accept that Sweden will slowly disappear as an industrial nation? This, of course, is an issue for general economic policy, but can it be separated from policies concerned with foreign direct investment or the continuous internationalization of Swedish industry? For the forseeable future, Sweden, from an economic point of view, is highly dependent upon the behavior and success of a limited number of large Swedish TNCs.

A conclusion that I would like to draw is that policies affecting foreign direct investment cannot be separated from general industrial policies.

FOREIGN INVESTMENT POLICY
INTEGRATED IN
INDUSTRIAL POLICY

The history of industrial policy (i.e., actions taken by the government directly aimed at affecting the structure of industry) is relatively short in Sweden. Basically it has been confined to measures to strengthen the backward areas, creating a state-owned conglomerate and subsidizing a few industries like apparel in order to keep local production above a certain limit in case of disturbed supply from abroad. During recent years the Ministry of Industry has concentrated its efforts on "restructuring" shipyard and farmer-owned forest industries. If for no other reason, this policy, which has been very costly, has now to come to an end because of budget reasons.

At the same time, there has been a public debate over the meaning of "industrial policy" and what the objectives and means of such a policy should be. Opinions seem to range from traditional Manchester liberalism to a wish to centralize decisionmaking in the Ministry of Industry. Opinions differ most often over the means to be used. But all parties seem to assume that we will continue to have an open economy, creating an internationally competitive and growing (if not in terns of employment then in value-added) Swedish industry.

However, before discussing future industrial policy for Sweden, I would like to discuss development in the surrounding world. I believe many industries will grow more slowly than before, and at the same time, competition will become more intensified because of new nations entering the group of industrialized countries. Therefore I expect governments will more or less voluntarily take measures in order to strengthen the competitiveness of "their industry." We have already seen how governments in some countries actually coordinate private business or try to stimulate the emergence of national champions in perceived important industries. Concentration continues and the weaker competitors are either forced out of business or forced to join with a stronger partner. Altogether, I expect the climate to be rather tough for Swedish industry.

In contradiction to such sweeping generalizations, I would like to underline the uniqueness of every industry, company, and investment, also including foreign direct investment. That is, of course, the reason why we believe in the superiority of the decentralized market system. However, it also means that general, as opposed to selective, political means are bound to be inefficient to some extent: because the situations differ, firms react very differently to common signals. Many political means also suffer from the obvious weakness of being tied to a political domain, that is, the nation, while firms are not. Several of the largest Swedish TNCs, for example, have more than 90 percent of their sales abroad. Of course, such firms will not react very much to Swedish measures taken, for example, in order to stimulate demand. Finally, the ongoing process of concentration has changed reality further away from the assumptions on which general economic policy builds, or in Muller's words:

> . . . the globalization of the world's largest private enterprises, industrial and financial alike, represents a structural transformation in the location

of their activities and a manner in which they behave as institutions. In turn this structural transformation has now increased significantly, the invalidity of the behavioral assumptions in the orthodox micro-economic theory of the firms, the underlying basis for modern Keynesian macro-economic theory and therefore policy. Because these corporations account for the dominant share of economic transactions within and between nation-states, it is hypothesized that their own transformation has brought about a structural transformation of the national and international economy. This change in the behavior of the U.S. economy including its foreign sector means that it no longer responds in a fashion predicated by the theoretical models underlying policymaking (Muller, 1976, p. 243).

I draw the conclusion from this that it is time to introduce selective measures in Swedish economic and industrial policy, directed not only toward unsuccessful but also the successful firms. For several reasons this selective policy could be limited to a small number of large firms. The largest TNCs would then automatically be included.

It is not within the scope of this chapter to discuss the content of this kind of selective industrial policy, or what kind of positive and negative sanctions could be used. What is important here is that future foreign expansion should be one of the important objectives of this policy with the goal of allocating as much as possible of the advantage-strengthening activities to Sweden, taking the international competitiveness of the corporation into consideration. I do not believe in the use of very specific and precise criteria. The tradeoffs that have to be made are far too complicated. For example, it may be absolutely necessary to locate a research laboratory in the home town of a certain U.S. university in one case, whereas it may not be necessary in another case.

I also think that discussions between the representatives of the government and the corporation in question will provide the government with useful information about the needs of industry. A recent series of articles in a Swedish business magazine points to the fact that managers do not have a very high opionion of Sweden as an environment for industry (Affärsvärlden, 26/28, 29/30, 31/32, 1980). Probably measures such as increasing the quality of university research and education would increase Sweden's attractiveness.

Finally, I think that awareness of the obvious fact that we are a small nation that is highly dependent on the surrounding world may increase. In addition, too many people in responsible positions behave as if the world ends at the Swedish border. This is not healthy in an environment of increased competition.

REFERENCES

Affärsvärlden 26/28, 29/30, 31/32. 1980.

Bank of Sweden. Balance of payment statistics. Stockholm, 1965–1978.

Konjunkturläget, No. 2. Government report, Stockholm, 1978.

Laestadius, S. D. *Produktion utan gränser*. Stockholm: Sekretariatet för framtidsstudier, 1980.

Muller, R. E. "The Impact of the Multinational Corporation." In *Markets, Corporate Behavior and the State: International Aspects of Industrial Organization*, edited by A. P. Jacquemin and H. W. de Jong. The Hague: Martinus Nijhoff, 1976.

National Central Bureau of Statistics. *SM F*, No. 1. Stockholm, 1977.

OECD. *Penetration of Multinational Enterprises in Member Countries*. Paris, 1977.

Swedenborg, B. *Den Svenska industrins investeringar i utlandet*. Stockholm: IUI, 1973.

——. *Den svenska industrins investeringar i utlandet, 1970–1974*. Stockholm: IUI, 1976.

Transnational Corporations in World Development Re-Examined. New York: Centre of Transnational Corporations, 1978.

Chapter 10

Belgian Industrial Policy and Foreign Multinational Corporations: Objectives Versus Performance

Daniel van den Bulcke *

It has been estimated that in 1975 33 percent of the employment and 44 percent of the total sales of Belgian manufacturing were "controlled" from abroad, that is, located in enterprises in which at least 10 percent of the equity capital was owned by foreigners. (In 90 percent of all foreign-owned subsidiaries in Belgium the degree of ownership was higher than 50 percent, while in only 1 percent of all cases did the foreign shareholders hold between 10 and 25 percent of the equity capital.) Involvement by *foreign multinational corporations (MNCs) in Belgium* is thus higher than in most other Western European countries.[1]

The recent attempt by the Belgian government to formulate "a new industrial policy" (1977) could not ignore the importance and influence of MNC subsidiaries. On the one hand, the government's

This chapter is based on the results of a study on "Foreign and Belgian Enterprises: A Comparative Analysis," which was published in Dutch on behalf of the "Belgian Fund for Collective and Fundamental Research." The study was carried out by the Seminar of Applied Economics (SERUG) of the University of Ghent (Director: Prof. Dr. A. Vlerick) and the Research Center of the Economische Hogeschool Limburg (LEHOC) Director: Prof. Dr. D. van den Bulcke). The author thanks F. Haex and E. Halsberghe, his collaborators and co-authors, for their permission to quote extensively from the global report.

*Director, Research Center, Economische Hogescchool, Limburg, The Netherlands.

white paper stresses from the very beginning that foreign direct investment has played a crucial role in Belgian industrial development since 1960, especially in the so-called "*secteurs do pointe.*" On the other hand, however, the government praises the advantages of an independent position as it is "too risky to depend too strongly on decision-centers on which one has little or no influence."[2] These introductory statements illustrate immediately the delicate position toward inward foreign direct investment of a small industrial country with very few MNCs of its own. Belgium actively courted foreign MNCs to invest in its territory but is becoming increasingly aware that its past promotional policies imply that an independent industrial policy is becoming unattainable. One should therefore not be too surprised to find, as one notable critic stated, that there is no trace of a clear and coherent Belgian policy toward MNCs.[3]

This chapter describes the most important characteristics of the MNC presence in Belgian manufacturing and begins with the premises or *main options* formulated in the government's report on industrial policy. The main planks of this industrial policy are a "restructuring" and modernization of the traditional industrial sectors; a strategy of specialization through diversification toward more sophisticated products; an extension of the foreign markets; and the promotion and reorientation of applied research and development. Each objective will be examined to see to what extent it is satisfied by foreign-owned enterprises. The question whether government measures that intend to limit the dependence on foreign decisionmakers can be carried out in the Belgian context is raised. This chapter does not attempt to judge Belgian industrial policy as such, but rather studies how MNCs facilitate or complicate the realizations of the governmental options of its industrial policy. Nor is the explicitly European context taken into account.

The data for this study are based, first, on the general results of an inquiry (1976) in which 221 Belgian indigenous firms (including 30 Belgian MNCs) and 262 foreign subsidiaries responded to a questionnaire. This "*global sample*" represents 27 percent of all foreign-owned enterprises in Belgium and 40 percent of their total sales and employment, on the one hand, 13 percent of all uninational Belgian firms with more than 50 employees and about 20 percent and 25 percent, respectively, of their total sales and employment, on the other hand. Second, to eliminate the sector differences between foreign subsidiaries and Belgian firms, a "*matched sample*" of 93 pairs is established. The pairing of a foreign firm with a Belgian firm is based on the preconditions of similarity in subsector, employment size, and age group. Third, and again to eliminate sectoral discrepancies, *simulated totals and averages* are used. Foreign-owned enterprises were examined to see if they had the same sectoral distribution as the Belgian uninational enterprises. In the tables the number of responding firms are mentioned because for some questions the rate of response may be somewhat lower.

RENOVATION AND STRENGTHENING OF THE COMPETITIVE POSITION

One of the main objectives of Belgian industrial policy is "the restructuring and modernization of traditional sectors in the new division of labor." The "improving the competitive strength of enterprises" is mentioned as a more general objective.

Although the competitive position of Belgian industry has been widely discussed, little or no attention has been devoted to its ownership. Nevertheless, the fact that a company is part of a larger multinational entity may very well affect its competitive position. MNCs incorporate the production factors of the host country ("location-specific advantages") into their global strategy and combine them with their own specific ("ownership") advantages, such as management expertise, organizational know-how, technological superiority, international brand names, marketing experience.[4] These ownership advantages are the main reason why MNCs are able to penetrate and dominate local markets.

That the MNCs succeeded in conquering a substantial *share of the Belgian market* is shown indirectly in Table 10.1. About one out of four foreign MNCs estimated that they controlled half or more of the Belgian market for their most important product. Only one out of seven Belgian uninational enterprises considered themselves to have a market share of more than 50 percent. If Belgian MNCs are included, however, this market share increases to 20 percent for the Belgian firms. American MNCs more often hold a relatively large slice of the Belgian market (28 percent). The same conclusions are derived when a 30-percent market share is taken as the point of comparison. The conclusions for the "matched sample" are somewhat less straightforward because relatively more foreign MNCs hold a market position of 30 percent or more, while relatively more Belgian firms control 50 percent of the market for their main product. These results, which vary according to whether the global or the matched sample is used, indicate that the dominating market positions of MNCs are sectorially determined and oligopolistic situations occur more frequently in some sectors than others. In nonmetallic minerals

Table 10.1. Market Share of Belgian and Foreign-owned Enterprises in Belgium (1976)

	Market Share of						Total Number of Companies (N = 100)
	+10%		+30%		+50%		
	N	*%*	*N*	*%*	*N*	*%*	
Global Sample							
Belgian enterprises	135	64	64	30	41	19	211
Belgian uninational enterprises	107	59	42	23	27	15	182
Foreign enterprises	138	68	83	41	46	23	203
American enterprises	66	76	37	43	24	28	87
EEC enterprises	61	61	38	38	21	21	99
Matched Sample							
Belgian enterprises	63	72	30	34	23	26	88
Belgian uninational enterprises	58	71	26	32	20	24	82
Foreign enterprises	51	61	35	43	18	22	83

Source: F. Haex, E. Halsberghe, and D. van den Bulcke, p. 114.

and electronics, not one Belgian firm attained a market share of 30 percent for its products, while MNCs controlled 38 and 60 percent, respectively, of the large market share.

Table 10.2 shows the *geographical origin of competitive pressure* for both foreign-owned and local enterprises. As 30 percent of the indigenous firms are exposed to "strong" competitive pressure from imports from developing countries (as compared with only 15 percent for foreign MNCs), it appears that Belgian firms are in a much weaker position than their foreign counterparts.

If the Belgian government is serious about using the new international division of labor as a criterion for its diversification strategy, more indigenous firms are going to succumb from the pressure of increasing imports from the developing countries. Another indication of the stronger competitive position of foreign MNCs is that only about one out of three foreign subsidiaries are exposed to any competition from Belgian firms as opposed to almost one out of two of the matched Belgian companies. Only about one-fifth of the indigenous firms in the matched sample compete with foreign subsidiaries, while one-third of the MNCs are direct competitors.

Foreign MNCs were not only exposed to less competitive pressure than their Belgian counterparts, but they were also more resistant to it during the period 1970–1976. More than half of the Belgian firms complained about the *increase in competitive pressure during 1970–1976* as compared with only 40 percent of the foreign subsidiaries

Table 10.2. Belgian and Foreign Enterprises with "Strong"[a] Competitive Pressure

| | Competitive Pressure from: | | | | | | | |
| | Imports from Industrial Countries | | Imports from Developed Countries | | Belgian Enterprises | | Foreign Enterprises Established in Belgium | |
	N	%	N	%	N	%	N	%
Global Sample								
Belgian enterprises	113	55	51	28	114	53	42	21
Belgian uninational enterprises	95	54	43	27	103	55	39	23
Foreign enterprises	130	62	24	15	74	34	67	33
American enterprises	67	72	8	12	25	27	28	33
EEC enterprises	55	54	16	19	44	40	35	33
Matched Sample								
Belgian enterprises	43	46	19	24	45	48	16	19
Belgian uninational enterprises	43	46	19	24	45	48	16	19
Foreign enterprises	51	61	11	17	31	36	29	35

Source: F. Haex, E. Halsberghe, and D. van den Bulcke, pp. 102, 104, 105, and 106.
[a]The other categories existed of "some," "little," and "no" competitive pressure.
[b]The percentages were calculated on the basis of the total number of responding enterprises.

(Table 10.3). Although approximately as many Belgian as foreign enterprises mentioned "some" increase in competition, the matched sample confirms that relatively more foreign subsidiaries fall into this category. About one out of three foreign MNCs mentioned that its competitive situation improved during 1970–1976, as compared to only one out of five for the indigenous firms. The matched sample and the simulation also point out that MNCs were better able to withstand competitive influences than local firms.

Increased competition during 1970–1976 manifested itself mainly on the price level as more than 80 percent of both foreign and Belgian firms mentioned this factor. An important difference in understanding the *origin of the competitive pressure* shows up in wage costs. While almost three-quarters of the local firms complained about wage increases, only about half (54 percent) of the foreign MNCs were worried by higher wage levels. The matched sample brings this percentage for MNCs down to 59 percent. This shows again that the differences between Belgian and foreign firms are to a large extent determined by sector. For other elements in the competitive situation, for example, increased imports or the price of raw

Table 10.3. Belgian and Foreign-owned Enterprises Experiencing a Change in Competitive Pressure during 1970-1976.

	Important Increase		Limited Increase		No Change or Decrease		Total Responding Enterprises
	N	%	N	%	N	%	(N = 100)
Global Sample							
Belgian enterprises	116	53	55	26	48	22	219
Belgian uninational enterprises	100	53	48	25	43	23	190
Foreign enterprises	91	41	60	27	73	32	224
American enterprises	40	42	27	28	30	31	97
EEC enterprises	45	40	30	27	36	33	111
Matched Sample							
Belgian enterprises	51	55	21	22	21	22	93
Belgian uninational enterprises	51	55	21	22	21	22	93
Foreign enterprises	34	39	27	31	27	30	38

Source: F. Haex, E. Halsberghe, and D. van den Bulcke, p. 124.

materials, the differences between MNCs and local companies are negligible.

An important element in the strength of an enterprise consists in its ability to renovate its production. To realize innovative investments enterprises must have sufficient funds at their disposal. During the 1970s it became not only increasingly difficult to borrow money because interest rates increased tremendously, but self-financing also became endangered by the low rate of return. The government's white paper on industrial policy states that an improvement in the competitive situation depends on a better management strategy for increasing the rate of return and that investment incentives will try to stimulate self-financing.[5]

Table 10.4 indicates that local firms are more dependent on self-financing than MNCs. Three-quarters of the Belgian firms *finance* their *new investments* with 50 percent or more from internal financial sources, as compared with only two-fifths of the foreign subsidiaries. External financing is used more often by foreign MNCs, which shows up most clearly in the matched sample. Foreign subsidiaries have a comparative financial advantage over local firms because they can apply for intragroup loans or borrow in foreign capital markets through the intermediary of the parent company or another subsidiary in the same multinational group.

The document on industrial policy issued by the Belgian govern-

Table. 10.4. Financing of New Investment by Belgian and Foreign
Enterprises (1976)

	At Least 50% Self-Financing		At Least 50% External Financing		Total Number of Enterprises
	N	%	N	%[a]	
Global Sample					
Belgian enterprises	165	75	82	38	219
Belgian uninational enterprises	139	74	76	40	190
Foreign enterprises	129	61	98	47	209
American enterprises	55	63	38	43	88
EEC enterprises	64	61	53	51	105
Matched Sample					
Belgian enterprises		79		32	
Belgian uninational enterprises		78		33	
Foreign enterprises		62		44	

Source: F. Haex, E. Halsberghe, and D. van den Bulcke, pp. 232–233.

[a] As a percentage of the total number of responding enterprises.

ment points out: "most industrial projects which offer interesting perspectives are *capital-intensive.* Capital-intensive investment not only offer long-term competitive advantages but also result in important spillover effects such as increased activity and employment in other sectors."[6] The global and matched samples as well as the simulation clearly show that MNCs are indeed more capital-intensive than their local counterparts.[7]

DIVERSIFICATION STRATEGY

By "specialization" the new Belgian industrial policy means, first, the production of more technologically sophisticated goods, and second, the introduction of production systems with a high value-added and an important technical content. The government's document also stresses "that an industrial policy which tries to diversify existing activities or increase specialization, necessarily has to be market-oriented. . . ."[8] Each of these points will be examined to see how foreign subsidiaries perform as compared with indigenous firms.

An indirect impression about the introduction of new products can be gathered from the absence of *competitors.* In 1968 one-third of the foreign subsidiaries had no competitors whatsoever on the Belgian market, while only one-fifth experienced any competition from other foreign MNCs.[9] An important qualification that has to be made here is that the foreign subsidiaries may have driven their local competitors out of the market. The data from the 1976 inquiry should be interpreted even more carefully. Only 8 percent of the Belgian firms did *not* have to bother about other Belgian competitors, whereas 22 percent of the foreign and 29 percent of the American enterprises did not need to worry about indigenous competition. The comparison between "pairs" of foreign and local companies (matched sample) confirms the difference between both groups, although the gap is somewhat narrowed.

A better way to measure the diversification effect of MNCs consists in comparing the *research intensity of the products*. The Belgian National Scientific Council affirmed in 1965 that three-fourths of the scientifically based products in Belgium resulted from foreign or mixed initiatives. It was concluded at that time that the relative weakness of Belgian enterprises in the innovative sectors was compensated by foreign—especially American—initiatives.[10] The sectors that were described as "scientifically based" were chemicals (including rubber and petroleum), machine construction, and electronics. A calculation of "sectoral concentration coefficients" (i.e., the ratio of the share in total industrial employment and the share of the employment provided by foreign enterprises located in Belgium) reveals that foreign MNCs are typically present in research-intensive sectors. (A coefficient of 1 indicates that the sectoral proportions are completely equal. If the coefficient is higher than 1 it means that foreign subsidiaries are relatively more active in these sectors than Belgian manufacturing *as a whole*.) For electronics (including miscellaneous metals), chemicals, and transport equipment, the concentration coefficients oscillate around 2, while rubber, oil, and plastics register 1.3, as compared with 1.1 for metals and 0.9 for machine construction and nonmetallic minerals.

Value-added normally increases with the degree of manufacturing. Intragroup trade seems to be responsible, however, for the relatively higher concentration of foreign subsidiares in semifinished products and raw materials. This characteristic shows up both in the global and the matched samples (Table 10.5). On the other hand, it is apparent from Table 10.6 that foreign-owned enterprises produce relatively more industrial and investment goods. Indigenous firms concentrate somewhat more on durable consumption goods. As was to be expected, these differences disappear completely with calculation of the matched sample.

The *average value-added* per enterprise and per employee is much higher in foreign-owned subsidiaries than in local firms. Value-added

Table 10.5. Foreign and Belgian Enterprises Producing Semifinished Products
and Raw Materials

	Semifinished Products		Raw Materials	
	N	*%*	*N*	*%*
Global Sample				
Belgian enterprises	48	22	11	6
Belgian uninational enterprises	39	21	12	6
Foreign enterprises	84	34	37	15
American enterprises	31	30	15	14
EEC enterprises	46	36	19	15
Matched Sample				
Belgian enterprises	22	24	6	7
Belgian uninational enterprises	19	22	5	6
Foreign enterprises	35	38	10	11

Source: F. Haex, E. Halsberghe, and D. van den Bulcke, p. 60.

was estimated by two different cost elements: wages, depreciation allowances, profits before taxes, interest, and rent, while the second method substracts total purchases from total sales. Although the data in both methods are not perfect, they keep their comparative value as the eventual shortcomings should be equally strong in foreign and Belgian enterprises. Only the cost method will be discussed here as it probably presents a more accurate measure of value-added (see

Table 10.6. Product Destination of Belgian and Foreign-owned Enterprises

	Durable Consumption Goods		Nondurable Consumption Goods		Industrial Goods		Investment Goods	
	N	*%*	*N*	*%*	*N*	*%*	*N*	*%*
Global Sample								
Belgian enterprises	60	27	72	33	83	38	42	20
Belgian uninational enterprises	52	27	65	34	70	37	33	17
Foreign enterprises	60	24	65	26	109	44	73	30
American enterprises	20	20	23	22	46	45	55	43
EEC enterprises	33	26	39	30	55	43	32	25
Matched Sample								
Belgian enterprises	19	20	28	30	39	42	29	31
Belgian uninational enterprises	15	18	25	29	36	41	39	29
Foreign enterprises	22	24	27	29	38	41	30	33

Source: F. Haex, E. Halsberghe, and D. van den Bulcke, p. 62.

Table 10.7). Value-added per company is almost four times as high in foreign MNCs as in Belgian uninational firms.

If Belgian MNCs are included in the comparison this difference is much diminished. The use of the matched sample also lowers the discrepancy between foreign and local firms, although the simulation technique still shows an average value-added per enterprise for foreign MNCs twice as high as that for Belgian firms.

Value-added per employee, which can be used as a proxy to measure productivity, is higher in foreign-owned enterprises (0.8 million Belgian francs) than in uninational (0.53 million BF) and all Belgian firms (including Belgian MNCs) (0.62 million BF). Although the matched sample and the simulated average diminish this supremacy of foreign-owned firms, their performance remains much better than that of local companies. The superiority of foreign subsidiaries is evident in practically all sectors (except in food and textiles where the differences are rather small) and size categories. American subsidiaries achieve a higher average in value-added than European

Table 10.7. Average Value-added per Enterprise and Employee in Belgian and Foreign-owned Enterprises (1976) (in million Belgian francs)

	Cost Method[a]			Sales Minus Purchases		
	N	Average per Enterprise	Average per Employee	N	Average per Enterprise	Average per Employee
Global Sample						
Belgian enterprises	196	469	0.62	195	552	0.83
Belgian uninational enterprises	172	138	0.53	172	193	0.77
Foreign enterprises	191	527	0.80	220	615	1.05
American enterprises	79	552	0.85	91	719	1.09
EEC enterprises	99	497	0.75	11	496	0.99
Matched Sample						
Belgian enterprises	85	192	0.85	83	251	0.76
Belgian uninational enterprises	80	162	0.57	76	222	0.77
Foreign enterprises	70	243	0.65	87	286	0.91
Simulated Average						
Belgian uninational enterprises		138	0.53		193	0.77
Foreign enterprises		298	0.66		371	0.94
American enterprises		358	0.66		582	1.11
EEC enterprises		267	0.58		283	0.91

Source: F, Haex, E. Halsberghe, and D. van den Bulcke, pp. 78 and 80, pp. 154 and 150.
[a]Wages + depreciation allowances + profits before tax + interest + rent.

Economic Community (EEC) firms and confirm the results of the 1968 study in which it was already noticed that productivity was higher for the American companies.

Marketing orientation can be measured by looking at the ratio of marketing personnel to total personnel and by taking advertising expenditures as a percentage of total sales. For the first indicator, the global sample is more favorable for uninational Belgian firms (Table 10.8). It is somewhat surprising to find that after adding the Belgian MNCs to the Belgian uninationals, the Belgian average of marketing personnel as a percentage of total employment decreases from 4.4 to 2.9 percent. The matched sample and the simulated averages indicate, however, that Belgian enterprises are not as marketing-oriented as their foreign competitors. This contradictory result might be explained by the differences between subsidiaries that sell to the local and neighboring markets and are very marketing-minded and the subsidiaries that sell entirely or to a large extent within their own multinational group and for which there is no need for promotional

Table 10.8. Marketing Orientation of Belgian and Foreign-owned
Enterprises (1976)

	Marketing Personnel as a Percentage of All Personnel		Advertising Expenditure as a Percentage of Total Sales	
	N	*%*	*N*	*%*
Global Sample				
Belgian enterprises	215	2.9	206	0.47
Belgian uninational enterprises	187	4.4	179	0.47
Foreign enterprises	243	3.8	226	0.41
American enterprises	100	3.8	91	0.42
EEC enterprises	124	3.9	116	0.41
Matched Sample				
Belgian enterprises	90	4.1	91	0.50
Belgian uninational enterprises	85	4.2	85	0.47
Foreign enterprises	89	6.1	89	0.98
Simulated Total				
Belgian uninational average		4.4		0.47
Foreign enterprises		5.4		1.34
American enterprises		7.2		2.21
EEC enterprises		4.8		0.90

Source: F. Haex, E. Halsberghe, and D. van den Bulcke, pp. 170 and 174.

activites. This latter situation is typical for Dutch and German subsidiaries in textiles and apparel.

The analysis reaches the same conclusion when the criterion of advertising expenditures as a percentage of sales is used. Within the global samples Belgian firms tend to be more market-oriented, while the "purer" comparison of the matched sample and simulated averages brings out a higher awareness of promotional activities for foreign—especially American—subsidiaries.

EXPORT PROMOTION

Export promotion is an essential characteristic of the new industrial policy as expounded by the Belgian government in 1977.[11] The report on commercial policy, published by the Minister of Foreign Trade in 1979, also insists on a consolidation and diversification of Belgian exports for the traditional EC markets, stresses the necessity of a systematic export promotion toward the industrial countries where Belgium experienced a deterioration in its trading position, and urges the penetration of the markets of developing and East European countries.[12] Both the texts of the new industrial policy and a new commercial policy state that Belgian direct investment abroad should be promoted to improve Belgium's export chances. This link between direct investment abroad and an increased export activity is not self-evident, however.[13]

In view of Belgium's great dependence on international trade, it is understandable that the authorities should be concerned about the influence of foreign subsidiaries on its trade balance. Before analyzing the contribution of foreign MNCs to the trade balance, two other trade aspects will be dealt with. First, data about the "export intensity" (i.e., exports as a percentage of total sales) of Belgian and foreign enterprises will be presented. Second, the question will be raised whether average exports per employee are different for local and foreign firms. The data for these trade aspects are presented in Table 10.9.

The *export ratio* (exports as a percentage of sales) indicates that foreign-owned subsidiaries are more export-oriented than indigenous enterprises. Foreign MNCs export 68 percent of their sales, while uninational Belgian firms send only about half of their production abroad. Belgian MNCs increase the ratio for Belgian firms up to 61 percent. The directly comparable data of the matched sample and the simulated averages confirm, however, that foreign subsidiaries export relatively more than indigenous firms.

Table 10.9. Export Ratio, Average Export per Employee, and Average Contribution to Trade Balance of Belgian and Foreign-owned Enterprises (1976)

	Export Ratio		Average Export per Employee		Average Contribution to Trade Balance per Enterprise	
				Millions of Belgian		*Millions of Belgian*
	N	*%*	*N*	*Francs*	*N*	*Francs*
Global Sample						
Belgian enterprises	207	61	207	1.12	170	372
Belgian uninational enterprises	185	50	185	0.95	151	131
Foreign enterprises	296	68	296	2.21	202	340
American enterprises	93	67	93	2.32	83	400
EEC enterprises	114	67	114	2.01	102	256
Matched Sample						
Belgian enterprises	87	51	87	0.93	76	80
Belgian uninational enterprises	81	47	81	0.88	76	77
Foreign enterprises	92	66	92	1.44	81	185
Simulated Averages						
Belgian uninational enterprises		50		0.95		131
Foreign enterprises		61		1.53		242
American enterprises		71		1.96		512
EEC enterprises		59		1.26		146

Source: F. Haex, E. Halsberghe, and D. van den Bulcke, pp. 308, 314, and 354.

The export intensity of foreign MNCs is much higher than their local competitors in textiles, wood, paper and leather, electronics, and the metal industry. Foreign MNCs also export more than uninational firms in the chemical sector, but the influence of Belgian MNCs is so strong that their inclusion eliminates the difference for all Belgian chemical firms. The higher export intensity of American MNCs as compared with European MNCs is only evident in the simulated averages and most outspoken in machine construction, metals, textiles, nonmetallic minerals, and wood and paper. This higher export tendency of foreign subsidiaries comes to the fore in practically all categories of employment size.

The export-intensive nature of foreign MNCs is also illustrated by their higher *average export value per employee.* Exports per employee become as high as 2.2 million Belgian francs in foreign subsidiaries as compared with only 1 million Belgian francs in local firms. The calculation of the matched sample and the simulated averages confirm the export superiority of foreign subsidiaries, on the one hand, and show that the export performance of American enterprises exceeds their EEC counterparts, on the other hand. The export per employee for indigenous firms is especially low in comparison with foreign MNCs in chemicals, paper and wood, and transportation equipment. Only in food do the Belgian firms succeed in jumping ahead of the foreign enterprises. The simulated averages especially bring out the outstanding American performance as compared with European firms. U.S. MNCs dominate their EEC competitors most explicitly in food, textiles, wood and paper, and transport equipment. All the above-mentioned conclusions also apply to the different categories of employment size.

Foreign MNCs in the 1976 study made a positive *contribution to the trade balance* of 68.7 billion Belgian francs. During the same year (1976) the overall Belgian trade balance registered a deficit of 98.6 billion Belgian francs, which was reduced to 79.5 billion Belgian francs when the nonmanufacturing sectors were excluded. Foreign firms in chemicals and transport equipment were responsible for about 90 percent of the positive result. Except for rubber and petroleum, (which showed a negative result of about 25 billion Belgian francs), and food, foreign subsidiaries in all other sectors contributed positively to the Belgian trade balance, for they exported more than they imported. The Belgian enterprises in the sample also contributed significantly to the trade balance, registering a surplus of 65 billion Belgian francs. In the matched sample the contribution of the foreign subsidiaries was about twice as high as that of the Belgian firms. This proves that the beneficial result for the Belgian firms was mainly realized by Belgian MNCs.

More attention should be given, however, to the average contribution to the trade balance by the individual enterprises. This effect amounts to 372 billion Belgian francs for all Belgian firms against 340 million Belgian francs for the foreign subsidiaries. If the comparison is limited to Belgian uninational enterprises (excluding Belgian MNCs), the average trade balance effect decreases to 130 million Belgian francs, however. The American average contribution is three times higher than that of the Belgian uninational firms. The matched sample and simulated averages confirm the foreign and American superiority as contributors to the Belgian trade balance.

During the 1960s and 1970s several Belgian Ministers of Foreign Trade repeatedly warned that Belgian exports were very vulnerable because they were too *geographically* limited to a small number of markets (especially EEC markets). To the extent that the EEC is becoming one economic area this vulnerability should not be exaggerated. It was already apparent from an earlier (1968) study that Belgian exports as a whole more often went to the EEC countries than did exports of foreign-owned enterprises taken separately. While more than half of the exports of American subsidiaries in Belgium went outside the former EEC market of the Six, this proportion amounted to only one-third of the exports of the Belgian–Luxemburg economic union.[14] Although a more recent analysis (1976) is less detailed, it appears that many uninational enterprises export only to the neighboring countries while foreign subsidiaries more often export to markets that are further away.

EMPLOYMENT CREATION

One of the main options of Belgian industrial policy is "the special attention to labor-intensive activities and the characteristics of the labor potential."[15] Full employment and improved employment conditions are stressed as points of primary priority. The same document mentions, however, as has already been pointed out, that the best investment projects are capital-intensive because of their beneficial long-term effects. These seemingly contradictory statements probably mean that labor-intensive activities should not be promoted as such, although they should have a place in the new international division of labor on which developing countries have put their hopes.

Contrary to what is often put forward, the employment performance of foreign subsidiaries, both from a quantitative and qualitative angle, has not been unfavorable. This does not mean that working conditions are altogether favorable and that negative aspects are completely absent. Certain employment aspects, for example, wages, are not determined so much by the multinational character of the firm as by their different sectoral distribution. Although the global sample shows a higher wage level in foreign subsidiaries than in local firms, this difference disappears completely with the calculation of the matched sample and the simulated averages. Only the quantitative contribution of foreign enterprises to the employment total and the level of qualification are studied here.

From 1968 to 1975 *employment in foreign MNCs* in Belgium increased by about 130,000 jobs.[16] As a result of this annual increase of 7.8 percent, the share of foreign-owned subsidiaries in Belgian manufacturing employment went up from 18 percent in 1968 to 33 percent in 1975. Even when the "employment switches" (i.e., takeovers of Belgian-owned firms by foreign MNCs) are not taken into account, the net effect (= gross effect — employment switches) still involves 80,000 new jobs. The net annual rate of increase between 1968 and 1975 amounts to 5.1 percent.

The positive contribution of foreign MNCs to the Belgian labor market is even more impressive when considering that during 1968–1975 the Belgian manufacturing industry as a whole lost about 30,000 jobs (annual decline of —0.43 percent). It is of course possible that, on the one hand, some of the Belgian firms that were taken over would have disappeared without the new financial and technological inputs from abroad, whereas, on the other hand, a number of Belgian enterprises may have been pushed out of the market by the foreign MNCs. If one assumes that both of these effects compensate each other, one has to conclude that foreign-owned enterprises stopped the tendency toward deindustrialization of the Belgian economy.

This employment expansion could not be kept up during 1975–1978, however. The economic crisis, which began in 1974, led to a downward trend in new investment projects, to collective dismissals, and to company closures. Even during this period, however, foreign subsidiaries did better than Belgian industry as a whole. While Belgian manufacturing registered an annual decrease of 3.97 percent during 1975–1978 (loss of 78,000 jobs), foreign-owned enterprises realized a net increase of 0.41 percent. The higher productivity and higher profitability of foreign subsidiaries and their integration in a larger multinational grouping undoubtedly have a beneficial effect on their competitive position and, consequently, on their employment situation.

Although editorials in the press about *company closures* such as Prestige-Tessenderlo, R.B.P.-Antwerp, Badger-Antwerp, and Sylvania-Tirlemont have given the impression that foreign and American subsidiaries close down more often than local firms, it would be inappropriate to conclude that more jobs were lost through the closure of foreign subsidiaries. Between 1960 and 1977, company closures in Belgium caused a loss of about 107,500 jobs. Twenty percent of this total could be attributed to foreign MNCs. Although foreign firms during 1975–1976 closed down relatively more frequently than indigenous enterprises (4.9 percent as compared with 3.2 percent), the "exits" of multinational subsidiaries resulted in a smaller relative loss of jobs than did the closings of local firms (1.6 as compared with 2.3 of their respective total employment). This contradictory finding is related to the smaller dimension of the closed foreign subsidiaries as well as their higher capital intensity.[17] It should be added here that the high closure rate and the resulting loss of jobs in foreign subsidiaries are highly influenced by European (especially Dutch) companies, and that the withdrawal of the American MNCs from Belgium is relatively less important than the closure of Belgium firms.

The above-mentioned results are concerned with the global employment evolution in foreign-owned enterprises and Belgian manufacturing. It was also possible to carry out a *direct comparison between foreign subsidiaries and local firms* (Table 10.10). One should be aware that the figures in Table 10.10 reflect the employment situation of companies that continued to exist throughout the whole period (either 1971-1976 or 1974-1976).

From 1971 to 1976 employment in multinational subsidiaries increased 9 percent (index = 109), while Belgian firms registered a decrease of 4 points (index = 96). As uninational Belgian firms succeeded in slightly increasing their number of jobs (index = 101), it becomes apparent that Belgian MNCs are responsible for the employment loss in Belgian firms. That the better employment performance of multinational subsidiaries is strongly influenced by their sectoral distribution is shown by the simulated index calculated on the hypothesis of a similar sectoral concentration of Belgian and foreign firms. Especially in the post-crisis period 1974-1976, the simulation

Table 10.10. Employment Effects of Belgian and Foreign-owned Subsidiaries (1971-1976)

| | Employment Evolution | | | | Degree of Qualification | |
| | 1971-1976 | | 1974-1976 | | University Educated as Percentage of Total White-collar Workers | |
	N	Index (1971 = 100)	N	Index (1974 = 100)	N	%
Global Sample						
Belgian enterprises	195	96	210	94	191	7
Belgian uninational enterprises	169	101	182	96	168	5
Foreign enterprises	201	109	235	99	233	7
American enterprises	86	108	97	100	97	9
EEC enterprises	101	109	121	99	117	5
Simulated Totals						
Belgian uninational enterprises		101		96		5
Foreign enterprises		104		95		6
American enterprises		117		95		7
EEC enterprises		94		96		5

Source: D. van den Bulcke and E. Halsberghe, *Effects of Multinational Enterprises on Employment: A Belgian Case Study* (Geneva: ILO, 1980), pp. 79-80.

results in a concurrent employment evolution for both foreign and local enterprises.

A previous study has already shown that the statement of the "Conseil professionnel du métal" that foreign subsidiaries employ fewer *university and technically educated employees* than local firms is untrue.[18] This complaint toward MNCs must again be rejected on the basis of the 1976 study, which was limited to university-trained employees (Table 10.10). According to the global sample, foreign and local firms both employ 7 percent of the academically educated persons. The average for foreign enterprises is the result, however, of a higher ratio (9 percent) for American subsidiaries and a lower ratio (6 percent) for German and French subsidiaries. Many Dutch companies run their Belgian subsidiaries from the Netherlands with only 4 percent of their white-collar workers having obtained a university degree. In Belgium uninational companies, 5 percent of the clerical job holders have gone through the university. As far as university-trained personnel is concerned, the foreign-owned enterprises showed the best results in machine construction and chemicals.

TECHNOLOGICAL ORIENTATION

"The promotion of applied technological research and its reorientation" is also part of the government's industrial policy.[19] The first question to be raised here is to what extent foreign enterprises are more "research and development" oriented than Belgian firms. The second question is what attention is devoted to the development of new products. The third question is especially interesting as it deals with the so-called research intensity, as measured by R&D expenditures as a percentage of total sales and the number of researchers as a percentage of total personnel (Table 10.11).

The global sample indicates that there is little or no difference in *research frequency* between foreign and local uninational enterprises 39 and 37 percent, respectively. Under the influence of Belgian MNCs the proportion of Belgian enterprises engaged in research activities increased to 43 percent, which brings their proportion to the same level as that of the American subsidiaries. According to the matched sample, Belgian firms (exclusive and inclusive of Belgian MNCs) are relatively more active in research than their foreign competitors. That a relatively small number (only one-third) of EEC firms are engaged in research is mainly caused by the low research activity of the Dutch subsidiaries. In comparison with the earlier inquiry of 1968 relatively more foreign subsidiaries have become engaged in

Table 10.11. Research Characteristics of Belgian and Foreign-owned Enterprises (1976)

	Research Frequency		Research into New Products as Percentage of Companies Engaged in Research		Research Intensity				Research Appeal to Other Enterprises	
					R&D Expenditures as Percentage of Sales		R&D Personnel as Percentage of Total Personnel			
	N	%	N	%	N	%	N	%	N	%
Global Sample										
Belgian enterprises	94	43	80	85	94	1.67	94	2.6	64	29
Belgian uninational enterprises	70	37	56	80	70	1.77	70	1.8	46	24
Foreign enterprises	98	39	69	74	59	1.52	69	4.9	189	76
American enterprises	47	45	35	78	33	2.17	36	6.0	85	83
EEC enterprises	41	32	27	69	18	1.09	26	3.9	90	71
Matched Sample										
Belgian enterprises	41	44	35	85	41	1.40	41	2.4		
Belgian uninational enterprises	36	41	26	72	36	1.34	36	2.2		
Foreign enterprises	34	37	24	73	22	1.80	20	4.7		
Simulated Total										
Belgian uninational enterprises	70	37				1.77		1.8		
Foreign enterprises	67	35				1.05		2.7		

Source: F. Haex, E. Halsberghe, and D. van den Bulcke, pp. 184, 189, 194, 196, and 202.

research in Belgium. At that time only 27 percent of all foreign firms, 32 percent of American firms, and 18 percent of EEC firms had started a research program in Belgium.

Belgian firms concentrate their research efforts more frequently on the *development of new products*, although this is mainly due to Belgian MNCs. On the basis of the matched sample, 73 percent of Belgian uninational firms and foreign enterprises are interested in new product research, as compared with 85 percent for Belgian manufacturing as a whole. Foreign subsidiares are engaged relatively more in research on the adaptation of existing products and production processes for the local market. Foreign subsidiaries often produce the same products as their parent company and have to adapt these products to the specific market situation of the host country and its local regulations. The concentration of research on new products by Belgian firms is most striking in chemicals, transport equipment, and electronics as well as wood and paper.

When *research intensity* is measured by expressing R&D expenditures as a percentage of sales, one finds a ratio of 1.52 for foreign-owned firms as compared with 1.77 for Belgian companies. The low foreign average results from a combination of the high research intensity of American subsidiaries (2.17 percent) and the low resarch intensity of EC firms (1.09 percent).

Although foreign subsidiaries are more research intensive, the elimination of sectoral differences through a simulated average results in a higher research intensity for Belgian enterprises. These results are limited to enterprises that are effectively engaged in research activities. When the calculation is carried out for all enterprises (i.e., firms that are active in research and firms that are not), it is clear that the foreign enterprises are less research intensive than their Belgian competitors. The corresponding ratios are 0.6 for foreign subsidiaries, 1.01 for Belgian uninational companies, and 1.42 for all Belgian enterprises, including Belgian MNCs.

The question of the research-intensive nature of Belgian and foreign enterprises is not settled completely if a second measure (research personnel as a percentage of total personnel) is used. According to this criterion foreign subsidiaries appear to take their research more seriously than do local firms. In foreign and American subsidiaries 4.9 and 6 percent, respectively, of all employees are employed in the research department, as compared with 1.8 percent for Belgian uninational companies and 2.6 percent for all Belgian enterprises. The supremacy of foreign and American subsidiaries is confirmed by the matched sample and the simulated totals.

A possible explanation for the contradictory results in R&D

expenditures and R&D personnel may be because of the relatively high number of researchers who are also responsible for other tasks in the smaller subsidiaries. In contrast, a high proportion of research personnel in foreign subsidiaries is concentrated in the chemical, electronic, and machine construction industries. In these sectors, the ratio of R&D personnel to total personnel is three to four times higher than the ratio R&D expenditures to total expenditures, while this proportion is only one to two times higher in the less scientifically oriented sectors. It has been pointed out that foreign MNCs are more active in scientifically oriented industries.

AUTONOMOUS DECISIONMAKING

From a different point of view the new Belgian industrial policy also stipulates that one should "try to limit the dependence on foreign decisionmakers, without neglecting the important contribution of foreign direct investment on employment."[20]

The size of the foreign presence in the Belgian economy increases the host country's *potential vulnerability*, especially if the subsidiaries have an ethnocentric relationship with their parent companies, which means that they are inclined to give priority to the interests of the parent country rather than the host country. A similar vulnerability may exist in the most multinationally oriented MNCs, which scan the world and look for optimal advantages for their globally flexible strategy on the basis of a great many subsidiaries scattered around the world. The subsidiaries of the "most multinationally oriented companies" are responsible for 22 percent of industrial employment in Belgium (two-thirds of all employment provided by foreign subsidiaries) while their sales and employment represent only about 1 percent of the sales and workforce of the multinational groups themselves.[21] The Belgian government is definitely in a weak bargaining position, especially if there is any collusion between the larger MNCs.

Another dimension of this vulnerability can be found in the fact that foreign subsidiaries dominate the "secteurs de pointe." Additional difficulties may crop up because of the issue of extraterritoriality, which means that foreign subsidiaries are urged to follow regulations specified by the parent country. American subsidiaries in particular have been exposed to measures from the country of origin (e.g., trade with countries from the East bloc, antitrust rules, balance of payment regulations) that upset the policy objectives of the host country. Belgium has been confronted with this problem in a Cuban order for combines from Clayson, a subsidiary of Sperry Rand, and President Johnson's balance of payment regulations (1965, 1968). In the latter case Belgium felt obliged to put up alternative funds for the American MNC to avoid a decrease in industrial investment in its economy.[22]

The study of the competitive advantages of MNCs points out that more than half of the subsidiaries see a definite *advantage in belonging to a larger multinational group.* They especially mention their direct access to the R&D potential of the group (one-third of the companies), or their use of brand names from the parent company (one-fourth), or the cheaper purchases that result from group imports (7 percent). About three-fourths of the responding firms, foreign as well as Belgian, thought that their productivity was one of their main competitive advantages, while two-fifths argued that their market knowledge and market experience gave them a competitive edge and one-fifth attached great importance to their superior management. The calculation of the matched sample showed that product quality and better management were more important for foreign subsidiaries than indigenous firms, while a more differentiated product package was quoted more often by local firms. Access to particular patents was valued more highly by foreign than indigenous firms (24 percent as compared with 6 percent).

There is little evidence about the extent to which the competitive advantages of foreign subsidiaries spill over to the national economy. There are few indications that these advantages spin off to the consumers or the buyers outside of the multinational group. Whenever the specialization strategy of an MNC is based on product differentiation or consists of a special product chain that stretches across national frontiers, the spillover effects tend to be limited. Antitrust policy should try to evaluate to what extent the dominating positions of MNCs on the national market do not exclusively accrue to the multinational group.

National authorities should certainly be aware that the *decision center for product development* of the foreign subsidiaries is outside their own frontiers. Somewhat less than half of the foreign subsidiaries in Belgium are unable to decide independently about launching a new product or carrying out important changes in an existing product.[23] Investment decisions are very narrowly regulated as they are at the nerve center of the control system of the multinational parent.

In 1968, only about 13 percent of the surveyed subsidiaries thought that they could decide autonomously about their investment priorities, while 6 percent believed that the influence of the parent company was rather limited.[24] The 1976 study confirms these results. Only 3 percent of the foreign subsidiaries in Belgium could freely choose their own investment projects and put up a new division, while only 13 percent were allowed to sell off their fixed assets without permission from headquarters. About one out of three subsidiaries could make these decisions about interference, although they were obliged to ask for the parent's company opinion beforehand. The choice of investment projects, the creation of a new division, and the sale of fixed assets were subjected to prior permission from head-quarters in 66, 63, and 57 percent of all cases, respectively. In addition, investment expenditures are often limited to a certain ceiling. Only 30 percent of the American and 40 percent of the non-American subsidiaries in Belgium can spend more than 500,000 Belgian francs without prior approval from the parent company.[25]

Decisions about the *marketing mix* are not altogether left to the subsidiaries either. The choice of suppliers and buyers is reserved for the parent company for one out of four subsidiaries, while the multi-national headquarters also works out the price policy for one out of three of their subsidiaires. Non-American enterprises are typically more free to carry out their marketing programs.

About one-fourth of the foreign subsidiaries experienced a parent company influence in the field of international trade. This again presents difficulties for the national government when its export strategy is not receiving sufficient response from the foreign subsidiaries. Export restrictions that rule within the multinational group may present a particular problem as they often imply that the subsidiary in the host country is not allowed to export to the home market of the MNC or to third markets reserved for other members of the multinational group. About 70 percent of the American subsidiaries in Belgium have no access to the North American market, while about 60 percent of them are excluded from the Latin American market. Fifty percent of the U.S. subsidiaries in Belgium have no permission to export to Asia, while 30 percent of them have no access to the African countries. The same phenomenon can be detected for MNCs of other nationalities, especially as far as the home market of the country of origin is concerned. To present a complete picture of the multinational practice of export restrictions, it should be added that as a rule the subsidiary in Belgium receives exclusive rights to the West European market, at least within the multinational system to which it belongs.

Personnel policy is generally the most decentralized. In 1968, one out of five EEC subsidiaries was strongly controlled from abroad in personnel matters as compared with one out of ten American affiliates. For recruitment and personnel selection in general, it was found that in 1976 one out of ten subsidiaries was strongly controlled by headquarters, while about two-thirds of them could carry out their employment policy independently. For the recruitment and selection of top managers, however, a strong parent company control is applied in 30 percent of all EEC-based firms and 25 percent of all U.S.-affiliated firms, while only 25 and 30 percent of the subsidiaries, respectively, could decide to engage top managers and middle managers without an explicit agreement by the parent company.[26]

It is often thought that multinational subsidiaries are closed down more often and more quickly than local firms during a period of economic decline or crisis. Indigenous uninational firms often lack sufficient flexibility to reorient their production activities with changing economic conditions. Closure of a division or a subsidiary does not have the same drastic consequences for an MNC as for an uninational firm for which the closure may be the end of its activity. It has been shown, however, that there was no tendency for MNCs in Belgium to divest more frequently than indigenous enterprises.

Research by the MNCs is mostly carried out by the parent company at headquarters. This undoubtedly implies that it becomes difficult for host countries to carry out an independent research policy of their own. In more than half of the foreign subsidiaries in Belgium the research program is decided upon in the country of origin, which means that the parent company makes the final research decisions after asking the opinion of the management of the subsidiary. Even when the MNC follows the research priorities of the host country, and especially if it accepts government funds for its research program, two important questions remain to be answered. First, there is the question of final ownership of the research results, and second, there is the question of where the product improvements or product innovations will be brought into production. Because there are many options available to the MNC, there is no guarantee that the product will be developed within the boundaries of the host country where the innovation was sponsored. In Belgium the Royal Decree of January 18, 1977 (about the development of the results of research that was financed with government funds), mentions certain provisions that intend to protect these results from the point of view of the Belgian economy.

CONCLUSION

When the Belgian government elaborated its proposals for a new industrial policy, its intention was "to catch up with the structural effects of the economic crisis in production and employment." The policy intends to "enable Belgian industry to look after its industrial creativity and employment in the coming ten years in a more autonomous way." This desire for an independent industrial policy is immediately weakened, however, by the remark that it "should not be chauvinistic and take into account the natural vocation of a small country to attract foreign direct investment, on the one hand, and to work in a multinational framework, on the other hand." A footnote explains that multinational framework means subscribing to the OECD guidelines, which were signed in 1976 and were extended in 1979.[27] This statement actually means, without really saying so, that Belgian industrial policy fully accepts the so-called principle of non-discrimination and does not intend to differentiate in its policy measures between national and multinational enterprises as such. This principle was a necessary linchpin in making the guidelines acceptable to a number of industrial countries. It remains to be seen if an industrial policy that tends to strengthen local industry without discriminating against foreign subsidiaries can be developed.

It follows from the above analysis that multinational subsidiaries in Belgium generally perform better than uninational firms and respond more closely to the government's objectives. The multinational subsidiaries were able to build a competitive position that withstood better the assaults of the economic crisis; to develop a more diversified production package; to realize a higher value-added; to be more market-oriented than their local competitors; to export more and span a larger geographical export area than the uninational firms; to increase the number of jobs during 1968–1975 while Belgian industrial employment stagnated; and to maintain their employment level during the post-crisis years of 1975–1978 while a great number of jobs were being lost in Belgian manufacturing.[28]

The performance of the multinational subsidiaries in research was not as good as that of the local firms, however. Multinational subsidiaries are also less interested in the development of new products and concentrate relatively more on development work than indigenous firms. This less vital research effort by the foreign subsidiaries is because of their permanent access to the research potential of the parent company. Other examples have been given of areas in which multinational subsidiaries are subject to the global strategy of the multinational group in which they are integrated. It is not possible to estimate the side effects of the multinational presence that might harm the economic development of the host country. Belgian governments have, especially since 1960, held the opinion that these negative effects were not important enough to restrict the activities of multinational subsidiaries on their territory. In fact, a very active

promotional policy was followed. There is, however, no escape from
the question of whether a more selective policy would not have been
able to eliminate or diminish certain drawbacks while increasing certain spillover effects.

The "new industrial policy" mentions a *new approach toward
foreign direct investment* in Belgium. Beginning with the decline of
new MNCs that have been established in Belgium since 1975, the
government's paper pleads for a renewed promotional campaign
toward foreign enterprises that are still in the first stages of the mul-
tinationalization process. The new industrial policy also insists that
"joint ventures" are preferable in order "to limit Belgium's dependence from abroad."[29] Such a policy is definitely outdated, however.
First, a larger indigenous participation in the equity capital of the
subsidiary does not mean that local influence on the decisionmaking
of the foreign MNC will be enhanced.[30] Second, there are few indications that the greater influence of local residents would result in
more respect for the objectives of the industrial policy. Third, the
financial resources that would be used to acquire a minority or
majority position in the joint venture might, in view of the technological dominance and marketing and management superiority of
MNCs be put to better use if they were spent on the development of
local industry based on technological contracts with foreign MNCs.
Measures like these that were mentioned in the government's document might be a good start.[31]

Most support should be given to plans for diversifying Belgian industry in activities that result in a higher value-added, employ more
qualified personnel, and have a larger technological content. As
MNCs perform better than uninational firms, methods to help indigenous companies without necessarily discriminating against foreign-
owned subsidiaries should be sought out. This selectivity might be
achieved by orienting governmental support to the specific needs of
the smaller local firms. Export promotion might be an example.
Instead of offering indiscriminate financial advantages and expecting
too much from direct investment abroad, export promotion should
be geared to companies that export only to a few neighboring countries and lack the funds and expertise to penetrate other markets.
Perhaps a certain amount of government funds could be set aside
for these firms. Another aspect is innovation. Instead of concentrating
only on innovative enterprises with the necessary knowledge, management, financing, and marketing to carry out a "breakthrough"
innovation, more attention should be given to improvements in the
production process. Product adaptations and quality improvements
might lead to an enlargement of the product package and sometimes

to backward linkages to new products. Participation in turnkey projects might improve the experience and extend the markets of these firms. The government should look for ways to stimulate these developments without neglecting the promotion of the transfer of technology to local industry.

When explaining the objectives of Belgian industrial policy, the government stresses that the small number of *Belgian MNCs* as compared with other small industrial countries such as Switzerland, Sweden, and the Netherlands, presents them with a handicap.[32] When discussing export promotion, the white paper also stipulates that "a selective support of foreign ventures abroad becomes more urgent in order to safeguard and develop employment in the industrial countries. For smaller enterprises investing abroad brings about difficulties, problems, and risks with which they are unable to deal alone. The government should therefore, with sufficient attention to the social implications of each operation, stimulate and support these investments abroad.[33]

The government's position toward Belgian direct investment abroad is thereby made official a number of years after this policy was actually started. In 1971 the government established the "Belgian Corporation for International Investment" (SBI) while in the same year the "Ducroire" received permission to insure against political and "catastrophic" risks for capital invested and profits realized abroad as well as loans to subsidiaries in foreign countries. Belgian Foreign Trade Office (OBCE) can also grant financial support to enterprises establishing commercial ventures abroad that may eventually develop into production units.

It cannot be denied that the internalization process could sharpen the competitive power of Belgian enterprises. There is a real danger, however, that the Belgian government will not be sufficiently selective toward outward investment, as was the case with inward investment. During the 1960s investment abroad may have been necessary to hold onto certain markets in the long term, but quite often negative short-term effects such as decreased exports and loss of employment are implied. As the positive effects of investing abroad work out only in the long term, adjustment measures, for example, retaining workers, have to be made far enough in advance. It will be necessary to test investment projects abroad for their microeconomic as well as their macroeconomic effects and, when the venture abroad has sufficient merits, level out the negative effects by preparing the necessary support.[34]

Although the white paper on industrial policy often points out the dangers of a loss of independence, one is inclined to think that the

Belgian government is not too serious about its pursuit of an independent industrial policy. Some proposals may be intended only to calm down certain groups that have expressed their concern about the possibility of Belgian manufacturing disappearing completely into the larger foreign multinational structures. Support of joint ventures will have little effect on the autonomy of Belgian industry, while measures to strengthen Belgian MNCs as a countervailing force are likely to result in even less government influence in the industrial field.

When evaluating the Belgian economic expansion law of 1970, J. Boddewyn concluded that for the dilemmas of industrial policy "much is of a symbolic nature that [it] is designed, at least in part, to prove to the electorate that government has vision and is ready and able to act on economic problems." He added that "much of what passes for an industrial policy is in fact of a social nature, since it amounts to various attempts to save or create jobs in order to alleviate or avoid serious dislocations and their political repercussions."[35] This latter remark applies very much to the part of the government's "communication" about public industrial initiatives and contractual planning, which was not dealt with in this chapter. The questions whether Belgian industrial policy can remain national in scope given the increasing frictions between the Flemish and Walloon region, and whether it should be integrated within the framework of an EEC industrial policy have not been addressed here.

NOTES

1. For more details see G. De Baere and D. van den Bulcke, "De buitenlandse ondernemingen in de Belgische industrie: Omvang, evolutie en kenmerken." In *Multinationale Ondernemingen in de Belgische Economie*, edited by D. van den Bulcke (Ghent: SERUG, 1978), pp. 79 and 84; and F. Haex, E. Halsberghe, and D. van den Bulcke, *Buitenlandse en Belgische Ondernemingen in de Nationale Industrie* (Ghent: SERUG, 1979).

2. L. Tindemans and W. Claes, "Communication du gouvernement concernant 'une nouvelle politique industrielle,'" Chambre des Representants, Session 1977-1978, 22 February 1978, p. 67. This "white paper" will be abbreviated as NPI.

3. E. van Lommel, "Het nieuwe industriële beleid in België," *Beleid*, June 1979, p. 15; and *Intermediair*, 11 January 1980, p. 3.

4. J. Dunning, "Trade Location of Economic Activity and the Multinational Enterprise: A Search for an Eclectic Approach," University of Reading, Paper No. 29, 1976; and P. Buckley and M. Casson, *The Future of the Multinational Enterprise* (London: Macmillan, 1976).

5. NPI, p. 22.
6. Ibid.
7. Haex, Halsberghe, and van den Bulcke, pp. 85-90.
8. NPI, pp. 21 and 57.
9. D. van den Bulcke et al., *De Buitenlandse Ondernemingen in de Belgische Industrie* (Ghent: SERUG, 1971), p. 201.
10. Nationale Raad voor Wetenschapsbeleid, *Wetenschappelijk Onderzoek en Economische Groei II* (Brussels, 1967), p. 50.
11. NPI, pp. 23-24.
12. Ministry of Foreign Trade, *Een beleid voor Buitenlandse Handle: Een Werkdocument* (December 1979), p. 63.
13. See, for example, F. Haex and D. van den Bulcke, *Belgische Multinationale Ondernemingen* (Diepenbeek: VWOL, 1979), pp. 126-133.
14. van den Bulcke et al., *De Buitenlandse Ondernemingen*, pp. 200-201.
15. NPI, p. 21.
16. D. van den Bulcke and E. Halsberghe, *Employment Effects of Multinational Enterprises: A Belgian Case Study* (Geneva: International Labor Office, 1980).
17. E. Halsberghe and D. van den Bulcke, "Desinvesteringen van buitenlandse ondernemingen in de Belgische industrie," in *Multinationale Ondernemingen in de Belgische Economie*, edited by D. van den Bulcke (Ghent: SERUG, 1978), pp. 133-167.
18. van den Bulcke, *De Buitenlandse Ondernemingen*, pp. 218-222.
19. NPI, p. 21.
20. Ibid., pp. 21 and 57.
21. D. van den Bulcke, *De Multinationale Onderneming: Een typologische benadering* (Ghent: SERUG, 1975), pp. 128-129.
22. Ibid., pp. 142-144.
23. D. van den Bulcke and E. Halsberghe, "Degree of Multinationality and Foreign Headquarter-Subsidiary Relationship in a Belgian Context," working paper, Stockholm School of Economics, 1980, p. 31.
24. van den Bulcke, *De Buitenlandse Ondernemingen*.
25. van den Bulcke and Halsberghe, "Degree of Multinationality."
26. Ibid.
27. Ibid.
28. A much smaller matched sample in the same sector (mechanical engineering industry) in Great Britain, however, showed better results for the uninational companies in labor productivity and export intensity and a similar performance in profitability and other financial criteria. (R. Solomon and K. Ingham, "Discriminating Between MNC Subsidiaries and Indigenous Companies," *Oxford Bulletin of Economics and Statistics*, May 1977, pp. 127-138).
29. NPI, p. 19.
30. E. Halsberghe and D. van den Bulcke, *Managementautonomie van buitenlandse industriële onderneming en in België*, working paper.
31. For a more detailed discussion of joint ventures, see van den Bulcke, *De Multinationale Onderneming*, pp. 355-359.

32. NPI, p. 21.
33. Ibid., p. 24.
34. For a more complete description of the effects of Belgian foreign direct investment abroad, see Haex and van den Bulcke, *Belgische Multinationale Ondernemingen.*
35. J. Boddewyn, "The Belgian Economic Expansion Law of 1970: The Levels and Ideological Content of Industrial Policy," in *Industrial Policies in Western Europe*, edited by S. J. Warnecke and E. Sulemein (New York: Praeger, 1975), p. 73.

Chapter 11

MNCs and the Australian Government: Some Emerging Policy Issues

Lawrence R. Welch* and
Finn Wiedersheim-Paul†

The subject of this volume is particularly appropriate to the current situation in Australia, for the policy issues surrounding the activities of multinational corporations (MNCs) in Australia and their contribution to the goals of the government are likely to be of major concern throughout the 1980s.

During the late 1970s persistent, high levels of unemployment emerged in Australia for the first time in the postwar period. Unemployment in August 1974 was still only 2.4 percent (a historically high figure), but it jumped to around 6 percent by the end of 1977 and has remained above this figure to 1980. The official figure probably understates significantly the real extent of unemployment because of the large pool of the hidden unemployed (see 18, p. 32). There appears to be little confidence that unemployment will disappear rapidly in the 1980s, yet political pressure has been mounted for a solution to the problem.

As an important element of its response to the situation, the government has embarked on a strategy of encouraging large-scale mining and mineral processing projects to provide the necessary impetus to economic growth and employment. A large proportion of

*School of Business Studies, Darling Downs Institute of Advanced Education, Australia.
†Department of Business Administration, University of Uppsala, Sweden.

these investments will come from MNCs, which will place great strains on the objective of maintaining Australian equity in natural resource development and exploitation. In addition, because of the highly capital-intensive nature of these projects, the employment-creating effects are likely to be somewhat less than is hoped for. As a result of their export orientation and the foreign capital inflow necessary to finance them, the mining and mineral processing projects are likely to cause the exchange rate to rise and thereby accentuate the problems of the more labor-intensive sections of the manufacturing industry. While the solution to the problems of the manufacturing sector is often couched in terms of a shift to a more technological and export orientation, such a change will be difficult to engineer because of the generally derivative nature of Australian technology, imported to a large extent via the MNC subsidiaries.

In this chapter we analyze the emerging policy issues concerning the involvement of MNCs in Australia and put forward some alternative approaches that the experience of other countries suggests might well be considered by the Australian government.

AUSTRALIAN FOREIGN INVESTMENT POLICY

Australia already has very high levels of foreign ownership in most areas of economic activity. United Nations data reveal that, among the advanced countries, foreign control in Australia's main industrial sectors is exceeded only by Canada (35, p. 265). That Australia has reached this degree of foreign penetration is partly explained by its past foreign investment policy and its colonial heritage. British investment has been important throughout the twentieth century, although it was relatively more important in earlier years. The colonial connection ensured easy entry by British firms, and helped to develop the derivative industrial structure that has remained a feature of the Australian manufacturing industry. During the post-World War II period American investment grew rapidly and played an important role in the expansion of the manufacturing and mining sectors. Taken over the 1950s and 1960s, Britain was still the most important source of investment, contributing 44 percent, but the United States and Canada accounted for 39 percent of the total (21, p. 101).

An interesting aspect of the two main sources of investment is that the beginnings of concern about foreign investment were associated more with the growth of American rather than British investment, as the then president of the American Chamber of Commerce lamented in 1963:

> A visitor to Australia might be pardoned for reaching the conclusion that overseas investment in this country is a synonym for American investment—for such a conclusion is to be drawn from editorials and letters from correspondents. . . . What is the peculiar ingredient that makes American investment suspect while investment capital emanating from Britain, France, Germany, Switzerland and other areas attracts unto itself no special nomenclature? Is U.S. money, then, some kind of monster? (8, p. 10).

While there was a growing concern expressed about the level of foreign investment during the 1960s, the government maintained a basic "open door" policy until the 1970s. The attitude of the federal government is perhaps best summarized in a comment by Prime Minister Gorton in September 1969:

> The importance to Australia of a strong and continuing inflow of overseas capital has never been questioned by my Government . . . Without that investment, it would have been impossible for us to develop as quickly as history demands we must . . . (15).

Not only were there a minimum of constraints placed upon the investment but it was also actively encouraged. Only in a few areas, for example, broadcasting, television, and civil aviation, was foreign investment specifically restricted.

The election of the Labor government in 1972 heralded a major change in the approach toward foreign investment, at least as the federal level. The Labor government was firmly committed to ensuring a larger Australian share of new investment projects. Its policy included financing of energy and mineral development projects through large-scale overseas borrowing rather than relying on capital inflow via the MNCs. It even aspired to the objective of "buying back the farm," that is active purchase of foreign interests so that assets were returned to Australian ownership. However, this government was removed from office before most of its policies in the field of foreign versus local ownership could be brought to fruition. A foreign takeover law, which provided a mechanism of control over takeovers of local firms by foreigners, was one of the few vestages of its three years if office.

Nevertheless, the new government fulfilled Labor's objective to some extent by setting up a broad framework of administrative controls over new foreign investment. In this sense, the government reflected perceived community concern about foreign ownership, reinforced during Labor's term in office. The foreign investment guidelines that have operated since 1976 are therefore a legacy of this Labor government.

The general stated purpose of these guidelines is to ensure a significant measure of Australian equity in new foreign investment proposals and that such investment conforms to the "national interest."

Each foreign investment proposal that is subject to screening is assessed for its contribution to the national interest on the basis of considerations such as:

The net economic benefits the proposal is likely to produce in relation to such matters as competition, technology, and export markets.

Whether the business concerned could subsequently be expected to pursue practices consistent with Australia's interests in matters such as local processing of materials, research and development, and industrial relations.

Whether the proposal would be in conformity with other government economic and industrial policies.

The main categories of foreign investment proposals that are screened, subject to certain minimum levels of investment, are:

1. Foreign takeovers of existing Australian businesses.
2. New foreign investments, including those by established foreign firms in new lines of business.
3. Purchase of real estate.
4. Proposals involving nonbank financial institution.
5. New mining or natural resource projects.

With regard to category 5, the government added two general rules:

1. *The 75 percent rule*—for uranium projects there should be a minimum Australian equity of 75 percent.
2. *The 50 percent rule*—apart from the national interest criterion, there should be a minimum Australian equity of 50 percent in new mining projects.

The application of these rules, and of policy in other key sectors of the economy, can be modified by a phased-in "Australianization" of the foreign enterprise. Investment is acceptable if there is a minimum of 25 percent Australian equity, an Australian-dominated board, and a public commitment to increase Australian equity to 51 percent.

In addition, when the application of the 75-percent uranium rule was regarded as likely to hold up a new uranium project in Western Australia, the government decided to reduce the benchmark to 50 percent in cases where:

1. Australian equity is unavailable in excess of 50 percent.
2. The project would be of significant economic benefit to Australia.

It should be noted that the Foreign Investment Review Board (FIRB), which administers the foreign investment screening mechanism, is only an advisory body. The government is not obliged to accept the recommendation of the board.

The true test of the outlined foreign investment policy of the Australian government is, of course, in the way in which it is applied. On the whole, it is possible to argue that the foreign investment guidelines have not been allowed to prevent the development of major new investment projects. For example, during 1978–1979, of 1052 proposals examined by the FIRB, only six were rejected outright, with 287 being approved subject to conditions. Of the rest, 168 did not require approval under the guidelines, while 591 were approved without conditions.

The chairman of the FIRB recently commented that:

> It is the practice of the board not to recommend that the Government reject a proposal until all avenues for amending it to make it compatible with the Government's foreign investment policy have been explored with the parties" (3).

In general, then, the approach of the government and the FIRB has been that, wherever possible, the rules are applied flexibly so that projects will go ahead. For example, the Worsley bauxite mine and alumina refinery (in Western Australia) was given approval in late 1979 despite an Australian equity in the project of only 20 percent (40 percent U.S., 30 percent Shell, 10 percent Japanese).

To some extent, of course, the foreign investment controls are ineffective in screening the expansion of foreign control as they do not apply to internal expansion by foreign firms within the same industry structure—apart from the movement into new mining projects. Given the high levels of foreign ownership already in both mining and manufacturing, the controls, such as they are, are bound to have only limited effects.

Therefore, while Australia does have a foreign investment policy demanding that such investment conform to a set of clearly articulated guidelines, the application of the policy has tended to maintain a relatively "open door" to the MNCs.

So far we have concentrated on the federal government's policy toward foreign investment. However, this is not the only factor in the MNC—government relationship, as an important part of the negotiation process occurs with state government. In the mining sector state government power extends to such areas as exploration rights, royalties, infrastructure, railways, and environmental rehabilitation. The state governments are in some sense in competition for MNC investment, because of the implications for jobs, revenue, and the supply of infrastructure. They tend to be less concerned about such national issues as export price, balance of payment implications, and the degree of foreign control. Thus, the federal government is often pressed by the state governments to modify equity guidelines or other controls to ensure that projects go ahead, as we shall see later in the case of the Blair Athol mine in Queensland.

MNCS, MINING, AND MINERAL PROCESSING

As stated already, the economic problems of the late 1970s, as evidenced by the high level of unemployment, have led the government to place great faith in the impetus provided by the large mining projects and associated processing activities scheduled to go ahead in the 1980s. For example, the minister for employment has recently stated: "I see no reason, given the energy imperative now working to Australia's advantage, why Australia cannot sustain high and rising economic growth, employment, and living standards throughout the 1980's" (22). The government is depending very heavily on this strategy as they have eschewed stimulation by traditional Keynesian methods, particularly via public sector spending, and have indicated that they are looking to improvement in the private sector as a basis for long-run recovery.

Before assessing this argument, it is important to stress that mining has not been a large employer of labor, even with the major developments of the last 15 years, while the increased unemployment in the late 1970s was very much associated with the decline in employment in the manufacturing sector, as Table 11.1 reveals.

There is no doubt that the energy crisis has worked to Australia's advantage in creating a strong and growing demand for the energy resources that Australia is well equipped to supply—especially coal. However, the abundance of energy-related natural resources not only results in the production and export of these resources to an energy-scarce world, but also affects the comparative advantage that Australia possesses with regard to the processing of minerals. This applies par-

Table 11.1. Employment in Broad Industries, August 1971–1978

Industry	Employment (thousands) at August			
	1971	*1973*	*1975*	*1978*
Agriculture	390.1	401.5	380.3	353.0
Forestry, fishing and hunting	22.4	24.7	17.4	24.4
Mining	89.1	69.5	79.1	79.5
Manufacturing	1364.9	1382.3	1262.9	1185.3
Food, beverages, and tobacco	201.6	215.4	193.9	192.3
Metal products, machinery and equipment	230.5	222.6	216.4	197.0
Other manufacturing	932.8	944.3	852.6	795.9
Construction	471.0	503.2	511.1	485.0
Wholesale and retail trade	1112.5	1187.1	1156.9	1238.6
Transport or storage	294.2	312.4	330.3	326.5
Finance, Insurance, real estate, business services	395.1	401.3	430.5	465.8
Community services (including education)	615.7	692.4	793.2	919.0
Entertainment, recreation, restaurants, hotels and personnel services	331.9	355.6	371.5	364.9
Other industries	428.8	453.2	508.1	527.6
All industries employment	5515.7	5783.0	5841.3	5969.6
Labor Force	5608.4	5888.7	6119.7	6365.3
Unemployment	92.7	105.8	278.4	393.7

Source: 9, p. 48.

ticularly to aluminium smelting, which is a heavy user of electricity. In the past the Australian aluminium smelting industry has mainly been aimed at servicing local demand. Now there is a major expansion in capacity to service export markets such as Japan, which is reducing its involvement in aluminium smelting (see 11).

A recent survey found that of $16.3 billion committed or expected to be spent on projects in the final feasibility stage, $9.1 billion was for mining projects and $7.5 billion for manufacturing. The manufacturing figures, however, included $4.6 billion to be spent on various integrated aluminium projects. Virtually all of the increased aluminium capacity will go toward servicing the export market, which could be worth about $1.8 billion by the mid-1980s as compared to $70 million in 1978 (14, pp. 13–14).

IMPLICATIONS OF ALUMINIUM EXPANSION

1. In all of the investments to be undertaken, there will be a heavy reliance on the vertically integrated MNCs, not only to under-

take the investment but also to establish world markets for the product. In 1972–1973 foreign control of the alumina and aluminum smelting industries was almost 60 percent of value-added. The dominant role of foreign interests will not be altered by the latest expansion because MNCs are instrumental in each new project. For example, a major part of the new investment will be undertaken by existing foreign-owned producers: Comalco (Kaiser, U.S. principal partner), Alcoa, and Alcan. In addition, new ventures such as Alumax (Alumax, U.S. principal partner) and Worsley (Reynolds, U.S. principal partner) have Australian equity figures of only 35 and 20 percent, respectively.

2. The new aluminium smelting projects have raised serious questions about the viability of the government's foreign investment policy and its attempt to ensure a satisfactory level of Australian ownership. The Worsley case has already been noted as breaching the guidelines, yet approval was nevertheless obtained. In addition, the expansions by existing producers have created a situation where a major export industry has been created with very limited Australian involvement and with Australian foreign investment policy unable to affect many change in this situation.

3. Given the electricity used by aluminium smelters, it is estimated that there will be heavy capital costs associated with the supply of power to the new smelters, on the order of $1 billion. Because of the premium on energy resources, this has led to questions regarding the price and availability of energy for the smelters, which are enclave-like operations. In negotiations with the state Governments the major aluminium producers have been able to negotiate very low bulk electricity rates. Already these are being put forward as evidence of a real transfer of wealth away from the community (36).

4. The employment question has been at the forefront of the government's support of the aluminium expansion, yet the employment generated by the new projects will certainly not be enough to reverse the decline in the manufacturing sector. The projects are highly capital intensive, with an investment of about $1 million in plant, equipment, infrastructure, and power generation for every extra job directly involved in the smelting operation. Overall it is expected that about 6000 permanent additional employees will be required in the new smelters and aluminium refineries (see 14, p. 13). A study of one of the new smelters estimated that the maximum additional number of jobs indirectly created throughout Australia would be of the order

of 3 : 1 (28). Thus, in total, about an extra 24,000 jobs might be created directly and indirectly by the developments in the aluminium industry.

However, the sheer success of expansion in the aluminium industry, and its dominant export orientation, alongside the growth of other export-oriented natural resource projects (e.g., uranium, liquefied natural gas, and coal) are likely to pose problems for other sections of the manufacturing sector—with negative employment implications. It is these other sections of manufacturing that represent the largest employers of labor (see Table 11.1), including the more labor-intensive activities like textiles, clothing, and footwear, in which the largest drop in employment has occurred. The export earnings likely to be generated by new mining and processing projects will ensure that the exchange rate for the Australian dollar is higher than would otherwise be the case. This will not only make exporting more difficult for the rest of manufacturing but will also maintain pressure from import competition, which has already made major inroads into the manufacturing sector in the 1970s. In other words, the exchange rate mechanism will be part of the adjustment pressure shifting manufacturing activity from more labor-intensive areas to capital-intensive fields like mineral processing (see 17). As a result, the net employment-creating effect of the aluminium industry expansion is likely to be somewhat less than the government is hoping for.

COAL INDUSTRY

The experience of the aluminium industry expansion is repeated to some extent in the coal industry—although the expansion process has been occurring for a long time. Nevertheless, the energy crisis has provided a new impetus to coal. In fact, coal is now Australia's largest single export earner, with nearly 40 million tons exported in 1978–1979, valued at $1519 million. Rapid expansion of this figure is expected in the 1980s with large investments planned, particularly to exploit the growing demand for steaming coal for use in electricity generation in such countries as Japan, Taiwan, and South Korea. In the past, Australian trade in coal with Japan has principally been in coking coal to service the iron and steel industry. However, recently the Japanese interest has moved more strongly toward steaming coal as it urgently seeks to reduce its dependence on imported oil. Japan is seeking to reduce its oil dependence from 77 percent in 1977 to 62.9 percent in 1985 and 50 percent in 1990. As a result, it is estimated that Japan will import between 18 and 22 million tons of steaming coal from Australia by 1985, and 37 to 43 million tons by 1990 (see 10). Although it is not as dominant as in aluminium, the export trade will take a large proportion of the new production. Some of the increased production will, of course, go to domestic energy production—including that for aluminium smelting.

In 1976–1977 foreign control of the black coal sector had reached 59 percent. Thus, like the aluminium industry, the expansion in coal mining is occurring from a basis of a very high degree of foreign control—with all of the attendant problems already mentioned for aluminium. Likewise, coal mining is a highly capital-intensive industry, so that there will not be a large expansion in employment to operate the new projects.

As with aluminium, the MNCs will be playing a key role in the new coal development projects. However, there is another side to this issue in Australia as the major oil companies are part of the new investment activity. Notable among the oil companies making the move into alternative energy stocks are Exxon (Esso Australia), Shell, and British Petroleum. The oil companies have also been investing in uranium. Already the interests of the oil companies in Australian coal mines are extensive. The debate surrounding this concentration of ownership in energy resources, however, has an international dimension, as the *Economist* has recently noted:

> . . . the political debate in Australia echoes a question that the governments of the world will increasingly have to face as the oil majors use their huge cash flows to diversify into coal and other minerals (31).

From what has been said about the foreign investment guidelines so far, it would appear that this policy will be tested as much by the investment activity of MNCs in coal as in the aluminium industry. While it is true that the foreign control, it is interesting that the most notable case where the government has held firm on its 50 percent local equity rule involves an international oil company (see 27). The Australian government announced in mid-April 1980 that it would not allow Japan's Electric Power Development Company to acquire a 19 percent interest in the planned Blair Athol steaming coal project from Conzinc Rio Tinto of Australia (38.9 percent Australian-owned but classified as "naturalizing" Australian). This would have meant a reduction in effect Australian equity to 25 percent. The oil company Atlantic Richfield holds a 38 percent equity in the project, although it is likely that some pressure will be applied to reduce this figure, thereby allowing Japanese involvement.

Blair Athol is an important test case for the guidelines as the government has previously argued that the benefits of Japanese utilities taking equity in such projects is a means of locking in the end market. The project was also considered important because it would further justify infrastructure developments for nearby coal mines. The state government concerned with the project has requested that it go ahead and that the foreign investment guidelines be scrapped.

The Blair Athol case exposes once again the acute policy dilemma that the government faces of a perceived reliance on MNCs for resource development while trying to maintain an acceptable level of Australian ownership. In addition, it has been shown that the capital-intensive and export-oriented nature of the various mining and mineral processing projects will mean that the net additional employment generated is not likely to produce a marked reduction in unemployment in the 1980s—especially in the manufacturing sector (apart from mineral processing).

MNCS, TECHNOLOGY, AND EMPLOYMENT IN THE MANUFACTURING SECTOR

The Australian manufacturing industry has developed in the postwar period with large inputs of foreign investment—as evidenced by the high levels of foreign ownership in the manufacturing sector. Until the 1970s, a large-scale immigration program ensured adequate opportunities for Australian growth—reinforced by high levels of protection against import competition. Not surprisingly, a study of American investment in Australian industry found that the principal reason for investment was "to take advantage of the expected growth of the Australian market" followed by the concern "to overcome tariff barriers" (8, p. 36).

Associated with the foreign investment has come a strong reliance on overseas technology. In fact, a recent investigation concluded: "the general picture that emerges is of an Australian manufacturing industry which derives most of its new technology from overseas, mainly through multinational corporations." A continuation of this pattern is expected because "the ratio of local R and R expeditures in manufacturing to overseas payment for technical know-how is lower than in most other advanced countries" (25, p. 244).

Manufacturing growth has stabilized in the 1970s, however, resulting in a relative and absolute fall in its position as an employer of labor. The pressures on manufacturing in the 1970s have come from two sides. To begin with, the growth of the internal market has diminished as a result of a reduced immigration program and a continued decline in the birth rate. On the other side, there has been an intensification of import competition, resulting in an increased share of imports in the domestic market as Table 11.2 reveals.

As well as the specific pressures noted above, there were also the general effects, in the mid to late 1970s, of inflation, recession, technological change, and equal-pay decisions.

In response to this situation, a committee set up to inquire into the future of manufacturing concluded in 1975 that it must become more internationally oriented: "Now that the domestic market is satiated and can grow only slowly, most manufacturing is stalled and lacks purpose. It needs to export to grow" (24, p. 1).

This philosophy was later endorsed in the government's White Paper on Manufacturing Industry in 1977:

> The Government's future approach to long-term industry policy is therefore concerned primarily with the development of a stronger and more specialized manufacturing industry in Australia than in the past. The Government endorsed the view expressed in the Green Paper (R. G. Jackson et al) that it is desirable to give encouragement to new investment that will be efficient, internationally competitive, and export oriented, particularly where it is based on Australian talents, skills, or resources, and where the degree of processing or transformation is the maximum consistent with international competitiveness (5, p. 1).

Table 11.2. Share of Imports in the Market for Australian Manufacturers (%): 1968-1969, 1973-1974, and 1976-1977.

	Share of Imports in Domestic Demand		
Industry Description	1968-1969	1973-1974	1976-1977
Food, beverages, and tobacco	3.6	6.1	7.6
Textiles	30.8	40.6	40.6
Clothing and footwear	5.4	17.0	22.7
Wood, wood products, and furniture	7.3	10.7	11.7
Paper and paper products, printing	16.7	16.5	18.0
Chemical, petroleum, and coal products	24.0	28.7	33.2
Nonmetallic mineral products	7.9	9.3	10.5
Basic metal products	7.2	9.3	8.0
Fabricated metal products	7.7	8.6	11.3
Transport equipment	27.5	30.9	32.3
Other machinery and equipment	32.1	36.0	46.2
Miscellaneous manufacturing	18.4	23.4	33.7
Total	16.5	19.9	23.7

Source: 23, p. 91.

The objective of greater international orientation will be difficult to achieve. It requires a shift from a structure and approach developed over a long period of time. In many industries, for example, motor vehicles and chemicals, optimal productive efficiency has not been achieved because an excessive number of MNCs, induced by high levels of protection, have set up production facilities in and for the small Australian market, often with suboptimal plants. This, of course, affects the export propensity of the Australian operations (see 32, pp. 176 and 180). The government has shown a reluctance to reduce tariff protection as a means of forcing a change. In fact, in some areas (e.g., motor vehicles) protection has actually been expanded through the application of import quotas and tariff increases. At a time of high unemployment, the electoral consequences of a wholesale reduction in protection make such a move not politically feasible. Because of its free enterprise philosophy, the government has in the main opted out of the idea of positively engineered structural adjustment. As a result, it has taken the softer approach of introducing a very much expanded export promotion policy. Cash grants are provided not only to develop export markets, but also for any increase in exports that is achieved.

THE ROLE OF MNCs

Given that so much of the control of the Australian manufacturing sector lies in the hands of MNCs, it is important to question whether the activities of the MNCs will fit in with the government's objective of greater export orientation and expansion. Apart from the mineral-processing possibilities, there is no reason to expect that the lack of growth in the internal market will not be reflected in the scale of MNC investment. Particularly in the more labor-intensive areas of manufacturing, Australia has little attractiveness as an export base for MNCs. What impact, then, are the MNCs likely to have on employment and export growth from the manufacturing sector?

1. The minerals-processing area has already been referred to, and it constitutes a special category of substantial export growth and some increase in employment.
2. The derivative nature of Australian technology, very much associated with the role of MNCs in Australia, has already been mentioned. With regard to the effect of this dependence on export capacity, Johns has noted: "The prospects for exports of 'technology-intensive' manufactured goods are not likely to be

good unless a considerably greater effort is made to increase local R&D expenditure in specific areas of technology" (25, p. 247).

It can be further argued that the dependence on overseas technology stifles the development of domestic technological skills.

However, greater spending on local research and development is not a sufficient condition for increased manufactured exports. Where such spending occurs by MNC subsidiaries (e.g., to take advantage of R&D incentives), it may only produce technological benefits that are exploited elsewhere in the MNC system. The MNC subsidiaries do actually spend proportionately more on R&D than do local firms. The Australian Bureau of Statistics found that 51 percent of expenditure in Australian manufacturing industry (1976–77) was undertaken by foreign-controlled enterprises—as against a 33 percent owner figure (see 3). Never-the less, there is also evidence that much of the R&D is directed toward modifying overseas technology to local conditions and is therefore unlikely to provide the basis of technological uniqueness and technology-intensive exports (see 33, p. 115, and 34).

3. As preeminent agents of technology transfer, the MNCs can be expected to play a major role in transferring the labor-saving technological developments that are set to flow through into industry in the 1980s for example, in the application of so-called chip technology (see 6). While the introduction of these innovations are a necessary part of the long-term viability of Australian manufacturing in a world context, they will inevitably pose some important employment dislocation and adjustment problems. In a study of foreign firms in Australian manufacturing industry, Parry found that foreign ownership was associated with higher levels of capital intensity—indicating a greater preparedness to use labor-saving production techniques (see 32, pp. 193–96).

4. Because of the attractiveness of the fast-growing East Asian economies as bases for servicing world markets, it can be expected that much of the attention of the MNC investment will be directed toward this region. Philips, for example, has reported that "it will have to develop its labor intensive activities in countries where production costs are low and reduce its concentration in high cost areas" (7). Even Australian-owned firms substantially increased their investments in near-Asian economies, especially Singapore, Malaysia, and Hong Kong, during the 1970s (see 12). There is no reason to believe that the growing trend of using offshore low-wage bases would be halted in

the 1980s, by MNCs as well as locally owned firms, which does not augur well for the development of export-oriented operations in Australia.

5. The likelihood of expanded MNC export operations from Australia may well depend on the extent to which they are prepared to incorporate a larger role for their Australian subsidiaries in an integrated global production system, rather than simply allowing them to produce for a limited growth, but increasingly competitive, Australian market.

POLICY ALTERNATIVES

While there is an almost uncritical acceptance of the need for foreign investment by the present Australian government, a lingering concern remains in many quarters that the overreliance on MNCs is not in the best long-term interests of Australia. This concern is being expressed in various ways, although the following statement by the chairman of Conzinc Rio Tinto of Australia (one of Australia's largest, though "Australianizing," foreign-controlled companies) is a typical example (20, p. 27):

> People don't realize the cost. If you get $2 in 1979 from overseas invested in equities, those owners want a dollar a year from 1990 onwards forever. What I'm saying is this: That's a very high price, but in political terms it doesn't seem a high price because they see the $2 coming in today, but in 10, 11 years' time, a dollar a year going out is an enormous price to pay . . . I think that at the present time the attitude is too often that we should continue our reliance on the international oil companies for source of capital. That's an easy way, but in the long term I don't think it's going to create the kind of jobs for young Australians which I want for my kids.

It is important therefore to canvass the alternatives to the policy approach adopted by the current government. Is MNC investment so necessary, or does the experience of other countries indicate an alternative, feasible path. Much of the argument in support of the present policy of allowing MNC investment on such a large scale centers around their provision of a total package of capital, technology, managerial know-how, and, most importantly, a marketing infrastructure that ensures the success of each venture. It is argued that development will occur far more slowly, if at all, when the elements of the package are broken up. Nevertheless, overseas experience demonstrates that it is possible to unbundle the package in various ways in order to obtain the best elements of the package without ceding ownership.

If the unbundling approach were to be adopted, a major question would be the availability of finance, because it has been difficult in the past to generate local funds even when MNCs have offered local equity participation. It would almost certainly require the tapping of international capital markets, perhaps through the medium of government borrowing. While such borrowing involves a debt burden to foreign interests, it would not carry the same foreign control effect as MNC investment. Given the present world premium on energy resources, the type of investment projects that Australia is able to offer would meet little difficulty in obtaining international finance.

A key aspect of the MNC package is technology. Under the present foreign investment guidelines the introduction of new technology via the establishment of an Australian subsidiary is a major factor supporting approval. Little attempt has been made to encourage the direct purchase of technology apart from MNC investment. Clearly though, countries such as Japan have demonstrated that technology can be obtained to develop industry without ceding foreign ownership. Japan is not unique in this respect among the Asian nations, and it is interesting to compare the position of the newly industralized Asian countries to that of Australia with respect to the mechanism of U.S. technology transfer.

Research by Davidson (13, p. 92) indicates that transfers of technology via licensing to independent producers is far more important in the rest of Asia than in Australia. The evidence suggests a more deliberate unbundling strategy (see 19). The South Korean government, for example, is heavily involved in encouraging the transfer of technology via simple licensing arrangements (26).

Particularly in the field of energy resources and their exploitation, there is a major role that governments can play to ensure greater local participation, in a way that involves greater spinoffs for local industry. Norway's strict insistence on local involvement in the exploitation of its offshore oil and gas reserves is indicative of the more favorable bargains that can feasibly be extracted. A major spinoff has been the acquisition of the technology of offshore oil rig design, construction, and operation. Norwegian expertise in this area is now being exported (16, pp. 20–1, and 30).

In Australia, the state governments have a long history of involvement in coal mining for power generation purposes (16, p. 17). It would seem, therefore, that the skills and technology developed in this area could be readily expanded to international sales. A key problem, however, would be market access, and this is where MNCs have been able to retain such a strong control position in Australia. Grant (16, p. 17) quotes the problems of two locally owned companies in obtaining long-term contracts for bauxite and alumina projects because of lack of involvement of the aluminium "majors."

CONCLUSION

Although alternative policy approaches to Australian development in the 1980s are feasible, there seems to be a lack of political will to pursue them. As a result Australia will remain highly dependent on MNCs for the direction and type of development that takes place. In the process, it is likely that MNC operations will fall short of achieving a number of policy objectives of the federal government, for example, in the areas of employment and local technological initiatives, while they are likely to conflict with other objectives in the area of local equity participation. It seems that Australia may well be already too highly dependent on MNCs to undertake a major change in approach even if it wanted to. Perhaps the colonial heritage and the lack of a struggle for independence (16, p. 24) has induced an acceptance of dependence that would not be tolerated in most other countries.

APPENDIX 11.1

Foreign Control and Protection in Australian Manufacturing

Foreign Control of Australian Manufacturing Industry: Percentage of Total Industry Value-added Accounted for by Foreign-owned Enterprise, 1972–1973.		Average Effective Protection in Australian Manufacturing Industry (%)		
Industry	1972–1973	1968–1969	1973–1974	1977–1978
Food, beverages, and tobacco	33	16	18	13
Textiles	33	43	35	57
Clothing and footwear	12	97	64	149
Wood, products, and printing furniture	7	26	16	18
Paper, paper products, and printing	17	52	38	29
Chemical, petroleum, and coal products	75	31	25	18
Nonmetallic mineral products	16	15	11	5
Basic metal products	38	31	22	14
Fabricated metal products	18	61	44	32
Transport equipment	55	50	39	61
Other machinery and equipment	42	43	29	21
Miscellaneous manufacturing	33	34	24	27
Total manufacturing	34	36	27	26

Source: 4 and 23, p. 83.

Foreign Control in 200 Largest Enterprises. In 1975–1976, the largest 200 enterprise groups in Australian manufacturing industry accounted for 50 percent of the value-added of all manufacturing industry. Eighty-six of the largest 200 enterprise groups were foreign controlled and they accounted for 43 percent of the value-added of the enterprise group and 22 percent of the value-added in all manufacturing industry.

In 1975–1976, foreign-controlled groups in the largest 20 enterprise groups accounted for over 50 percent of total value added in the following industries (*Source*: 1):

Tobacco products
Basic chemicals
Petroleum refining
Nonferrous metal basic products
motor vehicles and parts

Foreign Control in Australian Mining Industry

In 1976-1977, foreign-controlled establishments accounted for 59 percent of total value-added in the mining industry in Australia. (*Source*: 2.)

Foreign control was above 50 percent in the following industry classes:

Bauxite
Copper
Mineral sands
Silver–lead–zinc
Tin
Black coal
Crude Petroleum

Foreign control in:

Black coal	Value-added: 59.2 percent
Brown coal + crude petroleum (including natural gas)	Value-added: 84.2 percent
Total coal and crude petroleum	Value-added: 67.4 percent

Definitions

Value-Added: Turnover, plus increase (or less decrease) in the value of stock, less purchases, transfers in, and selected expenses. The item purchases, transfers in, and selected expenses refers to purchases of materials, fuel, power, containers, etc.

Foreign Control: An enterprise has been classified into foreign control if a foreign resident investor (individual, company, or group of related companies) or foreign-controlled enterprise held at least 25 percent of the paid-up value of voting shares in the enterprise, provided that there was no larger holding by an Australian-controlled enterprise or Australian resident individual.

REFERENCES

1. Australian Bureau of Statistics. *Foreign Control in Manufacturing Industry: Study of Large Enterprise Groups*, 1975–1976, Cat. No. 5315.0. Canberra, 1978.
2. ———. *Foreign Control in the Mining Industry*, 1976–1977, Cat. No. 5329.0. Canberra, 1978.
3. ———. *Foreign Control in Research and Development: Private Enterprise*, 1976-1977, Cat. No. 5330.0. Canberra, 1979.
4. ———. *Foreign Ownership and Control in Manufacturing Industry*, 1972–1973, Cat. No. 5322.0. Canberra, 1976.
5. Australian Government. *White Paper on Manufacturing Industry*. Canberra. Australian Government Publishing Service, 1977.
6. Barron, A. "Microelectronics Survey," *Economist*, March 1, 1980, pp. 1–18.

7. Batchelor, C. "Philips Is Confident of Longer Term Prospects." *Australian Financial Review*, April 17, 1980, p. 35.

8. Brash, D. T. *American Investment in Australian Industry*. Cambridge, Mass.: Harvard University Press, 1966.

9. Bureau of Industry Economics. *Employment of Demographic Groups in Australian Industry*. Canberra: Australian Government Publishing Service, 1979.

10. Byrnes, M. "Japan Report Sees Australia as Major Steaming Coal Source." *Australian Financial Review*, February 6, 1980, p. 54.

11. Byrnes, M. "The Japan-Australia Aluminium Exchange," *National Times*, April 6-12, 1980, p. 53.

12. Carstairs, R. T., and Welch, L. S. "Australian Offshore Investment in Asia." *Management International Review* 20, no. 4 (1980), pp. 17-25.

13. Davidson, W. H. "Trends in the International Transfer of U.S. Technology to Pacific Basin Nations." In *Proceedings of the Academy of International Business: Asia-Pacific Dimensions of International Business*. Honolulu: College of Business Administration, University of Hawaii, 1979, pp. 86-93.

14. Department of Industry and Commerce. "Aluminium Expansion and Its Impact on the Australian Economy." *Journal of Industry and Commerce* 21 (December 1979), pp. 13-15.

15. Gorton, J. G. Ministerial Statement. *Parliamentary Debates*. Canberra, June 16, 1969. Quoted in R. B. McKern. *Multinational Enterprise and Natural Resources*. Sydney: McGraw-Hill, 1976, p. 19.

16. Grant, P. "The International Transfer of Technology for Secondary Processing Projects in Australia." Paper delivered at the Fourth Australian Mining and Petroleum Law Association National Conference, Sydney, June 1980.

17. Gregory, R. "Some Implications of the Growth of the Mining Sector." *Australian Journal of Agricultural Economics* 20 (August 1976), pp. 113-120.

18. Gregory, R., and Duncan, R. "Wages, Technology and Jobs." *Australian Economic Review*, No. 45, First Quarter, 1979, pp. 22-32.

19. Helleiner, G. K. "The Role of Multinational Corporations in the Less Developed Countries' Trade in Technology." *World Development*, April 1975, pp. 161-189.

20. Hickie, D. "Who Owns Australia?" *National Times*, June 8-14, 1980.

21. Hughes, H. "Technology Transfer: The Australian Experience." In *Multinationals from Small Countries*, edited by T. Agmon and C. P. Kindleberger. Cambridge, Mass.: M.I.T. Press, 1977, pp. 101-127.

22. Hywood, G. "Pitfalls in the Primrose Path Back to Full Employment." *Australian Financial Review*, March 24, 1980, p. 12.

23. Industries Assistance Commission. *Annual Report: 1978-1979*, Canberra: Australian Goverment Publishing Service, 1979.

24. Jackson, R. G., et al. *Policies for Development of Manufacturing Industry*. Vol. 1. Canberra: Australian Government Publishing Service, 1975.

25. Johns, B. L. "The Production and Transfer of Technology." In *Growth, Trade and Structural Change in an Open Economy*, edited by W. Kasper and T. Parry. Kensington: Centre for Applied Economic Research, University of New South Wales, 1978, pp. 239-253.

26. Kim, H.-K. "Approaches to the Inducement of Foreign Technology: The Korean Experience." Paper presented at the International Licensing Conference on Technology Transfer: A Blueprint for Asian Pacific Development, Sydney, March 27-30, 1979.

27. Korporaal, G. "Government Blocks Key Coal Deal." *Australian Financial Review*, April 16, 1980, pp. 1-2.

28. Mandeville, T. D., and Jensen, R. C. *Economic Impact of Industrial Developments at Gladstone.* Brisbane: University of Queensland, 1979.

29. "Norway Squeezes," *Economist*, February 16, 1980, p. 81.

30. Ogg, T. "FIRB Admits Giving Every Aid to Foreigners in Takeovers." *Australian Financial Review*, March 4, 1980, p. 6.

31. "Oilmen Dig In." *Economist*, November 24, 1979, p. 20.

32. Parry, T. D. "Structure and Performance in Australian Manufacturing, with Special Reference to Foreign-Owned Enterprises." In *Growth, Trade and Structural Change in an Open Economy*, edited by W. Kasper and T. Parry. Kensington: Centre for Applied Economic Research, University of New South Wales, 1978, pp. 173-199.

33. Parry, T., and Watson, J. "Technology Flows and Foreign Investment in the Australian Manufacturing Sector." *Australian Economic Papers* 18 (June 1979), pp. 103-117.

34. Stubbs, P. *Innovation and Research: A Study in Australian Industry.* Melbourne: Cheshire, 1972.

35. United Nations. *Transnational Corporations in World Development.* New York, 1978.

36. Walsh, G. "Transfer of Wealth in Cheap Smelter Power." *Australian Financial Review* July 25, 1980, p. 46.

Chapter 12

The Relationship of MNC Direct Investment To Host Country Trade and Trade Policy: Some Preliminary Evidence

Andrew R. Blair*

This chapter attempts to shed some light on certain questions that have been raised in the literature concerning the international trade and trade payments policies of host country recipients of direct foreign investment. The study focuses on the extent of the relationship between the manufacturing direct investment in Latin America of U.S. -based multinational corporations (MNCs) and the trade of their affiliates in that region. While these findings are based on aggregative data from official sources, they should provide some insights into the nature of the impact of international trade in developing nations on MNC direct investment in such countries.

Thanks are due to my colleagues Michael Spiro and Dung Nguyen of the Graduate School of Business, University of Pittsburgh, for their valuable advice and comments. I also wish to thank my graduate assistants, Rosita Chang and T.S. Raghunathan, for their help with the data analysis. The comments of the participants in the Berlin IIM MNC/Government Relations Conference on the draft of this paper were also very helpful. However, the usual disclaimer applies concerning my sole responsibility for errors and inaccuracies.
*Graduate School of Business, University of Pittsburgh.

MNC DIRECT INVESTMENT AND
DEVELOPING COUNTRY TRADE

Considerable practical interest has been expressed in the increasingly important phenomenon of developing country exports of manufactured goods to the industrialized countries, as well as the multinational corporation as a possibly important vehicle for this type of trade (either on an intrafirm or conventional basis). Additionally, economists have recently begun to show more formal interest in the role of MNCs in the manufactured exports of "host country" developing nations. MNC direct manufacturing investment in developing countries has traditionally been viewed as being associated with production for the *domestic* market, much of it occurring as part of a process of "import substitution" (which for a number of years was deliberately fostered through government trade and foreign exchange policies in various countries, especially in Latin America). Now it is being suggested by some observers that manufacturing activity in many developing countries is beginning to swing more toward production for export markets, and that the MNCs are a major factor in this movement.

Both of these possible investment–production relationships (i.e., import substituting and export producing) can look to the theoretical literature for support. Mundell, for example, has demonstrated within the conventional factor proportions framework that a *substitutable* relationship should exist between trade in commodities and factor movements.[1] This occurs because free trade in commodities will result in the elimination of factor price differentials, thus also eliminating the incentive to the movement of capital (as well as other factors) between nations. A corollary of this view is that the erection of import barriers will permit factor price differentials to persist, thus providing the inducement needed to encourage the international migration of factors. In turn, this provides a rationale for the frequently observed tendency of MNCs who are faced with increasing import barriers to step up their direct investments in countries in which they had previously established export markets.

The product life cycle literature[2] also lends support to a connection (during a later phase of the cycle) between import substitution and direct investment. This approach involves a departure from the factor proportions theory and its assumption that production functions are always and everywhere identical. Instead, it recognizes that knowledge is unevenly distributed among nations and that possession of an innovation can initially serve as a basis for exporting a given product. However, according to this approach product innovations often are eventually disseminated to importing nations, where the underlying factor proportions (and factor prices) may be such as to result in import replacement by domestic production. Furthermore, as in the trade barrier case mentioned above, such production for the domestic market may well still be carried on via direct investment in the host country by the same MNCs that previously had served this market through exports.

A newer view, however, is that a close relationship exists between developing country manufactured exports and MNC direct manufacturing investment. This view also lies outside the factor proportions framework. An extended version of the product life cycle model, for example, envisions a subsequent phase (beyond the import substitution phase) during which MNC production in the host country attains a scale sufficient to take full advantage of a plentiful, low-cost indigenous labor supply. In this phase, MNC affiliates may then begin to produce for the export market (exporting to the home country as well as to third countries). Another approach linking exports and direct investment is based on the suggestion that there is frequently a "global strategy of established multinational companies.[3] Some companies, it is asserted, will engage in *horizontal* specialization—manufacturing different products in different countries and supplying the total world market from each. Others will specialize vertically—assigning the manufacture of specific components of an overall process to a subsidiary in a given country, with final production and assembly occurring elsewhere.[4] This latter pattern has been emphasized by Helleiner.[5] Aided, for example, by U.S. tariff items 806.00 and 806.30 (which provide for the levying of import duties on a product only on the basis of value-added abroad, if the manufactured inputs originated in the United States) Helleiner asserts that many vertically integrated multinational manufacturing firms are locating their specialized labor-intensive activities in various developing country subsidiaries. Thus, in this view, MNCs are currently "knitting the less developed countries into their international activities as suppliers not merely of raw materials but also of particular manufactured products and processes."[6]

Finally, and not unrelated to the above, Hufbauer, building on the ideas of Schmitz and Helmberger, has suggested a further basis for MNC specialization and export of labor-intensive products from the developing countries.[7] In the case of *primary* products, Schmitz and Helmberger had pointed out that foreign capital has served to develop highly specific, *immobile* factors (e.g., oil, mineral deposits) for subsequent export. However, according to Hufbauer this complementary relationship between direct investment and exports may well now need to be extended to more advanced forms of manufactures: "If the relaxation of trade barriers (in industrial countries) continues, the definition of specific immobile factors might be extended to include cheap labor in less developed countries."[8]

ALTERNATIVE TRADE–DIRECT INVESTMENT HYPOTHESIS

This review suggests two alternative hypotheses regarding the effect of a host country's international trade on direct investment from abroad. One alternative reflects the traditional (e.g., Mundellian) view that such investment responds inversely to changes in import barriers in the host country—an increase in such barriers, for example, attracting additional direct investment. In a subsequent section, we will discuss the formulation of a proxy variable capable of reflecting changes in the degree of restrictiveness of such government policy toward imports.

The other alternative might be termed the "export-induced" direct investment hypothesis. This position has not been formulated as rigorously, and thus it is possible to state three potential versions. The most basic version would simply suggest that the export sales of manufactures from MNC affiliates in a given country (overall and by sector category) exert a significant positive influence on MNC direct investment in these sectors. A somewhat stronger version would suggest the existence of a positive relationship between the ratio of a country's MNC export sales-to-total MNC sales in given sectors and the growth of direct investment in such sectors. Under this version, sectors with increasing export-to-total sales ratios would be expected to attract greater direct investment growth than sectors with decreasing (or less rapidly rising) ratios.

The strongest version of the hypothesis would address the extent to which MNC-manufactured exports are not only inducing direct investment, but are also playing a leading role in the host country's exports. Under this version, sectors with increasing ratios of MNC export sales to *country* exports would be expected to induce greater direct investment growth than sectors with decreasing (or less rapidly rising) ratios.

Each of these export-oriented versions asks a question of interest to those wishing to understand the relationship between MNC direct investment and MNC host country exports, and our review has suggested several plausible bases for linking such manufacturing direct investment in the developing countries to the growth of their manufactured exports. The older direct investment–import barrier hypothesis, however, is equally plausible on *a priori* grounds.

SCOPE OF THIS STUDY

Using the conceptual framework and alternative hypotheses outlined above, this chapter will analyze the nexus between U.S. direct manufacturing investment in Latin America and that region's U.S. affiliate export sales and overall trade in manufactures. Inasmuch as MNCs are apparently a more important factor in Latin American manufactured exports than is the case for most of the developing countries of Asia,[9] it is an especially relevant region in which to examine the extent of the relationships among MNC affiliate manufactured exports, government trade and payments policies, and MNC direct manufacturing investment. Unfortunately, our knowledge of the trade of MNCs in developing countries is quite limited, and only the United States has attempted to track systematically some of the export activities of the foreign affiliates of its home-based companies.[10] For the affiliates of other major industrial countries, the record is largely contained in a variety of research studies and monographs.[11] In view of the growing importance in the developing countries of MNCs based in Western Europe and Japan, it would naturally have been preferable to have included the Latin American trade and direct investment activity of non-U.S. MNCs in our study. However, the United States is currently the only country that generates the kind of data needed for a study of the type described below.[12]

Exclusion of non-U.S. MNCs will require us to exercise considerable caution in drawing conclusions from our data analysis, especially since U.S. MNCs have been declining in recent years relative to other MNCs. Nevertheless (and as will be shown below), U.S. MNCs are still a major element in the economies of other countries, especially the developing countries of Latin America.

The rest of this chapter is organized into the following sections:

1. A comparative review of manufacturing direct investment patterns, especially with respect to Latin America.
2. Recent patterns and trends in U.S. affiliate export sales of manufactured goods in Latin America.
3. Latin American manufacturing import substitution and export diversification trends.
4. Preliminary data comparisons of U.S. MNC affiliate export and direct investment patterns in Latin American manufacturing.
   Some regression results pertaining to the import barrier and export generating hypotheses.

The study is generally concerned with the period from the early and mid-1960s to about 1967. A lack of data precludes a detailed treatment of earlier years, as well as the period since 1976.

U.S. MANUFACTURING DIRECT INVESTMENT PATTERNS

The United States remains a major, if relatively declining, source of direct investment; in 1976 approximately 48 percent of the stock of foreign direct investment for all developed market economies was accounted for by the United States, as compared with 11 percent for the United Kingdom, and 7 percent each for West Germany, Japan, and Switzerland.[13] In addition, industrial sector direct investment stock data compiled by the United Nations for the United States, United Kingdom, West Germany, Japan, Canada, and Italy reveal a similarly continuing major role for U.S. direct investment as of the mid-1970s.[14] The preponderance of the stock of U.S. manufacturing direct investment (81 percent in 1978) is located in the industrialized nations. Comparable figures for the United Kingdom (1974 data) and West Germany (1976 data) were 85 and 79 percent, respectively. Japan, on the other hand, had channeled more than 40 percent of its stock of manufacturing direct investment to the developing nations as of 1974.[15] The absolute size of the stock of U.S. manufacturing direct investment in the developing countries, however, is such as to represent the largest source of such investment (roughly three times that of West Germany, four times that of Japan, and almost five times that of the United Kingdom as of the mid-1970s).[16]

The striking feature of U.S. manufacturing direct investment in the developing countries is its heavy identification with Latin America. As can be seen from Table 12.1 (which also summarizes the 1963–1978 relative distribution of the stock of U.S. manufacturing direct investment in selected Latin American Republics), the Latin American share of U.S. direct manufacturing investment in the developing countries has been consistently within the 81–88 percent range. The relative trend, however, has been in the downward direction, as such U.S. investment has grown more rapidly elsewhere in the developing world.

Table 12.1 also shows that Argentina, Brazil, Mexico, and Venezuela together accounted in 1963 for 82.3 percent of the stock of U.S. MNC manufacturing direct investment in Latin America. By 1978, this proportion was still essentially the same (81.3 percent). However, Brazil's share had expanded to 40 percent of the total (up

Table 12.1. Stock of U.S. Manufacturing Direct Investment in the Developing Countries and in Latin America, at Year-end 1963-1978

Year	Developing Countries (millions of dollars)	Latin America (millions of dollars)	Percentage of Which			
			Argentina	Brazil	Mexico	Venezuela
1963	$ 2516	$ 2213	20.5%	30.0%	22.7%	9.1%
1964	2890	2507	19.9	26.6	24.2	8.8
1965	4301	2945	21.0	24.6	25.7	8.4
1966	3525	2973	17.2	19.3	31.2	9.5
1967	3891	3238	16.6	19.4	31.4	8.9
1968	4439	3723	15.8	20.3	30.8	9.3
1969	5047	4202	15.7	21.4	30.4	9.0
1970	5477	4541	14.7	23.7	30.4	9.2
1971	6038	4995	14.3	24.5	29.9	9.2
1972	6767	5620	13.2	27.8	29.0	8.7
1973	7820	6456	11.9	31.7	27.9	8.0
1974	9200	7541	9.8	34.2	28.8	8.2
1975	10,459	8562	8.9	36.3	28.5	7.8
1976	11,395	9275	9.7	39.6	23.9	8.0
1977	12,324	10,063	9.2	39.1	23.8	9.3
1978	14,071	11,644	8.4	40.2	23.6	9.1

Source: 1963-1965, *Survey of Current Business*, various issues; 1966-1978, *Selected Data on U.S. Direct Investment Abroad, 1966-78;* both U.S. Department of Commerce, Bureau of Economic Analysis.

from 30 percent in 1963), while Argentina had undergone a sharp decline to 8.4 percent, as compared to just over 20 percent in 1963. Mexico's share expanded until 1967, but has since receded to its earlier relative position (23-24 percent). Veneuzela's share of U.S. MNC direct manufacturing investment showed little tendency to change during this period.

MNC EXPORT SALES OF MANUFACTURES IN LATIN AMERICA

As one would expect on the basis of the direct investment data in Table 12.1, Latin American affiliates of U.S. companies have accounted for a high proportion of total affiliate export sales of manufactures from the developing nations (see Table 12.2). This proportion was approximately 58 percent in 1967 but had dropped below 50 percent by 1970, subsequently recovering to 54 percent by 1976. However, despite its relatively modest share in total U.S. manufacturing direct investment in the developing nations, the share of exports from the "other Asia and Pacific" category (which includes India, Indonesia, Korea, the Philippines, and other countries not specifically identified, such as Taiwan) rose from 38.3 percent in 1976 to almost 45 percent in the early 1970s, later falling back to 38.4 percent in 1976.

Table 12.2 provides the basis for this disparity between export shares and direct investment shares among U.S. manufacturing affiliates in the developing nations: During this period, the other Asia and Pacific group generated export sales that ranged from approximately 22 percent to almost 30 percent of total sales, whereas the

Table 12.2. Affiliates of U.S. Companies in the Developing Countries: Overall Manufacturing Export Shares, 1967–1976

Year and Country Group	Total Sales[a]	Local Sales[a]	Export Sales[a]	Share of Export Sales in Total Sales	Share of U.S. Affiliate Total Developing Country Export Sales
1967					
Developing countries	7,773	7,044	729	9.4%	—
Latin America	6,558	6,136	422	6.4	57.9%
Other Asia and Pacific	1,034	755	279	27.0	38.3
1970					
Developing countries	11,347	10,331	1016	9.0%	—
Latin America	9,345	8,862	492	5.3	48.4%
Other Asia and Pacific	1,688	1,239	449	26.6	44.2
1973					
Developing countries	19,722	17,749	1,973	10.0%	—
Latin America	16,220	15,230	930	6.1	50.2%
Other Asia and Pacific	2,911	2,048	863	29.6	43.7
1976					
Developing countries	32,864	29,768	3,096	9.4%	—
Latin America	26,251	24,575	1,676	6.4	54.1%
Other Asia and Pacific	5,547	4,357	1,190	21.5	38.4

Source: Calculated from unpublished U.S. Department of Commerce data (for earlier years) and published data (later years) in "Sales by Majority-Owned Foreign Affiliates of U.S. Companies," *Survey of Current Business*, various annual issues.

[a]Sales data are in millions of dollars.

Latin American share ranged only from 5.3 to 6.4 percent. U.S. affiliates in Latin America thus appear to have generally been less export-oriented than those in this Asian–Pacific group of countries. Nevertheless, the dollar volume of Latin American affiliate exports of manufactures did rise significantly during this span of years; and, as noted, the share of such export sales in overall U.S. affiliate developing country export sales continued to be substantial throughout the period.

Tables 12.3 to 12.5 provide additional sectoral data relating to the manufactured export sales of U.S. affiliates in Latin America. As is evident from Table 12.3, such export sales, in general, are a relatively small share of total U.S. MNC sales of manufactured products in the region. Thus, U.S. manufacturing affiliates in Latin America have produced primarily for the *domestic* markets in which they reside. However, export markets are more important for affiliates in specific sectors and countries (e.g., food products in Argentina, electrical machinery in Brazil and Mexico, nonelectrical machinery in Argentina, transport equipment in Mexico). Moreover, many of the export sales ratios have been rising over time; the implications of this trend are discussed in a subsequent section.

As suggested in the literature review section, direct investment in a developing country by MNCs might be expected to be related to affiliate export sales *back to* the investing country. Despite the data gaps, however, it is clear from Table 12.4 (export sales to the United States as a percentage of overall sales, by manufacturing sector) that the U.S. market is currently a significant factor in only a handful of cases, most notably electrical machinery affiliates in Brazil and Mexico, food manufacturing affiliates in Argentina, and paper and allied products in Brazil.

Finally, as a means of comparing U.S. affiliate and host country overall export growth, Table 12.5 expresses U.S. affiliate export sales as a percentage of total *regional* or *country* exports for total manufacturing and its principal branches. (Inasmuch as the two sets of underlying data are derived from different sources, and thus inevitably involve timing and valuation discrepancies, a three-year smoothing procedure was employed in order to elicit the underlying trends in these ratios.) As is evident, trends tend to differ by country and category, suggesting no prevailing pattern for U.S. affiliates in terms of playing either a leading or a lagging role in the overall expansion of manufactured exports. An exception appears to be electrical machinery, where for Latin America as a whole, as well as Argentina, Brazil, and Mexico, U.S. affiliate export sales grew much more rapidly than total exports for this category. Another is probably transport equipment (although the U.S. Commerce Department's nondisclosure of the Mexican data prevented us from including the Mexican figures in the table). The other sectors, as well as total manufacturing, show varying regional and country patterns.

IMPORT SUBSTITUTION AND EXPORT DIVERSIFICATION WITHIN THE MANUFACTURING SECTOR

As we have seen earlier, Mundell's analysis (which in essence reflects the traditional view of the direct investment process) suggests a rationale for a possible association in developing nations between the erection of import barriers and an increasing volume of direct investment from the industrialized nations for the purpose of participating in an "import substitution" process. (The product life cycle literature also makes the case for a connection between direct investment and import substitution on different grounds).

Mundell made his observations in the late 1950s, and they seem accurately to describe the pattern in many developing nations (especially in Latin America) during the 1950s and early 1960s. A 1964 United Nations Economic Commission for Latin America study, for example, summarized the import substitution process for all branches of Brazilian manufacturing from 1949 to 1961.[17] Using imports plus domestic production as a measure of total "goods available" (not strictly accurate since exports should be deducted), the study showed that in all but two branches the share of imports in the total (the "import coefficient") declined during this period (in some cases quite substantially). A similar pattern of "import substitution industrialization" (ISI) was adopted by most of the other larger Latin American countries between the late 1940s and early 1960s.[18] Moreover, inflows of foreign capital and associated MNC technology apparently were closely identified with this ISI pattern, especially in the development of the automobile industry and other consumer durable goods industries, as well as some capital goods industries.[19]

The drive toward import substitution in postwar Latin America was motivated by a desire to pursue a program of economic development unfettered by sluggishly (or capriciously) performing world primary product markets. It is now recognized, however, that most countries soon found that only the structure, not the degree, of their dependence on imports changed. Import coefficients stopped falling or began rising under the need to import crucial capital goods

Table 12.3. Affiliates of U.S. Companies in Latin America: Share of Total Export Sales in Overall Sales by Manufacturing Category, 1967–1976

Year	Total Manufacturing	Food Products	Paper and Allied Products	Chemicals and Allied Products	Rubber Products	Primary and Fabricated Metals	Machinery Except Electrical	Electrical Machinery	Transportation Equipment	Other Manufacturing
Latin America										
1967	6.4%	16.4%	11.0%	5.3%	0.5%	2.0%	10.5%	1.7%	1.2%	3.6%
1970	5.3	11.4	11.9	5.4	(D)	(D)	7.0	3.2	(D)	4.4
1973	6.1	10.1	18.1	4.2	0.7	3.7	7.4	9.3	3.1	4.7
1976	6.4	3.3	17.4	3.5	0.7	3.4	8.5	10.2	5.7	6.6
Argentina										
1967	12.6%	52.0%	6.7%	2.9%	0.0%	2.1%	0.0%	0.0%	0.9%	0.0%
1970	3.2	36.9	4.8	3.0	3.1	1.4	0.0	0.7	0.9	1.7
1973	10.6	34.6	37.5	6.1	0.0	12.9	5.1	1.8	3.2	2.2
1975	10.3	35.4	40.0	2.1	0.0	6.5	24.5	3.5	4.1	2.0
1976	16.3	41.2	100.0	4.8	0.8	12.6	27.4	6.5	5.0	2.6

Brazil										
1967	3.8%	3.3%	23.3%	0.6%	0.0%	3.5%	20.0%	1.4%	0.5%	1.8%
1970	4.1	7.9	17.0	1.6	1.4	2.7	11.1	6.2	0.3	4.8
1973	4.4	5.3	16.2	2.0	0.3	2.7	8.8	12.6	1.9	4.9
1975	4.9	3.9	10.3	1.4	1.4	3.7	10.2	9.3	5.5	1.7
1976	4.6	4.7	11.6	0.9	0.9	3.8	7.6	10.6	4.6	5.2
Mexico										
1967	2.5%	5.5%	—	1.7%	(D)%	0.0%	2.6%	2.2%	(D)%	0.7%
1970	2.5	2.5	0.7%	2.9	(D)	1.6	1.9	3.7	(D)	0.9
1973	4.2	1.3	2.3	2.4	(D)	2.1	3.3	14.3	(D)	2.1
1975	4.0	0.4	1.9	2.0	0.0	2.0	4.5	17.7	8.4	3.0
1976	5.0	1.0	2.0	1.7	0.0	2.2	4.4	20.6	12.9	3.9

Source: Same as Table 12.2

(D) = underlying data suppressed by U.S. Department of Commerce to avoid individual company disclosure.

— = ratio could not be computed due to suppressed total sales data.

Table 12.4. Affiliates of U.S. Companies in Latin America: Share of Export Sales to the United States in Overall Sales by Manufacturing Category, 1967–1977

Year	Total Manufacturing	Food Products	Paper and Allied Products	Chemicals and Allied Products	Rubber Products	Primary and Fabricated Metals	Machinery Except Electrical	Electrical Machinery	Transportation Equipment	Other Manufacturing
Latin America										
1967	2.4%	6.3%	4.4%	1.7%	0.0%	0.3%	1.2%	0.8%	0.5%	2.8%
1970	2.0	5.4	2.0	1.6	(D)	(D)	2.6	0.6	(D)	2.4
1973	2.2	4.0	2.1	0.9	0.3	0.1	2.4	6.3	1.5	2.3
1976	2.4	2.7	3.0	0.1	0.1	0.1	1.2	8.2	2.9	3.4
Argentina										
1967	(D)%	(D)%	*%	*%	*%	*%	*%	(D)%	(D)%	*%
1970	5.1	15.6	*%	*	(D)	*	*	*	(D)	*
1973	2.9	12.3	*	*	*	*	*	*	*	*
1975	2.0	9.4	*	*	*	*	*	(D)	(D)	*
1976	3.6	11.8	*	*	*	*	*	*	(D)	(D)

Brazil

1967	1.2%	(D)%	20.9%	2.8%	*%	*%	(D)%	*%	(D)%	(D)%
1970	1.7	4.6	17.0	0.2	(D)	*	4.4	*	(D)	(D)
1973	1.7	2.3	(D)	0.3	*	*	3.2	(D)	(D)	1.2
1975	1.6	1.4	(D)	0.3	(D)	*	2.3	7.0	*	0.1
1976	1.6	1.8	10.8	0.3	*	*	0.5	8.5	(D)	(D)

Mexico

1967	1.1%	2.7%	*%	*%	(D)%	(D)%	(D)%	1.6%	–%	*%
1970	1.2	(D)	*	0.8	*	*	*	1.5	(D)	*
1973	2.8	0.8	*	0.7	*	*	1.5	12.8	–	*
1975	2.7	0.1	*	0.7	*	0.2	1.4	(D)	(D)	0.9
1976	3.8	0.7	*	0.3	*	*	(D)	20.1	(D)	1.5

Source: Same as Table 12.2.

(D) = underlying data suppressed by U.S. Department of Commerce to avoid individual company disclosure.

* = underlying data less than $500,000.

— = ration could not be computed due to suppressed total sales data.

Table 12.5. Ratios of U.S. Affiliate Export Sales of Manufactures to Total Country Exports of Manufactures Latin America and Selected Countries, 1967–1976

Category or Period	Latin American Republics	Argentina	Brazil	Mexico
Total Manufacturing				
1967/69	0.15	0.42	0.26	0.14
1970/72	0.18	0.35	0.19	0.20
1973/75	0.17	0.26	0.17	0.16
1974/76	0.19	0.28	0.17	0.21
Food Products				
1967/69	0.69	0.82	0.15	0.81
1970/72	0.47	0.75	0.13	0.35
1973/75	0.35	0.79	0.09	0.12
1974/76	0.33	0.85	0.09	0.12

Category or Period	Latin American Republics	Argentina	Brazil	Mexico
Machinery, Except Electrical				
1967/69	—	0.00	0.69	0.15
1970/72	—	0.00	0.44	0.05
1973/75	—	0.13	0.33	0.11
1974/76	—	0.17	0.29	0.16
Electrical Machinery				
1967/69	0.34	0.00	0.36	0.39
1970/72	0.48	0.10	0.98	0.42
1973/75	0.58	0.11	0.60	0.87
1974/76	0.65	0.14	0.58	(1.00)

(1.00) = numerator exceeds denominator, probably owing to valuation and timing differences

Chemicals and Allied Products

1967/69	0.21	0.14	0.07	0.13
1970/72	0.24	0.20	0.20	0.19
1973/75	0.22	0.14	0.21	0.13
1974/76	0.22	0.12	0.19	0.12

Primary and Fabricated Metals

1967/69	0.06	0.05	0.10	0.06[b]
1970/72	0.06	0.03[a]	0.06	0.08[c]
1973/75	0.09	0.10	0.06	0.10
1974/76	0.10	0.11	0.06	0.10

Transportation Equipment

1967/69	0.53	0.62	0.50	—
1970/72	0.27	0.26	0.27	—
1973/75	0.37	0.22	0.37	—
1974/76	0.42	0.18	0.34	—

Other Manufacturing

1967/69	0.04	0.04[b]	0.08	0.02
1970/72	0.06	0.14	0.03	0.06
1973/75	0.03	0.03	0.02	0.03
1974/76	0.04	0.03	0.02	0.04

Source: Underlying U.S. MNC affiliate export sales data, see Table 12.2; country export data compiled from *Yearbook of International Trade Statistics*, United Nations, various issues: both sets of data are reported in dollars. The country export data are reported in accordance with the Standard Industrial Trade Classification (SITC) system. These ratios were calculated by matching the U.S. Department of Commerce (*Survey of Current Business*) manufacturing categories with the comparable SITC categories as follows: chemicals and allied products = 5; primary and fabricated metals = 67 + 69; nonelectrical machinery = 71; electrical machinery = 72; transportation equipment = 73; other manufactures = 8 + 61 + 63 + 65 + 66; food manufactures are not reported as such in the SITC system, and thus this study has included estimates based on an approximation method used in United Nations (UNCTAD) reports (SITC categories 012 + 013 + 032 + 045 + 047 + 048 + 052 + 053 + 055 + 062 + 071.3 + 072.2 + 072.3 + 073 + 091 + 099); total manufactures = this food manufactures estimate + 5 + 6 + 7 + 8.

[a]1969/71.
[b]1968/69.
[c]1972/74.

and raw materials. Inevitably, the goal of import substitution was replaced by export promotion and diversification, as one of the major means of alleviating the "exchange contraints posed by a mounting external debt."[20]

While this description actually extends beyond the import of manufactured products per se, the Latin American manufacturing import data seem generally to be in agreement. Table 12.6, for example, shows that the overall manufacturing import coefficients for Argentina, Brazil, Colombia, Mexico, Peru, and Venezuela rose steadily from about 1965 onward. Table 12.7, which summarizes the import coefficients of the major manufacturing branches for Argentina, Brazil, and Mexico over the 1960–1976 period, reflects an essentially similar pattern at the industry level. Thus, if one looks solely at import coefficients, "import substitution" (defined as a declining import coefficient over time) seems generally to have come to a halt in the early or mid-1960s. Moreover, in only three instances (textiles

Table 12.6. Total Manufacturing Import Coefficients^a Selected Latin American Countries, 1960–1976

Year	Argentina A	Argentina B	Brazil A	Brazil B	Colombia A	Colombia B	Mexico A	Mexico B	Peru A^b	Peru B^b	Venezuela A^b	Venezuela B^b
1960	21.9	–	4.2	–	36.9	–	30.1	–	–	–	–	–
1963	19.0	19.2	4.1	4.2	32.7	–	28.5	28.6	31.2	13.4	–	–
1965	15.0	15.2	2.1	2.1	27.9	27.9	21.2	21.3	–	–	–	–
1968	15.0	15.4	4.3	4.3	33.5	33.5	28.5	28.6	25.1	25.4	41.8	42.1
1970	18.7	19.1	5.5	5.5	36.5	36.5	28.8	29.1	23.6	23.9	42.6	42.9
1973	19.7	20.2	10.1	10.2	38.1	38.7	37.3	37.6	29.9	30.2	48.7	48.9
1974	27.0	27.8	16.6	16.8	47.8	49.5	43.0	43.5	35.6	35.9	57.7	57.9
1976	24.7	25.5	15.9	16.2	44.8^c	45.3^c	43.7	44.1	–	–	66.8	67.1

Source: Calculated from original data appearing in *Yearbook of International Trade Statistics*, United Nations, various issues, and *Yearbook of National Accounts Statistics*, United Nations, various issues. Coefficients for Argentina, Brazil, and Mexico based on manufacturing GDP in 1960 prices and dollar export and import values converted to local currency at 1960 exchange rates; Colombia and Peru based on 1970 prices for manufacturing GDP and 1970 exchange rates; Venezuela based on 1968 prices and exchange rates. Exchange rates are annual averages used for trade data conversion purposes (line "rf," *International Financial Statistics*, IMF, various issues).

   Key: A = Based on underlying import and export data that do not include estimates for manufactured food products.

   B = Underlying import and export data include estimates for food manufacturers (see note to Table 12.5).

   ^{a}Import coefficient = manufactured imports ÷ (manufacturing gross domestic product + manufactured imports – manufactured exports).

   ^{b}1975 data.

   ^{c}Import coefficients based on import data only.

Table 12.7. Import Coefficients^a in Various Branches of Manufacturing, Selected Latin American Countries, 1960–1976

Industry Group	Argentina	Brazil	Mexico	Industry Group	Argentina	Brazil	Mexico
Chemicals^b				*Basic Metals^b*			
1960	12.1	—	42.5	1960	—	—	—
1963	12.0	11.2	43.5	1963	45.2	19.2	41.5
1965	14.3	26.3	40.6	1965	49.1	16.4	31.6
1970	17.6	21.5	32.3	1970	50.6	22.3	29.6
1974	35.8	34.3	55.7	1974	65.9	37.8	72.7
1976	30.7	—	47.4	1976	60.2	—	54.8
Paper Products^b				*Machinery and Transport Equipment*			
1960	—	—	16.4^c	1960	36.6	—	67.2
1963	—	12.2^c	14.0^c	1963	35.6	—	61.2
1965	—	8.6^c	13.5^c	1965	18.1	see below	57.2
1970	—	13.6^c	18.6^c	1970	23.7	—	58.5
1974	—	16.8^c	25.7^c	1974	24.7	—	68.0
1976	—	—	26.6^c	1976	29.6	—	71.8

Textile Products^b			
	Argentina	Brazil	Mexico
1960	4.9	—	—
1963	5.8	0.3	3.9
1965	4.6	0.2	4.1
1970	3.6	2.5	5.2
1974	4.2	6.5	9.2
1976	3.0	—	6.4

Brazil: Machinery and Transport Equipment^b

Year	Nonelectrical Machinery	Electrical Machinery	Transport Equipment
1963	55.3	17.1	14.5
1965	41.8	12.4	7.8
1970	42.6	26.9	17.8
1974	44.4	34.7	20.5

Table 12.7. (cont.)

Industry Group	Argentina	Brazil	Mexico	Industry Group	Argentina	Brazil	Mexico
Nonmetallic Mineral Manufactures[b]							
1960	—	—	—				
1963	4.9[c]	4.1	—				
1965	6.1[c]	3.3	11.3				
1970	8.9[c]	4.2	9.1				
1974	8.6[c]	6.4	12.4				
1976	11.1[c]	—	11.4				

Source: Same as Table 12.6.

[a] Argentina and Mexico coefficients computed on the basis of import and export data for each industry group and GDP data for each group; trade data (reported in dollars) converted to local currencies on basis of 1960 annual average exchange rates (line "rf," *International Financial Statistics,* IMF); GDP data expressed in 1960 prices. Brazilian coefficients computed on basis of industry group import and export data and "value-added" data for each group; trade data converted from dollars to cruzeiros on basis of current average annual exchange rates (line "rf," *IFS*); and value-added data expressed in current prices. Value-added data drawn from *Industrial Production Statistics* (United Nations), various issues.

[b] SITC Code/Industry Group (U.N. National Accounts Categories or ISIC Codes) "Match-ups":

Argentina and Mexico

5/Chemicals and Chemical Petroleum, Coal, Rubber Plastic Products

64/Paper and Paper Products (including Printing and Publishing)

65/Textile, Wearing Apparel, and Leather Industries

66/Manufacturing of Nonmetallic Mineral Products

67, 68/Basic Metal Industries

69, 71/Manufactures of Fabricated Metal Products, Machinery and Equipment

Brazil

5/351, 352

64/341

65/321

66/36

67, 68, 69/371, 372, 381

71/382, 383, 384

[c] Import coefficients based on import data only.

288

Table 12.8. Share of Manufacturing Exports in Overall Exports Selected Latin American Countries, 1960-1976

Year	Argentina		Brazil		Mexico		Colombia	
	A	*B*	*A*	*B*	*A*	*B*	*A*	*B*
1960	4.1%	–	2.3%	–	23.6%	–	1.5%	–
1963	6.1	12.8	3.0	4.4	27.1	28.9	3.6	3.6
1965	5.6	9.5	7.8	9.9	21.8	23.7	6.5	6.5
1968	12.3	22.0	8.1	12.5	28.0	30.0	10.4	10.4
1970	14.0	22.9	13.4	17.6	37.7	40.2	8.6	8.6
1973	22.5	28.9	19.8	24.8	66.0	68.8	26.5	26.5
1974	24.5	31.4	24.5	29.7	50.0	53.1	28.3	28.3
1975	24.4	30.6	25.6	29.7	37.9	40.3	21.0	21.0
1976	24.9	31.8	23.2	29.1	35.0	37.8	22.8	23.2

Source: Calculated from original data appearing in *Yearbook of International Trade Statistics*, United Nations, various issues.

Key: A = Underlying manufactured export data do not include an estimate for food manufacturers.

B = Underlying manufactured export data include an estimate for food manufactures (see note to Table 12.5).

and machinery-transport equipment in Argentina, and nonelectrical machinery in Brazil) were the 1976 coefficients lower than those for 1960. It should be noted, however, that these are still very broad groupings (data analysis below the two-digit SITC level was not possible, unfortunately). Consequently, it is possible that import substitution could still have been taking place in more narrowly defined branches of manufacturing.

Additonally, a significant expansion of manufactured export earnings (and a consequent diversification away from traditional primary products exports) occurred continuously during the 1960-1976 period. As Table 12.8 shows, in 1960 only Mexico (of the four countries listed) generated as much as a quarter of its export earnings from manufactures; the other three (Argentina, Brazil, and Colombia) were then only deriving a minor portion of their overall export earnings from manufacturing. By the 1970s, this picture had changed substantially: Argentina, Brazil, and Colombia having moved into the 20–30 percent category.

EXPORT PATTERNS AND DIRECT INVESTMENT—PRELIMINARY DATA COMPARISONS

This section focuses in a preliminary way on possible linkages between sectoral U.S. direct investment in manufacturing and MNC export performance in Latin America. Table 12.9 juxtaposes information on the direction of U.S. affiliate export sales ratios from Tables 12.3 and 12.5 with average annual direct investment growth rate data for total manufacturing and its major branches.

Inasmuch as many of the sectors experienced rising ratios of export sales-to-total sales, this at least suggests the possible operability of the "basic" export-induced direct investment hypothesis mentioned earlier (investment growth responds to export sales expansion). However, it is harder to find much ready evidence for the "stronger" affiliate export sales-to-total sales ratio version of the hypothesis (sectors with more rapidly rising export sales-to-total ratios will induce greater investment growth than sectors with decreasing or less rapidly rising ratios). Close linkages between the growth of this ratio (refer to Table 12.3) and investment growth rates are not obvious. Moreover, only a handful of branches had declining ratios (food products regionwide and in Argentina and Mexico; chemicals regionwide plus Mexico; paper and allied products in Brazil; and nonelectrical machinery in Brazil). Of these, direct investment in the food products sector for the entire region, and also for Argentina and Mexico, did grow less rapidly than the corresponding average for total manufacturing. The same can be said of the chemicals sector for the region as a whole, although direct investment in chemicals for Mexico grew on a par with its counterpart total manufacturing average. The absence of separate direct investment data for the two kinds of "machinery" (electrical and nonelectrical) makes it impossible to comment on the relationship of the declining Brazilian nonelectrical machinery sales ratio and direct investment in that sector; and we are similarly unable to comment on the declining Brazilian paper and allied products ratio.

Table 12.9 also provides no clear support for the "strongest" version of the export-induced direct investment hypothesis [sectors with more rapidly rising ratios of affiliate export sales to total *country* exports will induce greater investment growth than sectors with decreasing (or less rapidly rising) ratios]. A number of MNC affiliate export sales sectors did grow more rapidly than the comparable *host country* export sectors (i.e., increases occurred in the ratios of MNC export sales to total *country* exports), and also exhibited average annual direct investment growth rates in excess of those for manufacturing as a whole in the region and/or in a given country. However, "reversals" of this relationship are also evident in a number of cases.

Accordingly, the simplest of the export-inducing hypotheses appears to have the greatest potential validity. Moreover, it represents

Table 12.9. Comparison of U.S. MNC Latin American Manufacturing Affiliate Export Sales Ratios to Direct Investment Growth Rates, by Manufacturing Sector

Sector	Growing Export Sales to Total Sales Ratio, 1967–1976	Growing Export Sales to Total Country Exports Ratio, 1967–1976	Average Annual Rate of Growth in Stock of Manufacturing Direct Investment	
			1961–1976	1967–1976
Latin America				
Total manufacturing	No	Yes	11.9%	12.4%
Food products	No	No	8.3	8.2
Paper and allied products	Yes	—	—	—
Chemicals and allied products	No	(No)	11.9	11.4
Primary and fabricated metals	Yes	Yes	14.7	14.2
Nonelectrical machinery	No	— }	14.5	17.5
Electrical machinery	Yes	Yes }		
Transportation equipment	Yes	No	10.9	12.7
Other manufacturing	Yes	No	16.5	10.9
Argentina				
Total manufacturing	Yes	No		5.9
Food products	No	(Yes)		1.1[a]
Paper and allied products	Yes	—		—
Chemicals and allied products	Yes	No		4.5
Primary and fabricated metals	Yes	Yes		10.2
Nonelectrical machinery	Yes	Yes }		6.5
Electrical machinery	Yes	Yes }		
Transportation equipment	Yes	No		6.9
Other manufacturing	Yes	No		7.4
Brazil				
Total manufacturing	Yes	No		21.7
Food products	Yes	No		13.8
Paper and allied products	No	—		—
Chemicals and allied products	(Yes)	Yes		20.7
Primary and fabricated metals	(Yes)	No		20.8
Nonelectrical machinery	No	No }		26.1
Electrical machinery	Yes	Yes }		
Transportation equipment	Yes	No		22.2
Other manufacturing	Yes	No		19.9
Mexico				
Total manufacturing	Yes	Yes		9.1
Food products	No	No		8.3
Paper and allied products	(Yes)	—		—

Table 12.9. *(cont.)*

Sector	Growing Export Sales to Total Sales Ratio, 1967–1976	Growing Export Sales to Total Country Exports Ratio, 1967–1976	Average Annual Rate of Growth in Stock of Manufacturing Direct Investment	
			1961–1976	1067–1976
Chemicals and allied products	No	No		9.1%
Primary and fabricated metals	Yes	Yes		9.4
Nonelectrical machinery	Yes	(Yes) ⎫		
Electrical machinery	Yes	Yes ⎭		10.2
Transportation equipment	(Yes?)	(Yes?)		7.6
Other manufacturing	Yes	(Yes)		8.9

Source: Based on Tables 12.3 and 12.5, plus data appearing in *Selected Data on U.S. Direct Investment Abroad, 1966–1978*, U.S. Department of Commerce, Bureau of Economic Analysis.

[a]1966–1978.

the minimum in terms of a possible meaningful relationship between MNC affiliate exports and direct investment. The next section thus examines this relationship further in a regression analysis context, in conjunction with the older "import barrier" view of the direct investment process.

REGRESSION RESULTS

Formal statistical analysis is exceedingly difficult to employ in this area of research because of the paucity of usable data. Sectoral U.S. manufacturing direct investment and foreign affiliate sales data are available (on an annual basis) only from the early 1960s and 1967, respectively (and as of this writing data on affiliate sales are not yet available for the years after 1976). Nevertheless, this section presents some selected regression results for those countries and product groups for which we could gather continuous series— recognizing the problems inherent in drawing conclusions under such circumstances.

As suggested above, our results are based on a statistical model designed to test both the conventional import barrier hypothesis and the "basic" version of the export-induced hypothesis. Underlying the model tested is the following simple partial adjustment assumption regarding the relationship of the flow of direct investment to the total stock of such investment:

$$I_t = \beta(K_t^* - K_{t-1}) \qquad 0 < \beta \leqslant 1 \tag{12.1}$$

where I_t = the change in the stock of direct manufacturing investment by U.S. companies in selected Latin American
countries and product groups between periods $t-1$ and
t.

K_t^* = the desired stock of direct manufacturing investment in
period t.

K_{t-1} = the actual stock of direct manufacturing investment in
period $t-1$.

β = the "speed of adjustment" coefficient.

It is also assumed that:

$$K_t^* = \alpha_1 + \alpha_2 \left(\frac{M}{M + P - X}\right)_T + \alpha_3 MNCX_t + \alpha_4 RGDP_t \tag{12.2}$$

where $\dfrac{M}{M + P - X}$ the "import coefficient" for a given country
or product group, where M and X are country-
wide imports and exports, and P is total domestic production.

MNCX = the value of MNC export sales (in dollars) for
corresponding country or product group.

RGDP = a domestic market size variable (as available,
either real gross domestic product originating
in the product area, or an index of industrial
production for the area).

The estimating equation is derived by substituting equation (12.2)
into equation (12.1) and adding an error term, u_t:

$$I_t = \beta\alpha_1 + \beta\alpha_2 \left(\frac{M}{M + P - X}\right)_T + \beta\alpha_3 MNCX_t$$
$$+ \beta\alpha_4 RGDP_4 - \beta K_{t-1} + u_t \tag{12.3}$$

Accordingly, with the aid of this equation, we are investigating the
possibility that U.S. MNCs adjust their flow of direct manufacturing
investment to changes in the import coefficient for a country or
product category as well as to changes in the export sales of their
host country affiliates within the same country or product category.
The import coefficient is intended to serve as a proxy for the degree

of import ease or restrictiveness being pursued during a given period via host country government trade and foreign exchange policies. A reduction in the import coefficient suggests greater trade restrictiveness, perhaps resulting from a reduction of foreign exchange availabilities and a consequent tightening of various import and payments regulations. Under such conditions, the traditional (substitutable) view of the impact of trade on direct investment suggests an *increase* in the flow of such investment. Similarly, under conditions of rising import coefficients (which we have seen has generally been the case in Latin America during the period under study), the traditional view suggests a *reduction* in the flow of direct investment.

Thus, the conventional direct investment hypothesis requires a negative regression coefficient ($\beta\alpha_2$). The export-induced hypothesis, on the other hand, suggests a positive regression coefficient ($\beta\alpha_3$). The coefficient for K_{t-1}, moreover, should be negative in light of our stock adjustment direct investment model; and we would also expect the scale variable's coefficient to be positive.

Table 12.10 summarizes the results for the estimating equation for selected individual countries and categories, as well as for a pooling of data across countries for each of the categories. With regard to the individual country or category results, the Cochrane-Orcutt transformation procedure was employed as a means of adjusting for possible autocorrelation in the residuals. Similar results had initially been obtained using ordinary least squares. However, while none of the Durbin-Watson statistics generated as part of the OLS procedure suggested the rejection of the hypothesis of nonautocorrelation in the residuals, all were in the inconclusive range (owing to the small sample sizes).[21]

With regard to the country-pooled results, the original country data were first adjusted for possible autocorrelation by generating the transformed data employed in the above-mentioned Cochrane-Orcutt procedure. These data were further adjusted in order to correct for probable heteroscedasticity in the disturbance terms. For this purpose, an ad hoc procedure was employed in which all of the transformed data for each country were divided by the respective standard errors of the regression equations calculated as part of the individual country Cochrane-Orcutt regressions. Each of the pooling efforts consisted first of ordinary least squares regressions of these transformed or adjusted data involving the same independent and dependent variables specified in our original estimating equation, plus appropriate dummy variables representing individual countries and individual years, following a pooling procedure described by both Johnston and Kmenta.[22] However, since none of the resulting regression statistics for the dummy variables included in our three pooling efforts appeared to be significant, a second set of pooled OLS results was generated employing only the dependent and independent variables specified in our original estimating equation (adjusted for possible autocorrelation and heteroscedasticity). These are the pooled results reported in Table 12.10.

In terms of the hypothesis that MNC affiliate export sales induce direct investment, Table 12.10 shows that of the eleven export sales regression coefficients, six exhibit the correct (positive) sign. Only one of these, moreover, appears to be significantly different from zero (.05 level)—Mexican total manufacturing. Three others (Brazilian total manufacturing, Mexican machinery, and pooled Brazilian-Mexican machinery) could be included at a lower level of significance (.10). However, since two of the three total manufacturing coefficients for export sales (that of Brazil and Mexico) are positive, this perhaps suggests that at least the overall relationship is in the "correct" direction (although the pooled three-country total manufacturing negative coefficient does not confirm this conclusion). Of the five negative export sales coefficients, only two appear to be significant (three if we adopt the lower level). Nevertheless, the negative coefficients would seem to suggest that, other things being equal, the domestic sales market is in some instances exerting a countervailing influence on export sales.

With regard to the more conventional import barrier hypothesis, seven of the eleven regression coefficients for the trade and exchange policy proxy variable (the import coefficient) are negative, including two of the three individual country coefficients for total manufacturing plus the pooled three-country total manufacturing coefficient. Three of these negative regression coefficients also appear to be significant (as do, however, three of the positive coefficients—Argentinian total manufacturing and Brazilian and Mexican chemicals). On balance, the conventional view that direct investment responds inversely to the direction of the host country's import and payments policies thus seems to be supported. Other things being equal, the rising Latin American import coefficients of the mid-1960s and 1970s (signifying a less restrictive policy toward imports) appear in a number of instances to have exerted a restraining influence on the inflow of direct investment—just as the reductions in these coefficients from the late 1940s to the early 1960s apparently attracted direct investment flows.[23]

With respect to the scale variable used in the regression equation, Table 12.10 reports the expected positive regression coefficient in seven of the eleven cases, and five of these (six at a lower level of

Table 12.10. Regression Equation Results[a] Selected Latin American Countries and Product Categories (t statistics in parentheses)

Country or Category	Regression Coefficients				R^2	Standard Error of Regression	Durbin Watson Statistic	Number of Observations
	Import Coefficient	U.S. Affiliate Total Export Sales	Sectoral Real GDP Index	Direct Investment Stock (t-1)				
Argentina								
Total manufacturing[b]	490 (2.45)	-.51 (-5.12)	7.45 (3.81)	-1.30 (-3.84)	.95	10.31	2.53	8
Brazil								
Total manufacturing[c]	-7787 (-6.34)	.62 (2.02)	13.34[d] (11.71)	-.02 (-.17)	.99	18.91	2.72	8
Chemicals[c]	884 (11.72)	.77 (1.55)	3.14[d] (7.97)	-1.49 (-6.97)	.99	5.18	2.16	7
Machinery[c]	-406 (-12.90)	-.04 (-.13)	.58[d] (5.11)	.46 (2.39)	.99	2.60	3.48	7
Mexico								
Total manufacturing[b]	-1010 (-.67)	2.87 (3.01)	-1.27 (-.26)	-.35 (-1.71)	.90	45.73	2.10	8
Food products[c]	-358 (-3.02)	-1.38 (-1.73)	-.001[e] (-.31)	.16 (.65)	.94	3.93	2.75	8
Chemicals[c]	400 (4.37)	-4.48 (-1.71)	-.43 (-.72)	.92 (2.39)	.98	10.44	3.63	7
Machinery[c]	-48 (-.96)	.44 (2.56)	1.65 (2.26)	-.53 (-3.04)	.97	4.85	2.66	7

Pooled:

Argentina, Brazil, Mexico								
Total manufacturing	-305 (-.51)	-.61 (-2.53)	-1.07 (-1.02)	.51 (12.48)	.95	—	—	—	24
Brazil, Mexico								
Chemicals	159 (1.07)	.27 (.19)	2.87 (1.83)	-.85 (-1.45)	.49	—	—	—	14
Machinery	-10.2 (-.24)	.68 (1.59)	.47 (1.09)	-.15 (-.43)	.76	—	—	—	15

Source: Stock of direct investment data are book value estimates (in millions of dollars) at year end and are drawn from *Selected Data on U.S. Direct Investment Abroad, 1966–78,* Department of Commerce, Bureau of Economic Analysis; direct investment flow data (dependent variable) are year-to-year changes in the stock of direct investment; U.S. affiliate export sales data (see source note to Table 12.2); "Machinery" export sales data derived by adding reported data for nonelectrical and electrical machinery; import coefficient data based on original data appearing in *Yearbook of International Trade Statistics,* various issues (United Nations), *Yearbook of National Accounts Statistics* (for GDP data), various issues (United Nations), *Yearbook of Industrial Statistics* (for value-added data), various issues (United Nations); trade data converted to local currencies on basis of current exchange rates (line "rf," *International Financial Statistics,* IMF, various issues); sectoral real GDP and industrial production data are drawn, respectively, from *Yearbook of National Accounts Statistics* and *Yearbook of Industrial Statistics,* various issues.

[a] Cochrane-Orcutt iterative procedure for the individual country results; OLS employing adjusted data for the pooled results (see text).

[b] Underlying import coefficients computed on the basis of current GDP and exports and imports converted to domestic currency using current exchange rates.

[c] Underlying import coefficients computed on the basis of current "value-added" and exports and imports converted to domestic currency using current exchange rates.

[d] Based on sectoral industrial production index.

[e] Coefficient computed using actual real GDP figures.

significance) appear to be significant. Additionally, seven of the eleven lagged investment stock coefficients are negative (the expected sign). Two of these exceed unity (which one would not expect under a partial adjustment model). Neither of these, however, appears to be significantly different from one at the .05 level. Despite the small number of observations and the variety of other explanatory factors that potentially could intervene, these results thus tend to support the appropriateness of the overall regression model as a means of testing our two direct investment hypotheses.

CONCLUSION

This chapter has reviewed the literature on the relationship of direct investment to international trade with an eye toward developing testable hypotheses of interest to those who wish to understand the effects of the international trade and trade policies of developing nations on the manufacturing direct investment of MNCs. It has also placed in perspective the manufacturing direct investment in developing nations of the industrialized countries, and the predominant role of Latin America in U.S. manufacturing direct investment. The export sales patterns of U.S. MNC affiliates in Latin America have also been reviewed, as well as the general trend in Latin America since the mid-1960s toward rising import coefficients (signaling the end of widespread import substitution industrialization) and export earnings diversification in the form of manufactured products. Additionally, but certainly not definitively in view of the data limitations, we have examined the impact on U.S. manufacturing direct investment in Latin America of U.S. affiliate export sales of manufactures and of changes in Latin American government import policy.

In terms of the alternate direct investment hypotheses we have developed, the following conclusions appear to be warranted: Changes in trade policy continue to be a significant factor in inversely influencing MNC manufacturing direct investment flows into Latin America—Mundell's (conventional) view appears still to be supported. On the other hand, U.S. manufacturing direct investment in its Latin American affiliates does not appear to have generally responded to affiliate export sales expansion—thus, the Latin American internal market seems to have been the major attraction.

On the basis of our earlier data analysis, the following conclusions also can be drawn: U.S. affiliate export sales nevertheless appear to have been a dynamic element in total affiliate sales of manufactures, as evidenced by generally rising ratios of such export sales to total sales in the major countries. The U.S. market has also in several cases been an important component of total affiliate export sales (but this relationship is generally less significant than the literature on MNC trade would lead us to expect). Finally, however, while U.S. affiliate export sales seem to be growing in importance in terms of their own total sales, such exports do not yet consistently appear to be a significant element in the recent rapid expansion of Latin America's export earnings from manufactures.

While not directly addressed in our various data analyses, some implications can also be drawn for policy in the industrialized world toward MNC direct investment in developing countries. As is well known, some sectors of opinion in the industrial countries (e.g., representatives of American labor) assert that the establishment of MNC manufacturing affiliates in developing countries threatens domestic employment and the investing country's trade balance, either as the result of lagging production for export in the face of import substitution abroad, or because of import competition from MNC foreign affiliates.

With regard to import substitution in Latin America, we have seen that this pattern was generally reversed after the early 1960s. Thus, industrial country job losses and export problems emanating from this source should not have been a significant factor during the period studied in this chapter (which does not, however, rule out such losses during the earlier postwar period when Latin American manufactured import coefficients were forcibly contracted). Moreover, the still modest picture that emerges of U.S. affiliate export sales from Latin America—whether of total export sales or export sales back to the United States—does not suggest that such exports could have been a significant U.S. employment or trade factor in most of the industrial sectors studied. In formulating employment and trade policies that will affect MNC decisions to locate (or to continue) certain of their manufacturing activities in developing countries, the results of this study thus underline the need for industrial country governments to have a clear appreciation of the actual extent and market composition of MNC involvement in foreign production.

These conclusions have largely been extracted from an analysis of official U.S. Data. Subsequent research and additional insights should also be based, if possible, on official MNC sales and direct investment data from other industrialized countries, as well as similar information at the company level. Hopefully, these sources will become more available in the future.

NOTES

1. R. A. Mundell, "International Trade and Factor Mobility." *American Economic Review* 47 (June 1957): 321–335.
2. Usually associated with Raymond Vernon: see his seminal contribution "International Investment and International Trade in the Product Cycle," *Quarterly Journal of Economics* 80 (May 1966):190–207.
3. John H. Dunning, "Multinational Enterprises and Trade Flows of Less Developed Countries," *World Development* 2 (February 1974): 136.
4. Ibid.
5. G. K. Helleiner, "Manufactured Exports from Less-Developed Countries and Multinational Firms," *The Economic Journal* 83 (March 1973):21–47.
6. Ibid., p. 31.
7. G. C. Haufbauer, "The Multinational Corporation and Direct Investment," in *International Trade and Finance: Frontiers for Research*, edited by Peter Kenen (Cambridge: Cambridge, University Press, 1975), pp. 281–282; Andrew Schmitz and Peter Helmberger, "Factor Mobility and International Trade: The Case of Complementarity," *American Economic Review* 60 (September 1970):761–767.
8. Hufbauer, "The Multinational Corporation," p. 281.
9. Deepak Nayyar, "Transnational Corporations and Manufactured Exports from Poor Countries," *The Economic Journal* 88 (March 1978): 58–94. The statement in the text is based in part on the data Nayyar presents on p. 62. Four key latin American countries are said to have had the following MNC affiliate export shares of total country exports during selected years in the late 1960s or early 1970s: Brazil (43 percent), Argentina ("at least 30 percent), Colombia ("30 percent or more"), and Mexico (25–30 percent). These estimates (which are not inconsistent with estimates in the present study based solely on U.S. affiliate data–see Table 12.5) compared with MNC manufacturing export share estimates for Hong Kong (10 percent), Taiwan ("at least 20 percent") and South Korea ("at least 15 percent"). India's share was estimated to be lower still (approximately 5 percent). Singapore's share, on the other hand, was estimated to be considerably higher (almost 70 percent).
10. Reported in the U.S. Department of Commerce's annual review, "Sales by Majority-Owned Foreign Affiliates of U.S. Companies," *Survey of Current Business*.
11. Many are referenced in Nayyar, "Transnational Corporations." For additional information, see the United Nations study in note 12.
12. See, for example, Annex VII "Methodologial Note on Foreign Direct Investment Statistics," in *Transnational Corporations in World Development: A Re-examination* New York: United Nations Economic and Social Council, 1978.
13. Based on Table III-32 (p. 236), ibid.
14. Based on data in Table III-38 (pp. 242–243), ibid.
15. *Selected Data on U.S. Direct Investment Abroad, 1966–78*, U.S. Department of Commerce, Bureau of Economic Analysis, computed from data in Table

1, p. 15; and *Transnational Corporations in World Development*, United Nations, op. cit., computed from data in Table III-38.

16. Derived from data in *Transnational Corporations in World Development*, Table III-38.

17. "The Growth and Decline of Import Substitution in Brazil," United Nations, *Economic Bulletin for Latin America* IX (March 1964), especially Table 25, p. 40.

18. Werner Baer and Larry Samuelson, "Latin America in the Post-Import-Substitution Era"—Editor's Introduction, *World Development* 5, 1/2 (1977): 1-6.

19. Ibid., p. 2.

20. Ibid., p. 5, as well as the entire article in which this thesis is developed more fully.

21. For the same reason, the Durbin-Watson statistics generated under the Chochrane-Orcutt procedure and reported in Table 12.10 are also all in the conclusive range.

22. Johnston, *Econometric Methods*, 2nd ed (New York: McGraw-Hill, 1972), p. 180ff; Jan Kmenta, *Elements of Econometrics* (New York: Macmillan, 1971), pp. 516-17.

23. These negative coefficient results also conform to the results of Schmitz and Bieri pertaining to their trade policy proxy variables, which were based on EEC data for a span of years embracing EEC's founding. See Andrew Schmitz and Jurg Bieri, "EEC Tariffs and U.S. Direct Investment," *European Review* 3 (1972): 259-270. This conclusion had not been generally borne out in earlier EEC direct investment studies [e.g., A.E. Scaperlanda and L. J. Mauer, "The Determinants of Direct Investment in the EEC," *American Economic Review* 59 (1969): 558-568].

Chapter 13

International Industries, Multinational Companies, and Host Government Control: A Framework

*Yves L. Doz**

Many multinational companies (MNCs) operating in Europe have changed their strategies drastically in the 1970s. Instead of competing country by country, they have adopted coordinated approaches to the European market as a whole and integrated their operations across borders. Such integration may help maintain the international competitiveness of European firms in critical industries, but it also heightens interdependence among countries and further erodes government control over national economies. Based on the detailed analysis of a sample of eleven international industries this chapter analyzes the economic conditions that lead multinational firms to integrate their operations across borders, the responses of European governments, and draws implications for national industrial policies.

Until the 1960s, MNCs typically operated relatively autonomous national subsidiaries, each catering to its national market. Management tasks at MNC headquarters usually remained simple and limited in scope (mainly finance and treasury functions, technology transfer, and, sometimes, export coordination). Competitive pressures were mild, national markets were protected by tariff barriers, and the position of the firms in each national market was often negotiated with the government rather than decided by competition.[1]

*Graduate School of Business Administration, Harvard University

The growth of the European markets, the abolition of trade barriers within the European Economic Communities (EEC), and the enlargement of the EEC created the potential for more international competition. GATT negotiations, which lowered the EEC's common external tariff, and the emergence of major new export-oriented overseas competitors (led by Japan and followed by a number of newly industrialized countries) exposed European industries to renewed international competition. Imports of manufactured products from Japan and other countries increased rapidly. In many industries, manufacturing costs of non-European suppliers became lower than that of European suppliers, and the quality of their products were often higher. Technological innovation, automation, and higher scales of production became the only means to maintain the competitiveness of companies located in Europe.[2]

MNCs in Europe could respond to new competition by integrating their operations across borders. Instead of separately manufacturing a complete product range in each country, they specialized their plants so each national subsidiary produced only a small part of a common European product range and procured the large part of the product range it did not manufacture from sister companies located in other countries. When end products were complex (e.g., automobiles or television sets), specialization also developed by stage in the manufacturing process to exploit different economies of scale at the various stages, and different factor inputs. Significant numbers of European and American multinationals integrated their European operations in the 1970s, and more were in the process of doing so by the late 1970s.[3] In some industries, such as electronics, integration encompassed locating plants in cost labor countries in the Far East.

The integration of MNC operations posed a difficult dilemma to European governments. Integration strategies clearly reduce the effectiveness of conventional demand management economic policies and they also complicate the "negotiation" of strategies with host governments. Integration within the MNC means that demands from one government may directly conflict with that of another. As a result, MNC integration also makes supply management through national sectoral policies more difficult. Yet in some industries, only integration strategies may restore competitiveness and maintain employment, a key priority of European governments.

In some industries, considerations of national sovereignty make the dilemma outlined above even more acute. Concerns for national independence limit integration in such well-established industries as nuclear engineering, energy, aerospace, key raw materials, and shipbuilding. High technology industries such as microelectronics or data processing equipment also raise difficult questions, since they constitute the commanding heights of next decade's economy. Research and development costs and the need for large-scale production in many new industries put competitiveness beyond the reach of most countries. Even the maintenance of an autonomous capability lagging beyond the state of the art and serving a protected domestic market often results in forbidding costs. Accepting foreign control may be the only way to achieve competitiveness in high technology industries at an affordable price to the country, yet foreign control seldom satisfied all political forces. As a result, integration strategies have often been accompanied by growing outcries from host countries for more "national decision centers," an almost impossible combination.

Integration strategies have drawn a variety of responses from the European governments. Yet, from the myriads of discrete interaction incidents between MNCs and governments, some simple patterns can be identified and their policy implications can be drawn. This chapter first outlines generic multinational strategies and the economic characteristics of an industry likely to lead MNCs in that industry to adopt one or another strategy. It then discusses the policies of European governments toward industries in which economic pressures for integration are strong, and the type of industry structures that evolve as a result of government interventions. Finally some policy implications are drawn.

This analysis developed in this chapter draws on two samples of industries on which data were collected between 1976 and 1979. Six major industries were analyzed in detail: automobiles, trucks, microelectronics, data processing equipment, telecommunication systems, and heavy electrical engineering. Government importance as a customer for these industries varies greatly, from almost exclusively public sector sales in electrical equipment, to almost none in automobiles. These six industries were chosen to maximize the differences in government control over their markets. Within each industry, government control also varied significantly between product lines. Four-wheel-drive trucks are sold mostly to the military, or telephone switching equipment to postal authorities, but other trucks and office switching systems are sold primarily to business customers. All six industries, despite the differences in government control over their markets, attract much government attention, for they are all important to national economic development and to national independence. They also share economic characteristics that lead them toward oligopolistic structures such as high economies of scale, evolving technologies, complex product development activities, and high resource requirements. These characteristics, as will be analyzed in the chapter, also make multinational integration attractive to major competitors in these industries.

The structure of each of these industries was analyzed from published documents and industry sources and the strategies followed by the various international competitors identified. (Access to companies was obtained with a commitment that the information their managers provided would remain confidential until formally released by the company. Some companies have not agreed to release case studies detailing their management processes, and the detailed data therefore cannot be presented.) Detailed results of these analyses have been reported elsewhere.[4] For each of the first six industries, the management processes of at least one competitor following each type of strategy were then analyzed in detail and the internal rationale for its strategy explored in depth. Whenever possible, these company analyses have been reported in the form of case studies.[5] Typically, each company analysis involved from 20 to 100 interviews with senior executives. Another sample of six industries was selected in 1979: television tubes, agricultural tractors, ethical drugs, aeroengines, civilian aircraft, and military aircraft. Criteria for selection were similar to that used for the first sample, but each industry was studied largely from published sources using an already developed tentative conceptual framework. The framework was applied successfully to these industries, with the exception of ethical drugs. This appeared to be too broad an industry category to be meaningful strategically: Firms compete in one segment or another, not across the board. Published data on specific segments, however, were too fragmentary to allow a systematic analysis. The ethical drug industry was thus dropped from the study. The selection of industries ensured that each industry would be narrow enough economically and yet broad enough for its economical and political characteristics to be reflected in the strategies and organizations of the participating firms. A narrow economic definition was selected to ensure that firms identified as participants in the industry would compete for the same market with substitutable products, services, and technologies. A broad industry definition, such as "nonelectrical machinery," would not be meaningful economically; it encompasses a wide range of markets and firms, and it is not clear that there is a single competitive environment. A very narrow definition, such as "high intensity lamps," might not be significant strategically and organizationally. Major MNCs in the lamp business, such as Philips, ITT, or GTE-Sylvania, may not identify high intensity lamps as a separate business with its own strategy and organization, independent from that of related businesses. These considerations led to the choice of well-delineated industries (e.g., tractors and not farm equipment, or airframes and aeroengines, not jet aircraft), large enough to be considered as separate product divisions or product groups in multinational companies or in their subsidiaries.

Each major competitor's share of the European market in each industry was measured, as precisely as possible, and the strategy of the competitor was analyzed, through interviews with managers in the first sample, and through published information complemented by a few interviews in the second sample. Altogether, 42 strategies were analyzed. A typology of strategies was developed in the analysis of the first sample and tested on the second sample. It is presented in the first section of this chapter. A framework was developed, relating the type of strategy followed by a competitor to its share of an industry's markets and to the importance of governments as customers for the industry's products. This framework is presented in the second section of the chapter, and evidence from the two samples analyzed to support it. Finally, given the concern of European governments with the strategy of MNCs, policy implications are drawn in the third section.

TYPES OF MULTINATIONAL STRATEGIES AND INDUSTRY ECONOMIC CHARACTERISTICS

The types of strategies followed by multinational competitors in an industry can be clustered into three groups: integration strategies, national responsiveness strategies, and multifocal strategies.

Multinationals that follow a *strategy of integration* have global or regional centrally coordinated integrated production systems with little or no manufacturing duplications between manufacturing subsidiaries, and they rely upon extensive cross shipments of components and finished products among subsidiaries. High-volume, single-source production can permit the achievement of economies of scale in production. R&D can be centralized at headquarters or at specialized centers to avoid duplications and exploit potential economies of aggregation.

In contract, *nationally responsive multinationals* operate primarily "local-for-local" autonomous national subsidiaries, each serving its own market with a full locally manufactured product line. Manufacturing similar products in several countries does not permit the full exploitation of economies of scale and experience. Nationally responsive multinationals forego the potential economic benefits of integration but preserve flexibility at the national level by allowing their subsidiaries to behave as national suppliers. Their competitive advantages over national firms, however, include: (1) pooling financial risks; (2) spreading research and development costs over a larger sales volume than that of national competitors without the difficulties involved in license transactions; (3) coordinating export marketing in order to increase the overall success on export markets; and (4) transferring specific skills between subsidiaries.

Multifocal strategies reflect a desire on the part of the top management of a firm to combine the benefits of both multinational integration and national responsiveness. Instead of having a clear strategy, the firm attempts to trade off flexibly the pressures of competition and the demands of host governments. Some operations are run, and some decisions made, with integration as a priority, others with an overriding concern for responsiveness. Research and development, for instance, may be tightly managed from the center, with no duplication, but each subsidiary may be free to decide which products it will manufacture and which it will procure from other subsidiaries or headquarters.

Of course, national companies also compete in international industries though they manufacture in a single country. In internationally competitive industries that matter to governments they often are led to become "national champions," that is, they develop a relationship with the state that tends to lead them to the political negotiation of their strategies with their home government, to ensure them of the state's support in their international ventures, and to make them prime targets for government intervention, but also the priority recipients of their assistance.

More recently multinational and multigovernment sponsored consortia have taken a significant role in Europe's high technology industries. At first confined to the management of military equipment programs, these consortia were of limited efficiency because of their temporary and political character.[6] More permanent structures, enjoying greater autonomy from the various sponsoring governments, offer a better potential as effective competitors in open markets, Airbus Industries being a prime example.[7] These consortia usually attempt to obtain the economic benefits of integration while preserving the political advantages of flexibility in responding to their multiple "home" governments.

Industry economic characteristics can make multinational integration, national responsiveness, or multifocal strategies more or less attractive to multinational companies. Economies of scale, experience, location, product differentiation, the maintenance of export channels controlled by the firm, the firm's access to capital and its financial flexibility, and technology are most critical in making a strategy attractive. This list is not surprising; this is the stuff from which oligopolistic competitive advantages are built, and theories of foreign investment tell us that multinational companies have been successful largely to the extent that they exploited such advantages from country to country.[8]

Economies of Scale[9]

MNCs following a strategy of integration can best benefit from economies of scale. By specializing their plants across borders, they can achieve very large production volume at a single site for a particular product or component. National companies are likely to have a smaller overall market. They may not achieve similar economies of scale although they too produce in a single location. Where economies of scale are significant, multinationals following a strategy of national responsiveness often find themselves at an even greater disadvantage, compared to integrated multinationals, than national companies. They make a given product or component in many national subsidiaries in much smaller quantities than the large single plant of an integrated MNC. Their subsidiaries are also often smaller than national companies. Companies following a multifocal strategy fall somewhere between integrated and nationally responsive MNCs according to the extent to which they integrate their operations.

The specific cost disadvantage incurred by a firm will vary with the positions of companies in different national markets. A dominant national champion in a very large national market may enjoy a better cost position than a small integrated MNC with lower overall sales volumes scattered in a number of countries. Yet, in most cases, the presence of substantial economies of scale in an industry is likely to benefit integrated MNCs most and nonintegrated ones least, with large developed countries' national champions falling between these two extreme positions.[10]

Economies of Experience

Assuming that manufacturing operations are efficient and well managed, the average unit cost of a product to a company usually falls by a constant percentage each time its total historical cumulative production volume doubles. This effect is known as economies of experience. Cost decreases for each doubling of cumulative volume typically range from 15 to 25 percent, but vary with the industry.[11] Some economies of experience are location-specific. When a given workforce becomes more productive over time, production in a different location with a new workforce may derive little benefit from its experience. Other location-specific factors, such as the breaking in of new manufacturing equipment, may account for a large part of the total experience effect.

Some economies of experience may be transferred within a company from plant to plant, however. For example, the tenth subsidiary beginning to manufacture a given product in a nationally responsive MNC usually starts with an initial unit cost much lower than that of the first subsidiary. Its unit costs, at a similar cumulative volume manufactured locally, are also likely to be much lower than that of an independent national competitor. Much of the success of N.V. Philips in consumer products in Europe, before the development of the EEC, was based on the firm's ability to replicate efficiently organized plants from country to country. Economies of experience are thus likely to benefit integrated MNCs most, but also to give some advantage to nationally responsive MNCs over purely national competitors, unless the national competitors are much larger than the MNC subsidiaries.

Economies of Location

Factor cost differences among countries also favor integrated MNCs over national companies of nationally responsive MNCs active in high factor cost countries. Integrated MNCs can locate factor-intensive operations in low factor cost countries, such as semiconductor assembly and packaging operations in South East Asia. National companies with a large untapped potential domestic market in low factor cost countries, however, can establish an efficient large-volume production base by first selling on their protected domestic market, and then expanding internationally when the domestic market approaches saturation.[12]

Product Differentiation

Product differentiation can take place internationally along three dimensions. For some products, differentiation may take place among customers across borders. Such product differentiation often results from the need for a large number of subtypes. Among consumer goods, a striking example is that of the ski industry: the homogeneous worldwide market is separated into a series of multinational segments according to the types of skiing, the proficiency of the skier, and price brackets. In such circumstances, pooling demand from several national markets and building a large plant in one country to manufacture some subtypes efficiently results in substantial savings. Integration strategies thus have the better payoff.

Differentiation is also sometimes created by skillful advertising and marketing, particularly for some consumer goods. Where marketing approaches and product differentiation methods can be made common to several national markets, marketing knowledge and experience, as well as heavily advertised brands, can be transferred from country to country. For many consumer products, however, intrinsic product differentiation between countries can make integration of manufacturing unattractive: Food companies, for instance, seldom integrate their operations.[13] Nationally responsive MNCs are at an advantage here. Integration is possible only when staple goods are involved (fruit juices) or when new differentiated products are marketed through extensive advertising (breakfast cereals in Europe).

Finally, in some products intensive interaction is needed with local customers whose needs are specific. National companies are then at an advantage, as is found in some specialty food products or in residential construction. Multinationals seldom enjoy a large share of these sectors.

Export Channels and Intensity of Selling Tasks

The importance of export markets may be another industry characteristic that favors MNCs, their larger overall size making the maintenance of extensive company-owned efficient export distribution channels feasible. In contrast, a smaller national firm would have to resort to independent agents and importers, with lesser control on the distribution of its products and probably higher distribution costs and weaker marketing efforts. Nationally responsive MNCs also benefit from export contract allocation flexibility that can make access to third world and socialist countries much easier. They can supply similar products from several countries and take advantage of trade agreements, favorable financing, and cultural and diplomatic ties.

Access to Capital

MNCs may have a lower cost of capital than local national companies, since international lenders may desire to hold debts denominated in the currency of the MNCs' home countries rather than that of the host countries. Multinational diversification may also be valued by

MULTINATIONAL INTEGRATION AND NATIONAL POLICIES: A FRAMEWORK

The dominance of an industry by integrated multinationals ˗e discomforting for governments for a variety of reasons. ˳h the argument for such discomfort may be complex in its ˳s, its broad themes are simple and well represented in the ˳ure.[17]

˳ development of integrated MNCs—as major agents of inter-˳nal trade—reduces the effects of changes in domestic demand ˳e domestic industry. Demand regulation thus has less effect on ˳conomy than when MNCs left subsidiaries autonomous, since ˳diaries react to many changes outside the host country on which ˳overnment has no influence. Reactions of integrated subsidiaries ˳articular government policies are thus more difficult to predict ˳ndividual governments than those of nonintegrated subsidiaries ˳omestic companies. Furthermore, integrated MNCs have at their ˳osal a unique array of countermeasures with which to face ˳rnment regulations and intervention. These include:

˳nges in transfer prices.
˳ts in dividends, royalties, and remittances.
˳llocation of exports.
˳llocation of R&D facilities and budgets.
˳ernal financing and intersubsidiary credit.
˳nges in purchasing patterns.
˳cation of new investments.

˳ally, MNCs have more information available at a lower cost about ˳re alternatives than do domestic companies. Consequently, they ˳ome aware of more possible shifts in investment or strategy and ˳ir behavior, therefore, is less predictable.

˳Nonintegrated MNC subsidiaries can still draw substantial ˳vantages over national companies from their affiliation to a multi-˳tional company. Yet, because nonintegrated subsidiaries are less ˳fected by foreign conditions and because many of the integrated ˳NC's countermeasures are not available to nonintegrated MNCs ˳.g., sourcing or transfer price changes), a nonintegrated subsidiary ˳ likely to be more responsive to its host government policies than ˳ integrated subsidiary would be.

˳Concern over national decision centers has led most European ˳vernments to resist the mounting pressures for integration. In ˳any industries they substituted less formal barriers to trade to the

some investors.[14] In that case, nonintegrated MNCs are at somewhat of an advantage over integrated MNCs, other things being equal: Their autonomous subsidiaries represent more of a genuine diversification, and the stability of their earnings is less affected by shifts in exchange rates than that of integrated MNCs.[15]

Technological Intensity

High technology intensity (measured by the percentage of the company's revenues allocated to R&D expenses) favors MNCs that can spread their R&D expenses over larger production volume than smaller national firms. Though inventions seldom take place in MNCs, these firms account for a large share of innovations—the application of new inventions to products and processes—and play a key role in the diffusion of such innovations.[16]

Table 13.1 is a summary of how industry economic characteristics affect integrated MNCs, nationally responsive MNCs, and national companies that manufacture only in their home country. Companies following multifocal strategies fall somewhere between integrated and nationally responsive MNCs, whereas multinational consortia are usually set up to benefit from the same industry economic characteristics as integrated MNCs.

What is the cumulative effect of these characteristics on the competitive position of various firms? Integrated MNCs, of course, enjoy the most cost advantages in technology-intensive, scale-intensive, capital-intensive, geographically undifferentiated industries. The relative positions of nationally responsive multinationals and national firms vary with the importance of fixed and variable costs. MNCs can spread R&D costs over a larger volume and thus enjoy lower unit costs than national firms. The larger production volumes of national companies at one location may offset their fixed cost allocation disadvantages if scale or experience effects are strong.

Conversely, insignificant economies of scale (minimum efficient scale well below the size of most national markets), low technology, low capital intensity, and geographically differentiated markets give an advantage to national companies. Lack of proprietary technology and limited opportunities for product differentiation make multinational development even more attractive.

In the sample of industries selected for the research reported here, all economic characteristics heavily favor multinational integration. Yet, not all multinational firms integrated their operations. The policies and interventions of European governments limit the attractiveness of integration for many firms. Governments would often like to check integration moves by MNCs.

Table 13.1. Effect of Industry Structure Characteristics on Potential Profitability of Firms: Effect on Firms Following Each Type of Strategy

Industry Characteristics	Integrated Multinationals	Nationally Responsive Multinationals	National Companies
1. Economies of scale	Very favorable when manufacturing economies of scale exceed size of individual national markets.	Same as for national companies, but add vulnerability to forced merger of subsidiaries into national champions.	Unfavorable, except when low enough to be fully exploited within national market.
2. Economies of experience			
Location-specific	Very favorable, large plants	Unfavorable	Unfavorable
Firm-specific	Favorable	Favorable (replication capability)	Unfavorable
3. Economies of location	Favorable (flexibility to locate in low-factor cost areas)	Unfavorable	Unfavorable (unless country well endowed with cheap production factors)
4. Product differentiation			
By country	Very unfavorable (diversity among countries)	Favorable (different homogeneous national markets)	Favorable
By customer sets and product types	Favorable (similar segments in different countries)	Unfavorable (heterogenous national markets)	Unfavorable
By both country and customer set	Unfavorable	Unfavorable (fragmented markets)	Favorable (fragmented markets
5. Maintenance by company of own channels of exports, sales, maintenance, service, installation, etc.	Favorable because of volume only	Favorable, sourcing, financing, language flexibility, etc., and volume	Unfavorable
6. Financial flexibility, access to capital	Very favorable, potential to channel funds and profits between countries and hedges on currency markets and interest rates	Moderately favorable, access to markets, but fewer fund flow opportunities between countries	Less favorable
7. Technology intensity			
Product	Very favorable (economies of R&D aggregation)	Very favorable (economies of aggregation)	Very unfavorable
Process	Less favorable	Very favorable (replication	

can

Thou
detai
litera
The
natio
on th
the e
subs
the g
to p
for
or d
disp
gove

Cha
Shi
Rea
Rea
Ext
Cha
Loc

Fir
mo
bec
the

ad
na
aff
M
(e
is
ar

g
n

formal ones removed by EEC treaties and the GATT negotiations. Wherever possible the market power of state-owned customers was used to protect national industries. When such customers were dominant, for telecommunications equipment for instance, they effectively prevented the implementation of integration strategies.[18] Protection of the national industry was usually accompanied by the encouragement of domestic consolidations leading to a single "national champion" in key industries.[19] Government officials hoped such consolidations would sufficiently increase the effectiveness of the national industry to achieve some measure of financial self-sustenance.

The fate of these efforts varied with the extent of government control over the industry's markets. Where state-controlled customers are dominant, protection can succeed. In such industries the power of MNCs has been eroding steadily.[20] For instance, in telecommunications equipment, most developed countries now supply their needs from domestic suppliers, some with minority MNC ownership and others purely national. The surviving multinationals compete much as autonomous national companies. In Britain, for example, Standard Telephone and Cables, an ITT subsidiary, participates in the government-sponsored development of System X (an electronic exchange system) to the same extent as purely national Plessey though System X will compete against some of ITT's own exchanges.[21] France has put the control of telecommunication equipment manufacture in national hands. With original technology, one French supplier, CIT-Alcatel, has even been able to log sizeable export contracts.[22] Local national manufacture by nationally controlled companies often implies higher equipment costs than straight imports, but offers a number of advantages: self-contained capability guaranteeing safety of supply, employment, positive balance of payment effect and closer relationships with customers.

These advantages have been weighted differently against economic costs in different industries. Australia provides an example. Australia's telecommunication equipment is manufactured locally in subsidiaries of multinationals operating under close PTT supervision. Similarly, major foreign car manufacturers long had self-contained plants in Australia. In the 1970s, however, the need to retool to produce smaller cars, and the market share taken by Japanese importers, led to an impossible situation. Although Australian car prices were very high in comparison with world levels, multinationals threatened to close shop: The Australian market was too small and their profits too low to justify retooling to shift to small car production. Australia shifted to a policy of regulating integration. GM was allowed to offset duty-free imports of built-up vehicles with the export of components. Mitsubishi (which took over the Chrysler subsidiary) was given a similar treatment.[23]

The more a product is closely related to national defense and public procurement, the more likely it is to be produced locally at a great cost penalty (fighter aircraft provide the extreme case). The further away from national defense, the more likely countries will accommodate to integration strategies even when they retain formal control over foreign trade. Countries use such control to bargain successfully with MNCs, Ford in Spain or GM in Australia providing good examples.[24]

Where they exercise no control over markets, governments can hardly avoid integration strategies. Even their state-owned companies are led to integration by the economic characteristics of some industries. Volkswagen is developing into a major multinational, Renault follows suit. Where market success depends on low costs that only a large scale can achieve, the desire to keep a single-country orientation once some competitors take a worldwide perspective becomes illusory. Ford's and GM's integration of their European operations, and the Japanese attempt at gaining worldwide dominance, force all volume car manufacturers into global strategies.

Partial government control over markets raises more difficult trade-offs. Governments may be tempted to use whatever leverage they have to support local companies. Yet, the domestic public sector market may not be large enough to sustain even a marginally viable competitor, as the French came to acknowledge in their ill-fated attempt to nurture an autonomous national champion in the computer industry. Despite continuous subsidies, the firm's potential for competitiveness remained dim, industry economics favoring integrated MNCs too strongly.[25] International Computers Ltd., in England, with a long-established position in the computer industry and extensive government purchasing preference, was better able than C21 to withstand competition, but remained by and large dependent on public sector orders in Britain.

Despite the difficulties faced in maintaining autonomous national champions, governments seldom let integrated MNCs alone serve the market segments they controlled. A mix of privileged access to these markets, government-funded research programs, assistance for exports, and other forms of subsidies are often used to attract MNCs into cooperation with governments. Such cooperation often takes the shape of joint ventures, typical examples of which are the C21-Honeywell-Bull and the Compagnie Francaise des Moteurs and Saint Gobain-Pont à Mousson-National Semiconductors agreements.[26] Such ventures are particularly attractive to smaller MNCs facing larger integrated competitors. Privileged access to some markets and public assistance bolster their competitiveness at little cost. In most countries their operations remain integrated; in one they are nationally responsive. Such ventures are also very attractive to national governments: They usually provide for the maintenance of national decision centers and offer many of the economic advantages of integration.

Such policies lead to the development of *mixed industry structures*: Part of a national market in one industry is served by integrated MNCs and part by MNCs following a multifocal strategy, leaving much flexibility to cooperate with the host government. The promotion of such a mixed industry structure offers many advantages to governments.

First, mixed industry structures do not require a unanimous choice of priorities by all national customers: Some may buy from integrated MNCs and others from national companies or nationally responsive MNCs, according to the users' priorities in procuring a particular type of equipment. The French military could buy some integrated circuits for strategic missiles guidance systems from Texas Instruments, and the bulk of their requirements from Thomson-CSF whenever quality standards were not quite as stringent.

Second, a mixed industry structure increases the bargaining power of the government. By maintaining the coexistence of competitors following vastly different strategies, it is possible to bargain one against the other. Threats to increase support to national companies or nationally responsive MNCs can be used to lead integrated MNCs to comply with host government demands. Threats to limit or regulate integration are credible to the extent companies following other types of strategies can deliver the same goods.

Third, cooperation between national parties and selected MNCs usually decreases the needed level of government support. French national aeroengine manufacturer SNECMA could hardly expect to break into the world civilian market on its own: Their lack of credibility, lagging technical expertise, lack of a worldwide service organization, and lack of marketing expertise in dealing with airlines would have made success unlikely. A joint venture with General Electric, for which GE provided the technological and marketing expertise as well as an established worldwide sales and service organization, gave SNECMA the opportunity to enter the civilian market.[27] SNECMA brought to the venture developement funds and a privileged access to Airbus customers.[28] Similarly, the merger between French national computer champion C21 and Honeywell Bull allowed the French to end subsidies over a five-year period and to create a competitively viable entity.

Partnerships with MNCs usually require two conditions; (1) partial government control over markets and (2) extensive financial assistance. When free trade prevails, partnerships are unattractive and governments can only rely on subsidies, intrinsically attractive national conditions (lower factor costs), or indirect incentives (undervalued currencies) to attract MNCs. An example is provided by Ford's and GM's consideration of European investments in 1978–1979.[29] When governments by and large control markets, MNCs can be easily coaxed into national responsiveness strategies if the government so wishes.

Financial assistance is required to bolster the competitiveness of the partnership. Preferred access to a single national (or even regional market may not be sufficient to attract an MNC into such a partnership. Individual cases show that the French state supported such partnerships extensively. Aggregate data suggest that (together with some declining national industries such as steel or shipbuilding or textiles) aerospace, computers, and electronics received, over a number of years, a disproportionate share of all government assistance to industry in France and Germany, and to a lesser extent in Britain.[30]

Partnerships with comparatively weak U.S. MNCs have been particularly attractive to the French following de Gaulle's costly high technology ventures to recover past "grandeur." The British and German governments have favored other routes, often because their companies were better established internationally than the French (Siemens in electrical equipment or Rolls Royce in jet engines, for instance) or their ambitions more modest (Siemens in computers). As a result they have engaged more in selective cooperation with other relatively small national companies than in broad-based partnerships with U.S. companies. Examples are Siemens' agreement with Amdahl and Fujitsu to exchange products and jointly market them, or Rolls Royce's cooperative aeroengine development projects with Turbomeca, Motoren, and Turbo Union and, more recently, a group of Japanese companies. Such cooperative efforts undertake to obtain some of the economic advantages of multinational integration without relinquishing the national character of the various participants.

In summary, a few simple propositions can be made:

1. The more extensive government control is over the markets of an industry, the least likely integration strategies become.
2. Multifocal strategies are attractive to smaller MNCs where governments are willing to provide subsidies and export assistance to joint ventures.

3. The larger the international market share of a company within an industry, the more likely the company is to be integrated.

These propositions are supported by data from the sample of 42 firms (or businesses of diversified firms) drawn from 11 industries. Figure 13.1 (pp. 320-321) provides a graphic summary of the key data. Along the abscissa, industries are arranged according to the percentage of their sales going to government-controlled customers, that is, government agencies, local administrations, public authorities, and state-owned enterprises. Percentages run from about zero for standard television tubes to about 100 percent for military aircraft. Within Europe, there is little variation, for a given industry, in the percentages sold to government-controlled customers in different European countries.

Within an industry, firms are ranked by their market share, relative to that of the eight largest firms in the industry in Western Europe. A ranking of "1" would mean that the firm's share was just equal to the average share of each of the first eight firms. A ranking of "3," such as Daimler Benz's in trucks, means that the firm's share was three times larger than the average share of the largest eight firms. With that definition, a monopolist would rank "8," but since no market share was found to rank more than "5," Figure 13.1 has been truncated.

Each dot on the figure represents one firm, identified by its initials and characterized by the type of strategy it follows in the industry: (1) *W*: multinational integration; (2) *AC*: multifocal strategy; (3) *NR* or *N*: national responsiveness or national companies.

So far we have argued that the EEC treaties gave MNCs the opportunity to integrate their European operations. By reducing the EEC's common external tariff, the GATT negotiation opened the European market to competition from Japan and recently developed countries. Such competition—based largely on lower cost and higher quality—provided the needed incentive for integration. Though they acknowledge that integration may well be the only way to preserve the competitiveness of several critical European industries (such as automobiles or consumer electronics), governments are concerned by the more tangible international interdependence brought about by MNCs' integrated networks. In industries where they are the major customers, European governments have typically maintained a protected national industry populated by autonomous nationally responsive (often partly locally owned) subsidiaries of multinational corporations and by independent national companies. Only in the face of the most extreme economic costs have they allowed integration to proceed in these government-controlled industries and usually not through independent MNCs, but through government-sponsored multinational consortia, a prime example of which is provided by the

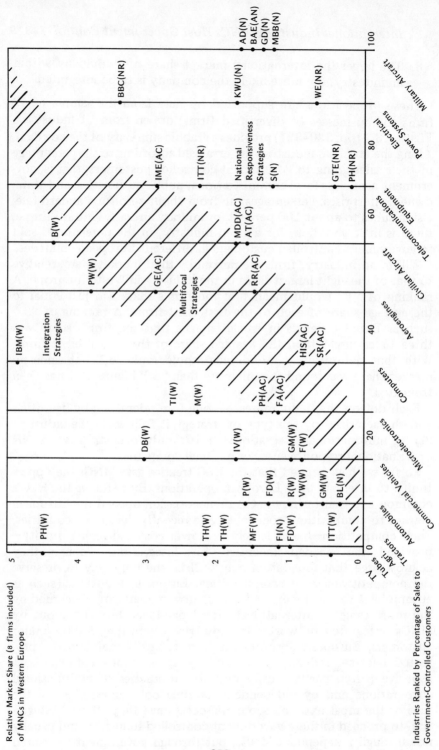

Relative Market Share (8 firms included) of MNCs in Western Europe

Industries Ranked by Percentage of Sales to Government-Controlled Customers

320

Legend:

1. *Types of Strategies*
are indicated next to company initials:

W = Worldwide (or regional) integration

AC = Administrative coordination

NR = National responsiveness

N = National company

2. *Company Names*
are represented by initials:

P	= Peugeot S.A.	M	= Motorola	S	O Siemens
FD	= Ford of Europe	PH	= Philips	GTE	O General Telephone & Electronics
R	= Renault	FC	= Fairchild	BBC	O Brown Boveri
VW	= Volkswagen	IBM	= International Business Machines	KWU	O Kraftwerk Union
GM	= General Motors	HIS	= Honeywell information	WH	O Westinghouse
BL	= British Leyland			FI	O Fiat
DB	= Daimler Benz	SR	= Sperry Rand	B	O Boeing
IV	= IVECO	LME	= LM Ericsson	AI	O Airbus Industries
F	= Ford	MF	= Massey Ferguson	IH	O International Harvester
TI	= Texas Instruments	PW	= Pratt & Whitney	RR	O Rolls Royce
TH	= Thomson-CSF	GE	= General Electric	MBB	O Messerschmitt Boelkow Blohm
AD	= Avions Dassault	BAE	= British Aerospace	MDD	O McDonnel Douglas
GD	= General Dynamics	ITT	= International Telegraph & Telephone		

Note: Some diversified multinationals, several businesses of which have been studied, are represented by several dots on the figure, one dot corresponding to their position in each of the selected industries.

Figure 13.1. Customers, market shares, and multinational strategies.

evolution of the European aerospace industry. Where they could not forestall integration governments have usually let their national companies join the integration bandwagon, Renault and Volkswagen being outstanding examples. Only when their national companies were quite weak have European governments reneged on their commitment to free trade and tried to keep non-European competition at bay through new barriers to trade, such as the "orderly marketing agreements" limiting the imports of some Japanese goods to Europe and the United States.[31]

Where governments had some control over markets, and for industries that mattered to national defense, national pride, or employment, some coexistence—at times uneasy—between integrated MNCs and multifocal MNCs cooperating with governments has developed. Integrated MNCs are profitable, pay large taxes, and are good citizens; nonintegrated MNCs enjoy privileged access to public sector markets and receive subsidies and export assistance, in exchange for their willingness to be nationally responsive. Some governments, the French in particular, have actively sought out MNCs willing to forsake integration and cooperate with national companies. Other governments, most prominent among them the German and the British, have rather resorted to multinational alliances among national companies for specific projects and programs.

POLICY IMPLICATIONS

The policies adopted by European governments in limiting the extent of integration strategies in a number of industries suffer from strong opportunity costs. Abundant evidence shows that significant economic inefficiency results from these policies. [32] Overcapacity, underutilization, high unit costs, and high prices plague such European industries as aircraft, electrical power systems, and telecommunication equipment.

In many industries, the maintenance of a national orientation is unfeasible, and clear choices have to be made between internationalization through integrated MNCs and withdrawals. This implies in a particular country the segmentation of the national industry between sectors in which national independence and international competitiveness are going to be sought, and sectors in which multinationals are given a free rein to integrate or divest. Such policies are known in Europe as "sectoral specialization" or "redeployment" policies. Though specialization is the result of free trade, given factor cost differences, it has been recognized as a national strategy only recently.[33]

Sectoral specialization, however, requires a high degree of political consensus in a country, or an authoritarian government. It involves the ability to shift workers from one sector to another and the commitment of massive resources to selected sectors. Social consensus in Japan, and the shocks of World War II, created propitious conditions. The peculiar pattern of interaction between the state, financial institutions, trading companies, and manufacturing companies exploited these conditions. Following de Gaulle's restoration of political stability, the sense of continuity brought by the orderly transition of power to his well-groomed successors made a consistent economic policy feasible in France. The International crises of the 1970s, the dislocation of the Socialist–Communist electoral alliance, and the dogged leadership of Prime Minister Barre made active redeployment possible. A major political problem of specialization strategies, however, is that whereas their benefits accrue to the population at large over a long period of time, their costs are felt immediately by well identifiable groups, particularly the workers in sectors not selected for growth and investment.

Letting MNCs integrate their activities in such sectors may offer a partial solution. Integrated MNCs alone can possibly maintain relatively small-scale activities in a number of countries and preserve their competitiveness by making them part of an integrated multinational network. Integration makes the need for sectoral specialization at the national level less acute, and may thus serve European governments.

Some control over foreign trade and investment may be kept by governments to improve their bargaining power with integrated MNCs. Beyond the example of the Australian automobile industry already mentioned, Brazil and Spain encouraged controlled integration. In 1972, when Ford negotiated entry, the Spanish government let Ford enter as an integrated MNC, but allowed Ford to sell only enough cars to make a new plant in Spain more attractive to Ford's executives than the expansion of existing plants in Germany. The majority of the cars built in Spain had to be exported. Similarly, Brazil extracted large export commitments from MNCs in exchange for access to the domestic market. When local labor or energy costs are relatively low, as is the case with Brazil and Spain, attracting integrated MNCs on restrictive terms may be relatively easy, provided control over market access is maintained.

Failure to decide, on the part of the government, whether to support a sector, or specific companies in that sector, or to let MNCs integrate their operations in that sector may be the most costly situation. When Chrysler took over Rootes in Britain, for instance, the British government was reluctant to let Rootes be integrated into

Chrysler's continental European operations. Hopes that Chrysler-UK could remain a viable operation autonomously were dispelled by the Chrysler's European car manufacturing.[34] Similar difficulties plagued Ford's acquisition of construction equipment manufacturer Richier in France.

The difficulties of the European civilian aircraft industry illustrate a parallel lack of clarity, on the part of the governments, about what policy to follow. Till the late 1960s, the British attempted to produce a full range of airliners tailored to the needs of British airlines. This led to a proliferation of types that found no market outside of the United Kingdom and were produced at a high cost.[35] The French segmented the world market successfully and introduced a product of much appeal with the Caravelle, but failed to exploit its breakthrough into the world market. The lack of a long-term strategy and of sufficient resource commitments led to followup types not being developed.

Assuming a national government decides to encourage integrated multinational operations, a subsidiary policy choice is whether to encourage the emergence of a single integrated firm or several. By controlling a very large share of the world's market a single very large integrated firm may offer the highest economic efficiency, provided it is well managed. It can also commit large resources to R&D and be technologically progressive. Not being in direct rivalry with any other firm, it may also be in a good position to achieve a fruitful exchange of value with host governments. The company may be willing to incur costs of citizenship to remain acceptable to host governments. Beyond taxes on profitable operations, costs of citizenship may take the form of progressive employment practices, research centers, responsiveness to regional development policies, low-cost services to government, and trade balance surplus. Despite the occasional grumbling, IBM's relations with European governments are fundamentally good because IBM has managed to strike a satisfactory balance between better, cheaper products and the broader needs of host countries. Larger countries, with more bargaining power, may find a single integrated MNC in an industry a more efficient, more flexible producer than several integrated companies locked in direct competition. In such case, each company may be reluctant to incur other than the minimal citizenship costs for fear they would decrease its competitiveness. Smaller countries, committed to free trade, may put more faith in competition than in negotiation to police the behavior of MNCs and thus not favor the emergence of a clear multinational champion in an industry.

Yet, where government favors a mixed structure, a single integrated company may well emerge, smaller integrated companies being driven by competitive pressures into alliances with governments that, in turn, make it difficult for these smaller companies to remain integrated.

Another potential advantage of encouraging integration is that, after the resulting shake down of the industry, concentration may become sufficiently high to allow a return to less integration. As a company becomes extremely large multinationally, it may exhaust all economies of scale at a fraction of its worldwide requirements. As a result it may return to a national subsidiary or to a regionally self-contained approach. Very large production volumes may also enable full use of automation methods and thus decrease the locational disadvantage of European countries. This automation strategy was clearly in evidence at ITT's European semiconductor operations and at SKF. The entry into the EEC of comparatively low labor cost countries from Europe's southern fringes may also contribute to make globalization strategies less attractive by offering within Europe the factor cost differences that MNCs sometimes sought in South East Asia.

The implication of the analyses made above is that, rather than encourage competition among several integrated MNCs, European governments may be better off to encourage the survival of only one integrated MNC is mixed structure industries. The mixed structure may give governments enough bargaining power over the sole integrated MNC to make it comply with their policies and to accept incurring significant citizenship costs.

As we discussed in earlier sections, well-selected partnerships may have significant payoffs. Such partnerships can be more successful with U.S.-based MNCs, the United States being the only country leaving managerial autonomy to high technology firms. If the government is not taking a major role in developing high technologies, the firms may be relatively free to pursue their own strategies.

Partnerships can also be more successful when other governments do not take a keen interest in the same firm. To a large extent the success of the C21-Honeywell Bull merger resulted from the lack of interest by other European governments in cooperation with Honeywell. Problems become extremely complicated when several governments are interested in the same multinational company. A good example is provided by Philips' semiconductors operations. Whereas it is relatively easy for Honeywell to provide national responsiveness to the French while remaining integrated in other countries, such an approach becomes much more difficult for Philips. With some of its plants located in England, France, the Netherlands, Belgium, and some very large plants in Germany, and most of these countries' governments interested in one or another aspect of Philips' operations, it is very difficult for the firm not to become the conduit of intercountry rivalry and still maintain the benefits of integration. The managerial issue also becomes extremely complex since it is not possible to jointly formulate a strategy with a partner to maximize only two operations without getting into problems with other countries. The company has to formulate a plan that makes economic sense and try to negotiate the various elements of the plan with different European governments and preserve its overall consistency.

It is therefore important for governments in negotiation with multinational companies to understand both the competitive position of the firm within its industry and the dynamics of intervention of other governments in neighboring countries. IBM would probably not accept the same terms as Honeywell or Sperry Rand from a host government. The most willing partner is likely to be a marginally uncompetitive integrated firm, that is, the largest firm that still finds it difficult to compete against larger companies. Another key to success is to avoid direct conflict with other governments. The Honeywell-C21 venture could work largely because other European governments were not particularly interested in cooperating with Honeywell or in setting up similar operations with other computer manufacturers. The British were supporting ICL and the German Siemens. Had both of these countries tried to bargain either with Honeywell or with some major competitors of Honeywell such as Sperry Rand or Control Data, Honeywell would have been put in a much more difficult predicament. Either it could have seen its access to various other European countries compromised further, or it could have been placed in the same position as Philips, having to bargain simultaneously with several governments instead of one.

In seeking a successful partnership, the corporate nature of the multinational may also be critical. Leading integrated MNCs are typically managed over the long term in a way very different from marginal divisions of diversified companies. Partnerships may work best in certain divisions of diversified companies. There the corporate level may feel less of a pressure to keep direct control over operations, less of a stake in their development, but also apply more pressures for the achievement of financial results. Leading integrated MNCs are usually run with a long-term strategy of external autonomy and internal unity. Their managers might find that partnership with a government could unduly restrain the future strategic freedom of the firm and compromise its internal unity. Integrated multinationals may accept well-spelled out restrictions to strategic freedom, but the type of limits to managerial autonomy that are implicit in a partnership are much more difficult for them to accept, because in the long run it becomes impossible to know what kind of a strategy the firm will be able to implement. The agreement between Honeywell and the French government, as an example, specified in great detail the strategy to be followed between 1975 and 1980. Firms may see their ability to preserve strategic freedom as a source of strength and thus be reluctant to enter into agreements with host governments.

The fact that none of the clear policy choices—commitment to an autonomous national industry competing internationally, acceptance of leading integrated MNC operations, or partnership with a competitively weaker MNC—brings a satisfactory resolution of host government dilemmas contributes to explain the development of mixed structure industries. Promoting mixed structure industries allows governments not to make a once and for all choice. Instead, governments keep their flexibility to trade off flexibly companies following one type of strategy against companies following another. The desire for mixed structure industries also helps explain the current revival of mercantilism in Europe: Regulated international trade facilitates the maintenance of mixed structure industries, and it may be that, over time, we will witness a convergence of international industries toward mixed structures.

NOTES

1. For detailed descriptions see L. G. Franko, *The European Multinationals* Stanford, Conn.: Greylock Inc., 1976.
2. See Y. Doz, *Multinational Strategic Management: Economic and Political Imperatives* (forthcoming).
3. No complete analysis of integration strategies has been carried out. Several surveys document their growing extent, however. See, for instance, S. Young and N. Hood, *Dynamic Aspects of U.S. Multinational Operations in Europe* (Farnborough: Saxon House, 1980). Integration strategies seem to have become increasingly prevalent in the late 1970s.
4. See Y. Doz, *Government Control and Multinational Strategic Management*. New York: Praeger, 1979; and *Multinational Strategic Management: Economic and Political Imperatives* (forthcoming), chapters 5, 6, and 7.
5. These case studies have not been gathered into a single publication. Three are summarized in *Government Control and Multinational Strategic Management* (chapters 7, 8, and 9). Many are available through the Intercollegiate Case Clearing House in Boston; a provisional list is given below:
   (a) On Ford Motor Company: *Ford in Spain* (A), (B1), *Ford Bobcat* (A1), (A2), (B), (C), and (D).
   (b) On Brown Boveri: *Brown Boveri & Cie.*

(c) On General Telephone and Electronics: *GTE's International Telecommunications Division.*

(d) On Compagnie Internationale pour l'Informatique: *Compagnie Internationale pour l'Informatique* and *Compagnie Internationale pour L'Information Honeywell Bull.*

(e) On International Business Machines: "IBM: A Strategic Profile" (in process), "IBM: A Managerial Profile" (in process).

(f) On General Motors: "General Motors Overseas Operations—Europe" (in process).

(g) On L. M. Ericsson: L. M. Ericsson (A) and (B) (in process), and also David Harkleroad *"L. M. Ericsson"* INSEAD mimeographed case, 198 1981.

(h) On ITT: "Internationale Telephone & Telegraph" (in process).

Other cases may be published within the next few years based on data collected in the course of the research.

6. See M. S. Hochmuth, *Organizing the Transnationals* Leiden: Sijthoff, 1973.

7. See J. de la Torre and M. Bachett, "Airbus Industries" INSEAD mimeographed case, 1979.

8. See R. Vernon, "International Investment and International Trade in the Product Cycle," *Quarterly Journal of Economics* 80 (May 1966):190-207. Also H. Gruber, D. Mehta, and R. Vernon, "The R&D Factor in International Trade and International Investment of United States Industries," *Journal of Political Economy* 75, 1 (February 1967); and S. H. Hymer, *The International Operations of National Firms: A Study of Direct Foreign Investment* (Cambridge, Mass.: M.I.T. Press, 1976, adapted from the author's 1960 doctoral dissertation). For a summary of several studies building upon dynamic models of international investments, see L. T. Wells, Jr. (ed.), *The Product Life Cycle and International Trade* (Boston, Mass.: Division of Research, Graduate School of Business Administration, Harvard University, 1972).

For theoretical bases on the importance of technology, see M. Posner, "International Trade and Technical Change," *Oxford Economic Papers* 13 (October 1961):323-341. For summary evidence see W. H. Gruber and R. Vernon, "The Technology Factor in a World Matrix," in Vernon, ed., *The Technology Factor in International Trade*, pp. 233-272. Several industry studies support similar conclusions; see, for instance, C. Freeman, "The Plastics Industry: A Comparative Study of Research and Innovation," *National Institute Economic Review* 16 (November 1963):22-62; or G. Hufbauer, *Synthetic Materials and the Theory of International Trade* (Cambridge, Mass.: Harvard University Press, 1966). Comparisons among businesses in the PIMS data base also support broadly the link between technology and international trade. See R. E. Caves and J. Khalilzadeh-Shirazi, "International Trade and Industrial Organization," in *Welfare Aspects of Industrial Markets*, edited by A. P. Jacquemin and H. W. deJong (Leiden: Martinus Nijhoff, 1977). Most prominent among the proponents of financial factors as a source of MNC competitive advantage is R. Z. Aliber. His "A Theory of Direct Foreign Investment," in *The International Corporation,* edited by G. P. Kindleberger (Cambridge, Mass.: M.I.T. Press, 1970), presents a summary argument.

9. Economies of scale, experience, and location are usually at work in some combination. The actual production costs for a particular product are thus a result of their combined influence. Though some generalizations are possible as to the likely direction of their impact or the relative cost positions of firms following different strategies, an assessment of actual cost differences requires a careful study of specific firms in an industry.

10. It is further assumed here that each firm successfully achieves the economies of scale made possible by its competitive posture. This assumption is not necessarily warranted. British Leyland, in the auto industry, for instance, has its production scattered among over 30 plants in the United Kingdom, and is far from fully expoliting its potential for economies of scale. Many national champions resulting from the forced merger of smaller firms have failed to exploit economies of scale made possible by the merger, hamstrung with social problems (e.g., plants that could not be closed or converted) or plagued by poor management (e.g., political operators rather than professional managers).

11. See Boston Consulting Group, *Perspectives on Experience* (Boston: Boston Consulting Group, 1968).

12. This has been a typical approach of Japanese companies in becoming internationally competitive. See J. C. Abegglen, *Business Strategies for Japan* (Tokyo: Sophia University, 1970); and E. Vogel, *Japan as Number One* (Cambridge, Mass.: Harvard University Press, 1978).

13. See U. E. Wiechmann, *Marketing Management in Multinational Firms* (New York: Praeger, 1976); and C. A. Bartlett, "Multinational Structural Evolution: The Changing Decision Environment in International Divisions," DBA thesis, Graduate School of Business Administration, Harvard University, 1979, Chapter 5.

14. See A. M. Rugman, *International Diversification and the Multinational Enterprise* (Lexington, Mass.: Lexington Books, 1979).

15. See S. M. Robbins and R. B. Stobaugh, *Money in the Multinational Enterprise* (New York: Basic Books, 1973).

16. For a summary, see E. Mansfield, "Technology and Technological Change," in *Economic Analysis and the Multinational Enterprise*, edited by J. H. Dunning (London: Allen and Unwin, 1974), pp. 147–183.

17. For a broad-based argument, see R. G. Barnett and R. E. Mueller, *Global Reach* (New York: Simon and Schuster, 1974). For a more analytic presentation of the argument, see R. Hall Mason, "Conflicts Between Host Countries and the Multinational Enterprise," *California Management Review* 17, no. 1 (Fall 1974):5–14. See also J. N. Behrman, "Governmental Policy Alternatives and the Problem of International Sharing," in *The Multinational Enterprise*, edited by J. H. Dunning (London: Allen and Unwin, 1971).

18. For a detailed argument, see Doz, *Government Control and Multinational Strategic Management.*

19. For specific examples drawn from key industries and several European countries, see R. Vernon (ed.), *Big Business and the State* (Cambridge, Mass.: Harvard University Press, 1974).

20. From telephones in Western Europe to automobiles in Latin America, there is ample evidence of continued high prices in protected national markets. Relatively ineffective national suppliers can develop, and more effective, more experienced subsidiaries of multinational companies can make windfall profits (in the 1960s, ITT's executives sometimes referred to France as the "Golden Cage"). See Doz, *Multinational Strategic Management*, chapter 6.

21. See "STC: 'Terribly British' and Willing to Stay That Way," *World Business Weekly*, June 25, 1979, p. 16.

22. See Doz, *Multinational Strategic Management*, chapter 6.

23. Industry sources.

24. For Spain, see Y. Doz, *Ford in Spain* (ICCH case; see note 5).

25. See Pierre Gadonneix, "Le Plan Calcul," doctoral thesis, Harvard Business School, 1975.

26. For C-21 Honeywell Bull, see *Compagnie Internationale pour l'Informatique* and *C21-Honeywell Bull* (ICCH cases; see note 5). For Compagnie Francaise des moteurs, see G. W. Weiss, Jr., *The General Electric-SNECMA Jet Engine Development Program* (ICCH case 9-380-739); and Jack Barenson, *Technology and the Multinational* (Lexington, Mass.: Lexington Books, 1978), pp. 23–29. For Saint Gobain-Pont à Mousson-National Semiconductors, see "France's Glassmaker Bids for an Electronic Future," *The Economist*, November 17, 1979, p. 81.

27. See Barenson, *Technology and the Multinationals*, pp. 23–29.

28. Rolls Royce's belated interest in the Airbus program and the early British government's withdrawal from the program avoided a possible conflict with Rolls Royce. Airlines could specify other engines than GE's but they had to agree with engine manufacturers to certify the aircraft with the different engines, a costly process that deterred Airbus customers from selecting Rolls Royce engines. Pratt & Whitney, however, became a supplier to Airbus customers who already used Pratt & Whitney engines on other aircraft types in their fleet, mainly the Boeing 747.

29. See "Won't You Come into My Parlour: Europe Courts a Finicky Ford," *World Business Weekly*, March 5, 1979, pp. 9–11.

30. For Britain and Germany, see W. M. Corden and G. Fells, *Public Assistance to Industry* (London: Macmillan, 1976). For France, see *Rapport Hanoun* (unpublished Ministry of Industry report).

31. Despite the severe loss of domestic market share suffered by British Leyland and Fiat to foreign European competitors, both the British and Italian governments have so far refrained from building intra-EEC barriers to trade or from evoking "injury" clauses in the EEC treaties.

32. See Central Policy Review Staff, *A Market for Aircraft* (London: Her Majesty's Stationery Office, 1973); Barbara Epstein, *The Politics of Trade in Power Plants* (London: The Atlantic Trade Study Center, 1970); A. Surrey, *World Market for Electric Power Equipment: Rationalization and Technical Change* (Brighton: University of Sussex Science Policy Research Unit,

1972); Central Policy Review Staff, *The Future of the U.K. Power Plant Manufacturing Industry* (London: Her Majesty's Stationery Office, 1976).

33. Japan's Ministry of International Trade and Industry has been the first public body to actively pursue such a strategy and to articulate it clearly. This strategy is documented in Groupe d'Études Prospectives Internationales, *Croissance Mondiale et Stratégie de Specialisation* and *Une Economie à la Recherche de la Spécialisation Optimale: Le Japon.* (Paris: Centre Francais du Commerce Extèrieur, 1976).

Among European governments, the French had given most explicit attention to sectoral specialization strategies. See R. Coubis, *Competitivé et Croissance en Economie Concurrencèe* (Paris: Dunod, 1975); Christian Stoffaes, *La Grande Menace Industrielle* (Paris: Calmann Levy, 1978); and Alain Cotta and Christian Stoffaes, *Le Redéploiment Industriel* (Paris: La Documentation Francaise, 1977).

34. See Stephen Young and Neil Hood, *Chrysler-UK: A Corporation in Transition* (New York: Praeger, 1976).

35. See Robert Gray, *Rolls on the Rock* (Salisbury: Compton Press, 1971.

Indexes*

AUTHORS

A

Abegglen, J. C., 309, 329n
Abell, D. F., 45
Abernathy, W. J., 44, 51, 52
Ahmed, A. A., 6, 182, 190
Alexander, G. J., 111
Aliber, R. Z., 44, 46, 55, 308, 328n
Ashton, D. J., 39
Atkins, J. C., 111

B

Bachett, M., 307, 328n
Baer, W., 285, 301n
Baliga, B. R., 13, 16, 17, 19, 41n, 42,
    45, 51, 56, 72
Ball, G., 150, 157n
Barenson, J., 317, 330n

Barnet, R. J., 42, 55, 151, 157n,
    314, 329n
Barron, A., 262
Bartlett, C. A., 310, 329n
Batchelor, C., 263
Behrman, J. N., 168, 314, 329n
Bell, J., 41n
Beranek, W., 111
Bhattachanyya, S. K., 110
Bieri, J., 297, 310n
Bierman, H., 111
Black, F., 111
Blair, A. R., 204, 205, 270
Boddewyn, I., 248n
Bourgault, P. L., 177
Bradbury, F. R., 167
Brash, D. T., 251, 259
Braudel, F., 132, 156n
Brennan, M.J., 111
Brigham, E. F., 108

*This index is subdivided into six sections: Authors, Countries, Enterprises, Industries, Institutions and Organizations, and General Topics.

INDUSTRIES

INSTITUTIONS AND ORGANIZATIONS

About the Editors

Walter H. Goldberg is Professor of Management at the Graduate School of Business Administration, University of Gothenburg, Sweden. In addition, he has served both as Senior Research Fellow and as Director of the International Institute of Management at the Science Center Berlin. His experience in international business is extensive, ranging from work in highly industrialized to less developed countries. He has been a consultant to several governments on matters of development policy, industrial policy, and innovation policy and has served as director and board chairman of various multinational corporations. Professor Goldberg has also organized many management training courses and international conferences on international business. He has published numerous articles and books, including *The Multinational Firm and National Policy* (1975) and *Mergers and Interorganizational Cooperation: An International Outlook* (1982).

Anant R. Negandhi is Professor of International Business at the University of Illinois at Urbana-Champaign. He earned his B.A. and B.Com. degrees from the University of Bombay; his M.B.A. from Texas Christian University; and his Ph.D. from Michigan State University. Prior to joining the faculty at the University of Illinois, he 'aught at the University of California at Los Angeles and at Kent Stat.   ersity. During the years 1976–1978, he served as Senior Research Fell   ،c the International Institute of Management of the Science Center Berlin. Professor Negandhi has published over sixty articles in various scholarly journals; in addition, he is the author of *Quest for Survival and Growth: A Comparative Study of American, European, and Japanese Multinationals.* He was founder-editor of the quarterly journal *Organization and Administrative Sciences.* His most recent publication is *TABLES ARE TURNING: German and Japanese Multinational Companies in the United States* (1981).